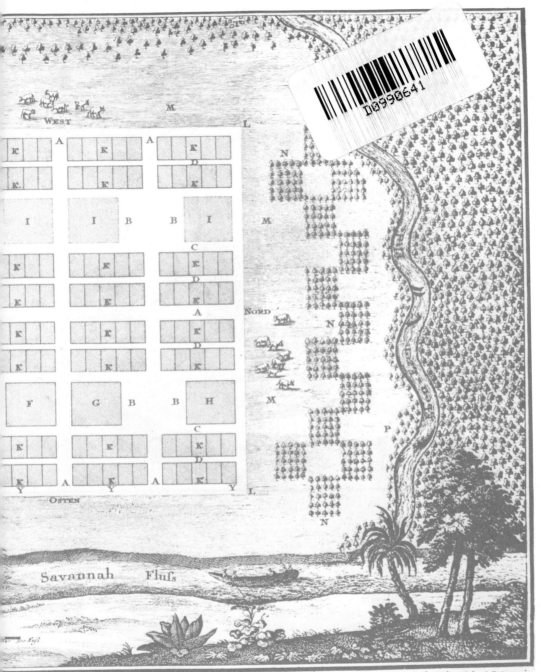

Nachrichten, 13te Continuation, Erster Theil (Halle and Augsburg, 1747).
Collection, University of Georgia Library.

This volume consists of an annotated English translation of the reports sent in the year 1738 from the Lutheran clergymen in Ebenezer, Georgia, to the authorities of the Francke Foundation in Halle, Germany. While the chief concern of the two clergymen was the saving of their parishioners' souls, their reports reveal much information about such secular matters as cattle-raising, farming, disease, slavery, game, and predatory animals. As a keen observer of human nature, one of the clergymen, John Martin Boltzius, made shrewd observations about various people, including the Englishmen in Savannah such as Oglethorpe, Causton, Wesley, Whitefield, Habersham, and Noble Jones.

George Fenwick Jones is professor of German and comparative literature at the University of Maryland. Renate Wilson is a writer and editor at Johns Hopkins University.

Detailed Reports on the Salzburger Emigrants Who Settled in America . . . Edited by Samuel Urlsperger

VOLUME FIVE, 1738

Translated and Edited by
GEORGE FENWICK JONES
and
RENATE WILSON

WORMSLOE FOUNDATION PUBLICATIONS
NUMBER FOURTEEN

THE UNIVERSITY OF GEORGIA PRESS
ATHENS

Set in 11 on 13 point Mergenthaler Baskerville type
Printed in the United States of America

Library of Congress Cataloging in Publication Data

Urlsperger, Samuel, 1685–1772, comp.
    Detailed reports on the Salzburger emigrants who settled
in America . . . .
    (Wormsloe Foundation. Publications, no. 9–   )
    Includes bibliographical references and indexes.
    Translation of Ausführliche Nachricht von den saltzbur-
gischen Emigranten, die sich in America niedergelassen
haben.
    CONTENTS:—[etc.]—v. 3. 1736.—v. 4. 1737.—v. 5. 1738.
    1. Salzburgers in Georgia—History—Sources.   2.
German Americans—Georgia—History—Sources.   3.
Lutherans—Georgia—History—Sources.   4. Ebenezer,
Ga.—History—Sources.   5. Georgia—History—Colonial
period. ca. 1600–1775—Sources.   6. Stockbridge
Indians—Missions—History—Sources.   7. Indians of
North America—Georgia—Missions—History—Sources.
I. Jones, George Fenwick, 1916–   II. Title.   III. Series.
F295.S1U813   975.8'004'31   67-27137
        ISBN 0–8203–0482–4 (V. 5)

The preparation of this volume was made possible in part
by a grant from the Program for Translations of the National Endowment for the Humanities, an independent
federal agency.

Contents

Vierte
CONTINVATION
der ausführlichen Nachricht
von den
Saltzburgischen
Emigranten,
die sich in America niedergelassen haben.
Worin enthalten sind:

I. Das Tage-Register der beyden Prediger zu EbenEzer in Georgien vom 1. Iul. 1737. bis auf den 31. Mart. 1739.

II. Gedachter Prediger, wie auch einiger Saltzburger und anderer Briefe, vom Jahr 1739.

III. Ein Extract aus Georg Sanftlebens kleinem Reise-Diario, als derselbe zu Ende des Ianuarii 1739. mit etlichen Colonisten wieder nach Georgien gegangen.

IV. Ein Verzeichniß aller Personen, die theils den 19. May 1739. in EbenEzer gelebet, theils von Anno 1734. bis dahin gestorben.

Nebst
einer Vorrede
herausgegeben
von
Samuel Urlsperger,
Des Evangelischen Ministerii der Stadt Augspurg Seniore und Pastore
der Hauptkirche zu St. Annen.

HALLE, in Verlegung des Wäysenhauses, M DCC XXXX.

Fourth

CONTINUATION

of the Detailed Reports

of the

SALZBURG

EMIGRANTS

who have settled in America

in which are contained

I. The Diary of the two ministers at Ebenezer in Georgia from 1 July 1737 to 31 March 1739.

II. Letters from the above-mentioned ministers and also from several Salzburgers from the year 1739.

III. An extract from Georg Sanftleben's short travel diary, when he returned to Georgia at the end of January 1739 with several colonists.

IV. A list of all persons who were living in Ebenezer on 19 May 1739 and of those who died from the year 1734 until then.

together with

A PREFACE

edited

by

SAMUEL URLSPERGER

Senior of the Evangelical Lutheran Ministry of the
city of Augsburg and pastor of St. Anne's Church

HALLE

Published by the Orphanage Press, M DCC XXXX

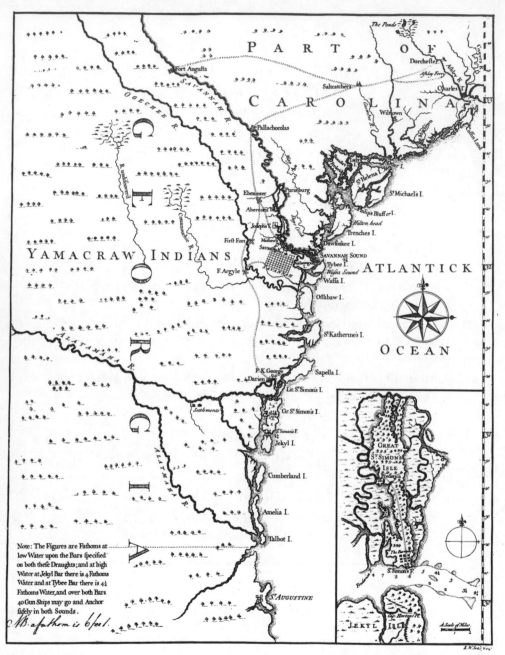

From an original in the De Renne Collection, University of Georgia Library. It is supposed to have been drawn during the period 1741–1743. It has been reproduced in several publications, including Urlsperger's *Ausführliche Nachrichten, 13te Continuation, Erster Theil* (Halle and Augsburg, 1747).

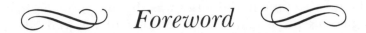 *Foreword*

THE Wormsloe Foundation is a non-profit organization chartered on December 18, 1951, by the Superior Court of Chatham County, Georgia. In the words of its charter, "The objects and purposes of this Foundation are the promotion of historical research and the publication of the results thereof; the restoration, preservation, and maintenance of historical sites and documents and the conduct of an educational program in the study of history in the State of Georgia, and in states adjoining thereto."

As its first important activity, the Foundation has begun the publication of a series of historical works and documents under the title of "Wormsloe Foundation Publications." They consist of important manuscripts, reprints of rare publications, and historical narrative relative to Georgia and the South. The first volume appeared in 1955, written by E. Merton Coulter, the General Editor of the series, and entitled *Wormsloe: Two Centuries of a Georgia Family*. This volume gives the historical background of the Wormsloe Estate and a history of the family which has owned it for more than two and a quarter centuries.

The second publication of the Foundation was *The Journal of William Stephens, 1741–1743*, and the third volume was *The Journal of William Stephens, 1743–1745*, which is a continuation of the journal as far as any known copy is extant. However, there is evidence that Stephens kept his journal for some years after 1745. These volumes were edited by the General Editor of the Wormsloe Foundation series and were published in 1958 and 1959, respectively.

The fourth volume of the series was the re-publication of the unique copy of Pat. Tailfer et al., *A True and Historical Narrative of the Colony of Georgia . . . With Comments by the Earl of Egmont*. This volume is in the John Carter Brown Library of Brown University. In this publication there appears for the first time in print the comments of Egmont. With the permission of Brown

University, this volume was edited by Clarence L. Ver Steeg of Northwestern University, Evanston, Illinois.

The fifth volume in the series was the long-missing first part of Egmont's three manuscript volumes of his journal. It was edited by Robert G. McPherson of the University of Georgia. This volume contains the journal from 1732 to 1738, inclusive, and is owned by the Gilcrease Institute of American History and Art, Tulsa, Oklahoma, which gave permission for its publication.

In 1963 the Foundation published its sixth volume, *The Journal of Peter Gordon, 1732–1735*, which was edited by the General Editor of the series. Gordon came tŏ Georgia with Oglethorpe on the first voyage; he began his journal on leaving England. The original manuscript was acquired in 1957 by the Wormsloe Foundation, which presented it to the General Library of the University of Georgia.

The seventh volume in the series was *Joseph Vallence Bevan, Georgia's First Official Historian*. It is a departure from the nature of the five volumes directly preceding, which are documentary. It was written by the General Editor, who brings to light a historiographer who was appointed Georgia's first official historian by the state legislature.

The eighth volume, *Henry Newman's Salzburger Letterbooks*, begins a series within the general series, for it is to be followed by several volumes of translations of the Urlsperger Reports (*Ausführliche Nachrichten . . .* , edited by Samuel Urlsperger, Halle, 1735ff, and dealing with the Georgia Salzburgers). This volume was edited by George Fenwick Jones of the University of Maryland, who has also edited later volumes of the Salzburger translations.

The ninth volume of the Wormsloe Foundation Publications is the first of several volumes of the Urlsperger Reports in translation to be published in this series. It appeared in 1968. The second volume of the Urlsperger Reports (being the tenth volume in the general series) was published in 1969, edited by George Fenwick Jones of the University of Maryland, as was the first, and extends over the years, 1734–1735. The third in the Urlsperger series (the eleventh in the general series) covers the year 1736, and was published in 1972. It was translated and edited by Professor Jones with the assistance of Marie Hahn of Hood College. The fourth volume in the Urlsperger series (twelfth in the general series) covers the year 1737, and was published in 1976. It was edited by Professor Jones and translated by him with the assistance of Renate Wilson of the Johns Hopkins University. The present volume, fifth in the Urlsperger series and fourteenth in the whole number of the Wormsloe Foundation Publications, was edited and translated by those listed directly above.

E. Merton Coulter
General Editor

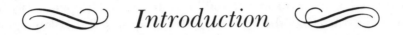 *Introduction*

THE first three of the following paragraphs may be passed over by the reader who has read the earlier volumes of this series, since he will already know why and when these reports were written. For the newcomer, suffice it to say that most of these reports were written by Johann Martin Boltzius, the Lutheran pastor assigned to the Protestant exiles from Salzburg who settled at Ebenezer in the colony of Georgia in 1734 and the following years. The remainder were written by Boltzius' assistant, Israel Christian Gronau, who kept the diary only when Boltzius was away in Savannah or Purysburg or else incapacitated by sickness.

Being destined for the Francke Foundation at Halle in East Germany, where Boltzius and Gronau had been educated, these reports were sent from Georgia to Halle via Augsburg in South Germany, where they were first edited for publication by Samuel Urlsperger, the senior Lutheran minister of that city. The edited texts were then published in Urlsperger's *Ausführliche Nachricht*, which was printed at irregular intervals by the Waysenhaus (Orphanage) Press in Halle.[1] Meanwhile, the original unedited reports were transcribed into copy books by professional scribes at the Francke Foundation.[2] There they have lain largely ignored by Georgia historians, who have had to rely on Urlsperger's greatly bowdlerized edition.

Like the previous volumes of this series, this one restores [in brackets] all matter deleted by Urlsperger; and it reveals that this deleted matter comprised all statements discrediting the English authorities and the behavior or conditions of the Salzburgers. It seems surprising, therefore, that Urlsperger did not suppress or disguise the appalling death list reported by Boltzius on 1 January. Some of Urlsperger's deletions are difficult to explain. For example, he consistently suppresses the name of George Whitefield, despite that missionary's great kindness to the Salzburgers; such antipathy must have been caused later by Whitefield's admiration for the Herrnhuters or Moravians, a German sect in Savannah that had strayed from orthodox Lutheranism.[3] It will be noted that Urlsperger withheld the fact that the barrel of dried apples the Salzburgers received from Pennsylvania had been donated by the Herrnhuters (7 February).

In addition to his many deletions, Urlsperger also made a few additions, mostly harmless little explanations or justifications, or else expansions of Biblical verses abbreviated by Boltzius. It is possible, of course, that some of these apparent additions had actually been written by Boltzius but had then been inadvertently omitted by the Halle scribe. To obviate the need for many footnotes, this volume will indicate such additions by setting off / with slashes / all matter found in Urlsperger's edition but not found in the Halle manuscripts, that is to say, all matter either added by Urlsperger or omitted by the Halle scribe. At this point it may be advisable to prepare the reader to expect statements like "Christ is restless again" (5 September) or "Christ has become obstinate again" (10 November), since such comments refer to Johann Gottfried Christ, a converted Jew from Frankfurt, not to Jesus, whose cognomen in German is always Christus. It is to be remembered that the spelling of proper names was not always standardized, especially with regard to single and double consonants, as in names like Kiefer/Kieffer. Also, z and tz were interchangeable in names like Boltzius/Bolzius and Hertzog/Herzog, the sound t being pronounced even when the name is spelled only with a z.

Although typical of eighteenth-century letters, Boltzius' literary style would be unacceptable today in even an undergraduate composition; and it has taken much will power to refrain from making stylistic improvements in the translation. Boltzius is clearly following the "plain style" (*genus humile*) rather than the "grand style" (*genus grande*) as befitting the Christian who wishes to report beneficial truths without garnering personal glory. In general he seems to have begun his sentences without planning what he was going to say; he merely wrote down whatever words came to his pen and neglected to edit his text to enrich his vocabulary or to remove repetitions.[4] Consequently, a few basic words like *good* (*gut*), *honest* (*ehrlich*), and *edifying* (*erbauend*) are much overworked. Nearly every newborn baby is a "young baby," as if Boltzius were unaware that all new babies are young; and the few babies that are not "young" are "small," which hardly indicates their relative size. These words express neither youth nor smallness, just endearment.

When judging Boltzius' vocabulary, we must remember that he used many common terms in an uncommon way, namely, as the Pietists used them. For example, *äusserlich* (external) referred to worldly and therefore unimportant matters, such as food, clothing, and shelter. A person was "honest" (*ehrlich*) if he shared Boltzius' Pietistic views, or at least pretended to. Boltzius was skeptical of "natural honesty" (*bürgerliche Ehrlichkeit*), through which some misguided souls hoped to achieve salvation on their own merits without even admitting their depravity and crawling into the wounds of Jesus to be born again; and this explains his amazement that Sigmund Ott, although not yet resigned to divine dispensation, nevertheless returned money that did not belong to him (7 January). Only those can be saved who evince true "poverty of the spirit," true recognition of their own perdition: in other words, only those can be saved who believe in the New rather than in the Old Law. Not nature, but only grace can win salvation (13 March); and fallen man can be redeemed only by the blood of the Lamb. As a result of such attitudes, which are an integral part of the Pietist tradition, Boltzius judged people by a yardstick quite alien to our own. When he complains that a parishioner is "indolent" (*träge*), he may mean that he spends too much time in chopping and hoeing and not enough in praying.[5] Likewise, if he says that a certain German in Purysburg or Savannah is worthless, he may merely mean that he does not profess Pietistic convictions. Likewise, when he calls people *unordentlich*, it is sometimes better to translate the word as "inordinate," rather than as "disorderly," since he may not be implying that they are rowdy or disreputable, but merely that they overstep their divinely ordained order, like the inordinate sectarians in Heidelberg who arrogate to themselves the prerogatives of the proper clergy (14 July).

As a minister, Boltzius felt that his chief duty was to save the souls of his flock. However, having rid himself of the two secular leaders, Baron von Reck and Jean Vat, he found himself responsible for the physical as well as spiritual welfare of his parishioners. The previous volumes show how quickly he adapted himself to the challenge and how cleverly and diplomatically he handled Oglethorpe, the founder of Georgia, and Thomas Causton, the keeper of the storehouse, as well as the authorities in London and the benefactors in Germany.

The first volume of this series cites a proverb from German colonizers in the undeveloped lands of Eastern Europe: *Dem Ersten, Tod—dem Zweiten, Not—dem Dritten, Brot* (Death for the first, hardship for the second, bread for the third). By the year 1738 the Salzburgers, through Boltzius' wise guidance, had reached stage three, even though bread was not yet plentiful and death and hardship were still ever present. However bad conditions were in Ebenezer, they were even worse in Savannah, especially among the indentured servants from Germany.[6] These poor redemptioners, who had sold their bodies for a number of years of servitude to pay their passage, were usually called Palatines, regardless of their actual origin, since the majority did come from the Rhenish Palatinate.

The thing most needed by Boltzius' parish was better health; sickness had not only carried off a third of the parishioners, it also kept many others bedridden or otherwise incapacitated. Through constant entreaty to his superiors in Halle, Boltzius at last obtained a Halle-educated physician to take the place of the poorly trained and unsuccessful apothecary, Andreas Zwiffler, who had since removed to Pennsylvania. Christian Ernst Thilo, Georgia's first bona fide physician, was enthusiastically greeted on 13 January by the whole congregation, who had already constructed a comfortable house for him; and on 25 January Boltzius made note of his spiritual concern for his patients. But Friday the thirteenth must have been an inauspicious day, for Thilo soon became chronically sick and Boltzius began to observe that he was not following the methods of Dr. Christian Friedrich Richter and Professor Johann Junker of Halle, whose remedies had previously proved successful (9 August). Also, as was revealed later, Thilo did not attend divine services and caused much disorder with his outlandish religious beliefs.

Also of vital importance for the survival of the community was a surveyor; for Boltzius had finally received permission for his parishioners to exchange their sandy pine barrens for swamp land which, being occasionally flooded, would remain rich without manure. Boltzius saw that agriculture could not prosper until the farmers knew precisely which land was their own. Having been dissatisfied with the service of the Savannah surveyor, Noble Jones, who had laid out both Old and New Ebenezer, he had engaged a certain Ross; but Ross in turn disappointed him by procrastinating and even interrupting his work to take up a more lucrative assignment at Port Royal. Above all, Ross insisted on placing the Salzburgers' plantations in the sterile pine barrens, where the going was easy, rather than in the fertile, but densely overgrown, bottom land. It was only after the Salzburgers tried to help the surveyor in his difficult work that Boltzius realized what a thankless and unprofitable task Ross was performing. Since their survival depended upon his success, it seems strange that the Salzburgers did not begin helping him sooner, rather than letting him struggle unproductively for so long with only his two sick Swiss redemptioners.[7]

Of perhaps less importance than the physician and surveyor, yet of great concern to Boltzius, was the acquisition of a proper shoemaker. To be sure, Reck of Purysburg did good work; but he was a worldly man who drank heavily and was a bad influence on the pious Salzburgers. Besides that, he drained away much money from Ebenezer that could have been spent there. On 7 January Boltzius even interceded with Causton to permit Reck to settle in Ebenezer; yet Reck failed to keep his good resolutions and slipped back into his evil ways. Eventually, after Reck helped a discontented Salzburger abscond, Boltzius was so enraged that he even removed his seven-year-old son from the orphanage and sent him back to his father (17 April). To fill Reck's place, he persuaded Oglethorpe to give him a shoemaker from among the newly landed Palatines. This poor man, Solomon Adde or Ade, made a good start but soon misbehaved and left Ebenezer.

Ebenezer suffered no shortage of carpenters. With such men as Kogler, Sanftleben, and the clockmaker Mueller, construction progressed rapidly and efficiently as long as the Salzburgers had sharp tools. At first they could get their tools repaired by an English smith at the neighboring settlement of Abercorn; and, when the smith ran away to Port Royal, Boltzius advanced three pounds to one of the Salzburgers on 18 April to buy his smithy.[8] The one profession represented in excess was that of the tailors; for, in addition to Herrnberger and Christ, the community acquired the retired soldier Kikar.

Boltzius declined the services of one man who would have been of great practical value to the Salzburgers, namely a professional hunter indentured to the recorder in Savannah, who offered to donate him to the Salzburgers (19 December). In Germany hunting was restricted to the nobility and their well-trained gamekeepers, and therefore this hunter should have been skilled in his profession and able to adapt himself to the local game and thus provide the Salzburgers with abundant flesh and fowl, as well as teach them his art. Unfortunately, German gamekeepers were reputed to be inveterate tipsters; and this man seems to have been no exception, unless perhaps Boltzius judged him by his professional stigma rather than by observation of his personal behavior. Medieval theologians had always deprecated hunters, including the mighty Nimrod. Perhaps they were prejudiced by the double meaning of the word *venery*; for in literature hunting often symbolized erotic pursuit. It should be noted, however, that the Herrnhuters in Savannah had a gamekeeper in their group who provided them with game, apparently without offending their moral scruples.[9]

The preface to the previous volume of this series noted that Boltzius made little mention of hunting. Possibly his parishioners, knowing his disapproval, failed to report all their booty; or possibly he omitted game in his reports because they were supposed to convince the benefactors in England and Germany that the Salzburgers still lacked food and needed continued support from the storehouse in Savannah. Not until 19 December did Boltzius mention that the Salzburgers had shot a hundred turkeys during the previous summer, at which time he also mentioned that the wood ducks, which the people had previously shot, had not returned that year. In these generally dreary reports it is refreshing to read that the naughty Helfenstein and Rheinlaender boys, both of them non-Salzburgers, squandered their time in hunting and fishing (25 August); so let us hope that their parents, despite their wickedness, were well supplied with flesh, fish, and fowl. Only on 10 April of 1738 did Boltzius learn from the miller at Old Ebenezer that the creek on which the Salzburgers had been settled for two years abounded in fish.

In addition to guarding his parishioners' souls and feeding their bodies, Boltzius dispensed justice; for, as long as they settled their own affairs quietly, the Salzburgers were exempt from the far harsher justice being meted out in Savannah. However, it was only with Oglethorpe's written permission that Boltzius allowed the widow Resch to marry four years after her husband was lost in the woods and presumed dead. Boltzius' extreme caution may have been intensified by his learning, some months earlier, of a man in Purysburg who pretended to be lost in the woods in order to desert wife and children and go to live better near Charleston.[10]

Boltzius was able to procure both justice and mercy when evidence came to light that Andreas Grimmiger had stolen three pounds from Johann Pletter three years earlier (3 July); and the punishment, far less severe than it would have been in Savannah, was of benefit to the community. Apparently Boltzius considered this theft less serious than the charge of fornication made against Paul Zittrauer and Barbara Maurer on 5 June, which, because it was neither proved nor confessed, was ordered into oblivion, along with Grimmiger's expiated sin. Because his authority did not extend across the Savannah River, Boltzius was less successful in coping with the French tavern-keeper who persisted in selling rum to some of the Salzburgers; but he was at least able to persuade Leonhard Rauner to cease collaborating with him (12 August).

Boltzius' greatest danger during the year 1738 was Thomas Pichler's and Stephan Riedelsperger's resolution to leave the colony; for, although Boltzius would not have missed them, their desertion might have caused an exodus to the promised land of Pennsylvania. One must marvel at, even if not admire, the devious diplomacy Boltzius used to balk the two men. Poor Mrs. Pichler seems to have intuited that she would die if she did not leave Ebenezer, and she confirmed her fears with her untimely death (1 March). Pichler almost followed his wife to the grave, in fact he became so ill that even Boltzius almost believed in his penitence; but then a wonder came to light and he rebounded from his deathbed (17 June) and settled into a marriage bed, for he soon married Theobald Kiefer's daughter.

Although Boltzius could leave the actual management of the orphanage to the saintly Kalcher, he still had to provide the means and make all policy decisions, and his detailed entry of 11 January reveals how closely he was involved. Even if the consumptive tailor Christ was dissatisfied with the "soul food" given in the menu of 15 March, the fare and treatment at that institution seem to have been much better than at other institutions of the time and even later, if we may believe what we read about Oliver Twist and other orphans. Although this was an age in which no loving father spared the rod, we read of only one incident of severe punishment at the orphanage (23 August). Boltzius' favorable report on the orphanage was confirmed by none other than George Whitefield, the famous preacher and philanthropist, who wrote in his journal under Tuesday, 11 July: "Returned this evening from Ebenezer (whither I went yesterday) the place where the Saltzburghers are settled; and was wonderfully pleased with their order and industry. Their lands are improved surprisingly for the time they have been there, and I believe they have far the best crop of any in the colony. They are blest with two such pious ministers as I have not often seen. They have no Courts of Judicature, but all little differences are immediately and implicitly decided by their ministers, whom they look upon and love as their fathers. They have likewise an Orphan House, in which are seventeen children and one widow, and I was much delighted to see the regularity wherewith it is managed. Oh that God may stir up the hearts of His servants to contribute towards that and another which we hope to have erected at Savannah. Mr. Boltzius, one of their ministers, being with me on Saturday, I gave him some of my poor's store for his orphans, and when I came to Ebenezer, he called them all before him, catechised and exhorted them to give God thanks for all His good providence towards them; then prayed with them, and

made them pray after him; then sung a psalm, and afterwards
the little lambs came and shook me by the hand, one by one,
and so we parted, and I scarce was ever better pleased in my
life. Surely, whoever contributes to the relief of the Saltzburghers, will perform an acceptable sacrifice to our blessed
Master. They are very poor; but with a little assistance might
live comfortably and well. They want a place for public worship, and money to buy cattle, and other necessaries for the
Orphan House and people. May the great God raise up instru-
ments to assist and relieve them, for surely they are worthy."[11]

Boltzius' journal usually reveals him as an astute man
endowed with a keen understanding of human nature; yet
occasionally he seems to be duped by people who know his
weaknesses. For example, when a parishioner tells him on 11
February that he feels too sinful to attend Holy Communion,
we suspect that he may prefer to spend his time some other
way. Boltzius also seems to have devoted too much time to
moral hypochondriacs like Mrs. Schweighofer, who was always
suffering from some scruple concerning her or her children's
souls (2 January), although perhaps she merely enjoyed the
young minister's attention. On the other hand, he seems to
have misjudged Mrs. Pichler in interpreting her desire to seek
medical treatment in Savannah as a sign of excessive self-will
(12 January), for her prompt death proved her point. Boltzius
called it divine guidance that caused Thilo to arrive in Ebenezer
just before Mrs. Pichler's planned departure for Savannah (13
January); yet he fails to mention that, even though God led
Thilo to Ebenezer, He did not guide him well in his treatment
of the sick woman. Boltzius was correct, however, in predicting
that the tailor Christ would cause annoyance in the orphanage
(11 April). Whereas Boltzius was sometimes gulled by smooth-
talking people, he was not too proud to admit that he had been
taken in, as when he realized that the younger Zuebli, whom he
had highly praised, was a gossip and troublemaker (7 February,
9 March).

Boltzius showed faith in divine aid, and human help, when
he built sheds for the cows and a hut for the cauldron that he
expected from the hand of God (9 January), feeling well assured that some human agency would have to make good this

trust in the Lord. We may almost suspect similar motivation, even if subconscious, when Boltzius magnanimously pressed for a fitting habitation for his assistant minister; for naturally the authorities would eventually appreciate both his magnanimity and the discrepancy of having the assistant better housed than the minister himself (20 April).

Besides informing us about the Salzburgers, Boltzius' diary throws light on other people and events of the general area. His frequent weather reports may help explain some of the activities in Savannah, for which no such consistent meteorological records survive. His accounts of the Palatines in Savannah are almost the only intimate information we have of that important segment of the population, which was so little understood by the British authorities and inhabitants of the town. It is only regrettable that Boltzius, like most eighteenth-century chroniclers, so often neglected to give proper names (which would, of course, have meant nothing to most of his German readers), since it would interest us to know the identities of many of the persons he mentions, for example, the German Indian-trader who passed through Ebenezer on his way back from the Cherokees (3 August) and the German slave-driver from near Charleston who attended Holy Communion with the Salzburgers (18 September). One wonders whether such people survived and left descendants to the present day and whether these descendants have anglicized their names. As an aid to genealogists, the footnotes to this volume give Christian names, when possible, for even the least conspicuous characters.

Some of the events mentioned by Boltzius would make romances in their own right, such as the escape of the indentured girl who was smuggled out of the country in men's clothing (26 February) or the plight of poor Abraham Grüning, who left Ebenezer and married a Scottish lass, only to become jealous when her beauty attracted other men (13 October). Or perhaps we should sympathize with the poor fun-loving wife who was torn from her father and countrymen and forced to live among righteous strangers who could not understand her Gaelic tongue. Other fates were even more pitiable: we might think of the Huber girl who lost both parents and all her siblings (10 January) or of the two elderly Swiss, Pastor Zouberbuhler (11

July) and the unnamed carpenter (29 July), who lost most of their loved ones in the unhealthy country.

The editors again wish to thank the authorities of the University and State Library at Halle in the German Democratic Republic for their hospitality and for graciously providing microfilms of Boltzius' diary. We also express our thanks to the American Philosophical Society for granting travel funds for research at Halle, to the General Research Board of the University of Maryland for defraying typing costs, and to the National Endowment for the Humanities for a grant to do research at the Georgia Historical Society in Savannah.

GEORGE FENWICK JONES
University of Maryland

RENATE WILSON
The Johns Hopkins University

Daily Register

Of the two pastors, Mr. Boltzius and Mr. Gronau
From January 1st to the end of the year 1738

JANUARY

Sunday, the 1st of January. Before the afternoon divine service I received a visit from a man who recently sinned grievously against God and His commandments, but whose heart is now penitent. It is very difficult for him to win God's grace again after he has once been unfaithful; but, if the Lord helps him through it, he will surely guard himself his life long from such vexation of his soul. He could hardly speak because of his tears; and it was hardly necessary for him to do so, because I had already known for a long time of his sin and his pangs of conscience caused by it. Such souls who begin to feel their sins and the anger they cause God will surely receive comfort and the wealth of God's mercy in due time, provided they remain faithful. Concerning this, we preached from the twelfth chapter of Isaiah briefly at the beginning of the morning prayer meeting and in more detail in the repetition hour. God be praised for all the blessings he has bestowed already today on us two and on several of the congregation from the sweet gospel of Jesus our Savior. May He allow some fruit therefrom to remain into eternity to the praise of his glory!

Already two days ago N. [Pichler] announced that he had resolved, through God's mercy, to partake of Holy Communion together with his sick wife. This time he was able to bear better witness of her than he had been able to the last time. Previously his wife had always resented it when my dear colleague and I could not consider her to be what she wanted us to think she was; and she usually expressed her anger about this more against her husband than against us. We hope from our hearts that she will so arrange her affairs that she will not stand naked and disgraced on the Day of Judgment.

In the past year one couple has been married in our congregation, seven children have been born, twelve persons have died, and from the very start up to this time sixty-four persons have died.

Monday, the 2nd of January. Mrs. Schweighofer visited me before the prayer hour and asked me about the meaning of the dear words of Christ in Matthew 5: "Blessed are the poor in spirit," etc., likewise, "Blessed are the merciful." She wished to know whether she too might partake of this blessedness. I gave her examples of both of these that she herself practiced daily and tried to apply to her the goodness that flows to us from the heart of our dear Savior. And, because she constantly complains and worries about her perdition and great spiritual wretchedness, I referred her again to the well-spring of salvation in Christ, to which she should flee or crawl as a sick and miserable wretch; for here everything that pains us will be removed and everything we are lacking will be abundantly restored. She is joyful in her heart that she will soon move into the orphanage and will enjoy, both mornings and evenings, not only bodily food but also the divine Word as the food much desired by her soul. Since she is being relieved of her two other children, who have been causing her much care and worry, she hopes to be all the less hindered in preparing herself for eternity. She prays diligently and with faith and will help to petition divine blessings as compensation for all our dear benefactors whose charitable donations supported the beginnings of our orphanage.

Tuesday, the 3rd of January. Today my dear colleague, Mr. Boltzius, returned to Savannah in order to preach the word of the Lord to the newly arrived Germans[12] and to administer Holy Communion. May the Lord Jesus bless all this and let much good be caused by it!

After school this morning three children came to me and said they would like to learn to believe. This may well be the occasion for such a resolution: yesterday in the prayer hour my dear colleague said how much it would please him when he returned from Savannah, if one or more children would bring him the joyful tidings and could truthfully say that the Lord Jesus had accepted them and had shown mercy on them, in which case he would at once kneel with such a child and heartily praise God for it. I spoke with these three children and told them I was pleased that they had made such a resolution, but they should not let matters rest at that but should not cease until it had come to pass. It was not enough to begin well (as they had often done before), but they must give their hearts entirely unto the Lord. I also told them to their comfort that the dear Lord would so bless them in Christ that each of them could turn himself from evil. He had exalted Jesus to be a prince and savior in order to give Israel penitence and forgiveness of sins, these last words being the ones I had used this very morning in the prayer hour.

Wednesday, the 4th of January. Mrs. H. [Helfenstein] visited me this morning and told me with joy how the dear Lord had greatly blessed her soul at the last prayer meeting that Mr. Boltzius had held on Monday.[13] When she had come home she had not found her daughter and had waited for her a long time.[14] When the daughter finally returned, she learned that the dear Lord had also blessed the prayer hour in her, for which reason she (the daughter) had gone out immediately after the prayer hour and had called upon the dear Lord with all her heart to make her truly poor in spirit and to bring her to a recognition of her sins. She also told her that it had always seemed to her that she should first go home and get warm and then pray, but she did not wish to let herself be deterred from her resolution. At the same time she[15] gave her good advice and admonished her how she should continue in this way so that she would someday come straight to Jesus. She told me that God is working on both[16] her sons, but that they are still much too frivolous.

Recently one of them dreamed that he had to hurry, for the axe was already placed at the root of the tree and, if it did not soon bear good fruit, it would be cut down and cast into the fire. Thereupon he prayed diligently to God in bed until he got up. The other one also dreamed that he was standing at the edge of the water with many other people, when a crocodile came out and approached him alone and wished to eat him.

Therefore she admonished him not to be so frivolous but to think of his salvation: Satan, who is compared in Holy Scripture to the Leviathan, wished to swallow him up completely. These were merely dreams, she said; yet she thought one should not ignore them entirely. She also said that her daughter had told her how there were still some children in the school who were giving themselves to Jesus. She had asked one of the girls how she was doing, whereupon she answered that she was earnestly trying to improve.

After the evening prayer meeting the previously mentioned three children came to me and said they would not slacken until they had won Jesus and that I should pray for them. One sees how these children now pray diligently in the prayer meeting, as they have not previously done.

Thursday, the 5th of January. In the evening after the prayer hour not only the first three children but also two other ones from the orphanage came to pray with me. First I told them something about the joy the Lord Jesus would have if they came to Him in truth, and I told them that they should not rest until they had come to Him entirely and given themselves to Him. They would have to undertake this with true seriousness and with great daring, they must be concerned only with the Lord Jesus and His mercy, even if they were to be ridiculed for it by ill behaved children. For all this the Savior Himself would give them strength, for without Him they could do nothing. Thereupon we knelt down together and prayed. Now may the Lord Jesus, as the good Shepherd, let these lambs be commended to His pastoral care and may He also give me wisdom to advise them rightly.

Friday, the 6th of January. Shortly before the noon service my dear God brought me (Boltzius) home again. At first I was of a mind to spend this day, the Feast of Epiphany, preaching the divine Word in Purysburg; but I was too weak physically and I also heard there that they knew nothing of this holy day, and therefore I traveled home as quickly as I could. I was already indisposed at my departure from Ebenezer; but, since the trip had to take place, the Lord strengthened me so much in Savannah that I was able to consort with the German people there both Tuesday afternoon and also on Wednesday and to prepare them from God's word to receive Holy Communion. Now that they have received spiritual guidance and have been clearly shown the way to the Kingdom of God, we must wait to see whether any fruit will result from it. There are dreadful swearers and other ill behaved people among them, as the Salzburgers who took me down noted. If they should be disobedient or unfaithful in the service of the Lord Trustees and thus cause great annoyance, we will withdraw from them or at least exclude the misbehavers from Communion as an example for the others, after first warning them sincerely and kindly.

They consider themselves unfortunate for having come to this province of Georgia and not to Pennsylvania, from where some of them have received good letters. However, because I know from oral and written reports of the miserable condition of the people there, who have been sold by the ship captains as indentured servants for several years, I showed them all in an hour what advantages they had not only over the servants in Pennsylvania and Carolina but also over the other servants here in Georgia because of the concern of the Lord Trustees so that, through these remonstrances, they might be restrained from all grumbling, recalcitrancy, and other misbehavior. If they behave themselves they will profit from it and Mr. Causton will take all possible care of them and their children. At my request he will compensate one or two schoolmasters with clothing, provisions, etc., if they will teach the children. But there is no time here for that except before day in winter and evenings after the work has been done: men, women, and children must apply the whole day to work. In the summer they have a few hours free when the heat is too great, at which time school could be held. I was asked for ABC books for children and for New Testaments and Bibles for the adults, which are to be brought down for them in the future when one of us comes down. They would be pleased if the Word of God were preached to them at least once every four weeks, which, with God's help, is to be done. If we should come down to Savannah from time to time for other reasons (as has often been necessary up to now), then we will hold an evening prayer hour with them. Mr. Causton is very pleased with all this and will give provisions and one shilling per day as pay for the Salzburgers who bring me or my dear colleague down for this purpose.

[Capt. Thomson[17] was still in Savannah with his ship, and I would have liked to give him a letter to Court Preacher Ziegenhagen, if only I had not been interrupted after starting to write. We are expecting a ship from London any day, at which time we will immediately answer the letters for which we are hoping.]

Saturday, the 7th of January. Mr. Causton is willing for me to accept the Purysburg shoemaker Reck into our congregation; but he reminded me of the hypocrisy of N. [Rheinlaender], who was accepted upon my intercession. I told him clearly that he had not lived well in general but that he was resolved to improve his ways and to tear himself away earnestly from his dissolute comrades. After my return I reported Mr. Causton's worries to shoemaker Reck and let him know that I would not allow him to entertain old acquaintances or to drink or misbehave, etc. He promises much, and we can only hope for the best.

N. [Ott] came to me and reported that a young Salzburger had brought him several shillings with which he wished to repay him for some damage for which he felt responsible. However, he was not to blame, rather the damage was caused by something else; and therefore he felt pangs of conscience at keeping the money. I advised him to return it and, if the Salzburger did not wish to accept it, to bring it to me. His overly sensitive conscience may have been touched again by God's word; and therefore he wishes to be freed from anything that might cause him any disquiet, even though he is very poor. Ott will not yet resign himself to the divine dispensation, yet I am pleased that he will not accept and keep money that does not belong to him.

Because the chapters concerning the particular unrighteous acts of the Children of Israel have been completed in the previous prayer hours, I spoke this evening about the general purpose God has in presenting them. This cannot only be so that we will know what kind of uncleanliness and repulsive sicknesses His people had and the means he ordered against them, but rather that we will recognize sin as the source of all, even physical, evil and the resulting repulsive spiritual uncleanliness because of which we would have to be expelled from communion with God and the holy angels and so will seek purification from it in Christ and his blood of reconciliation. For an explanation and application of this matter I read from, and briefly explained, 1 John 1:7–10 and 2:1–2; and, from this, frivolous and confident people were warned, whereas penitent and sin-laden souls were comforted in Christ. After the prayer hour a certain man [the schoolmaster Ortmann] complained to me that he could lay hold of no hope because he had spent his youth so disgracefully and in such worldly pleasures and had served the devil so much and had become such an old tree that he did not know what would become of him. For his comfort I spoke a bit with him about the above-mentioned passage and also about 1 Peter 4:3.

Sunday, the 8th of January. Today has been a most refreshing and blessed Sunday for me and, as I have learned, also for others, for which may His holy Name be for ever and eternally praised and exalted! In today's prayer hour, which was again held in the medico's hut as has been done before, we repeated that part of the morning sermon that we could not complete in the repetition hour because of lack of time. Today the children caused me more pleasure than usual.

The day before yesterday Mrs. Rothenberger bore a young daughter, who was baptized publicly today.

Monday, the 9th of January. Last Sunday the surveyor[18] returned to us from Purysburg to complete his work once and for all [because he surmises that Mr. Oglethorpe will come soon and may not be pleased with his negligence]. He is now surveying all the land that belongs to the city, as well as all the gardens, as we would have liked long ago. He led both of us to the piece of land which he is planning to measure out for our gardens. It lies in the angle made by the Savannah River and Ebenezer Creek and therefore could not be surveyed for the Salzburgers according to Mr. Oglethorpe's plan. It is large enough for each of us to receive a well laid out garden.

Last week, with divine assistance, we completed all the structures which were required for our home for orphans and widows.[19] In addition to the orphanage, which consists of three sitting rooms and three bedrooms, we have built: 1) a spacious kitchen with an attached pantry, 2) a large cowshed for the cows we now have and for those we hope to receive from divine providence, 3) a firm pigpen with a chicken coop above it under its roof, 4) a spacious toilette with three separate booths for married people, boys, and girls, 5) a spacious hut for the mill, bake-oven, and wash cauldrons, which we are expecting from the generous hand of God. These structures, which are indispensable for our housekeeping, have required so much money and expense that neither we ourselves nor the builders could have imagined it. But everything has been built so solidly, neatly, and comfortably that everyone who knows about it must evaluate it even higher than the expenses have run.

Now, even if we have expended the provision that God has granted us for it, and even a bit more, it will be easy for the Lord to grant enough more to enable us to accept poor children and impecunious widows or at least to maintain those whom we have already accepted with His blessing. [Nothing can be expected from Savannah, for promises from there are subject to many changes and exceptions.] During the entire construction God has averted all injury and strengthened all the workers right noticeably in their bodies. They in turn began their work every morning and ended it every evening with prayer; and, to my joy and to the furtherance of the work, they showed great diligence, loyalty, and unity, as befits Christian workers.

Now that they have moved from the doctor's hut into this new home to take care of the children, Kalcher and his wife are in great distress and consider themselves entirely unqualified by their previous experience for this important office as directors and parents. I had to make every effort to raise their troubled and depressed spirits and to direct them to the true source from which all strength for good works may be obtained. In my duties concerning the orphanage they are truly my right hand; and through God's grace they are the kind of people whom the Lord has prepared as vessels of his mercy and whom he already uses and will continue to use as tools of his mercy on the children and others. And therefore I am very pleased that they are growing smaller and smaller in their own eyes and see better and better the importance of their office and therefore strive all the more zealously to ask, seek, and knock. They administer the housekeeping so orderly and exactly that they could serve as models for others. The children whom they have under their supervision so far have, through God's mercy, become much better behaved and much better mannered and at ease in their social conduct; and this gives us good hope also in regard to those who will be added. The Salzburger Herzog has requested, through other people and in person, to be accepted and cared for in the orphanage; because, as a result of his natural simplicity and special circumstances, he is not in a position to earn his bread. At times his physical circumstances have made him miserable in body and soul; and, because, as all those familiar with his circumstances know, he would perish, he has been accepted and is doing right good service in the housekeeping for Kalcher, who is now supervising him. He genuinely fears God but has his weaknesses, which we must bear. The Lord be praised for everything!

Tuesday, the 10th of January. This evening our regular prayer meeting was canceled and the time destined for it was used for the dedication of our new orphanage. To be sure, no signal for this was given by the bell as is made for the prayer meeting; yet almost the entire congregation had gathered, and we attempted to pass our time together in the new house with singing, praying, and the contemplation of the edifying example of the Lord Jesus in order to urge both adults and children to follow in His steps. The text was from the recent Sunday gospel Luke 2:49–52; and, after quoting it, I especially stressed the two major points, the godliness and obedience that can be presented in the dear example of Christ for imitation by children and adults; and I designated Psalms 99:4 as a source from which they could gain strength for such imitation. After the sermon we fell on our knees together and praised God for all the physical and spiritual blessings he has granted us so far and implored Him, for us and for our benefactors, all gifts and benefactions necessary for this life and for the life to come.

The people who live together in the house are 1) Kalcher and his wife and child, 2) Mrs. Schweighofer, a true Hannah (Luke 2:3), 3) the Salzburger Herzog as handyman, and 4) the orphans, namely three boys and eight girls. The ninth, to wit, Margaret Huber, remains for cogent reasons under the supervision of Peter Gruber and his wife but receives her subsistence from the orphanage. Four children are still expected from Purysburg, whose parents promise to repay their rations after the harvest.

The names and the conditions of the orphans are as follows: 1) Catharina Holtzer, 14 years old. Her mother died here as a widow on 28 August 1737. She is now being prepared for Holy Communion; afterwards, if she is strong enough, she will be trained for housekeeping and domestic chores. 2) Sophia Catharina Elisabeth Arnsdorf, 14 years old, and 3) Dorothea Catharina Arnsdorf, 6 years old, are the children of the shoemaker who lost his life in the water at Purysburg on 1 July 1737.[20] The widow is still living with us and is still keeping two of the children with her to help in her work. 4) Thomas Schweighofer, 9 years old, and 5) Maria Schweighofer, 11 years old, and 6) Ursula Schweighofer, 5¼ years old, are the children of the above-named widow who was paralyzed by a stroke. The father died in Old Ebenezer on 21 March 1736. 7) Susanna Haberfehner, 16 years old, and 8) Magdalena Haberfehner, 14 years old, are the children of a pious Austrian. The father died on 29 April 1736 and the mother on 28 October 1736. The oldest girl is weakminded and must still go to school in order to learn to recognize the path to salvation. 9) Johann Jacob Helfenstein, 12 years old, and 10) Jeremiah Helfenstein, 10 years old, are the children of the tanner who came to us with the third transport. He died on 23 October 1736; and his widow leads an edifying life among us in great physical poverty. Besides these two children she has four others. The oldest daughter is a maid in my service; the oldest son is to learn the shoemaker's trade in Savannah, the middle daughter helps her mother, and the youngest son of four years still needs his mother's care. 11) Eva Rosina Unselt, 10 years old, is the youngest daughter of the old schoolmaster who came to Purysburg four years ago with his wife and four daughters. Both parents are dead. 12) Margareta Huber, ten years old, is the only surviving daughter of the entire Huber family, which consisted of six persons. She is still under Peter Gruber's supervision.

In addition to these children, we also take care of the widowed Austrian Grimmiger's child Catharina, 2 years old; and, since it cannot be taken into the orphanage because of its tender age, Mrs. Rieser is being paid from the poor box, as previously, to take motherly care of this child. The father of this child is almost always sick and unable to support it. To maintain a child, when large and small are averaged out, requires at least three pounds sterling, which, to be sure, is very much according to German money; but here in this country, where everything is very expensive and money is scarce, it will buy very little. No matter how much the maintenance of the orphanage and the education of the orphans may cost, our dear Lord cares more about one soul, if it can be saved from physical, spiritual, and eternal death, than for all the treasures and wealth of this world.

How miserable it would be if our orphans were scattered here and there throughout the country to earn their bread; for then, like other miserable children, they would grow up not only in ignorance but also in wickedness and heathen horror and would be of no future value either to God or man. Our Salzburgers are so occupied with their own poverty that they are unable to contribute towards the maintenance of the orphans. For our part, we could not help but risk this undertaking in faith and await divine approbation through God's granting of support for it. Our loyal Savior, who so dearly loves children and wishes to have them led to Him so that He may bless them, has sufficient physical blessings and will surely grant enough to enable us to maintain the few lambs that we now have as well as others. Yesterday, while I was inspiring the childish fear of and love for God that have been presented to us for our imitation of the example of Christ, it occurred to me what is meant by Psalm 34:11: "They that seek the Lord shall not want any good thing." We have accepted this word of God in faith and will await its fulfilment.

The program with the children is as follows: they all arise early in the morning before five o'clock, wash, and get dressed, whereupon one of us sings a song with them and lets them read a chapter from the Bible in regular order. We then discuss it briefly for their edification, and finally we kneel to pray and close with one or two versicles. When they are completely dressed, they are assigned some housekeeping task until breakfast; or, if they have something to learn, they have time for that. After breakfast, which is always a hot meal, they go together to school, which lasts until midday. After the noonday meal, as also after the afternoon school, which lasts from two to four o'clock, the boys, who are still very little, are put to some work in the garden or to something else useful, whereas the girls are put to some female work (to which more attention will be paid from now on). As can be easily guessed, their work does not amount to much but is necessary for its own sake so that they will soon be accustomed from youth up to useful things and be kept from idleness. When evening comes, which is now at about six o'clock, they are led to the prayer meeting and afterwards they repeat in their private prayer what they have already had in catechism. Everything for the glory of God!

Wednesday, the 11th of January. I assembled the men to discuss general matters with them in order to maintain good order and good understanding among all members of the congregation. This time we have a very pleasant winter. The frost, which has fallen a few times, has never lasted but has soon changed into a right pleasant and temperate warmth by day and sometimes at night too.

Mrs. Kalcher has attested to me her right sincere pleasure that God has ordained for Mrs. Schweighofer to be accepted into the orphanage, because she finds in her a right serious companion in prayer and spiritual struggle. She applies her sojourn like the godly Hanna (Luke 2) and is trying, through the grace of God, to make careful use of this beautiful example of a righteous widow. She has always wished sincerely before the Lord for her three children to change; and now it appears that the Lord has looked with mercy on her prayers and tears, since both the boy and the girl are now giving more hope than previously.

Thursday, the 12th of January. Mrs. P. [Pichler] is still sick and yearns to go to Savannah to be cured by a doctor there; and her husband has agreed to this because he cannot contradict her in her excessive self-will. We have wished to treat her with medications, as we have done for other people in her condition with good success, God be praised! However, because they did not take effect at once, especially since she did not care to take them according to the given directions, she considered them more harmful than helpful. Her worldly nature longs for comfort and greater relaxation for her body than she finds here; and therefore she will surely nag and drive her husband until he finally resolves to leave here completely, since he himself is not yet firm in his Christianity but has it more in thoughts and resolutions than in deeds. He has had to put up with a great deal from her so far, and she has blamed him for all her physical and spiritual misery and made the most bitter and dreadful reproaches so that, when he complained to us about it, we were horribly shocked. Her head is full of Pennsylvania and the alleged good times there, but things could go very wrong for her there and it might be well if she would let herself be warned. The most horrible thing about it is that she is risking the most extreme danger of going to eternal damnation yet does not wish to believe it.

Today, in the course of my work, I paid a visit to H. F.'s [Hans Floerel's] wife, which she herself recognized, with tears, as a fatherly dispensation of the Lord. She is deeply aware of her sins and stands as a right poor sinner in a pure and sincere yearning for her salvation in Christ, which she herself, however, cannot recognize as sincere and pure. She only said that she would have prayed but that she could not find any words for it, for which reason she was holding the 55th Psalm in her hands when I found her. I read the Psalm to her and showed her that in it our Lord Jesus had prayed for His suffering and struggling members those things that they should pray after Him in His spirit. From His own experience He assured them with these words, among others, that they would be heard: "Cast thy burden upon the Lord, and He shall sustain thee." I then spoke further with her according to her condition and prayed with her as simply as I could, and the Lord gave His blessing.

Friday, the 13th of January. Yesterday N. [Eischberger] asked me to drop in on him sometime, and I did it today and led a very necessary discussion with him and his wife concerning what pertains to salvation. For some time God has been awakening the man mightily with His word, and now he well recognizes that he is lacking in a thorough conversion and change of heart and that he cannot yet say with truth: "For I know whom I have believed and am persuaded"; yet he has made the good resolution to hurry and save his soul. For some time his wife has not been able to come to church or to the prayer meeting because of her situation, since she has been sick some of the time and has borne a little child. We can notice bad consequences of this very much in that she has become more indolent and careless, and for this reason I attempted to awaken her today to a real seriousness.

God has caused us an unexpected pleasure through the unexpected arrival of Mr. Thilo. He came to us with our boat, which had been sent already on Monday for provisions, and brought some very enjoyable letters from Court Preacher Ziegenhagen, Senior Urlsperger, and Professor Francke, from which we could again take much material for the praise of our merciful Lord. God brought our dear Mr. Thilo here healthy and happy on the ship that has brought provisions from Ireland for this colony;[21] and today he joined us in humbly praising the Lord for all the mercy that has been shown him. Praise be to the Lord, who has fulfilled our wish even sooner than we expected. An unusual joy has arisen among the congregation at his arrival, especially since they still remember clearly the good recommendation I once read to them out of a letter from Professor Francke. Those things he brought for himself, for us, and for the congregation are still in Savannah; and arrangements will soon be made to fetch them. Now God has shown us again in our want that His river is full of water and that he has awakened various benefactors to various charitable gifts; and may He reveal Himself as a gracious and bountiful rewarder of them.[22]

Saturday, the 14th of January. This morning my dear colleague, Mr. Boltzius, has gone to Savannah with Mr. Thilo in order to fetch his and our things and to speak with Mr. Causton concerning Mr. Thilo's provisions. He hopes, God willing, to hold divine services with the German people in Savannah. The reason that he hurried so much is this: there is a sick woman here who would like to be treated by Mr. Thilo. However, he has none of his medicines here and would therefore like to fetch them. It is very peculiar about this woman:[23] as previously reported, she had always wished to go to Savannah, but the trip was always postponed. Finally it was firmly resolved that she would go down as soon as our boat returned. But, when the time came, our dear Mr. Thilo arrived with our boat; so it was not necessary. This sick woman's husband could hardly speak a word because of his tears and amazement. Thus does our dear Lord provide! [Meanwhile, he has prescribed some of our pulv. bozoard. for her.][24]

Sunday, the 15th of January. I tried to show the congregation from today's gospel, John 2:1 ff., how the dear Lord guides his people, amazingly to be sure, but also gloriously and blissfully. May the Lord bless this on them all! This evening in the prayer meeting, which was held for the first time in the kitchen of the orphanage, I read to those present about the edifying death of the late Römer from the *Collection for the Building of the Kingdom of God.*[25] Our so loyal and loving God greatly blessed this for me and the others.

Monday, the 16th of January. Last Saturday four more children came to us from Purysburg who have been taken in by the orphanage and whose parents wish to repay their rations after the harvest. Now there are thirty-two children altogether in the school. May the Lord Jesus have mercy upon them, and may they let themselves be gathered as lambs in His arms! In the evening during the prayer meeting we had the verse: "But unto you that fear my name shall the Sun of Righteousness arise with healing in his wings, etc." That's the way it is: no one is better off than he who fears the name of the Lord! This will be revealed on Judgment Day. Here the world is blind; but there one shall see what a difference there is between the righteous and the godless, between him who serves God and him who does not.

Tuesday, the 17th of January. By Mr. Thilo's return everything in his hut will have been put into good order so that he will be able to enjoy the greatest possible comfort in it. The hut, like the roof, is well guarded all around against the wind and rain and is furnished with two bedrooms, both of them provided with thick oaken floor boards. The courtyard is separated from the garden by a firm fence. In the yard, in addition to the house, there is a spacious kitchen along with a hearth, also a pigpen and chicken coop and other necessary conveniences.[26] Across the street on the right side is the orphanage, and behind the garden lies the place where, with divine blessing, the church and school are to be built.

Wednesday, the 18th of January. I (Boltzius) was held up along with Mr. Thilo in Savannah longer than we had imagined. The ship did not arrive before Savannah until Monday noon, and yesterday morning his things were delivered to our boat so that we departed at about noon and came to our dear Ebenezer at about noon today with comfort of body and soul. The captain of the ship could not yet give us what was sent to us and the congregation in the way of money and things, but he comforted us with the knowledge that everything could be fetched next week. Captain Daubatz has proved friendly to Mr. Thilo. We told him how meanly the ship captains are accustomed to treat their passengers and that the good treatment he gave will serve as material for the praise of God and for intercessions for those who helped him in the task. Also, he was unable to tell of any storm or danger at sea. Mr. Causton has shown Mr. Thilo every kindness and was ready to give him the allotted provisions, kitchen utensils, and house tools, that are usually give by the Lord Trustees. However, since there are now few in the store-house, he will get them later.

On Sunday morning and afternoon I held divine services for the newly arrived German people in the regular church. In the morning I preached those truths from the gospel for the Second Sunday after Epiphany, John 2:1 ff., first those that lie in the text, namely that the friends of the Lord Jesus have, to be sure, their hardship and distress of soul and body in this pilgrimage yet do not despair in them but exercise themselves in praying, waiting, and obeying according to the example of the mother of the Lord Jesus Christ. Help will come at a certain and already ordained time; at which hour the Lord Jesus will appear to us all the greater and sweeter in His glory and loving qualities. As an application I explained to them what an important difference there is between the hardship and distress of the righteous and that of the godless; and I told them that they should consider it to be the real affliction of unconverted people in Christendom and in every congregation that such people lie in their sins and under the anger of the Lord and yet neither know it nor believe it. In this regard they have received sufficient instruction for their salvation.

In the afternoon I briefly repeated the morning sermon and applied the verse 2 Peter 2:9 to it as a basis for edification; and I showed what godly and unrighteous people may finally expect according to the witness of the Holy Spirit. These people from the Palatinate come, to be sure, diligently and show a desire and reverence for the Word of God; but I have not yet been able to recognize any other fruit but this. They know very few edifying songs, so that we must accommodate ourselves to them. Most of them are full of grumbling and complaints, although Mr. Causton takes good care of them and they receive more kindness through the good orders of the Lord Trustees than other servants in the colony. They would like to be free, but they have engaged themselves as servants in writing. The most grievous thing is that their children must serve until they are twenty-five years old even though the parents and adults are free after five years. They besieged me with requests to speak to Mr. Causton on their behalf and to ask for this or that for them, which I gladly did as far as was feasible. Unreasonable demands we refuse to accept.

Senior Urlsperger has written a very edifying and affectionate letter to our congregation, which, with God's grace, I shall put to use for our listeners in the prayer meeting. According to church order I am to treat a very edifying and pure evangelical matter in Leviticus 16 concerning the typical reconciliation in the Old Testament, and in this I shall refer my listeners constantly to Christ and the reconciliation he has instituted, which is the principal treasure of the New Testament and is recommended to us by the gospel. Today the example of the high priest showed us that the day of reconciliation of the New Testament was, to be sure, a bitter and burdensome day for our High Priest but that He embraced it with the greatest willingness in order to win salvation for us. How willing He shall be to grant it to all poor distressed sinners! Likewise, our High Priest has gone to the Allhighest with prayer and blood, which,

in Hebrews XII, is speaking blood which cries out for reconciliation and mercy, again a glorious comfort for penitent souls
who would gladly be saved [but cannot].

We shall soon receive from the ship the charitable benefactions that have again flowed to us abundantly through the
hands of our righteous Fathers in Christ in London, Augsburg,
and Halle. We can already take much in advance for our edification, comfort, and instruction from their strength- and
pith-filled letters. May our dear Lord, whose goodness is renewed over us every morning, bless all this in us for His glory
and our true salvation; and may He be a rich rewarder in
Christ's name for all the physical and spiritual gifts that have
flowed to us so far from their love and care. [This time we have
received no letter from Secretary Newman. Perhaps something
will arrive soon when Mr. Oglethorpe comes.]

Thursday, the 19th of January. An unknown benefactress
from London has sent the two sisters who are our helpmeets
a welcome gift of all kinds of useful linen things, which Mr.
Thilo delivered today. The letter that was enclosed with it reveals, in addition to the truly kind gift, the glorious treasure
of righteousness and the sincere humility that dwells in the
heart of this unknown benefactress, who is so dear to God; and
the edification that all of us received from it to the praise of
the Lord is worth more than the value the benefactress, in her
humility and disdain for temporal things, could place upon the
gifts she sent. May our loving Jesus, who has filled her with His
love that also flowed out so lovingly even to His poor members
dwelling in the wilderness, endow her further with the garments of His salvation as a complete possession of her soul!
Instead of a simple recompense, we and our helpmeets wish
this worthy person the heart and the treasure of the God-
devoted Maria, Luke 10:42. And, since I was greatly edified
with the children today by the extremely delightful song: "One
thing is needful, oh Lord, this one," etc.,[27] we shall send her
the same as a token of our love and respect. May the Lord Jesus
fill all his children with the spirit of faith, love, and humility.

A student of theology from Halle, Mr. N. [Hirte], sent me a
short letter in which he reminded me of several things that led
me back to the great mercy of God and His fatherly guidance

that I experienced in Halle. In it he said with great simplicity
that the dear Lord had blessed my poor services in him, etc.,
for which may the name of the Lord be praised. May He make
this Mr. N. [Hirte], who is no longer known to me, loyal in the
grace he has received and make him into a vessel of His mercy
and an instrument of His grace so that the blessed orphanage
there, as well as other people, may have in him a righteous and
loyal worker!

Friday, the 20th of January. I learned in the case of two
people in an evening prayer meeting that God had so blessed
the few words "Have thanks for Thy love"[28] from the glorious
song "Bridegroom of the Soul" that this is now the content of
the prayers every day. On the occasion of the 16th chapter of
Leviticus, when we were recalling our Lord Jesus' bitter day of
suffering, the words "Thou hast wearied me with thine iniquities" cried out to each and every one of us from the mouth and
heart of the Lord Jesus; and we encouraged each other to learn
to call back to our Lord Jesus, our meritorious Savior: "Have
thanks for thy love," which, however, should not be mere lip
service.

In today's evening prayer meeting I read the letter of Senior
Urlsperger, which he wrote this time to the congregation, with
a few observations aimed at its application to our circumstances.
With divine blessing this made such an impression that I heard
someone say afterwards: "I would not have missed the prayer
meeting for anything." The Lord has certainly inspired our
dear Senior to write precisely what was in the letter, because it
exactly fitted the circumstances of the congregation. The example of the late Riedelsperger, who was mentioned in it as a
victor, was without doubt impressive for all those who knew
him well. At the same time I cited the example of his brother
who, during his good days in the Empire, learned to love the
world again and even became a Papist.

Oh, if only everyone would believe that the paths of the Cross
which God has walked with us so far are the surest and most
blessed paths! I attempted to present this matter to my listeners
as simply and earnestly as our dear Lord granted me to do so.
I promised to begin house visitations as soon as I have finished
writing letters to England and Germany and to ask around

what effect was had by the prayer hours we have had so far concerning reconciliation and salvation in Christ and also by today's prayer hour and all the other good things that God has
shown us this week so that the name of the Lord will be praised
here and also elsewhere, when word spreads about the righteous paths of our people here.

Saturday, the 21st of January. The men of the congregation
gathered again today at noon in order to discuss a few material
things together. Especially, they hired new herdsmen, of which
there are three for two herds, for an entire year. Because of
their need, we have given the congregation some of the blessings that have flowed to us so that they may help them with
money and clothes. [And, because the Salzburgers are unable
to pay such people for their work as a result of the hard times
and the poor harvest and the holding back of provisions by
the storehouse, they will be given not only the necessary clothes,
as was done last year, but also 2 £ sterling as support from these
blessings.] If this arrangement with the three herdsmen had not
been made last year, most of the cattle would have perished,
since they must be grazed in various places.

[Since my return from Savannah I have been occupied in
writing letters, which were finished today and are to be given
to Capt. Thomson next Monday when my dear colleague journeys to Savannah on account of our things and money that are
still on the ship. Because we have written this time in haste
and not to all benefactors and friends, the remainder will be
added in about fourteen days with Capt. Daubaz, who brought
Mr. Thilo to us with letters and other things. The present letters are from me and my dear colleague to Court Chaplain
Ziegenhagen, Court Preacher Butjenter, Senior Urlsperger,
Professor Francke, also to an unknown benefactress in London
and to two theological students in Halle. The diary, up to this
point, accompanies them.]

Continuation of the Diary

Sunday, the 22nd of January 1738. Some of the girls among
the school children have shown more seriousness in their Christianity recently than formerly; and Kalcher reports that some

of the orphans secretly kneel in diligent prayer. They are, to
be sure, often awakened; but their frivolity hinders them from
achieving a righteous nature and entering into a communion
with the Lord Jesus. It is of great value if we can talk and
pray with each individual child in private; and for this reason
I would like to be freed of the burden of administrating the
provisions, which compels me to travel so often and takes so
much time.

H. Floerel brought me a letter that he had written to Senior
Urlsperger and asked me to enclose it. Our dear Lord blessed
in him the Senior's edifying letter when it was read aloud last
Friday for general edification; for it moved him to write to him
about what is going through his mind through the blessing of
God. For the good of our congregation we try to make use
of all the letters that come to us from our dear Fathers in
London and Germany, as occurred last evening and will occur
in further prayer meetings. From the letters we reveal to them
only that which suits them and serves for their edification.
[What is written privately for our information is kept secret.]

Today we discussed the gospel for the Third Sunday after
Epiphany, Matthew 8:1 ff., concerning true faith; and, to clarify and emphasize this important material in the evening prayer
meeting, we read and applied a pertinent passage from the
blessed Luther's golden foreword to the Epistle to the Romans.
Oh, how greatly both old and young in all places are hindered
from a true faith by superstitious belief in the use of the means
of salvation and in natural honesty[29] (Galatians 6:6). The de-
scription of true faith in said preface is worth being learned
by heart, and it will be taught to our children. [We also find
it very useful on occasion to teach the children some edifying
apophthegmata and emphatic sayings of pious clergymen; and
they have already learned several of these.]

Monday, the 23rd of January. We were told that a member
of the congregation had fallen into such sorrow because of his
sins that he might founder in them and even risk mortal danger. When we learned about it yesterday evening it was already
too late to speak to the person, so this morning I sought the
earliest opportunity to bring a word of the gospel and of comfort to his anguished conscience. May the Lord give His bless-

ing! Oh, how easily is sin committed, but how much it costs later to return to grace! All my life long I shall remember this example and another in the congregation; and, as long as my eyes remain open, I shall warn with love and sincerity against the deceit of sin and will call out to pious people: "Let him that thinketh he standeth take heed lest he fall." [I had intended to go to Savannah this morning to fetch the benefactions that we had received from Europe and to terminate the provision accounts for once and for all; but I was prevented, and the trip must take place tomorrow, God willing.]

In the evening prayer hour I again read an inspiring letter from those that have just arrived; [and on this occasion I could not help but pour forth, more with tears than with words, the distress that is weighing upon me because of my usual lack of time for my spiritual office.] May God grant, however, that the emotions that were aroused will not remain only as such but that each and every one will become serious and loyal and that all limping will stop on both sides.[30]

Tuesday, the 24th of January. This evening in the prayer hour I (Gronau) began the contemplation of the stories of the New Testament, and I plan to continue with them as often as my dear colleague is not at home or is prevented from holding the prayer meeting. I have undertaken this task in the name of God, and He will stand by me. Without Jesus I can do nothing; but with him I can do everything. Also, my Savior, let me learn to believe both right firmly!

Wednesday, the 25th of January. This morning Mr. Thilo and I visited a sick person who showed us a certain song and pointed at a verse in it with her finger, and from this we could see how dark it appeared in her soul. Mr. Thilo spoke to her about it and showed her what she should do: she should merely persist in asking, seeking, and knocking, for Jesus would finally help. It is a great joy for us that dear Mr. Thilo takes such care of the sick both spiritually and physically. The sick too are happy that they have received a doctor who not only gives them medicine but who also cares for their souls. May the dear Lord be praised for that, and may He stand by him and us!

Thursday, the 26th of January. Mr. Thilo believes that our huts, where the wind can blow through, may be contributing

much to the sickness that has been prevailing among us. Therefore he wishes nothing more than that we might receive better
huts; and also, for the same reason, he would like to see Mr.
Boltzius do something soon towards building his house. Perhaps the dear Lord will help him start soon, especially since
some money has recently been sent for this purpose.

Friday, the 27th of January. Last night the boats arrived,
but my dear colleague remained down there to balance the accounts completely. The boats returned immediately and will
fetch more provisions.

Saturday, the 28th of January. Toward evening one of the
boats returned and brought up the things that were sent from
England, among other things three iron mills and an iron
wheel, with which the mills can be driven all the faster. [The
chest of books, medicines, and linens which were sent from
Halle to England and were reported by Mr. Ziegenhagen to
be coming with them was, however, forgotten but will probably
be sent after them on Mr. Oglethorpe's ship.] May the dear
Lord mercifully and bountifully repay everything that we now
have and that will be sent later!

Sunday, the 29th of January. This morning the daughters
of both Hans Floerel and Hans Maurer were baptized. We
have tried all day long to arouse people from the word of God
to a true seriousness in their Christianity. May the dear Lord
lay his blessing on this endeavor. [My dear colleague has probably preached the Word of the Lord to the Germans in Savannah today, since he had to remain there because of the
accounts.]

Monday, the 30th of January. This evening in the prayer
meeting I told the story of how Mary visited Elisabeth and
how God laid such a blessing on the visit. Thus I showed how
God would not fail to bless us assembled in the prayer meeting
or elsewhere, if only we continue to strive for His blessing.
The dear Lord did not fail to bless this and the other things
recalled in the prayer meeting, as I have learned. For that may
the Lord be praised, and may He make us hunger at all times,
for He fills the hungry with good but leaves rich men empty.

Tuesday, the 31st of January. In the evening after school
I visited a woman in our congregation who, like her son, sel-

dom comes to church. To be sure, she is not very well; yet we see that she goes elsewhere. She tells how previously at home in Upper Austria she had liked to pray and read God's Word; but, when I asked her whether she still did so, she had to confess that she was no longer so serious. Therefore I showed her that she could know from that how bad things stood with her. If St. Paul, who went so far in his Christianity and with whom we cannot compare ourselves, said: "Brethren, I count not myself to have apprehended: but this one thing I do, forgetting those things which are behind, and reaching forth unto those things which are before," yea, how much more seriously we should take it; for the Lord Jesus would spew the lukewarm out of His mouth, as she herself knows how to cite from the Revelations of St. John. Even though I spoke to her in that way, I did not notice that she took it so ill as she used to do when we told her that she could not be saved in such a condition. The Lord have mercy on her!

FEBRUARY

Wednesday, the 1st of February. Today our large boat arrived again and brought up the chest of books, linen, and medicines for us [which had been sent from Halle and was said to have been forgotten]. This is truly a great blessing. [May the dear Lord richly reward Professor Francke for it and bless him and all the Orphanage in compensation.] Oh what the Lord does even for us poor people here in the wilderness! How can we begin to tell of His benefactions, Oh my God, we are too insignificant for all the mercy and loyalty that you show us miserable exiles! Let Thy goodness lead us all to true penitence and let us give ourselves to Thee truly as a sacrifice that is living, holy, and pleasing to Thee. Amen.

Thursday, the 2nd of February. This afternoon I (Boltzius) returned to Ebenezer wet with rain but sound in body and joyful in spirit about the goodness and loyalty of the Lord that I have experienced. And again I have reason enough to praise the name of our merciful Lord for all the kindness and benefactions that He has shown me and my dear people. My absence from the congregation lasted longer this time than I had expected; but now, God be praised, all the accounts have been fully examined, closed, and signed, and Mr. Causton knows how much the storehouse in Savannah still owes us. In the past we have suffered for want of some of the provisions due to us; but this has not harmed us, since it is now very opportune for the poor people to receive the outstanding provisions in these hard times, since some foodstuffs cannot be bought for money. Mr. Causton immediately delivered to me meat, flour, rice, butter, cheese, and soap, all that he had on hand; and I let these be brought to an empty house near the water so that the Salzburgers would not disturb the storehouse and Mr. Causton's employees when fetching the provisions and so that they could stay there themselves and I could make new accounts. He could not give me the additional rice, corn, beans, sweet potatoes, and syrup for making beer; but he will deliver it all as soon as what he is expecting arrives in Savannah. To be sure, there are some corn and beans there; but at the present time we are lacking containers for storing them. In Purysburg we are going to get a big boat for a couple of weeks so that everything can be brought up in a few trips and our people will not have to be kept so long from their agriculture. Mr. Causton again showed me every possible kindness and was satisfied with all the remonstrances I made on behalf of the congregation; and he also proved ready to advance certain foodstuffs against future payment to those among us who prove themselves diligent and orderly.

[From Court Chaplain Ziegenhagen I received a new letter with a copy of the letter he had sent to us by Mr. Thilo. Likewise, a chest has arrived from Halle with linen, books, and medicines that Capt. Daubaz must have forgotten and which another ship's captain brought to Charleston, from where it was sent to Mr. Causton. Mr. Causton was writing to London and, because he was willing to forward some letters for me, I wrote to Court Chaplain Ziegenhagen and also to the praiseworthy Society and to the Lord Trustees even though I had recently sent the letters I had written on the 20th of January and the enclosed diary by safe hands to Capt. Thomson for him to forward to Charleston.]

On Sunday I preached the Word of God twice to the Palatines in Savannah and distributed a few Bibles and New Testaments to those who had requested them and ABC books to the children. The Lord Trustees have commended these people to the good care of Mr. Causton and have ordered that those who have already paid the merchant in Rotterdam some money for their passage should be refunded such money. Therefore, any who can reimburse the Trustees for their passage will be released from their service and become free. [They are mostly restless and displeased, and many of them of a very mean nature. They quarrel and bite each other so that we hear many complaints. In Purysburg on my return trip I was given a letter from Mr. Secretary Newman, also one from Court Chaplain Butjenter to us and one from Dr. Gerdes to the schoolmaster, which I should have received several weeks ago, if the bringer had not been so dilatory. We plan to write again soon and then to answer all these.]

In my last letter of the 30th of January I thanked the Society for their kindness in sending the doctor, the three iron mills, and our salaries; and I also gave them a short account of the building and purpose of our orphanage. Through Mr. Vernon I likewise thanked the Lord Trustees for all the benefactions they have shown us so far, especially because they have given our Salzburgers at our new place provisions for six quarters, the accounts for which have now been signed and which will soon be forwarded to them by Mr. Causton. I recommend our poor people, especially in these hard times, to their further care and affection. I am also sending Mr. Vernon a short report on our orphanage. [I enclosed a copy of this letter for Court Preacher Ziegenhagen. Mr. Manitius sent us a continuation of the work he has been performing among the Jewish people, along with a few lines. I am sorry that I could not answer him, since he has already written to us for the third time. Our friends will be so good as to excuse us if we do not write as often and to everyone as we would like to.]

Friday, the 3rd of February. This evening the prayer meeting was held in the orphanage because the distribution of the gifts we have been sent, which is to occur this evening, is more convenient here than in the old hut where church is usually held. We sang together the edifying song: "Praise and glory be to the Highest Good."[31] Then I spoke a bit with the dear congregation about the beautiful words in Psalms 68:20–22 and showed them with what we must provide ourselves if we wish to fit ourselves into the order of salvation of our Savior, who has received gifts even for the apostates. I also told them something about the value of the tribulations, after which God refreshes us again. In this I reminded the congregation about their previous experiences and especially about the many provisions which they have received and are to receive from the storehouse in Savannah. Finally, we fell on our knees and thanked the dear Lord for his goodness, as well as for the benefactions that came with the last ship; and we called on Him with one voice to repay everything which we have received from charitable hearts.

Next the beautiful supply of linen, which had been sent through the care of Mr. N. [Prof. Francke], was distributed as far as it would go. Married couples received an entire piece sewn together, and two unmarried persons must share a piece [which can be done easily by separating the seam]. The names of those who receive something are always written in a book so that those who have not received anything this time will be remembered in the future, if God again grants something. The [young] children who behave well and follow the gospel of Christ have been promised at this time that they will receive shirts made of this linen, and for this purpose two pieces were reserved. One piece was put aside for table cloths for the orphans. Finally the twenty florins that were sent by Pastor Riesch as a gift and amount to 2 £ 6 sh. 8 p. sterling were distributed to thirteen Salzburgers, men and women, who came to America from Lindau. The names of those who received something are as follows: Simon Steiner, Ruprecht Steiner, Kogler, Kalcher, Eischberger and his wife Maria, née Riedelsperger, Brandner and his wife Maria, née Hürl, Rothenberger and his wife Catharina, née Piedler, Gabriel Maurer, Burgsteiner, Christian Riedelsperger. The remainder of those who came from Lindau are dead and surely all in heaven. Each of these people received 3 shillings 7 pence. May God richly repay these and all other benefactions we have received and arouse us all to praise of His name.

Saturday, the 4th of February. The surveyor is now finished

measuring all our land down to those fields that are called "gentlemen's lots" and is asking me for a certificate for the work he has done so that he can be paid by Mr. Causton in Savannah. He has proved himself loyal and diligent in his work, so I can recommend him well to Mr. Causton.

The weather is very variable at present—now warm, now cold, now sunshine, now rain. Some people are now noticing the fever again, which, however, does not last long at this time.

Sunday, the 5th of February. [The prayer meeting held in the orphanage at night after supper is not only visited industriously by young and old, but has today and on other occasions brought much blessing for our edification. We either repeat from the sermon, or else we read an edifying example and pray to the Lord on bended knees. We trust in the Lord that He will legitimize this house as his abode if He attracts some souls to Himself in these surroundings and strengthens the spirit of others in the grace received.]

In the evening after the repetition I received a letter from Purysburg in which I was asked to marry the German and French preacher there, Chifelle. My dear colleague will take over this task for me because, after my return from Savannah, I would like at least to remain for a time with my congregation and to perform my duties undisturbed. The matter of provisions still causes me much work and worry; but God will soon free me from this as soon as what is still owed us from the storehouse is brought up and distributed.

Monday, the 6th of February. The good people who recently received some linen hardly know how to give enough thanks for it and to wish the benefactors God's blessings for it. The beautiful supply of books, which were enclosed in this same linen-chest, are worthy of much thanks and praise. With them we serve both young and old for their edification, and we have our own enjoyment from them. May the Lord graciously deign to hear our prayers for His rewarding of these and other benefactions!

After the evening prayer meeting, a Salzburger invited me to dedicate his new hut, into which he and his wife moved today, with prayer and the word of God. All the neighbors assembled there. After we had sung a song of praise, I read, explained, and applied the words of the Lord Jesus: "And into whatsoever house ye enter, first say, Peace be to this house." Finally we prayed for blessings for us, for this hut, and for our entire village; and we parted from one another with blessings and peace. The man to whom the hut belongs was especially joyful at the emphasis of the divine Word, which he felt in his heart; and, while accompanying me home with a lighted pine torch, he assured me that he would remember this dedication all his life.

A widow from Purysburg and also a German man from Old Ebenezer, who is an indentured servant of the Lord Trustees, urged us to accept their children into our orphanage. And there are surely many others both near and far who would like their children to be with us. However, it not yet possible to accept as many as request it; but first we must observe what the Lord will show us as the footsteps of His care and at the same time of His will. Besides that, it is good for us not to be crowded with children while first getting established. May the Lord do what pleaseth Him, and may He grant us wisdom and loyalty to do His will in all things.

Tuesday, the 7th of February. We have been sent a barrel of dried apples from [the hands of the Herrnhuters in] Savannah, which have been sent here from Pennsylvania and are for refreshing our sick people. God be praised for this and all other benefactions! The two Zueblin brothers who left Purysburg some time ago and moved to Ebenezer with Mr. Causton's permission are showing great diligence in winning their salvation, after God has let them recognize out of His Word that more is demanded for being saved than external appearances, blameless behavior, and good practices, for which they were not lacking previously.[32] They are very poor and receive not the least aid from their wealthy brother in Purysburg.[33]

[Soon after his arrival, that good man learned to love the world, and he strays deeper and deeper into it. The letter he wrote me about these two brothers when I asked about them was so written that one could clearly recognize his fall. Mr. Causton recently complained to me that this Mr. Zueblin in Purysburg advanced some money to a subject of the Lord Trustees in order to alienate him from them; and this came close to causing prejudice against these two brothers who have been accepted by us. However, I showed Mr. Causton of what mind these were and how they could not harmonize with the other brother and much less take part in this deed.]

Mrs. Pichler is coming closer and closer to death. God has brought her to a recognition of her misery and perverted heart; and she now considers herself an unworthy worm and realizes that God means well with this long lasting and painful sickness and that she would not have fared well if God had snatched her away in her self-assuredness. She appears to me as a penitent and fearful sinner who is crying with all her might for help and salvation in Christ. May God help her along and grant her a blessed end for the sake of Christ and His death!

Wednesday, the 8th of February. We intend to go to Holy Communion next Sunday; and therefore our listeners visit me daily and give me an opportunity to speak and pray with them. A young man asked me whether I thought he should go to Holy Communion. He says that he recognizes himself, to be sure, as an abominably sinful worm and that he cannot believe that the Lord Jesus wishes to accept him. To be sure, last Sunday the Lord blessed His word in him so that he could grasp some comfort and even felt rather good about it yesterday evening when he commended himself to the mercy of God both in communal prayer with some children of God and also in private prayer before going to sleep. However, during the night he was awakened two times in a row and greatly daunted by a frightful dream in which he was damned with other godless people before the judgment seat of God to eternal death and cast into a bottomless pit. He got up twice, he said, and prayed to God and again achieved some comfort of soul; yet even then it seemed to him that someone had said into his ear: "Your prayer will not help you, it is all over, etc."

In this discussion I led him over and beyond anything that might ever occur to him and led him only to the firm and certain word of God, where he will find that God has promised the penitent sinner mercy in Christ and forgiveness of sins. I also read him something about a man whose life the devil embittered during his conversion with all sorts of temptations and suggestions, yet who finally succeeded and overcame through the strength of Christ. I also told him that the Lord Jesus would not exclude him from the use of His body and blood, but rather invites precisely those who are laden and heavy of heart. Since he needs strength for struggle and victory, he must fetch it from Him and therefore go to Holy Communion. The sacrifices that please God are a fearful spirit. God will not disdain a fearful and battered heart, even if the burdened sinner thinks so.

A woman complained to me that she would have signed up for Holy Communion but that she did not know whether she dared do so. Whenever she thinks of Holy Communion, the time for which is so near, she gets such a blow and pressure on her heart that she can keenly feel it. Before registering she had prayed to God with tears to cause me to hold her back if she would suffer harm from going. I told her, however, that the Lord Jesus calls poor sinners, receives them, and eats with them; and now it is right for a servant of the Lord to consort with poor penitent sinners as He did, etc. Her husband was not present, but we were joined by a couple others whom the husband had promised to call when I came to his hut. The condition of the woman and also of the others called for me to read the fourth chapter of St. John and to apply briefly to their profit what is written there about the Lord Jesus' uncommon desire to save sinners and about His gentleness toward the woman of Samaria, who was mired down in her sins. The loving Savior did not leave this without his blessing, as they let me know by their bright faces and by giving me their hands in thanks for the gospel I had proclaimed.

Thursday, the 9th of February. This morning I visited a few people who had assembled for the purpose of preparing themselves for Holy Communion. They were all very attentive before the Lord in order to hear what was to be told them for the sake of their salvation. I spoke with them a bit about Malachi 4:2. They were all fearful of the Lord Jesus, because they felt themselves sinful; so I attempted to lure them under the widespread merciful wings of the Lord Jesus, who, since He sought and wished to assemble even the hostile Jews, would certainly not scorn souls that were awakened yet were still timid. In doing this, I showed them how it had come about that many souls still remained so pitiful: it resulted from the fact that, even though they did practice the denial of themselves and the crucifixion of their sinful pleasures, they did not wish to enter and penetrate rightly into Christ and into the gospel as the rich pasture, for which they still considered themselves unworthy. Let Him call: "Come unto me, all ye that are, etc." Hereupon I knelt down with them and reminded the Lord Jesus of all His promises and asked Him to fulfill them for these souls who had sighed and longed for Him for so long, etc.

After the prayer a woman complained to me with tears that she did not know whether she should go to Holy Communion: she was afraid that she was still mired under the law and she saw herself fully portrayed in the seventh chapter of the Epistle to the Romans, etc. Thereupon I told her that the verse from the eighth chapter applied to her better: "There is therefore now no condemnation to them which are in Christ Jesus, who walk not after the flesh, but after the Spirit." The children of God, I told her, not only have the flesh of original sin in themselves but also feel the desires and temptations of the flesh, which they do not consummate but against which they earnestly struggle. Doing this is often as bitter for them as having an eye plucked from the head or a hand and foot cut off (as the Lord Himself presented it in Mark 9:43, 45, 47). This struggle results, not as in the case of those who obey the law only through fear of hell while feeling a secret love for, and joy in, sin and secretly murmuring against the Law Giver and holy God, but rather from a general and serious hate against sin and an honest love for God, whom one does not wish to sadden with sins even if it should cost his life a thousand times. And what causes a child of God such distress is precisely the fact that his flesh is so active. Wherever this takes place in a person's soul, I told her, as I knew it was doing in hers, that was a sign that she was in Jesus Christ and was not damned, for she was living not according to the body but according to the spirit. To be sure, the flesh struggles against the spirit, but the spirit also struggles against the flesh so that it will not do what the flesh wishes, etc.

Another woman stepped up and showed me what she had chanced upon in the *Treasure Chest* but had not, as she said, been able to apply to herself. The right golden words, which impress me greatly, are found on p. 365 and are worthy of being written down here for my own refreshment because of their more than balmy strength: "In those days and at that time, the iniquity of Israel shall be sought for; and there shall be none" (Jeremiah 50:20) and "I will remember their sin no more" (Jeremiah 31:34). I am ashamed, oh Lord, when I think of my sins and consider how Thy pure eyes have seen all my sins. But Thou wilt not only forgive and no longer reproach or be angered as a man does; but Thou wilt actually forget everything and act as if Thou didst not know what I have committed in the years of my sinful life, so that I in time and eternity shall be considered a dear child as if I had never done anything evil in all my life. For Thou seest in me no sin, yea, no spot nor wrinkle, but only Thy dear Son and his blood and therefore only what is loveable. Therefore Thou lovest me too, like Thy Son himself.

> If the sin falls into the sea,
> It must vanish like a mist:
> Who will find my sin?
> No, it must be forgotten,
> Now and forever,
> Because I am entirely in Jesus.[34]

A man there was likewise so comforted and edified that he took courage to go to Holy Communion too, although he had previously been timid and worried.

Mrs. Landfelder showed me three verses in the Bible that she wished to send to Senior Urlsperger in thanks for the love he bears our congregation; and she asked me to write a few lines for her, for which she told me the content. The verses were Psalms 41:2, "Blessed is he that considereth the poor," etc.; Psalms 68:20, "Blessed be the Lord who daily loadeth us with benefits," etc.; and Psalms 37:19, "They shall not be ashamed in the evil time," etc. [My dear colleague is kept quite busy with such letter writing, because many of the people wish to have letters written to express the gratitude of their hearts.]

Friday, the 10th of February. We have had very little rain all summer, fall, and winter; but now a rainy season seems to be starting which the earth greatly needs. [Our people brought fifty-three bushels of beans from Savannah that had gotten rather wet. They had to be distributed at once in the boat in a most violent rain, because they had been poured in loose without containers; and otherwise they would have been spoiled entirely. In this way, the loss was not great.]

Sanftleben, a carpenter, has resolved to travel to Silesia, his fatherland. I have not wished to disapprove or advise against this trip altogether, because he has assured me that he has been brought to this difficult and costly journey by his sincere love for his sister, who is being tempted to return to Popery. He is leaving his cattle and whatever else he has behind and hopes to return as soon as possible and to bring his sister with him.[35] He has been a diligent and loyal hearer of the word of God among us, through which God has brought him to a recognition of himself and of the order of salvation; and he is earnestly resolved to penetrate earnestly through the narrow gate and to save his soul. Mr. Causton is well pleased with this intended journey. With this opportunity we and several people of the congregation will write to our friends and benefactors.

The shoemaker Reck of Purysburg brought his seven year old son to us with the request that we accept him into our school. He must provide him with food, which he can well do [since he has plenty of money left over to drink away in evil company.]

Saturday, the 11th of February. I notice that the Lord Jesus has been active this week in bringing some souls to Christian struggle and seriousness; but I have also noticed, and I have been told by several people [souls], that Satan is also trying to make their struggle and the salvation of their souls difficult for them in every way or even to mislead them from it through all sorts of delusions that lead them to frivolity or desperation. After some of them have their consciences awakened, they have restless nights, dreadful dreams and fantasies, etc., even though they have previously slept very well. Late in the afternoon one of them came to me and said that, because of his feeling of great sin, he would have been pleased if I had kept him from Holy Communion, because he considered himself a great sinner. However, I could not do this, since he greatly needed this spiritual medicine of the soul and reinforcement in his difficult struggle. I let him precede me into the prayer meeting, which we held in the orphanage for those who wished to go to Holy Communion and for others who joined us. After the singing of two songs, I read the passion story from St. Matthew and we prayed to our Lord Jesus on our knees.

Sunday, the 12th of February. [Mrs. Pichler has come very close to her death, yet I cannot accept the condition of her soul. To be sure, he and she have made good pretences so far; yet we cannot make heads or tails out of some things that have occurred from time to time. He believes that God is letting things take place in him for his conversion such as he has never experienced before. Time will tell whether there is any truth in it. Otherwise he belongs among those who place their Christianity in good intentions and rationalizations. He does not lack in conviction. Mrs. Rheinlaender sent me a pious widow[36] and let me know that our merciful God has brought her to the recognition of and remorse for her sins but that she was too timid and fearful to come to us herself because, as she said, she had deceived us from time to time in the past with her pretences. This widow told me much about her earnest prayer and struggle and said that she has high hopes that the truth will be found in her. She[37] hopes her husband will soon return from New York because she wishes to tell and explain to him real soon that he is as blind as she, etc. Because of her obvious wickedness and annoyance she has been kept away from Holy Communion until now, which greatly hurt the Old Adam in her.]

Today there were thirty-four persons at Holy Communion. May God transfigure His Jesus-love in all of them so that their hearts and mouths will be filled with Christ crucified!

Monday, the 13th of February. Mrs. Pichler died this morning before day. I was called to her from bed late last night, but she could understand neither my consolation nor prayer. In previous times she had sinned against me and my office with as much blasphemy as N. [Paul Lemmenhofer] did, who went to eternity without penitence. [To be sure, this once caused her a great fright; but we must hope in Christian love that she has done proper penance for this and her other sins, since] on her sick bed she at last gave appearances of doing so. God is a holy God! From the very time that she so greatly sinned, to the scandal of many in the congregation, she had bodily pain and great suffering right to the end of her life.

Both children and adults are now very busy in writing letters to send with the departing carpenter Sanftleben to our benefactors in England and to friends. The recent benefactions have made an especial impression on many in the congregation. For some time the people have been showing themselves much more contented with the dispensations of God, which are surely good and salutary, than ever before. Therefore many of them wish that their kinsmen might also be here, and that is what they are writing for. If the Lord should ordain that still more honest Salzburgers should be sent here, they would surely find their subsistence here. There are still many pieces of land that have been surveyed for gardens and that have the richest soil in our region, but which our people will not be allowed to cultivate because they already have their gardens and now also their plantations. Because their plantations were surveyed so late, they will not be able to plant anything on them this year, with the time for planting being already at our door. Meanwhile they have cleared lovely pieces of land around the town and prepared them for planting. This is very useful for them, and gives the town a pretty appearance; and now everything is beginning to be airier and healthier.

Tuesday, the 14th of February. A Frenchman[38] has begun to build a tavern not far from us in Carolina and is selling rum and brandy. I sent him word via the shoemaker Reck as to what I was intending to do, namely, first to complain in Savannah and then to have the matter carried further by Mr. Causton so that his business will be suppressed. I also told him that I would earnestly forbid the congregation to buy anything whatever from him and that I was assured in advance that they would obey me in this. He sent very good words as an answer and promised to remove the present supply of rum and not to bring any more up. He had not known that it would matter.

Yesterday and today we have been busy writing letters to our patrons and benefactors, which Sanftleben is to take with him.[39] [We are writing to Court Preacher Ziegenhagen, Senior Urlsperger, Prof. Francke, Court Preacher Butjenter, Mr. Lau, Privy Counselor Walbaum, and several merchants in Venice who have sent the congregation some benefactions.] Through Sanftleben the Salzburgers are inviting several of their countrymen in the Empire to come here, and for this reason they are writing letters. Should some of these join together, they could come here very well with this Sanftleben and have in him a loyal helper, adviser, and companion in prayer. Should it come about that a transport were sent here and our benefactors wished to help my mother come, I would especially thank the Lord for it. Perhaps it would serve to save her soul (as I trust the dear Lord would). [My brother, who has yearned for a long time to come here, I do not desire to come except under the conditions which I once sent to Senior Urlsperger and Prof. Francke.] We greatly need a shoemaker and a smith.

Continuation of the Diary

Wednesday, the 15th of February. [An Englishman wrote me a rather rude letter because he thought I was to blame that he could not get any of our people to work for him for a couple of months. I prefer for the people to remain here rather than go away, especially now that the time for planting is nearing. The young people who have hired themselves out elsewhere have tired of such work because the loss has been greater than the gain.] Sanftleben's trip has been delayed for a few more days, for which reason we have written letters to several friends [especially to Court Chaplain Lau in Wernigerode]. I have also requested the merchant Mr. Evelcigh in Charleston to see to it that Sanftleben can journey to London with a good captain, and my dear colleague is writing to a German carpenter in Charleston for the same purpose.

Thursday, the 16th of February. For some days we have had beautiful spring weather, and therefore the peach trees quickly became full of blossoms; but now a heavy frost has fallen again, which we did not expect. The weather here is very inconstant. Our people have already brought up all the provisions from Savannah, at which Mr. Causton is much amazed. As mentioned previously, I had all the outstanding provisions that Mr. Causton had been able to give me transferred to a house situated on the water, and from it the Salzburgers could fetch them without being held up in the least. Also, the trading boat that we borrowed in Purysburg did us good service. If they had supplied us in the beginning with a large light boat, then we would not have had such difficulties and lost so much time in bringing up the provisions. [Coming Saturday, God willing, I intend to go to Savannah to hold divine services there with the German people and to let Mr. Causton deliver the still remaining provisions due us.]

Friday, the 17th of February. [This time Mr. Thilo has not written with us to England and Germany but is waiting for the chest of medicines which was given to him in Halle.] Our Salzburgers have written many letters in which they not only show their contentedness and praise God for all the good things that have come to them so far from near and far but also advise their countrymen and friends to follow them here. They tell them that there are many trials and tribulations here, but there is also much good.

Saturday, the 18th of February. My dear colleague Mr. Boltzius went to Savannah this morning [in order to preach the word of the Lord to the Germans there.] May the dear Lord be with him and let such journeys redound to His glory!

A pious widow[40] visited me today and complained of the naughtiness of her children; but at the same time she said that this drove her all the more to prayer and that already God had often heard her prayers. Recently she had a special request, for which she prayed to the dear Lord and reminded Him that He was a living and a true God who had, as we know, said that He would take care of widows so now He should prove it and ordain this particular matter according to His pleasure. It was in the evening that she had so prayed, and in the morning God let her experience His hearing of her prayer and petition. This strengthened her in her faith that God would not let her pray in vain in regard to her children.

Sunday, the 19th of February. This afternoon we began the passion story from the gospel of St. John. May the dear Savior let it be blessed and reveal Himself to us as the crucified Jesus. If He revealed Himself to His enemies, how much more will He do it for His friends who seek Him with all their heart?

[Something else occurred of which I cannot approve and which has caused me much worry.]

Monday, the 20th of February. This afternoon the Lord helped me (Boltzius) back home again. We left this morning at about two o'clock from Savannah; and, because I had two good oarsmen, we reached our dear Ebenezer very early with good weather. Mr. Causton again showed me much affection and is doing everything for our Salzburgers that is possible and in keeping with his orders. I recommended to him the carpenter, Sanftleben, who is journeying to Germany; and he agreed readily and will find a good opportunity for him to go to Charleston. Meanwhile, he is having him provided with food from the store-house.

The Lord Trustees' German servants, to whom I preached the word of God again yesterday in the morning and afternoon, ask me for Bibles, testaments, hymnals, and other books. The last of these we lack, and there are even some people in our congregation who have recently learned to read but are not yet provided with them. We also desire more Bibles of smaller size, which are also cheaper. [These people have almost no books, are in great ignorance, and are so wicked that one complains to us about the other. There are also some Catholics among them who have probably slipped in without the knowledge of the Lord Trustees.]

Tuesday, the 21st of February. Because Sanftleben is remaining a few more days in Savannah, I have found time to write to the praiseworthy Society and also to Court Chaplain Ziegenhagen, which letters are to be sent along with our boat that is going for provisions. Enclosed with them is a letter to Mr. Manitius, who has written to us several times. God let everything serve for the glorification of His name! The hard freeze has turned into a right cold rain, which affects us more than when things are frozen. Some of the peach blossoms are falling and will probably suffer damage from it.

Wednesday, the 22nd of February. The nights have again become as cold as any we have had this winter, and even in the day the winds are rather raw. Some people have been misled by the past lovely spring weather to plant something, but perhaps nothing will come of it. The time for planting actually begins in the middle of March, when the cold night freezes are over. [When we sent away our latest letters, which were recently forwarded to Sanftleben, something happened to us of such a nature that we could not have expected it. Our friends will hardly be able to believe it when we have to report it to them, which we are trying diligently to postpone until the matter either improves (since we would like to bury the matter entirely) or comes to light even more. In this regard a pious woman told me that she suspects that the letters will serve for the glory and praise of God and that the devil well sees this and therefore is opposing it with all his might, even under good appearances. Meanwhile it extracts many a sigh from us, and it also prevented me from holding the prayer meeting this evening. How wonderful art Thou, oh God, in Thy ways that Thou lettest so many kinds of unfamiliar trials come over us! Now Thou shall help us through: we trust in Thy word.]

Thursday, the 23rd of February. Yesterday our boat brought sixty bushels of corn, which had come from New York into the store-house in Savannah. Today it was sent back to fetch more. Our dear people cannot marvel enough at the wonderful care of our heavenly Father, who lets so much flow to us during this famine, since none of us had expected it. This morning someone told me that he had never been so rich as now and that he often talks with his wife about such especial blessings of God. The long omission of provisions in the past has served only to our benefit. When I was with Mr. Causton on Saturday and Sunday, he gave me a bill of exchange for fifty barrels of rice each of 500 lbs., that our people are to fetch from Mr. Montagut's plantation. I often think of the text of Psalm 81:14–15, which we had at our memorial service last year.

A pious woman finds her present condition fully expressed in the song "Release me, Lord, from all my Bonds";[41] and, because she would like to learn the melody, she asked me to sing it with the children, in which manner she hopes to learn it quickly. The songs in our hymnal are a great treasure for us and bring much edification with divine blessing. It is too bad that several right excellent songs are in neither the *First Part* nor in the *Extract*, but only in the *Second Part*, e.g. "Crucified

Lord, my heart seeketh."[42] Also, we cannot sing such songs well publicly which stand only in the *First Part* or only in the *Extract*, because some members of the congregation are provided only with the *Extract* and some others only with the *First Part*. The songs "Jesus is the fairest Light", "It is finished, etc.", "Break through, my troubled Heart, etc.", "To Thee, Lord Jesus", "My God, Thou knowest best of all", "When Thy dearly beloved Son, oh God",[43] and so forth are right dear songs; yet they are lacking from one or the other of the aforementioned songbooks.

Friday, the 24th of February. Hernberger told me that he praises God for having saved him and brought him to our congregation from all kinds of sects with which he almost became entangled in Germany and also from his uncertainty as to which religion and teaching might be the right and true one; for God has fully assured him and convinced his heart that the right way and order of salvation is taught by the Evangelical faith, even if few really accept it. When he abjured popery he had observed the life of Christians and met up with various parties and had therefore sought a congregation who lived the true teachings as they professed them with their mouths, but he had sought in vain and could therefore not actually join any party for a long time. He is a man who is honest at heart and useful to us. In his *Treasure Chest*, which a pious tailor in Augsburg [by the name of Wendel] gave him, I found these words written in his own hand: "On the 5th and 6th of August 1737 my dear and true Savior had mercy upon me and showed me that His Holy Communion should be my love-feast."

Saturday, the 25th of February. The bitter cold is now abating and it is becoming mild and lovely again. The fever is already bothering some of the people again among both children and adults. I too seem to have had some fever yesterday, of which, however, I notice nothing today. All winter long there has been something in our family, which God has surely ordained for some very salutary purpose. We too can say, "It is good for me that I have been afflicted; that I might learn Thy statutes."

[This afternoon I found enough time to read the recently arrived letters through, since I had been hindered from reading them carefully. God be praised for the blessing which He has granted to me this time again from them. May He repay

our dear Fathers and friends for what they have accomplished
in us through their wise and edifying writings.]

Sunday, the 26th of February. [The ill-behaved Purysburg
shoemaker, who has been working here for a while, still continues his evil custom of going to Purysburg on Saturday and
remaining over Sunday; and therefore he is to get no more
work from us unless he improves. Mrs. Ortmann kept him
company yesterday and travelled with him to make some pur-
chases, and this scandalized our congregation and the people
in Purysburg, who well know how seriously we observe Sundays
and holy days. I spoke with the schoolmaster Ortmann and
showed him what his wife had heard last Friday in the prayer
meeting (in which she, but not he, was present) about Leviticus
19:3, namely that God wishes the third commandment to be
observed as well as the fourth, for which reason He brought
the two commandments together as if one and proclaimed
them one with the other.[44]

[I also showed him that those who transgress the third commandment by neglecting the Sabbath and divine service are
sinning at the same time against the fourth commandment, in
which God demands obedience not only from children but also
from adults towards their ministers and all good church regulations and orders made by the authorities. His wife, however,
does not observe these commandments and thus rejects the
blessings of the third and fourth commandments. She had already done this several times, and she is not improving. He well
recognized that she was doing wrong but could not hold her
back. Now he assured me that he was freeing himself more and
more from harboring wicked people, because it caused him
nothing but loss. They have let a young fellow go in and out of
their house whose wickedness was otherwise generally known
but has now become public in that he disguised a girl in men's
clothing in Savannah and helped her to Purysburg and beyond.[45] Because we have not wished to put up with such company, he and she have been very angry at us. Now he thinks he
has learned from his loss, and he is making a better pretence.]

Afternoons, instead of the Sunday epistle, we are again contemplating the passion story, this year from the gospel of St.
John, of which my dear colleague made the beginning a week

ago. So far our dear Lord has always laid a blessing of edification on us and on others, and He will surely have mercy upon us this time too. With regard to our office, since last Sunday there has been a time of tribulation, in which may our merciful Lord stand by us! We shall be able to be a bit more explicit in letters.

Monday, the 27th of February. Since yesterday the cold has again become very intense, and thus the winter has actually begun this month, since it was formerly rather tolerable and not so cold as last year. [Yesterday morning before dawn our boat returned with sixty bushels of very beautiful corn, which I distributed this morning. I shall send the boat back to Savannah today because the congregation is to receive more corn or beans.] Much corn and flour is now brought from New York and Pennsylvania to Savannah in sloops, because nothing has grown in this country and in South Carolina.

Yesterday I received a letter from Savannah in which I was asked to baptize the child of a German family there. My dear colleague will undertake this journey today and [I shall give him a letter to Prof. Francke for Sanftleben, who is still there, to forward.]

Continuation of the Diary

Tuesday, the 28th of February. N. [Spielbiegler] visited me at my request, and because of certain circumstances I had to reveal to him his miserable blindness and wickedness. One would not expect to find such darkness in people who enjoy the abundant preaching of the divine word as I find in this man and his mother. It is unbearable for him and for her if we prove to them that they cannot achieve salvation in their present condition. If we cannot be content with their Christianity, but admonish them sincerely to reform and do penance, then they look upon it as hate and hostility or even as a new kind of dogma that they have not heard in other places, where, they claim, people were not treated so severely and were not damned forthwith. If the Lord does not open these people's eyes, they will surely remain blind and perish in their sins.

[The shoemaker from Purysburg took not only Mrs. Ortmann but, as I was told, also Rauner and Michael Kiefer (both of whom are worthless) and thereby gave them an opportunity to desecrate the Sabbath. This compelled me to mention this vexatious behavior yesterday in the evening prayer meeting and to remind the listeners of what had been preached in last Friday's prayer meeting about the third and fourth commandments, which God has joined together most exactly.[46] I also expressed my displeasure at such willful transgression of the Lord's commandments. Today I called the two men to me and told them my opinion in the name of the Lord and admonished them to penitence. They admitted their guilt, accepted the chastisement well and promised to accept the advice I gave them to convert themselves earnestly to God. I shall also speak seriously with the shoemaker and advise him that we shall expel him entirely from us if he wishes to continue in his vexatious practice of desecrating the Sabbath.]

MARCH

Wednesday, the 1st of March. N. [Stephan Riedelsperger] is a very inconstant person. He had firmly resolved not to move away from us, as he had gotten it in his head to do some time ago; and for this reason he wished to buy back some of the cattle he had sold at that time. Now, however, he yearns for Pennsylvania and promises himself there many advantages over Ebenezer, which, however, he could enjoy here if he wished to work. But he was already used to a vagabond and disorderly life in Germany, and therefore it has been painful for him to sit still in one place. With all his selfish seeking he will surely run into his misfortune. P. [Pichler], who lost his wife through death a few weeks ago, told me of R. [Riedelsperger's] intention and has an inclination himself to move with him, if it were not against my wishes. Mrs. R. [Riedelsperger] wished to take on his child as if it were her own, and he wishes to work jointly with R. [Riedelsperger] in Pennsylvania and keep house jointly, otherwise he cannot bring up this young child properly without a wife. Someone in Savannah, he says, praised Pennsylvania, etc. I told him that, if he had no other reason for moving away except that he had a two year old child and no wife, then this reason was not adequate. I myself would give him some help in raising the child and we would easily find a Christian woman in the community who would take care of it. Otherwise he would have to help himself as other unmarried Salzburgers have to do. I warned him against being too hasty and asked him to consider his plan well; and I told him also that it would displease Mr. Causton and our benefactors, who had spent so much on the Salzburgers, and that they would consider it a sign of shameful ingratitude if a Salzburger wished to leave this colony without adequate reasons.

Thursday, the 2nd of March. After my school hour I summoned the two men P. [Pichler] and R. [Riedelsperger] to me again in order to express clearly my opinion of their thoughtless, ungrateful, and repugnant attitude. I sincerely warned them against harm and predicted for them what righteous indignation their moving away would cause our dear benefactors, [and what sighs it would cause the servants of God who care and pray for us.] And because P. [Pichler] asked me yesterday to present his intention to God and give him good advice and because R. [Riedelsperger] requested the same this morning, I read the two of them the 42nd chapter of Jeremiah, to which, however, they said nothing. I reminded them of this chapter again upon their departure. I offered them reasons enough regarding the danger to their souls and their physical circumstances to hold them back; but they choose their reason as their guide and will therefore surely run into perdition.

[We are sorry for Pichler's child, which he will sacrifice to Moloch, since he wishes to move to a place where churches and schools are lacking; yet he is neither able nor willing to believe this.] Neither of them suffers any want here, they have enough provisions, better land for gardens and plantations than the others have, and also a few pieces near their houses that they themselves have fenced in only recently and fully prepared for planting. And now they are hurrying away so fast that they are already selling their belongings, provisions, cattle, etc. They will probably have to leave behind them those things they have received from the Lord Trustees such as cattle, household utensils, etc. for use in this colony; and they must and desire to speak to Mr. Causton himself about them. To be sure they do not say so, but I hear it from others that N. N. [Mr. Zwiffler] had praised the splendor of the Pennsylvania land, which well agrees with his worldly nature. I warned them sincerely against such letters if they should ever get to Pennsylvania; for through shame they would not wish to report that things had turned out badly, etc. This much they well know, that there they must buy their land, which they receive and possess here for nothing. They wish to work as day laborers there; and it seems to me that they wish to earn some money there and return to Germany.

A few weeks ago, when so many letters were being written by the congregation to Germany, they had not yet thought of moving away; and therefore P. [Pichler] himself had written to his brother-in-law to come over here but to consider everything well in advance and to be certain of the divine will. Moreover, R. [Riedelsperger] had begun to cut boards for the orphanage floor, from which he would have earned rather much money. They do not have as much taste as true Christians should have for God's Word, which usually restrains people from such thoughtless undertakings; for they have withdrawn from hearing it publicly with many pretexts and to the great scandal of other people. They are neither cold nor warm, but lukewarm, and the Lord will spue them out; and I am concerned with what God has said in the 22nd verse of Leviticus 20 (which chapter we have just had in the evening prayer meeting): "Ye shall therefore keep all my statutes, and all my judgments, and do them: that the land, whither I bring you to dwell therein, spue you not out."

Friday, the 3rd of March. A Salzburger told me that he was actually driven out of his fatherland by the lascivious dancing, gambling, and other vexatious things; for he had been in such circumstances that he might well have become entangled in that wicked company. He had thought, he confessed, that he was well grounded in his Christianity and that he would be saved if only he would learn a few more songs and prayers by heart. However, once he had come to God's Word, he had realized for the first time how much he was lacking and that he had not yet recognized his sins, nor had he laid a firm foundation for his Christianity. He now earnestly desired to attain salvation. He noticed, much to his grief, that his wife was lazy in spirit and much addicted to the things of the world. For some time now he had begun reading a chapter every morning, noon, and evening; and he would not let himself be distracted from this by any work. However, his wife did not seem to be truly involved in this, etc. [This pious man told me that everything that is said in my hut can be heard from outside, with the result that many misunderstandings arise among the people and they are afraid to come here, etc.] From this pious man's story I notice how necessary it would be to have a house instead of a hut, where one can hear everything from outside. However, I can not help myself but must be satisfied with this hut until God grants a house. Sometime I shall ask Mr. Causton whether I may dare to have the wood cut for a house so that it can dry out. I do not dare do it on my own until I have explicit orders and authority.

Saturday, the 4th of March. There have been many annoying things this week and again today; yet the dear Lord has always helped and will continue to help. [From time to time our office becomes very difficult for us and becomes a burden from which we would otherwise hope for relief.] P. [Pichler is not taking his child to Pennsylvania] is giving his child, that is somewhat more than two years old, to a pious Salzburger here to take care of. May God convert him and bring him onto straight paths so that he will not err!

[The shoemaker Reck promises to behave more orderly among us, and he claims that his wife's dangerous condition has obliged him to leave here some Sundays. We very greatly need a shoemaker.]

Sunday, the 5th of March. Frantz Hernberger declared his banns with Anna Justina Unselt, and Michael Rieser declared his with a Swiss widow from Purysburg.[47] The first pair will be married tomorrow, but the latter pair must declare their banns three times both here and in Purysburg, for which reason I have written to the preacher in Purysburg. The dear Lord let us preach His word abundantly several times again today, so that we feel in ourselves a noticeable blessing from it in the disquiet and worry that has been oppressing us for the last few days.

P. [Pichler] and R. [Riedelsperger] heard the morning sermon about the actual work of the Lord Jesus in the soul of man based on Luke 11:14 ff.; and, if they had even the least desire to begin and to lead a true Christianity, they would soon change their shameful resolution and prefer to remain with the Word of God at a place where there is opportunity to save their souls rather than to move to a spiritual desert. They have been warned publicly and often enough; for only the day before yesterday my dear colleague told P. [Pichler] as much and even more than he cared to hear.

[There are several other inconstant, ungrateful, and frivolous people among us who are not averse to following this example, provided they find an occasion and the means to do so. Some of the young Salzburgers, as they have been heard to say on occasion, have come to America in a way not unlike that of the young journey-men in Germany, who like to travel to far-away cities and foreign countries but return home if they do not find it to their liking there. Now for some years, however, they have heard so much advice from God regarding their salvation and have been told every day so clearly what is necessary for Christianity and salvation that they will have no excuse on that day of judgment.]

Monday, the 6th of March. I have considered it necessary and according to my duty to report to Mr. Causton about the two men's intentions. [The letter, which is to go to Mr. Causton with the first opportunity, reads thus: "Here are 2 Men in my Congregation, Pichler & Riedelsperger by name, who have sold all their Provisions & things, & design to leave the Colonie & to go to Pensylvanie by next Opportunity, which they have resolved to do with such a start of fancy, that we cannot but be supprised at it. No body can tell, what reason they have to such a foolish & scandalous thing, which, I am afraid, will be of Consequence, if they succeed well in their shameful, Intention. I endeavoured my self to the utmost of my power to turn them from it, but all was in vain. It is a scandalous thing & and plain proof of Ingratitude towards all the Benefits, which the Honourable the Trustees as well as the Society for promoting Christian Knowledge have bestowed upon them in bringing them with Great many charges from Germany to London, sending them over to Georgia, & providing them with Provisions & other Necessaries. They tell me, that Mr. Vat hath assured them, to have liberty to leave the Colony, after 3 years are past. I believe, a sweet letter from Mr. Zwiffler, who is still at Philadelphia, has encouraged them to such a sudden Resolution to my & Mr. Gronaus very great Grief. Please to advise me, what must be done in this matter, especially in regard to their Cattel, Hoggs, Poultry & Utensils, which are given them by Charge of the Trustees, some of them, they say, are lost & killed by misfortune. Pichler came to my Congregation under Conduct of Mr. Vat, & Riedelsperger with the first Salzburgers; but his Wife 2 years ago under Conduct of Mr. von Reck. I suppose, they would abide in Pensylvany, but will go to Germany having some money in their pockets, which will happen to many sorrows of our frinds in Europe & to their own Ruin. Relying on your Wisdom & long Experience, I hope, you will do in this melancholy matter, what will redound to my Consolation & to a Stop of ill Consequences. Wishing you the Conduct of God Almighty & good success in your weighty Affairs, . . ."]

This morning I sent our boat to Mr. Montagut's[48] plantation to fetch some of the rice from the twenty barrels still due us.

Tuesday, the 7th of March. A sick woman complained to me that she thought she had gotten fever and suffered attacks as a result of her troubled mind; because ever since Friday her conscience has been disturbed by a sin that she committed in her youth when, in a certain place, she took something with which the children were playing and which did not belong to her and then threw it away again. She would have no rest, she said, until she confessed it and gave something in its place to a poor person, which she is now arranging to do. Last Sunday she was very pleased that, in the evening prayer meeting in the orphanage, my dear colleague had prayed to our dear God to forgive youthful sins in the name of the Lord Jesus because this had well applied to her, and she had thought of the verse "The effectual fervent prayer of a righteous man availeth much" (for others too). At the same time I pointed out to her the complete reconciliation that occurs through Jesus, who has atoned for her youthful sins too and gladly forgives her everything, since she has a displeasure in it and turns to His blood of reconciliation like a poor sinner in faith. I was very pleased to hear her acknowledge the value of common prayer, [because even among us there are people who are opposed to it in word and deed.[49]]

If anyone among us sincerely contemplates being saved and learns to feel his need and danger, he makes use of everything that can advance him to his purpose. Moreover, this does no harm when, in addition to the dear teaching of the gospel (which, to be sure, should be a Protestant minister's chief point of instruction), the law is practiced in its order and application, as we, God be praised, have experienced in many souls! Granted that some troubled souls here and there might apply it wrongly to themselves and would become even more troubled and depressed, still this would not do as much damage as the false or premature appropriation of the gospel does to impious people or merely awakened souls.

We make it our business to be concerned about each and every one in our little congregation and to follow after the troubled and tired souls to hear whether they have heard the sermon correctly and profitably according to their circumstances. If they have not done so, we put them right, just as we make distinctions among our hearers according to their condition every time we preach the Word of the Lord; and we distribute the Word according to the Lord's precepts. [We cannot and will not be divided by idle criticism.]

The raw wind is lasting long this time and will do damage to the blossoms and other things that have sprouted. Last night and today we had a very cold north wind, which also prevented us from holding regular school. In the hut where school is held the wind, which blows in from all sides, will tolerate no fire. A few days ago it appeared that spring was starting seriously.[50]

Wednesday, the 8th of March. For a long time our Salzburgers have wished for some German seeds such as barley, wheat, corn, oats, buckwheat, etc. in order to make a try with them here; but they have not been able to get any of them. Soon after our arrival in Old Ebenezer the first Salzburgers received many such seeds; but some of these were eaten up and the poor soil there and the lack of experience in this strange land did not suit the others. I was told that in the corn that was brought from New York and Pennsylvania to Savannah and then distributed among us some grains of the above-mentioned seeds were found, which they carefully collected and sowed in the ground. When these sprout and ripen, they can serve to produce more seeds. Last year some of the Salzburgers did that with barley and oats, from which they gained a couple of handfuls and can now sow a few small patches. They have tried diligently with flax and are still trying; but it seems to be too hot here for such seeds: the hemp simply did not wish to grow. Perhaps they will gain more and more experience.

In today's evening prayer meeting we began the 23rd chapter of Leviticus, whereby we showed what, after the symbol of Christ, was the second purpose of the holy days, especially of the three chief holy days: Easter, Whitsuntide, and the Feast of the Tabernacles. This is, namely, to remember the spiritual and physical benefactions we have received from God and to bring him especial offerings of thanks and praise for them. That is, I said, also the purpose of our commemoration and thanksgiving festival, which is to be held next Saturday in accordance with the announcement made last Sunday. Now, in order that the devil cannot bring disgrace upon our thanksgiving feast, the congregation has been sincerely warned not to forget, because of this or that trial or tribulation, the benefactions they have enjoyed or to belittle them, as is so often done.

In general I reminded them of what especial benefactions the Lord had showed the Salzburgers when He saved them from their spiritual Egypt [and from Popery] and inclined the hearts of good people who soon took them up and cared for them and even aroused entirely strange people, like the English, to expend so much money on bringing them here from Germany and maintaining them so far. Further, I reminded them that ministers and a teacher had been provided, that they enjoy all liberties and much good, and that anyone who wishes to reflect about it must well marvel at it. They should remember these and similar benefactions and begin to praise the Lord. [Because the two men who are leaving, as well as others of their kind, think they are mistreated because they may not sell their land if they move away and because the female sex may not inherit their property after their death, I both explained and showed how such a regulation aimed only at their best interest and how the Lord Trustees wished to further the welfare of the land and of the inhabitants thereby. E.g., if cleared land were for sale here, then rich people would buy it and gradually oppress the poor folk.]

I also read to them the four points that Secretary Newman had written to Senior Urlsperger on behalf of the Lord Trustees and which announced not only the hoped-for inheritance through the female line but also other points that are advantageous to us. From the newspapers of the year 1737 I made them familiar with the dangerous wars, inundations, great famines, and other tribulations which are afflicting many thousands of people in Europe and Germany and showed them their advantages, which many thousands of people would wish to have. It was therefore a shameful and irresponsible thing if one or the other wished to move away from us for trivial reasons and from pure lack of faith, by which he would bring down on our necks the sighs of our honest friends and benefactors and the displeasure of the authorities. At the same time I reminded them of what I had observed when the Appenzellers wished to lay out their new city of New Windsor and some young and inconstant Salzburgers wanted to move with them because the said people had praised the place as a paradise: now, however, they see what advantages we have here. [Therefore it is very regrettable, I said, that on the occasion of Pichler's and Stephan Riedelsperger's intended departure several others have gained the desire to move away and to seek their luck in the world in heathen fashion. Therefore I again expressed my opinion clearly to them so that they will all know that they have been warned against their perdition, if they run into it.]

Sunday, the 9th of March. This morning P. [Pichler] and R. [Riedelsperger] announced that they wished to go to Savannah and inform Mr. Causton of their designs and therefore requested the letter I had already written to him. They were also at the prayer meeting yesterday and seemed to be very confused and depressed because they had been deprived of their foolish reasons for their departure, [and now they are seizing any excuse in order to be able to say something. They claim, for example, that there is so little love among the Salzburgers that they have never experienced the likes of it even in dark Popery, also that various people, including the recent Zuebli brothers, have been taken into our village even though Senior Urlsperger had expressly promised that none but Salzburgers would come to them. We have, they said, had nothing but inconvenience and annoyance from such people, as has been the case so far with the Rheinlaender family; and this matter is making many people restless and will motivate them to move away. This is, indeed, a miserable reason. We have, to be sure, always wished that only Salzburgers might be here; but, since others have come to us too, we have been neither able to nor desirous of opposing them, because God may perhaps have let it occur for their salvation or at least in order that they will have no excuse on the day of judgment. From that I see that some people must have been displeased by what I reminded them of concerning their behavior towards strangers according to Leviticus 19:10 & 33 (cf. Exodus 22:21 and especially Exodus 23:9), along with other verses.

[In the case of the first mentioned point, I remember how, in my time, some people in the Orphanage in Halle always complained violently of the lack of love the workers there were said to have for one another and took that as a very evil sign. When Pastor Freylinghausen thereupon addressed the people who were in the service of the Orphanage and mentioned Psalm 133, he also mentioned this complaint but said in this connection that he knew how much of it he should believe; and he revealed the basis of his complaint, which lay for the most part in the complainers themselves, in that they looked upon others but not upon themselves and demanded that others should practice love first yet let themselves lack it. As far as the younger Zuebli is concerned, we had not expected such impure behavior on his part, through which he has made himself very suspicious to the congregation by causing grief and misunderstandings through his gossip and unkind judgments. The older Zuebli behaves better, and the community is quite contented with him. Rheinlaender is still in New York or Pennsylvania; and his wife has been using means to salvation diligently and has resolved, she says, to convert her heart through the grace of God.]

Friday, the 10th of March. Last night rainy weather began,

with somewhat warmer temperature than we have had for some days running. The flax, the blossoming peach trees, the sprouting grape vines, and other green things that cannot stand much frost are frozen because the cold was too severe. Now our people are very occupied in putting their sweet potatoes into the ground. Mr. Causton wished to give us sweet potato seeds but could not get any; but we do not need them, because all the seed potatoes that the people buried in the earth here, if they have not been damaged by either the mice or the frost, have remained as fresh as when they were buried. For setting or planting, one needs only the smallest and thinnest, which are cut into several pieces; and therefore one can plant a rather large area with one bushel. As soon as the vine has grown three or four feet out of the ground (which generally occurs about the month of May), it is cut off and laid in piled-up earth so that the ends stick out of both sides of the pile; and the potatoes from these are better than those from the roots.

Because Mr. Thilo is a great fancier of this root, the entire garden belonging to the storehouse is being planted with them for him. In the garden at his house all sorts of garden plants are being sowed such as parsley, squash, melons, cabbage, etc. and other things that belong in the kitchen. On the other hand, the large garden of two acres is being planted with corn and beans; and with all this he has not the least work. The potatoes have dangerous enemies not only in the many field mice but also in hares and deer, the latter of which not only devour the leaves but also dig up the roots, for which reason the people must plant them not far from their huts and keep watch over them. Last year the hares, which are very small in this country, got into several gardens by the huts and did much damage to the cabbage, peas, and potatoes, even though the fences were well protected with six-foot high shingles or split pallisades. But now this is of less concern, since the many trees and bushes all around the town have been completely cut down.

Saturday, the 11th of March. Today we celebrated together our commemoration and thanksgiving feast in grateful memory of all spiritual and physical benefactions that our gracious and merciful God has so abundantly shown us on our pilgrimage by water and land. The morning text was from Psalm

33:18–19: "Behold, the eye of the Lord is upon them who fear Him, upon them that hope in His mercy," and the afternoon text from Psalm 9:10–11: "And they that know Thy name will put their trust in Thee." In the application for the listeners I utilized what I had read yesterday in the recently received Halle newspapers from 1737, namely how miserable things stand in some places in Germany with respect to foodstuffs, [where poor people have dug up the cattle that had died and had been buried], and also that in Regensburg they had resolved upon a weekly tax for the emigrants who have had to suffer much there because of financial difficulties and winter scarcity and are in great need of help.

With the grace of God we make every effort to convince our dear listeners of the many advantages, both physical and spiritual, that they enjoy in Ebenezer from the hand of the heavenly Father so that they will be grateful to God and man. God is also giving his blessing so that the intended purpose is being attained, and the two Salzburgers who wish to move from us have much aggrieved most of the congregation for persisting in their obstinate resolution. Honest souls sigh at this, and this can not be good for such annoying and ungrateful people. Before anyone else knew that they had wished to move away, they suddenly sold their provisions and things, perhaps because they feared they might be dissuaded by honest people, a thing that is even less possible now because they have nothing of their own except what they wear on their backs. It occurred to me today on the occasion of the morning text what I once said to the congregation in Old Ebenezer about the words in Amos 8:11–12, namely, how miserable it is in Pennsylvania with regard to the word of God and the holy sacraments and what a spiritual famine is afflicting the land, and yet these are running into such a famine.

Sunday, the 12th of March. Today, using the regular gospel for Laetare Sunday, John 6:1 ff., we contemplated the loving provision of the Lord Jesus for his people; and during the sermon and repetition hour we again had opportunity enough to remind one another gratefully of the many fatherly benefactions of God that we have experienced so far and to strengthen ourselves in our trust in His continued care, both from His promises and from our previous experience. We see it as a special proof of the Lord's loving providence that He has awakened various ones of his righteous servants [the Protestant ministers] in England and Germany to embrace us before God and men; and therefore during the repetition hour I read our congregation something from the last letter of our very dear Court Chaplain Ziegenhagen, in which he announces for the strengthening of our faith that, when he contemplated the gospel on the seventh Sunday after Trinity and again on the fifteenth after Trinity, our dear congregation was especially on his mind at the words "But seek ye first the Kingdom of God," to which he added this: "Perhaps at the hour at which I am writing this, they are already enjoying some of the fulfilment of the delightful promise that lies in such words." If anyone among us has eyes to see, he sees and says that the Lord has done great things in us and is doing them daily. In these days we have often called to each other: "The works of the Lord are great, sought out of all them that have pleasure therein."

The two Salzburgers who wish to move away [Pichler and Riedelsperger have lapsed so far that they] traveled to Savannah shortly before evening last Friday and thereby willfully missed and scorned both our memorial and thanksgiving ceremony and also this Sunday, as well as all the spiritual good that our Lord has offered us. The Lord will certainly not allow them to succeed in such shameful transgression of the third commandment and to insult and affront the ministers contrary to the fourth commandment. I hear that they returned very late this evening, and now we shall soon learn what they have arranged with Mr. Causton concerning the journey they have planned.

Monday, the 13th of March. [A few days ago a Frenchman asked me to change some Carolina paper money for him and to give him English and Spanish money for it; but we are not accustomed to enter into such deals even though some advantages are supposed to be connected with them. Now I have learned that he has deserted to the Spaniards or the French and that he had stolen the trading boat that he was to take upstream to the Indians with a full cargo, and therefore I am happy I rejected him outright with his money exchange. He won't get far with Carolina paper money.] There are many secret Papists here in this and the neighboring country, who make all sorts of intrigues here and then desert.

A woman [Schweiger's wife] is claiming that God is working mightily on her with His word; and in the presence of her husband she gave good testimony of a recognition of her very corrupted heart and of the inevitable necessity of changing it. I cannot accept the protestations of the wife of N. [Mueller, the watchmaker]. She speaks very edifyingly and thoroughly about the way to salvation and about the proper preparation for blessed eternity, to which she is coming nearer and nearer because of her age. Yet much is revealed in her that does not rhyme with this blessed dogma, and one cannot just consider it mere weakness and the kind of frailty that is accustomed to cling to the children of God. Time will gradually manifest what is in her. We shall often stress and call to mind the dogma of the difference between nature and grace and how easily nature can imitate grace and how often it appears to go a long way.[51]

Tuesday, the 14th of March. [The shoemaker Reck, who is still working here, told me about the recent death of a man in Purysburg, whom we knew very well and who was repugnant to everyone because of his injustice and wickedness. He was one of those French Swiss who were sent a few years ago to Mississippi but compelled the captain of the ship to go to Carolina. On this occasion I warned the shoemaker movingly to turn himself to God and to guard himself carefully from the frivolity in which many people are mired as if they could be saved without conversion on their death beds through sighs, partaking of Holy Communion, etc. I gave him the booklet *Dogma of the Commencement of Christian Life*[52] with the request to read it through not just once but many times. He testified that he had been awakened mightily several times by God's word, especially a short time ago when we catechised the passion story. He had also acknowledged this to Mr. Gronau yesterday evening and had accused himself greatly. He is very fond of lying (as of other vices); and therefore I will believe nothing until I see that it is the truth. I also warned him sincerely against evil company.

[Pichler brought me the news] I learned that Mr. Causton was very angry about the departure planned by [him and Riedelsperger] the two Salzburgers and would not agree to it at all unless they repaid the expenses that were spent on them. I too think it quite proper that such people not be allowed to leave whenever it occurs to them and they think it a good idea; for 1) it is apparent that an unusual amount of money has been spent on them to bring them and their belongings from Germany to England and from there to here. [Nothing like it has been spent on any Englishman.] 2) They were provided with chaplains for their journey and with regular ministers in such a way that it did not cost them a thing, and every conceivable effort is being made to make things easy for them and to further their physical and spiritual welfare, and not the least contribution or payment is demanded of them or their children, who are maintained entirely free in school. Therefore, 3) it is an ungrateful and irresponsible act if the listeners, out of invalid and entirely wordly reasons, wish to abandon their ministers, who have undertaken such a journey out of love for them and are still prepared to sacrifice their health and strength for their good right to the last drop of blood. 4) They are lacking nothing here, and they have a better living than most peasants in Germany have under strict authority. They have provisions, cattle, and their own land, and all the liberties that they could desire in Christian fashion. No man oppresses them, they do not need to pay anyone any tax or tribute, they and their children are provided with God's Word and the holy sacraments, in case of accidental shortage they are assisted from the poor-box, they are cared for in sickness, and a new doctor has been sent here for their good at great expense, even after Mr. Zwiffler (like Mr. Thilo now) had received considerable presents from the Society. Even though, with all the physical and spiritual advantages, there are some tribulations, most of these have been borne with God's grace; and righteous souls have found them more useful than harmful.

The Lord Trustees take care of this colony in every way; and we could not wish for better authorities, especially since we have their promise that they will continue to take an interest in our Salzburgers in every way and take care of them. Mr. Causton has orders to give our Salzburgers every assistance, and none of them who works loyally will suffer want. 5) After the honorable Trustees have risked settling this colony with people, the Spaniards and other enemies have become jealous and are anxious to harm this colony in every way; and therefore it is improper to move away and leave others in the lurch who, because of their smaller number, will be less able to be formidable to the enemy. And 6), what kind of salvation will such people find in another place like Pennsylvania? Even if it is cheaper there and there is more food, money is scarcer and the opportunity to earn something is all the rarer, whereas in this colony, where there are no Negro slaves, every laborer can earn at least 25 sh. Sterl. per month and receive complete provisions at the same time. 7) Such removal does not become a Salzburger who has the reputation of having emigrated for the sake of the gospel; and nothing else can arise from that but defamation and suppression of the true good that God is doing in the emigration work. Everyone who hears about it will have to believe that the people have not been concerned with the word of God and the free practice of religion, as they claim, since they have it in Ebenezer; they must[be restless characters and vagabonds who] wish to withdraw from good order and their obedience to the authorities. I shall not mention 8) what damage such renegades would do in other places; for, having no scruples against distressing God and His people through such ungrateful behavior, what scruples would they have against broadcasting lies and calumnies against the land and its inhabitants whom they had abandoned, especially since they would have to give some excuse for not having remained.

[These and other reasons require me to hinder the Salzburgers from moving away as best I can; yet I must guard myself in this against all violence and evil appearances and pray to God and communicate our concern to Mr. Causton.] Therefore I think that Mr. Causton has done very well in not agreeing to their request. For ingratitude is a punishable sin; and it, along with their obstinacy and worldly attitude, could not be more gently chastised than in that manner. Should these ill-behaved people accomplish their design and if others should follow them because of letters they send, then our little flock and congregation would not only become smaller, against the intention of the praiseworthy Society (which wishes to accept 300

Salzburgers), but it would also change the affection of the authorities into indifference towards, or repugnance against, the Salzburgers remaining here; and therefore the innocent would pay for the ingratitude and wickedness of their renegade countrymen. To this I may add merely incidentally that the enemies of truth act without grounds when they hear of the evil and especially of the ungrateful behavior of these or those Salzburger emigrants and therefore suspect that entire emigration work; / because no one has ever wished to maintain that there are no tares among this Salzburg wheat.

Wednesday, the 15th of March. [Kalcher], the master of the orphans, who is showing all possible loyalty in caring for their spiritual and physical needs, has made several suggestions concerning the economy. [is subjected to the criticism of several people. Some think that he expends too much on the housekeeping, but others think he saves too much, and therefore he cannot please any of those censorious people. Hertzog, who was accepted into the orphanage at his own request and out of commiseration for his physical and mental state, is making secret but obviously ungrounded complaints about the food, which, however, is so good that one has reason to thank the good Giver for it.] The meals they receive consist of flour, rice, ground Indian corn, beans, cabbage, beef, and pork, and are well prepared three times a day [as well as cooked with sufficient lard]. In addition they always have good bread and strong well-brewed beer. [If God grants the house manager and his wife something exceptional, he lets Hertzog and others enjoy some of it too, as far as it will go. It customarily happens that people value less and less what they at first appreciated highly, or they even scorn it when they have enjoyed such benefactions daily and abundantly. Otherwise this Hertzog is an honest, yet very simple, obstinate, and suspicious man; and Kalcher tries to help him in his weakness in every way. For this reason I have admonished him even more and given him some suggestions about managing the economy; and finally I prayed with him for us, his orphanage, and for others.]

Since yesterday the wind has been as violent and cold as it is accustomed to be in the middle of cold winter; I have never felt the wind in Germany so raw at this time of year. The flax, which

the people had sowed and which had sprouted up nicely, is totally ruined along with other tender plants. It is planted here so
early because otherwise it is burned up by the great heat of
summer.

Thursday, the 16th of March. Some Indians have come to
our place again with their wives and children and are bringing
the people pieces of meat for rice. One of them brought an
entire deer to the orphanage, presumably because he had seen
that many people were eating there at one table and therefore
needed more than individual persons. We like to do as much as
we can for them; but then we have them around our necks all
the more, as long as they are at our place. At our recent memorial service an Indian received some food and drink from us
and also some rice for his journey; and that must be what
motivated him to return here on horseback all the way from
Palachocolas a couple of days later with two others. They were
all very drunk and had more rum with them, therefore they
caused much shouting and annoyance. In addition, they were
bolder than they are when they are sober; and they therefore
demanded whatever occurred to them, especially bread and
also syrup, in which they dunked the bread. They came without
their muskets, which some sober Indian must have taken away
from them with good grace as is customarily done, so that they
will not harm anyone. I have been told that, after waking up
from their intoxication, they are accustomed to give thanks for
this service. At such times we must bear all annoyance patiently
and not let them notice any anger or displeasure at it.

[Yesterday towards evening I received a written report from
the minister in Purysburg that he had declared the banns three
times for Michael Rieser and the widow Ihler, named Maria, of
Purysburg and that there were no impediments to postpone
their marriage, and, because this couple had also posted their
banns here for the third time last Sunday, they were married
today.]

Friday, the 17th of March. The cold weather has abated, and
today we have had a right pleasant day. It appears as if the
weather wishes to change now completely and gradually become warm. On Fridays I still hold a conference with the leaders of the congregation, if neither they nor I am prevented,

about those things that concern the good of the entire community. [Today we took up the case of the ill-behaved Ernst, who had not only attacked a Salzburger family with scandalous words but had even uttered wicked threats. He denied both in his usual way, because no witnesses were present. Meanwhile, he was warned sincerely against carrying out his threats and was shown that, if any harm were inflicted or any trick played on the Salzburger and his wife, the strongest suspicion or blame would fall on him. Because he willfully mistreated one of the three iron mills we recently received from the praiseworthy Society, the use of the iron mill was denied him until he improves. Meanwhile, he will have to help himself with the stone mill, which is now in good condition and which he cannot so easily damage. The man will probably behave like this until the country, or our Ebenezer through God's judgment, spues him out.]

Saturday, the 18th of March. Very early this morning my dear colleague journeyed to Savannah to hold divine services again for the German people there. We must always schedule our departure according to the flood and ebb tides so that we reach Purysburg just at the time of flood or ebb, otherwise it is very difficult if one must go against the current.[53] When the water in the Savannah River has not risen too high, one can observe the tide as far as Purysburg. My dear colleague also took along a couple of Bibles and Arndt's book *Of True Christianity*, for which some people have recently asked. May the Lord accompany him and let much good be accomplished through the word of the gospel when he preaches it in His name.

[Sunday, the 19th of March.] A pious Salzburger told me that he had recently read in a booklet that those who had not learned the catechism could not be saved. He had told his wife that, and she was not a little disquieted by it because she had never been sent to school in her youth and she now found it so hard to understand the catechism with Luther's explication.[54] She could, she said, recite it somewhat without the explication. The wife was present herself while the man was pouring out his and her troubles. I let them show me the booklet and the cited passage; and then, as I had expected, I did not find the expression so severe as the man had understood it. The question was posed thus with the answer: "Whither will you come if you learn the catechism and live according to it?" Ans. "To the joys of heaven." "But whither will they come, who do not wish to learn the catechism or to live according to it?" Ans. "To hell."

To comfort them I told them that it was a loving benefaction of God if He granted someone the opportunity to go to school and to learn to read, and the parents in our place should recognize with gratitude the benefaction that God is granting their children. Meanwhile, no one's salvation is really being damaged because he cannot read or has too weak a memory to learn the words of the catechism fully. It is good, I continued, if grown people who were neglected in their youth make the effort, with prayers to God, to learn by heart at least five chief items of the catechism without the explication, as some among us have done. But, even for the simplest man who wishes to be saved, the most important thing is to understand and wish to believe the basic truths of the Christian dogma that are found in the catechism. For example, according to the content of the ten commandments he should learn to know his fall and deep perdition and, at the same time, according to the three chief articles he should know that our most merciful God, through His only-begotten Son, has redeemed His noble creation, which has become so corrupted through Satan's seduction and his own guilt, and that He is now working on it through His spirit in order to put it aright. For this purpose, however, man must make loyal use of the means of salvation in the divine order. In this regard I referred to several very simple people of humble class whom I knew and who have nevertheless come to a living recognition of the salvation in Christ, even though they could neither read nor write. This woman is a diligent house-keeper, but because of that she sometimes neglects the necessary seriousness and zealousness in her use of the means of salvation, a fact which causes her husband to worry and struggle. Therefore I spoke a bit about the example of Martha and Mary in Luke 10 according to their circumstances and read with them the song "One thing is necessary."[55]

A pious widow told me that a few days ago she had learned to practice and understand the words "Truly my soul waiteth upon God: from him cometh my salvation." She said she had been in peculiar circumstances, which she hesitated to reveal to me because of the presence of some people; but the Lord had helped her.

Monday, the 20th of March. Yesterday we had a thunder storm that soon passed over, and in the night a cloudburst. Yesterday and today the wind has been stormy and cold again, and the pleasant springtime just won't start rightly. Most of the peach blossoms are falling off and are spoiled by the frost. Some people are worried that their sweet potatoes that they planted before the last cold may have frozen in the ground. One supposes, however, that this has happened only to those that were not buried deeply enough in the earth.

A German man who heard us preach a couple of times some months ago and had come to a recognition of true Christianity called on me and said he was coming from the newly built fortress of this province, Augusta, via Savannah-Town, where he was serving as a soldier. They have built a fortification of pallisades, together with a house for the captain and lieutenant and also a hut for the soldiers; but otherwise there is nothing there. They have nothing at all to fear from the Indians, who harmonize fully with the [English] Europeans in drinking, misbehavior, and in the most dissolute things, that no one holds against the other. He could not sufficiently describe the shameful manner of life [the swinish behavior and lewdness] that he had to witness there. The captain[56] is otherwise an honorable man but has been lying sick at his plantation near Savannah with epilepsy,[57] which he is said to have contracted from drinking and anger. Things are miserable in that land. However, because there are still some just men and children of God there, who step up to the abyss,[58] our merciful Father in heaven will probably withhold His judgment over the country and its inhabitants. Just now we hear nothing more about the Spaniards' designs against this colony.

Tuesday, the 21st of March. It was very cold again last night, and the wind was so violent that the ships at sea must have run a considerable danger if this wind struck them. It is a northwest wind and therefore exactly opposite those that come from England to Carolina or this province. [My dear colleague, as well as the Salzburgers who are fetching rice, will be greatly hindered in coming back up or will have to remain on shore,

because the violent wind is still blowing. Nevertheless,] my dear
colleague arrived this noon safe and sound; and God had
strengthened him in Savannah to preach to the people there
both in the morning from the regular gospel John 8 and in the
afternoon from the passion-text John 19:1–11, which follows
in our order. [In answer to my recent letter, Mr. Causton sent
the following one, which we judge necessary to quote here:
"Your favour of the 7th Inst. was delivered past Saturday by
Pichler & Riedelsperger, I must own the Contents little sur-
prized me, & as I was apprehensive, how dangerous it would be
for Resolutions of that Kind to grow, I thought it necessary to
stop them in the bud, & I hope those people are convinced,
that it is nither just nor reasonable to quitt a Countrey without
repaying the Charges anvanced in bringing & settling them
there, when such bringing & Settling was at their Intercession
et Request.

["As to the term of Continuance for the particular time of 3
years (which they might be possibly be told of by Mr. Vat or
others) they could have no Pretence to make any Claim thereby,
since it is hardly 2 years, since they were removed from their
old Town, & new Charges defryed (defrayed) on that account.
In my Discourse to them, I acquainted them, that the Trustees
did not intend or would desire, that any man should be kept in
the Province contrary to his liking, therefore if they were able
to pay their Charges, they might as well go the first Week, first
Month or first year as the last. Upon the Whole, I told them,
that if they had any desire to preserve the Character of honest
men, their business was to petition the Trustees, & set forth
their Reasons, because without their Authority I could not suffer their desire to be put in Execution. As you was pleased to
write fully to me your Sentiments, you will see, I have not been
behind hand in giving you mine, earnestly recommending you
to the Disposer of all Things, hoping that by his Assistance you
will comfort the feable minded, who seem to stagger under di-
versity of Opinions. I take liberty of using this Expression, as
being well acquainted with the artful Insinuations, that all our
industrious people are attacked with, but if they draw their
Conclusions from Reason, it cannot be supposed, that the
Trustees, who have taken so much Pains to distribute the Bless-

ings of this Life to the Industrious, will ever let them sink under Disappointment whatsoever, I am etc. Savannah, March 15th 1738. Th. Causton."

[Because even before my dear colleague's return the two men asked about a letter that Mr. Causton had wished to write to me on their behalf and because they returned after his arrival, I told them the contents of the letter, which was, however, very offensive to their worldly desires and designs so that they revealed their anger in a rather rude way. Pichler remained behind with me and let me know that he would be content if we would help take care of his child because, not having a wife, he could not keep it with him, since it would greatly hinder him in his work. Recently, when he used the child as an excuse for moving away, I had promised to do as much for the child as was in our power; and I repeated that this time. We shall gladly do what we can just to avoid the vexation that would doubtless arise if one or more Salzburgers were to leave Ebenezer and move elsewhere.]

Wednesday, the 22nd of March. We have very little profit from the Indians when they are at our place; and therefore it is good that our village does not lie on their path, or otherwise we would have them here more often. Their dogs almost tore a poor young man's cow apart and made her useless for giving milk. [Some time ago the Salzburgers' pigs were wounded or even killed.]

Mrs. Schweighoffer was sick for a couple of days, of which circumstance she made very good use. For her the words are very true: "He must wax, but I must wane." I received much edification from her, and Kalcher and his wife cherish her as a jewel and receive no little advantage from her prayer and Christian conduct. While they were telling me about her spiritual condition, I remembered the late Prof. Francke's sermon, "The First Kösteritz Memorial,"[59] which I promised to lend them and from which I hope they will receive good instruction and encouragement in their troubles and anxiety.

Thursday, the 23rd of March. Among the children who are being prepared for Holy Communion daily from two to three o'clock in the afternoon there are some who are becoming obedient to the gospel and wish to leave a place for grace in their hearts. We are planning next time, which will be on Maundy Thursday, to present some of them to the congregation, to confirm them, and to let them attend Holy Communion for the first time, provided they continue to give us and others a dependable proof of a changed attitude.

Since the boy Zettler has been under the supervision of Ruprecht Steiner, he has become better behaved and more obedient to the word of the Lord, so that one can well see what an impression persistent admonitions and a good example can make.

On the occasion of the 25th chapter of Leviticus, which follows for our contemplation in the prayer meeting, the listeners were shown, among other things, what merciful care God takes of the poor, whom He does not wish to be oppressed by the rich. For this reason He has wisely and earnestly ordained not only the remission of debts and redemption from servitude but also the restitution of land that was pawned or sold because of bitter poverty. For, if the rich among the people had been permitted to buy and keep whatever they wished, it would finally have gone so far that many a poor man would have to leave the country because of poverty and thereby remove himself from the practice of the proper public services, to the great danger of his soul. With this I had an opportunity to say something about the good intentions of the authorities of this land, the Lord Trustees, who, in their ordinance that no one might sell his land, were thinking mainly of the poor in the land, who would otherwise soon be pushed out. In this I could refer not only to experience in Germany, but also in neighboring Purysburg. As I could again assure them in Mr. Causton's very own words from his last letter, the Lord Trustees wish to let no diligent and honest worker fail but to help him as best they can. Therefore no one should be moved by poverty to sell his land and the work he has put into it. Nor were disorderly, frivolous, or dissolute people allowed to do so in the Old Testament, etc.

Friday, the 24th of March. For some time our dear Lord has granted Mrs. N. [the wife of the Austrian, Schmidt] much grace for her conversion, so that we who knew her previous condition are glad in heart about it. Today she told me this and that about the condition of her soul, and from this I could clearly note her growth in goodness. Again she assured me, as she has often done before, that our wilderness has become an opportunity for her salvation through God's mercy, which she would never have achieved if she had remained in her former place in Germany. She marveled at her previous blindness, when, for example, she took it amiss that her husband admonished her to love her enemies and to repay evil with good, which she had considered unnecessary and impossible. For instance, she continued, she had not been able to understand it in N. [Regensburg][60] when other people had made so much of a Biblical verse and had found edification in it, whereas she found it as insignificant as any human words. Now, however, God is letting her feel the strength of His word, law, and gospel.

Saturday, the 25th of March. A Salzburger woman could not thank God enough for having given her His blessing in learning to read, which brings her so much advantage in her edification. A few days ago I heard a very similar thing from another woman who wished to reward a man, if he would only accept it, for his efforts in giving her some initial instruction in reading. The aforementioned Salzburger woman praised her neighbor for often coming to her and being very useful to her with edifying conversations from God's Word and also with singing and praying. While at work during this Passion Season her mind was always on our suffering Savior and His love. Concerning this woman one can well say that humility and simplicity well rule her heart and lead her to heavenly wisdom. She considers herself the most useless and lowly creature in the world; yet, as she says, God is doing much good to her unworthy person and is letting her gain a better and better recognition of Him.

[Pichler called on me with Brandner because of his child, which he wished to entrust to him and his wife, in order to make this definite and to ask my approbation and help. The matter was agreed upon in the following manner: "Thomas Pichler has agreed with Matthias Brandner to entrust him with the care and education of his child and to pay him 4 £ sterling yearly for food and care (which includes washing and mending). From the poor box he will receive 2 £ sterling assistance, provided he remains in this colony and pursues his profession in Ebenezer, for otherwise we have no authority to grant such a benefaction."]

Sunday, the 26th of March. The booklet *Dogma of the Commencement of Christian Life*[61] is in the hands of some Salzburgers, some of whom received it from Senior Urlsperger for the trip; and it does much good to those who read it devoutly. During our visits we discover in what kind of books our listeners seek and find their edification; and at the same time we always recommend the chief book, namely, the Holy Scriptures; and in the said booklet there are excellent instructions for useful and edifying Bible reading. Some people make good use of our hymnal and of the songs in it. While walking past, I heard that a family had several children in their hut and were singing "So I am a stranger no more."[62] The children, especially girls, who were with me today are giving me good hopes in this Holy Week that they will vie with one another in loving and praising the Lord Jesus, who loved them unto His death; and for this reason, as I hear, they have gathered together. I sang with them the song, "Crucified Lord, my Heart is seeking,"[63] which some of them know by heart and without prompting. I spoke to them about the beautiful behavior of the children in Matthew 21:15, for them to imitate, prayed with them, and gave them the pious wish to take home with them: "Let my soul be a little bee on Thy roseate wounds, etc."[64]

Monday, the 27th of March. N. [Rieser's] middle son has been in preparation for Holy Communion too up till now and would like to go if we would let him. The great frivolity to which he is more devoted than his brothers has hindered him from receiving the divine word rightly. The older brother was on good paths both before first partaking of Holy Communion and afterwards in his sickness, but now he has fallen by the wayside and become frivolous and careless. I called them both to me and spoke to their consciences and gave them the advice not to be too hasty with Holy Communion but to prepare themselves with sincere prayer so well that they can go to Holy Communion with profit. I gave them Prof. Francke's little book: *Necessary Self-examination before Taking Holy Communion*,[65] in which very fine and inspiring instruction is given not only for those who wish to go to Communion for the first time but also for others.

[The parents of these boys, particularly the father, will also find their lesson in it; for, although he always reads and hears much good, he still does not wish to tear his heart away from all sins and to devote it to Jesus, and therefore he is still limping on both sides.[66] At the same time he knows himself very well and can say clearly what it is he is lacking.]

Today I distributed the last rice from the twenty barrels that the Salzburgers have fetched from Mr. Montagut's plantation. There has never been so much rice in our place as now, even though the last harvest did not turn out well. And similarly no one is lacking corn, beans, and meat; and all this is a manifest blessing of the Lord and is recognized as such by those who are understanding.

After Easter I shall have to go to Mr. Causton to put our accounts entirely into order and especially to obtain the cattle the third transport should receive, and also a few tools.

Tuesday, the 28th of March. At last we have had a gentle rain that has lasted since yesterday and which the soil needed for planting corn, from which the people have been kept so far by the continuous cold and drought. Yet nothing has been lost, because one can plant on good soil until May; that is not too late, provided the weather is favorable. The sweet potatoes that were planted deep enough in the soil have, I understand, received no damage from the heavy frost.

[Eischberger and his wife have been living for some time in disharmony; and therefore last Sunday one of them complained about the other to my dear colleague. I spoke with both of them today separately and will speak to them jointly when I have more time. They are probably both to blame; and the husband tried to hide his rashness, anger, and foolish behavior behind all sorts of good appearances, but they were easily revealed. Neither he nor his wife can now be permitted to take Holy Communion until everything is in Christian order again, a fact which he has accepted and recognized as necessary. I told him something concerning the verses 1 Corinthians 16:13–14, and likewise something about our Lord Jesus, who is the head of our congregation and rules over it with great meekness and gentleness (2 Corinthians 10:1). In this manner Christian men, who are their wives' heads, should imitate the Lord and rule with wisdom, love, and gentleness over the female sex, which is like a weak tool in its weakness. I also gave the woman a lesson appropriate to her understanding. She complained especially that her husband would not remain at home with the child on Sundays or during the prayer meeting but preferred to go to church, so that, if she wished to hear something, she would have to take the child along and thereby be hindered in hearing.]

Wednesday, the 29th of March. Ott came to me this morning and announced that he could not go to Holy Communion this time because he wished to prepare himself better beforehand. Last evening at Rieser's house he heard someone read from the booklet *Necessary Examination of One's Self*,[67] and he must have become even more aware of the disloyalty and ingratitude he has shown since he first took Holy Communion. He requested said booklet; but I could not serve him this time, since we have only one copy left.

A [Salzburger] woman told me that her husband had become irritable and angry several times because he had been told by my dear colleague both during his field work and also in his hut that his condition was not yet adequate and that he was still lacking in true conversion. However, she directed him to prayer and kept after him with admonitions and remonstrances until he finally recognized that such chastisements were meant not badly but sincerely. She too is fully convinced that, despite all his knowledge and reading, he still lacks faith and that his unbelieving and worldly heart often betrays itself, of which she divulged to me several especial illustrations. This news will help me to work on him in all possible ways.

In the private preparation for Holy Communion we contemplated Christ's first words on the cross: "Father, forgive them, etc." As I learned later, they immediately caused a blessing; for a righteous young man came to me and, for the sake of his conscience, told me something about another man of whom he had seen and heard something for which he had already admonished him, but without accomplishing what he had wished. Therefore he asked me to speak with him too. I did this right away; and, God be praised!, it had very good effect in that he not only recognized and regretted his deed but thanked me for my admonition with hand and mouth and with great emotion.

In the evening many of us gathered together for prayer in the orphanage, because we have a better opportunity there [for kneeling because of the well laid floor] than in the hut, where divine services are otherwise held. Here I read out loud the last part from the afore-mentioned booklet *Necessary Examination of One's Self*, after I had already used the first part in the morning prayer meeting for the good of the children and others who are going to Holy Communion from the orphanage. This booklet has been of great use to us for our edification and confirmation in the dear dogma of the right use of Holy Communion. From it our people learn that what they hear from us out of God's word is also the well founded dogma of other people, especially of the dear servant of Christ, the late Prof. Francke, and this is a beautiful answer against our calumniators.

Thursday, the 30th of March. Today fifty-six people of our congregation went to Holy Communion; in addition came the shoemaker Reck and two families or four persons of the Trustees' indentured servants from Old Ebenezer. Of the children who have been prepared for Communion, three girls, namely, Sibylla Friderica Unselt, Catharina Holtzer, and Susanna Haberfehner, were confirmed before the congregation after a public examination on today's epistle 1 Corinthians 11:23 ff. and then admitted to Communion with the others. We believe that the congregation was edified by their example and good conduct as well as by the entire company in which they participated. Zettler and my English boy Bischoff,[68] whom I have taken on, were also among those who have been prepared. However, because the former had already gone to Holy Communion several times in Germany and the latter was baptized and nurtured in the English Church, they were both admitted without any such confirmation ceremony after previously having received enough instruction and after we were able to detect some certain signs of the grace of God that was working on them and for which they had made room. The said English boy speaks German, can read German books well, and attends our divine services gladly and diligently. May God let all this be commended to His blessing!

In today's evening prayer meeting we completed the last chapter of the book of Leviticus; and, God willing, we shall begin the fourth book after Easter. May God be humbly praised for all aid and blessing which He has graciously granted so far! May He let His Son with all His virtues and acquired merits be painted right before our eyes and written in our hearts as the One who has been presented to us so far on almost every page of the book of Leviticus which we have been contemplating, so that what He himself has said will come true: "Moses has written of me," "Search in the scriptures," and "They are they which testify of me."[69]

Friday, the 31st of March. N. [Rauner] complained to me yesterday with many tears about his plight and testified that, to be sure, his great poverty was depressing him but that that was negligible in comparison with his spiritual misery. I summoned him to come to me today, at which time he told me in more detail how badly he is faring in his child raising and what an obstacle it is to his conversion. The oldest son of his wife, whom he married three years ago in Purysburg, is full of cunning and wickedness and cannot be brought to order by any discipline on his or his wife's part. He brought this misery on himself through his rash marriage, against which we warned him at the time with all our might. It will probably come to the point that he will put this evil boy to a profession or into the service of a strict master. But this is not poor N. [Rauner]'s only obstacle to a serious conversion to God, as he himself will well see once he has gotten rid of this troublesome and wicked boy. Meanwhile, however, it is good that he recognizes what he is still lacking and claims to be resolved to turn fully to God. I told him that, if things were better with him and his wife, then it would also go better with the child raising.

This year, as we do every year, we have spent Good Friday as a regular holy day by holding public services both morning and afternoon; and in the evening we held a prayer meeting with the congregation in the orphanage. May God be humbly praised for all the blessings that He has granted us publicly and privately during this passion season through the contemplation of the suffering and death of our Savior!

APRIL

Saturday, the 1st of April. This evening in the orphanage we attempted to prepare ourselves for our holy Easter Sunday with our dear congregation on our knees before the countenance of the Lord. Before the prayer we read out loud the biography of the late Provost Porst, as it appears in the ninth *Contribution to the Building of the Kingdom of God*;[70] and we reminded them of some of it for closer application. It contains some beautiful Easter matter, namely, the revelation of Joseph to his brothers, which is an excellent prefiguration of the merciful and compassionate love of the Lord Jesus for His weak children and all those who would like to be saved through Him; for this was the very matter which our faithful God blessed in that blessed man for his complete penetration into the living recognition of our dear Savior and which granted him the forgiveness of sins.

Although the dear Lord does not walk the same paths with the people who let Him lead them to heaven on the narrow way of the imitation of Christ; and, although no one may demand from Him the specific experiences that this or that person has had, one nevertheless has a good opportunity to show the listeners what seriousness and struggle are required for true Christianity, and that it is not only necessary but also possible to be changed in heart, mind, mood, and all one's forces and to become a new man, especially if one carefully perceives the great loyalty of the Savior that is revealed in His guidance of His children. We are already experiencing profit in our congregation that is encouraging us to read such examples from time to time. Sometimes we hear that this or that person about whom something is read has had to fight the very same sins, temptations, obstacles, etc. as this or that person among us. Therefore, if God has helped in these cases, then such fighters in our congregation grow in courage so that they will attack the matter afresh and in the name of Jesus, our predecessor and victor. And behold, the Lord Jesus helps, yea, He is still helping. Hallelujah!

Sunday and Monday were Easter. During these holy days both of us had a strong catarrh and hoarseness; but the dear Lord so helped that we were not hindered in either the public service or the repetition hour and prayer meeting, even though the sermon was a bit more difficult for us. In so far as it was possible, we also visited our listeners in order to bring closer home to them those things that had been read from the dear gospel during the public service. Before Easter Mrs. N. [Arnsdorf] came to a deep recognition of her sins and great perdition and therefore she celebrated Easter this time only with sighs, moans, and weeping. However, this will be many thousands of times more pleasing to the Lord Jesus than the worldly Easter joy of secure people. Her heart was somewhat comforted by the exposition on Easter Sunday of the resurrected Savior's patience and love for those of weak faith and the troubled souls as exemplified by the godly women of Galilee. After the Easter holidays we shall probably see what other good has been caused in our congregation through the preaching of the gospel of Jesus, the resurrected, glorious, sweet, most beautiful, dearest Savior, to which all the congregation, both large and small, found their way often and in Christian order.

A weak timid little lamb called me to him last Saturday to complain of his troubles, but I have not yet had time to go. The Lord Jesus will surely have gone to him, for He wishes to wait upon the weak and to care for all, as is right.

A young Salzburger complained to me that he had begun to pray after God had mightily awakened him to penitence; but it seemed only to get worse, for he was remembering more and more the dreadful sins of his youth which he had committed as apprentice and journeyman and now he was experiencing what is meant by: "To be a Christian costs you much." I cited to him the verse: "Yet the effort it is worth," [71] and related the parable about the manure pile or the filthy cesspool. If one disturbs it or wishes to remove the filth, then it stinks all the worse. As reading matter I gave him the late Prof. Francke's *Preparation for Easter Sunday*[72] concerning John 11:25–26, which God had recently blessed in me.

Tuesday, the fourth of April. My dear colleague Mr. Boltzius went to Savannah this morning in order to speak with Mr. Causton about this and that circumstance concerning the congregation. May the Lord give him wisdom for this and let it advance His glory!

I have spoken with one and the other of our community and learned with joy how our dear Lord has not left this Easter celebration unblessed. They could say that the Lord is living, that He is truly arisen. A woman said that last year she had had a troubled Easter and that this time she had been very worried before the celebration, but the dear Savior had had mercy upon her and refreshed her. This person cannot read, yet in spite of that she has such a recognition that one can soon hear from what kind of foundation it comes; and we can consort with her most edifyingly.

A certain man said that he had been very sad on the first Easter day but that he had seen the light during the evening repetition hour. Still another told me how hard it had been for him to believe that all his sins would be forgotten, but now God has wrought such a faith in him. This is N. [Gschwandl], who came to America with the first transport. In such a manner the right hand of the Lord wins victory in many souls, even among us. The Lord be praised! This encourages us to continue conducting our office ever more loyally; for it is not in vain. May the Lord let us ourselves experience the strength of His resurrection better and better so that we can praise it ever more to our listeners.

Wednesday, the 5th of April. So far God has given N. [Mrs. Rheinlaender] much grace at the commencement of her conversion; but for some time it has seemed to me that she does not mean it honestly and that her love for Jesus is not yet right, for she loves the world and pleasure even more than the glory of Jesus Christ. Therefore I sincerely admonished her to begin with true earnestness in the name of Jesus Christ to free herself from everything, let it cost what it will. Should the Lord Jesus see that there is truth in her, I told her, He would help her through the greatest difficulties. Because she prays more now than formerly, and God's word goes more to her heart than in former times, this poor woman thinks that everything is now all right. Nevertheless, although her heart has expelled so many things, it does not yet belong entirely to the Lord Jesus and she cannot yet believe. Among other things, she said that she has been among us for a long time, has listened to God's word, and has sung and prayed with us; and with all this she thought she was pious. Some time ago, however, she had learned to know it had been hypocrisy previously. Thereupon I told her that, even though she had considered herself pious then, we had not been able to recognize her as such and, if we had spoken to her about it, she would not have been able to believe it.[73] That is the way it still is, I told her; for now she has begun to show more seriousness in her Christianity and thinks that things stand all right with her. She would not be able to believe it if we told her that she does not yet mean it honestly. But she would recognize it quite differently if she would accept good advice. She accepted, with many thanks, this and other things that were told her. May God make her sincere!

Thursday, the 6th of April. Mr. Causton has been sick for several days and has therefore remained at his estate,[74] to which I had myself directed in order to settle my business with him. Because very little could be accomplished this time, I have been summoned to him again in fourteen days, when everything that concerns the Salzburgers' provisions will, hopefully, be taken care of. One must resign oneself to making a trip almost in vain from time to time; yet this one was not entirely in vain, because I could get the provisions due to Mr. Thilo and the two Zueblin brothers from the store-house for them and adjust some matters. I found a letter to me from Mr. Verelst from 24 December 1737, in which he answered mine of 29 July. [It appears that the Lord Trustees were not happy with everything that was written in my aforementioned letter, yet] The Lord Trustees have consented to most of the things which were requested on behalf of the Salzburgers, and they sent a very friendly letter.

[In Savannah I wrote a letter in answer but could not mail it because of my hasty departure. Next week there will be an opportunity via Purysburg to Charleston, so we will forward several letters to London then. The merchant of St. Gall, Mr. Schlatter, sent me from London two copies of the letter he had sent me some time ago together with a barrel full of linen. He has not yet received my previous answer, so he wonders how things must be going. Mr. Causton accepted the linen; but, as he told me, he cannot dispose of it anywhere because the people here have no money. Nevertheless, he again promised to send the money for it to London, and I shall remind him of it as soon as I come to Savannah. We hope very much that this man, who had very honorable intentions in this deal, will not suffer any loss.]

Mr. Causton has had the picture of Mr. N. [Urlsperger], which was recently sent to him, mounted under glass and set up in his room; and under it are the English words: "This Print was transmitted from Germany by himself to Mr. Thomas Causton at Savannah Jan. 31, 1737, as a Token of his particular Regard to him for Kindnesses shown to the Salzburgers at Eben Ezer in Georgia."

Friday, the 7th of April. I had to speak to a Salzburger about some external matters; and, when I could not agree to his request or let him commit a wrong against a widow, he revealed his considerable anger; but later, when he had thought it over, this caused him to shed many tears and to make a sincere apology. External matters cause us much difficulty, yet the dear Lord always helps us through them.

So far the weather has been very pleasant; we have had penetrating rains several times. The nights are quite cool, but without frost. The people complain not only that the large birds are pulling up the sprouting corn[75] but also that the field mice are doing much damage, and therefore they must plant again and guard diligently against the birds.

Saturday, the 8th of April. N.'s [Rauner's] wife is suspected by several people in the congregation of having let herself get intoxicated with strong drink on a neighboring plantation in South Carolina; but I could learn nothing certain except conjectures. Nor could I get any confession out of her, rather she wept and complained much about calumniators and false people. This may serve to cause her to avoid evil appearances and not keep close company with such an ill-bred lot like the people on said plantation. It is good if tipsters, and even those who appear to be such, are chastised and denounced in the congregation. This vice is far too common in this country, and therefore we must try in every way to prevent such a plague in the congregation. I have spoken with Mr. Causton about the Frenchman who sells rum and wine on this plantation and he has consoled me with the arrival of the new governor in Carolina; he is said to be a good friend of our colony who will soon put such disorderly people out of business.

Sunday, the 9th of April. A German man in Old Ebenezer is still hoping that we will accept his oldest girl into our school, since she cannot help him in his work now and can therefore go to school all the better. I have promised the man to speak to Mr. Causton about it, because I would not like to do this without his permission. He generally insists that children from eight to ten years old who get provisions from the storehouse be kept at work and therefore be spared from going to school. No arrangements are yet being made for the German children in Savannah to go to school. Perhaps it will happen when Mr. Oglethorpe returns to this country. We continue to hear that he is coming, but no one, not even Mr. Causton, knows when.

Monday, the 10th of April. For exercise this morning we took a trip to Old Ebenezer in order to see how things are going with the saw mill there. A small ditch has been dug through the garden we used to have; and the water in the regular river is held back by a dam so that it collects and the collected water then drives the mill, which stands on the new ditch. Two saws cut the outside parts from the wood, and on the other side as many saws as one wishes to apply cut the wood entirely into boards, at which time the two remaining rough sides of the wood are cut off. As a favor to us the miller had a piece of wood placed on and the mill run; but there did not seem to be enough water on hand, and therefore it was cut only slowly and with only one saw.[76] The entire works must have cost a lot of money; yet the mill run is not yet furnished with posts and thick boards, and there is still much else to be fixed. The greatest value that they see from their work so far is that, after they have let out the water, they can catch the most beautiful trout, pickerel, carp, and other fish with their hands in great quantities and as often as they wish.[77] The miller gave the Salzburger who had gone with us eight large trout for us, and he offered to give us more like them as often as we might send for them.

We were told that Lackner, who is grazing the second herd of cows on a grassy spot in the forest, had stepped on a large snake that had wrapped itself around his foot but could not hurt him any more because he had crushed its head when he accidentally stepped on it. This is an example of God's fatherly providence which, in this instance too, has swayed over this man, who fears Him. So far, our dear Lord has mercifully kept all of us from the misfortune of being bitten by a snake, although many have come close to that danger. A year ago a cow was bitten and quickly swelled up and collapsed. There are many such vermin in this wild land. Whenever a person sees one, it is killed or shot so that gradually there should be fewer of them.

Tuesday, the 11th of April. [Christ, the baptized Jew, who learned the tailor's trade in Germany, cannot earn his bread with his profession, especially since he does not work diligently without supervision. He is entirely unsuited for working in the field because of his many hemorrhages.[78] He has often requested to be taken into the orphanage and to be provided there with food and clothing in return for his work. We may finally come to do it from pity for his sick and needy circumstances, although we are afraid he might become a burden to Kalcher and his wife because of his obstinacy and laziness. Kalcher does not refuse to accept the burden gladly just so the poor man will not suffer harm, since he is lacking everything, except that he now has more provisions than previously. I told him both today and recently in what way we are worried about him, and therefore I suggested to him that he work in his profession for perhaps fourteen days in the orphanage and see how the set-up there pleases him. At the orphanage, proper conduct is observed both by day and by night, and everyone has to be satisfied with the food God grants. He should hope to get no more from his work than maintenance, necessary clothing and, against the winter, a better bed than his present one. In return for this he must work for the orphanage in his profession to the best of his ability and in anything else for which his help is needed; and he said he would gladly do so. He has made some start in Christianity and shows much love and reverence for the preaching of the gospel.

[Herzog, of whose conduct mention has recently been made,

now appears to be more content; but he gives others in the orphanage occasion to practice their patience. He is often told that he is at liberty to move out of the orphans' home again and to work on his own if he cares to; but now he himself considers this more of a punishment than a benefaction.]

For the past two years Grimmiger's little child has required much work and care because of its sick and miserable bodily condition, and therefore also much expense; its mother died when it was scarcely half a year old and its father was not in a position to raise it himself or to have it raised because of his poverty and long lasting sickness. All this time Bartholomew Rieser's wife has had it in her care and has received 6 £ sterling yearly from the poor box for her considerable effort and right motherly loyalty. Now that the child is over the worst and is fully strong and healthy, we have come to an agreement with this woman and her husband to give her 3 £ sterling for the current year; and the child's father must also contribute as much as is in his means, especially since he is now healthy and able-bodied.

Wednesday, the 12th of April. Last night we had a very violent cloudburst with lightning and thunder, which had already begun last evening. During the day some hailstones fell with the rain, and now it has become cool and fresh again. The soil has now become softened, and the planted corn is sprouting. [Susanne Haberfehner is the third of the girls who were recently admitted to Holy Communion for the first time. Although the other two no longer go to school but must do regular work like other people, it will nevertheless be necessary for her, because of her simple and rather restricted understanding, to attend the two catechism lessons, namely, the first in the morning and the second in the afternoon.]

A woman in the congregation assured me that God is opening her eyes more and more through His word to recognize the path to salvation. She often thinks, she said, that she would have gone to hell if she had remained in N. [Memmingen].[79] To be sure, she had disliked obvious wickedness and had even disapproved of it and was ridiculed because of that; but, she added, that is still not Christianity. This woman, along with her likewise honest husband, has suffered much here because of sickness and poverty; and therefore this speech and witness are all the purer.

Thursday, the 13th of April. I hear and see in some of the Salzburgers' gardens that in the present fruitful spring weather the flax damaged by the long-lasting freeze has recovered, and that that which was planted later is growing well too. The people show great zeal in raising flax because string and linen are very expensive. They have noticed that, if the frosts do not last too long in the spring and the heat is not too great at first, the flax will flourish on well manured soil, provided rain is not lacking. Everything is growing very nicely in our people's gardens; for their cattle they are planting much cabbage, which grows well here, but without heads, only with leaves.

[The shoemaker Reck of Purysburg is leaving his child, a boy of six,[80] with us and is putting him under the supervision of the orphanage, for which he will pay 2 shillings sterling per week for food, laundry, and care.]

Friday, the 14th of April. [When I was in Savannah the last time, Mr. Causton summoned me for another time; he was out of town because of sickness and could not expedite my business.] The day after tomorrow the German indentured servants of the Trustees wish to have Holy Communion; and I find it necessary to go there already today in order to have all the more time to talk with those who wish to confess and to give them cause for a worthy preparation for the Lord's Table. Perhaps God will give His blessing so that the matter of the Salzburgers' provisions, which is almost settled, will be finally completed and that the other things that the Lord Trustees have ordered for our congregation will be carried out.

Saturday, the 15th of April. In the afternoon Mrs. N. [Schweighofer] came to me and tearfully complained of the troubles of her heart. Last Sunday, she said, she had felt very well, for the Lord Jesus had especially refreshed her and made her joyful; but now she was again so miserable and, even if she prayed ever so much, her heart was and remained as hard as stone. Thereupon I read to her the song: "Away, my heart, with all such thoughts,"[81] and spoke with her of the heart of the Lord Jesus, referring to the 16th chapter of Ezechiel and the 11th chapter of Isaiah. In the latter place it is written of the

Lord Jesus: "He shall not judge after the sight of his eyes, neither reprove after the hearing of his ears," and: "The spirit of wisdom shall rest upon him." He knows therefore how to consort with miserable people and to have compassion on them. We also prayed together, and finally I read something from the historical commentary that the late Dr. Anton added to his *Household Conversations about the Redemption*[82] and especially what is written on pages 180 and 183–186, which is appropriate for such souls as are earnestly seeking to be saved. Praise be to our dear Lord, who has not failed to grant His blessing to this simple affair.

Sunday, the 16th of April. Yesterday evening we received the news from Savannah that the Spaniards were intending to attack this colony. Therefore I arranged the prayer meeting accordingly, in that I had reached the second part of the second chapter of Matthew for contemplation in the story of the New Testament.[83]

Both in the morning and afternoon today we have heard good things about the Lord Jesus as a good shepherd, and all this has led to making our hearts right familiar with His shepherd-like heart.

After the afternoon divine service I visited a certain family and spoke particularly with the husband, who remembered the 23rd Psalm, which I had used as an exordium, and said: "Oh, if I could only say with truth, 'The Lord is my shepherd.'" Thereupon I asked what was preventing him from it, and he answered, "sin." So I showed him fully how He had given up His life in order to take away our sin. In the evening I held the prayer meeting in the orphanage and, because I had heard much today about the heart of the Lord Jesus, I read a letter from the *Contribution to the Kingdom of God*[84] that was written concerning Ezechiel 34:24 and presented the heart of our heavenly Father most gloriously. Among other things, it showed how a child of God, who had God as His God, could derive comfort from all circumstances, for it knew that the Father in heaven would do nothing that might cause harm to His children. Finally we prayed together and presented our special troubles to the heavenly Father and begged Him, if it were His will, that He might leave us still longer in quiet and peace for

Christ's sake so that we might make even better use of His gospel. We asked that He might treat us not according to our sins, but according to His mercy.

Monday, the 17th of April. Stephan Riedelsperger has taken a very angry departure from us and has dragged his wife, the Valentin woman, who was at first of a docile and agreeable disposition, with him on his disorderly paths. Early yesterday morning he embarked on the boat of the Purysburg shoemaker, Reck, and went secretly to Purysburg with this shoemaker after, as is being said, he had sent his heavy copper money, which he had exchanged here, in advance on a trading boat that recently passed here on its way from Savannah-Town to Charleston. By this, the shoemaker has revealed himself as a treacherous and evil man, who, while wicked, wishes to keep up good appearances. In Purysburg he told the Salzburgers who had travelled up from Savannah with me that Riedelsperger had journeyed to Carolina to buy cattle; yet he concealed the departure of this disorderly man from me entirely; and the Salzburgers accepted his story as true so that they told me nothing about it until we were nearly home. With his departure yesterday morning, the shoemaker has now broken the third commandment[85] again so grossly despite all previous warnings and remonstrances that we can no longer tolerate it but wish to free ourselves completely from him and from his work, with which he has earned much money up until now. I sent our small boat to Purysburg to learn about the circumstances of the runaway Riedelsperger and to demand from the shoemaker the money he had received as advance payment for his shoes, and also to let him know my anger at his shamefully ungrateful conduct. I also sent his child, which he had put in our orphanage, home to him so that all connections between him and our congregation would be cut until he finally improves.

His wife in Purysburg tearfully complained to me that he is squandering in dissolute drinking company what he has earned in Ebenezer as a result of which she and her children must suffer lack of food and clothing, etc. He had seriously forbidden her to tell us of his new disorderliness, otherwise he would beat her and go to the West Indies and leave her behind with the children. This woman has a timid disposition and could be won over if she were with us for some time and understood German better.[86] After my arrival in Ebenezer I sent news about this to Mr. Causton, who will doubtless be as annoyed by this as we are. So far Riedelsperger has not been working but has been consorting with Reck and another dissolute Frenchman, who have also helped conceal his treacherous designs.

Tuesday, the 18th of April. In my absence Mr. Causton had sent a letter to me here, of which he had told me the contents when I came to him last Saturday. I reported it today to the congregation, especially because so much gossip and frightening reports had been spread through our community about the threatening war and the attack we feared from the Spaniards. The facts are as follows: Mr. Causton has received unexpected reports that the Spaniards intended to attack this colony from four directions; and for this purpose several warships had come from Spain to St. Augustine and a body of Florida Indians had gathered together with Negro slaves who had run away from Carolina and other English plantations and who had been promised their freedom, along with others who would run away and join them when the drums beat. Just as they wished to carry out their designs, and before the arrival of the English troops that are being expected daily, an order came from Madrid that the warships should return but that the small vessels and also the said Indians and the other assembled rabble should wait for new orders.

Now, since the Spaniards have nothing good in mind, the order has been given in this and the neighboring colony of Carolina that everyone should be on guard and should march at the first indication to the place where they are needed. In Purysburg the inhabitants had assembled from the plantations there to practice in arms and to hear the orders that had come from Charleston, and with this there had been much drinking and disorder. Through drinking, shouting, and shooting, the Indians, too, showed their joy that there was to be war with the Spaniards; and in N. [Savannah] people are almost making a joke of these plans, instead of letting the unpleasant news serve a good purpose according to the will of God. [There is no minister there at all now.][87]

There is a smithy for sale in Purysburg; and, because one of the Salzburgers can practice this profession and thereby be of great use to the community, I advanced him three pounds sterling for it.[88] The smith in Abercorn who worked for our people has moved to Port Royal; and in Savannah, as in Purysburg, it is excessively expensive, and therefore we would be very pleased to have a smith at our place. We are in equal need of a shoemaker.

Wednesday, the 19th of April. I have now completely finished the Salzburgers' accounts with the storehouse in Savannah; and Mr. Causton owes us no more than eighty-eight gallons of syrup and four hundred and ninety-two pounds of brown sugar, which he is now sending up to us on our boat. Praise be to God, who has helped so far and has so abundantly and clearly fulfilled His promise: "I will never leave thee, nor forsake thee." He will also show Himself to be a helper and guardian in the threatening danger of war. My soul now hangs on the words of the Lord in Philippians 4: "The Lord is at hand. Be careful for nothing; but in every thing by prayer and supplication, with thanksgiving let your requests be made known unto God."

On Saturday and Sunday I worked on the German people in Savannah with all the strength that the Lord granted me; and with God's grace I presented the order of salvation and the way to life so clearly and simply that several of them told me themselves that they had never heard and understood it that way anywhere else. God caused some of them to be moved now and then. Some [Reformed people] are very obstinate and expect to be saved through their [old] faith. Yet they hear the word and approve of it. I have shown these people who are served by our office that we wish to hold Holy Communion every eight weeks for them so that those whom we find unprepared can be instructed for the next time. I also told them that I had made their elders morally responsible to observe each individual's conduct and way of life and to report to me as often as I or my colleague comes to them in our office in order to prevent the sacrament from being cast to the dogs and the pearls to the swine. This despite the fact that we do not yet at this time know any [true, let alone] well grounded exemplary

Christian among them whom we might appoint as leader, but we must do what we can.

The wife of a [Reformed] German man has become delirious; and the main cause of this may have been above all her great distress at her present condition of servitude and the home-sickness,[89] which was very strong in her. Some time ago both these people yearned to be accepted at our place; but I see no possibility of this because we could not pay so much passage money for them or furnish them with provisions. If they had been accepted and if the woman had fallen into such miserable circumstances here, then we and the word of the Lord, which is earnestly preached, would be held to blame. This is the case with the Herrnhuters in Savannah, where she had been several times and where she is now being treated by their doctor;[90] they are now being blamed for her condition. Because the man is poor, I gave him five shillings sterling from the poor box.

In yesterday's prayer meeting we discussed, following chapter 5 of Numbers, God's statute according to which all unclean persons had to be put out of camp. This was applied to the discipline ordered by God in the Christian Church according to I Corinthians 5:13, and II Corinthians 6:17; and in this I could not help reminding the listeners, in reference to the renegade N. [Riedelsperger], how God acts with those who not only are unclean and unbelieving but also skillfully conceal their uncleanness and wickedness and can always extricate themselves. To wit, He finally does through His judgments what His servants are prevented from doing and puts the wicked out of the community; all of which such people may later consider not a judgment of God but a kindness and even pride themselves on their artful deceit of others and on how they can disentangle themselves from Christian statutes and shackles (as they probably call good order). Finally I emphatically reminded both children and adults of the two verses, Revelations 21:27 and 22:15. I also asked those who can pray to commend to God and his mercy poor N.'s [Riedelsperger's] and his wife's deplorable ways so that they will not plunge into eternal damnation.

This evening we contemplated the second part of the fifth chapter[91] concerning sinning against one's neighbor with regard to the seventh commandment[92] and concerning absolution according to divine decree, which should proceed 1) through an openhearted confession of the sin, 2) through an expiatory offering, 3) through restitution, to which a fifth part must be given in addition. In this we referred to I Corinthians 6:9; and I emphasized particularly these words: "Be not deceived" (not even by the false heart that so gladly excuses and belittles the sin against the seventh commandment with all sorts of pretexts.) With this I earnestly warned against the very common self-deception and false comfort of being saved without such confession and without being freed from sin and unrighteousness through the merits of Christ.

Likewise, I showed that the runaway N. [Riedelsperger] is to be pitied, not only because he so wickedly withdrew from his obedience to and from the orders of the authorities, but also because he had neither repaid nor made good what could rightfully be demanded of him, and that no excuse would help him before God. Those who knew of his designs and did not prevent them but even secretly helped him in them, have made themselves guilty of the sin of collusion[93] and will not succeed either unless they are truly penitent. We must show the people that such misdeeds are not to be taken lightly but that we should rightly be disgusted and displeased by them so that others should have no excuse on the day of judgment if they followed their example or made intrigues or deceived and took advantage of the authorities or their neighbors.

Thursday, the 20th of April. Yesterday two soldiers came to us on horseback, whom Mr. Causton had promised me to send so they could ride out every day and give prompt reports here and in Savannah of anything they may discover. They will not cost the congregation anything but will be maintained at the expense of the Trustees. One of them is from Hamburg,[94] but he has almost forgotten the German language because he came to America already as a child and has lived among the English.

Last Saturday I delivered to Mr. Causton, for forwarding, a letter to the Lord Trustees dated 13 April. It is addressed to Mr. Verelst. In it I reported that I had received their letter of 14 December of last year; and I thanked them for the benefactions they had shown to us and to the Salzburgers, especially by increasing the sixteen pounds destined for the building of the parsonage and school house to thirty pounds and for sending new orders that five persons of the third transport would receive a cow, pig, Welsh hen, and goose, and every family a hen and rooster. In my letter that was answered by this one of 14 December I had requested that each family might have a cow, but they merely repeated their first order. Even though, as one can easily guess, thirty pounds is by no means adequate for building three houses, I shall give no more thought to having it increased because [from the letter of Mr. Verelst, who usually writes to us in the name of the Trustees,] I see that they think they have allowed much for the construction.

My dear colleague finds it necessary for reasons of health and his office to build a dwelling that is larger than a hut; and I shall gladly help him to further this because I can well see its necessity. I, however, am almost accustomed to the disquiet and will therefore be satisfied with what I have until it pleases our dear Father in heaven to provide for me too and let me recognize the traces of His good will. The said house, which the carpenters will soon begin, will cost about 27 £ sterling; and even then we will economize as much as is possible, and it will lack outbuildings such as kitchen and stable, as well as chimneys and windows. The circumstances and the love I owe as a colleague (because of which I do not begrudge my dear colleague what I wish for myself) require me to let him have the 14 £ sterling which we recently received from Court Chaplain Ziegenhagen and Senior Urlsperger to help with the construction until God lets His river of providence flow in another manner.

Friday, the 21st of April. Yesterday we received a letter from Savannah in which we were asked to baptize the child of a German family there. My dear colleague undertook the journey and hopes to be here again by Sunday. Yesterday and today I have distributed the last syrup, rice, meat, corn, and sugar; and I rightfully thank our dear Lord for all the assistance He has granted. He has looked upon my sighs graciously and so legitimated me and my efforts that everyone, even those who are usually not too satisfied or content, must recognize that the previous distributions had been handled rightly and fairly and that each family has received its provisions as fully and properly as was possible. Only today I asked a suspicious man, who had formerly checked on my accounting, about a certain item of provisions in order to avoid any error and to be certain; but I received the answer that he had ceased to write down and calculate these because it seemed to him that he had long ago received his and his wife's allowance and that he would consider anything given later to be a mere gift and benefaction. If another transport should come here some time, I could not undertake such work again.

Saturday, the 22nd of April. [My dear colleague came back from Savannah already this afternoon, having travelled all night in order to be home again sooner. One of the two Salzburgers who rowed him down in the boat fell sick and has remained with the Herrnhuters' doctor in order to take some of his medicines.[95] Meanwhile Mr. Causton let one of the German indentured servants in Savannah help bring the boat back.]

I knew that a couple of members of our congregation deeply feel the sins they committed in their previous life and are therefore very troubled and depressed. Therefore I took the occasion to speak with them and to tell them, from the gospel, of the gracious Friend of man. May the dear Lord place His blessing on all this and lead them and all suffering souls to the dear wounds of His Son, so that they may be well advised!

Sunday, the 23rd of April. After the afternoon divine service a member of the congregation came to me to speak with me about the condition and guidance of her[96] soul, for there had been too little opportunity to speak with me quite alone in her hut while I was there yesterday. She was a very contrite soul, much bowed in her heart, to whom God had granted a beautiful blessing through the preaching of His word both last week and also today, when we treated the gospel for Jubilate Sunday concerning some of the causes of the sorrow and joy of good souls and when, as an exordium, we preached something about the words Psalms 30:5-6. This caused her to shed many thousands of tears, but she well recognizes how necessary it is for her false and frivolous nature to be properly bowed under the cross of Christ and to be divinely distressed in the true recognition of her sins.

Among other things, she said that God had granted her the resolution to free herself from everything through His grace and that she could not sufficiently lament the sins of her youth or describe them as disgustingly as they were. She also regretted with many tears that she was not in a position to restore what she had ruined for other people through her disloyalty and carelessness. It touches her to the very marrow when she hears in the sermons the beautiful title of true believers, namely, the children of God; and she desires nothing so keenly as to appropriate this beautiful name for herself in truth. As soon as she came home she was compelled to kneel before the Lord in the very first corner to call out to Him for His grace and to be accepted as His child. The comfort and splendor of the gospel is, she thinks, still too brilliant and overwhelming; and she will work very hard to apply it. She has great need, she said, of sermons about the law in which the deep perdition of her heart is rightly revealed and her conscience is made active.

Another suffering person told me that she[97] had been in very low spirits at Easter because she could not possibly presume to have the comfort of the gospel, since it was all too good for her; yet the dear Lord had granted her a little blessing on the Sunday after Easter from the words Isaiah 27:6: "He shall cause them that come of Jacob to take root." She also referred me to some words from the song "Help Jesus, help Conquer," verse 2: "I have heard your praying, and I have seen the misery in your heart, the bitter pain," and this gave her hope that the Savior will have mercy on her too.

Tuesday, the 24th of April. The heat is very great by day, and the soil is very dry because of the lack of rain. The Lord, who looks from heaven upon the earth and knows the needs of His creatures, will come with His help at the proper time. Well for him who trusts Him in all things! [Michael Rieser still remains the old angry and spiteful man who simply cannot bear it if we do not approve of his disorderly ways. I fear that sometime it will turn out as badly with him as it has turned out with Riedelsperger, whose language he is already speaking and of whose godless conduct he seems clearly to approve. We hear neither good nor evil of his wife, whom he married not long ago from Purysburg.[98] She appears to be a quiet, simple, and tolerable woman, who adapts herself best in this way to him and his violent temperament.]

Tuesday, the 25th of April. Now that my dear colleague has resolved in the name of God to build himself a house, for which I shall advance the recently received 14 £ sterling until perhaps the Lord Trustees pay the expenses, I have learned with joy that the members of our dear congregation will contribute their part toward it according to their ability, in that some of them will help the carpenters every day in felling trees and boarding the house; and this will greatly decrease the construction costs and make them bearable. At first the carpenters had wished to build the house in the same way the orphanage was built so that it would be panelled on the inside with boards and thus have a double wall, namely, on the outside with shingles and inside with boards. However, because they now have so much help from the men in the congregation, they intend to build a house of pure wood that will be neatly panelled and jointed in just the manner that I have recently written to the Right Reverend Court Chaplain Ziegenhagen.

Because we had resolved to build one spacious house for the two of us in which both my dear colleague and I would have private studies separated from the household, the costs would have amounted to as much as 100 £ sterling. However, now that the congregation is so eager, it would come to much less if it were built with their help, which, however, we really could not presume upon. I hope that the dear Lord will provide for me too in His time. At Mr. Causton's request a few months ago, I had sent him the itemized expenses for our house for him to present to the Lord Trustees. However, because I could clearly read out of the Lord Trustees' last letter that the 30 £ sterling which they had destined for two parsonages and a school seemed very much, I asked Mr. Causton not to forward my report. I am resolved not to insist upon a house and would rather remain in my hut than to live in a wooden house like the ones they are accustomed to build in Savannah and thus cause new expenses. The dear Lord knows what is good for us, and therefore He shall and certainly will act according to His will. I would that my dear colleague rather than I receive a well constructed house soon, and I thank the dear Lord for having made the members of the congregation so willing to help through love for Him and his office, too.

Wednesday, the 26th of April. [I have asked at the Eischbergers' hut several times since their last discord whether the two of them are getting on better together after the advice we gave them, since recently, and even more now, we have heard that God has blessed our exhortation. The woman said that we must have prayed diligently for her and her husband, because God quickly gave His blessing for their betterment, and that she was heartily and joyfully thanking God for it.]

A woman with whom I had briefly spoken in her hut for edification asked me at my departure to drop in again often, for she considered it a great benefaction and honor. At the same time she told me how much good it had done for her recently when my dear colleague reminded her on the street about her indolence and frivolity; because of it she had humbled herself before God and had received a new grace for a new seriousness. It was pleasing to her, she said, if anyone would say something to her to reveal her sins and to encourage her; on the other hand she did not like it if anyone wished to flatter her and keep quiet about her faults. All of this she said with many tears and great emotion. She could now say more good about her husband than she usually could; among other things, she said that he was learning more and more to recognize how useful a zealous prayer is, whereas he had previously thought and said that his prayers did not help him.

[On Monday I had sent our small boat to Savannah to bring back some things for the congregation that could not be loaded recently and also to bring back Pichler, who could not return at the time because of bodily weakness. He had become even sicker there and has had to spend much money for little medicine, even though the Herrnhuters' doctor had not demanded anything for his troubles.[99] May God convert him thoroughly and free him from his own righteousness and intentions. I fear that this sickness came to him, as it did to his late wife, from the sorrow of the world (II Corinthians 7:10), whereas he, as his wife had done, will probably lay the blame on others.]

Thursday, the 27th of April. A Salzburger sought as much opportunity as was possible in my hut to speak entirely alone with me and to tell me something privately about the sins of his youth, which are only now occurring to him, and to receive instruction from me. To be sure, the world would probably not make much of such matters and only laugh if anyone made a scruple of them. But it is a different matter for those who are being saved with fear and trembling and wish to penetrate into the Kingdom of God through the narrow gates, and their hearts must be freed of everything if they wish to get through. He wished Senior U [Urlsperger] thousandfold divine blessings as a reward for having helped him to the journey to America and Ebenezer; because, as he said, it was God who had done it through him. He had long considered himself saved and yet had never really made a proper beginning. God had, however, now given him the resolution to renounce everything through His grace and to turn himself entirely to Christ, for otherwise he would not find peace. He considers his wife and another pious soul, with whom he often has occasion to consort, to be much further in their Christianity than he. Consequently he thinks that he is not worthy to attend their prayers, even though they earnestly request it of him; and therefore he wished to hear my opinion. I told him, however, that the heavenly Father loves all His children, whether they speak clearly or mumble, jubilate, or weep. The stronger person's prayers must be useful for the weaker one, just as the stronger, if he stands in poverty of the spirit, would know how to use the weaker one's help in prayer.

I could tell him that his wife had the very same worry that she did not consider herself worthy to share in his prayer or in that of the previously mentioned person and therefore preferred to pray alone, against which, however, I had strongly advised her. In the poverty of her spirit the good woman values her husband's piety and seriousness so highly that she considers herself entirely unworthy to have him as a husband, especially since she is conscious of so many youthful sins, which, if he had known them, would have held him back (as she thinks) from entering wedlock with her. However, by this she should realize that this marriage will be her opportunity to save her soul. This Christian simplicity in marriage made a deep impression on me. In her spiritual trouble this woman asked me where the verse was written which she had heard several times from me to her comfort: "The Lord Jesus' merits extend over all sins and over all sinners." Thereupon I showed her from Biblical verses and examples that it is written in the scripture of both the Old and the New Testaments, if not in just those words, then at least with that meaning.

N. [Pichler] has been taken by N. [Kogler] into his well constructed cool house that he has recently built so that he can be better cared for here, since he has no wife. When I spoke and prayed with him today he pressed my hand with tears in his eyes and asked me to stop in on him often, for he appreciated my consolation greatly. It seemed to me that he wished to confess something, perhaps concerning his previous ill-bred behavior towards me; but his bodily pain, difficult breathing, and tears prevented him from doing it. Upon leaving, I cited the verse II Corinthians 7:10: "For godly sorrow worketh repentance to salvation not to be repented of: but the world worketh death." I also told him of its *prodromos*[100] and applied it to him, because he had only shortly before been worried because of such temporal things, of which he might now well be freed.

Friday, the 28th of April.[101] The dry weather is still lasting and causes us both publicly and privately to present our plight to the dear Lord. I spoke with the poor N. [Herzog] while he was working in the field, since elsewhere [at the orphanage] we cannot speak to him as necessary [because of his hard hearing.] To be sure, it seems that he is now more content [with his treatment at the orphanage] than previously; yet his soul is full of disquiet, doubts, and distrust toward God; and he has even revealed his spiritual condition several times in the presence of the children in offensive expressions. I warned him against this and requested him to come to me or to my dear colleague with his doubts to discuss them and pray with us, since that would be healthier for him than to seek out those for whom such things are unsuitable and to speak incautiously. I called his attention to several Bible verses, especially those that treat of the general love of God in Christ and also of the order which He wishes to help us obtain. He well comprehended all of this and agreed with the word of the Lord.

To be sure, he diligently practices in God's word and prayer; but at the same time he neglects his vigil and earnest struggle. He himself had to admit that his heart still clings to self-will and other inclinations; and thus it is no wonder if a man can [not become a Christian and can] achieve no peace despite all use of the means of salvation. There are, to be sure, people among us who wish to be Christians merely through the use of the means of salvation but without struggle and without rightly attacking the enemy in their hearts through the strength of Christ, yet this is in vain. If they make no progress because of their wicked hearts, then the dear Lord must be to blame, or they come upon the evil idea that it is not possible to become as is demanded according to God's word in the sermons and prayer meetings or even in private intercourse. It is said: "Drop all, and join with Christ, then the matter is settled." [102]

[Today I reminded Pichler that he had distressed me no little bit with his wilful absence from our thanksgiving ceremony and the following Sunday when he had travelled to Savannah with Riedelsperger, which sin against the third commandment he would have to recognize penitently. He wept at this and said: "I have thought well about that and am deeply sorry. Alas, no matter how depraved Riedelsperger was, I still had a chance to speak with him. I feel, for sure, that his conscience will disturb him and he will be sorry; but his pride will not allow him to return." At these and other words he was very depressed, especially because he had been implicated with Riedelsperger in one matter, namely, leaving this colony; and it almost seemed as if he were to blame that he had run away. He was at least pleased by the fact that he had told him and his wife that he would not go along unless he could leave in joy and love, at which both had become indignant and angry and had begun to pretend to him and others that they would remain too; and to give this appearance he had planted a little. [Pichler believes that Riedelsperger's wife is more to blame than he for this running off; she had driven him into moving away. She had not taken part in the farm work and she had not economized in the

housekeeping and cooking but had squandered much unneces-
sarily and in luxury, so that it was impossible to prosper here,
especially since they did not like the local diet such as rice. He
had wished to buy a couple of Negro slaves; but, because it is
not allowed in this colony, he had preferred to go to Pennsylvania and, if he did not succeed there, he was thinking of going
to Holland, where he knew of a merchant with whom he
thought he could achieve his purpose.]

N. [Pichler] told me that since yesterday the dear Lord has
again given him some bodily strength as well as the grace of
penitential tears at the recognition of his sins, by which his
heart has already been softened. Nevertheless, he was somewhat worried by the fact that he remembered having heard that
penance on one's sick bed or death bed does not count. I told
him, however, that he had not heard correctly. The thought
must have been that the people who postpone their penitence
until they reach the gates of eternity, generally wish to be penitent and to convert themselves to God only out of fear of hell;
and, when they are well again, they show well enough through
their new godless nature that it was only hypocrisy. Therefore,
when they were called to account, they would die in hypocritical
penitence, as I could illustrate in the example of the renegade
N. [Riedelsperger]. In his sickness he had once accused himself
so severely and made so many good resolutions that one might
have thought that there was truth in him, yet soon thereafter he
fell so dreadfully. And that is just the way it was with his wife in
her last illness. But the dear Lord in His mercy earnestly wishes
to offer and grant the sinner grace for conversion to the very
end of his life and even in the eleventh hour, as is taught in
Holy Scripture and as he has also heard in the beautiful examples that are read from time to time.

Saturday, the 28th of April. [However much a married
couple in Old Ebenezer would like to send their girl to our
school, it will not be possible because Mr. Causton will not allow
it but wishes to have even such children of the Trustees kept at
some kind of work according to their abilities.]

N. [Rottenberger] and his wife belong to the well-meaning
people who would gladly be saved, if only it could occur without
self-denial and serious struggle. I spoke with her today and

asked her to take serious care that she might truthfully say that she is a child of God and has surely received forgiveness of sins, at which time I described the children of God's state of grace as delightfully as I could. She recited a few verses from the sixth psalm for me and wished to know what the number of the psalm was, and I looked it up for her. Since she had learned it almost by heart, I told her that many people learn this psalm by heart as a penitence psalm and pray it but do not consider what they are praying, for they often confess something about themselves with the words of this psalm which they could not truly find in themselves if they would only examine themselves a little. For example: "I am weary with my groaning, all the night make I my bed to swim, etc." But out of all the words that David uses here, and all other penitent sinners with him, she should recognize what is going on in her own heart, where true recognition and remorse for sins is found.

Sunday, the 30th of April. [A man from Purysburg[103] asked me to accept his ten-year-old girl into our school whom he would board with his brother-in-law Michael Rieser. We will see whether the child will be cared for here; if not, some change will have to be made.]

We treated the gospel for Cantate Sunday concerning the condition of man before, during, and after conversion and took as our exordium Acts 7:51: "Ye stiffnecked and uncircumcised in heart and ears, ye do always resist the Holy Ghost."[104] In the repetition hour, as is always done, these words were discussed more extensively and applied, at which time I showed, among other things, what good emotions and resolutions the dear Lord has wrought in the hearts of many (even if not all) of our congregation during the past four years while we have been together as a congregation in this land. These resolutions, however, have been to a good part rejected and expelled again, for which reason many are still lacking a true conversion and state of grace. At the same time I warned with all my might against disloyalty and resistance, for the harm gets greater and greater and it finally comes to a point that the heart becomes insensitive and incapable of faith.

At that point I had to think again of poor N. [Riedelsperger] and tell the congregation how mightily God had worked on him

during the sea voyage and also afterwards during his dangerous sickness and how much good he had promised his Creator
and Savior in my presence; yet he had subsequently become disloyal and ever worse. Because he had revealed his hardheadedness in many ways, I had him tearfully in mind, I told them,
and sincerely wished for his improvement once as he sat in
church before me while I was stressing the verse Habakkuk
2:4: "Behold, he who is stiffnecked shall find no peace in his
heart." However, he has remained hardheaded; and only yesterday an honest Salzburger who had consorted with him often
told me that he had such a hard head that, if he had once
planned something, he could not be dissuaded from it even if it
were to his great detriment; in fact he would do it just to spite
other people. As a warning in this connection I reminded the
listeners of the verse II Timothy 4:10: "For Demas hath forsaken me, having loved this present world, and is departed unto
Thessalonica." I wish from the depth of my heart that it will
turn out as well for this poor man as it did for Onesimus, who,
to be sure, left the family and supervision of Philemon after
committing disloyalty but came to the Apostle Paul through the
grace of God and was brought by him to conversion and finally
to recognition and absolution of his sin and was sent back to his
former master no longer as a useless servant but rather as his
dear brother.

MAY

Monday, the 1st of May. I reminded a Salzburger woman
about yesterday's sermon concerning people's varying condition with regard to conversion, and asked her in which class she
counted herself. The answer was that she was still an unconverted person; and she greatly complained about her temper,
which her neighbor had recently provoked. She thanked the
Lord for her husband, who always worked on her like a tutor,
examined her according to the sermons, and recited one or two
Bible verses every morning before he went to work, about
which she could think all day and with which she could edify
herself. When he came home he would ask her about them
again. I reminded her how much earnestness her husband

would have to use, and does use, since he wishes to be saved, and that God demanded the same of her; and after our prayer I left her the verse: "Work out your own salvation with fear and trembling."

Another woman recognized it as a great benefaction that she had an opportunity here to find the way to life. Previously, while she was in service, the order of salvation had seemed, she said, very dark; but the dear Lord now had her in His service, and only her disloyalty was to blame that she was not progressing better. It will be hard work for her, but she trusts that the Lord will not cast her away. She remembered a song of which the third verse was very dear to her. It runs: "Jesus, thou Comfort of Souls, no one hast thou rejected who would have liked to remain with you. Lord, thou wilt not now begin." [105] I cited for her good the words of a hopeful and penitent soul: "He will turn again, he will have compassion upon us; he will subdue our iniquities; /and thou wilt cast all their sins into the depths of the sea."/ Micah: 7:19.

Mrs. N. [Schweighofer] complained to me [in the orphanage and again in my hut] of her spiritual plight; and she was especially troubled that she is, she said, still so lacking in understanding and can scarcely remember anything from Holy Scripture when she reads in it herself, and therefore has little profit from her Bible reading. I told her that I too could not understand many things in the Bible, but I restricted myself to the clearest verses. She should do likewise and pray diligently and the Holy Ghost would reveal to her, one after the other, the things that are necessary for her salvation. I gave her a pencil to mark, while reading, those verses that she would like to remember and note; and, as soon as she has collected some of them, she should let me underline them with red ink so that they will catch her eye all the better. This suggestion pleased her very much. We read a few chapters of the prophet Isaiah and prayed; and it seemed as if the dear Lord had again blessed in her the reading, encouragement, and prayer. She is like a parched soil where the rain comes just right; but it sinks soon again, and she is therefore again full of panting, thirsting, and languishing.

Tuesday, the 2nd of May. The wind was very violent today

and at the same time so cool that we would have had a frost if it were not already so late in the spring. There is still no rain, and the Lord is teaching us to wait for His goodness with faith and patience. Mrs. N. [the old Mrs. Spielbiegler] is not to be convinced that she is not yet in a state of grace and therefore not ready to die a blessed death. And another person with her [her son] is just as blind. They both rely on their reading and praying at home and go to church when they see fit. And even from the simplest sermon they do not have the benefit that we seek and wish from our listeners. Their right pitiful blindness and dreadful disbelief distress me greatly, and we do not know how we should undertake to convince them that their *opus operatum* and their trust in it, as well as in the merits of Christ, will not help them without a change of heart. We wish to present their miserable condition to the merciful Savior even more diligently.

Because she so highly values her faith, which she claims to have received already twenty years ago, and does not consider a godly life to be necessary for salvation, or even possible, I opened her Bible to the passage about real faith of Christians in the late Luther's preface to the Epistle to the Romans, which she marked and promised to read again [with her son, who was not then at home.] She can make neither heads nor tails of why I am not satisfied with her; after all, she is not doing anything to anyone, evil people must be telling stories about her. With such a distressing example I sometimes think of what the worthy Pastor N. [Sommer] told me once about the piteous blindness of some of his listeners in C. [Köthen], among others about a woman who made a confession to him which suited only an unmarried serving girl, and, when he wished to straighten her out in this matter, she became angry because, as she said, he wished to ruin God's word.

Wednesday, the 3rd of May. I took the opportunity to talk with poor N. [Herzog] in the field, where he confessed to me a double sin against the seventh commandment,[106] which unrighteous act, as he said, was lying on him like a curse; and therefore it is no wonder that the word of God has, so far, had the effect on him that he has merely become more miserable and has never been converted. He wishes to free himself from this sin externally too, and he promised to accept the advice I gave him. He is full of mistrust, and even secret calumny, against God and cannot believe that God wishes him to be converted and saved; and at the same time he is sinning through severe and offensive expressions. I explained to him what the devil is, namely, a calumniator, and that his purpose is to calumniate our good Lord among people as if He did not mean well with them. However, because He, as the one good God and the highest goodness, cannot wish any evil and has explained Himself that way sufficiently in His word, then one does Him the greatest insult and outrage if one does not believe the evidence of His love but wishes to follow one's own suspicious and scandalous thoughts.

I admonished him to come to me often and also to put aside all external work[107] [that he is doing for the orphanage] for the time rather than to neglect a zealous and lasting prayer in the extreme danger to his soul. I assured him that the good shepherd Jesus was seeking him and would accept him with a thousand joys. In his presence I indicated that I would remember the troubled condition of his soul in my prayer, and this pleased him very much. Many a man may have a curse on himself; and, because he does not honestly wish to free himself from it but wishes to be confounded by his sin, things will get worse and worse. This poor man himself recognizes that he is standing on the very brink of his eternal perdition.

[At the home of a woman who had been present during my conversation with old Mrs. Spielbiegler, I inquired whether she had understood me better than the former. I then learned that she had told her husband of her miserable excuses and the evidence of her blindness, and both of them gave testimony of great repugnance for her godless behavior and sincere pity for the danger to her soul. Here I heard clearly what I had previously feared, namely, that Mrs. Spielbiegler had been happy that I had left. She thinks I do not like her and her son; and she uttered other angry words, for which this woman chastised her but without accomplishing anything.]

Thursday, the 4th of May. Last night we had a gentle rain which, to be sure, lasted only until morning yet was very useful for the soil and conducive to growth. Toward evening I met the woman from whom N. [Herzog] had purloined some things;

and, because I knew that he had already spoken with her about it yesterday and had offered her restitution either in *natura* or *specie*,[108] I asked about various things of which I had to know. She told me something about N. [her husband], who did not wish to let go of a thing which, to be sure, is insignificant yet does not belong to him; and he resents any admonition from her about this or anything else. He is often mightily moved by God's word and also disquieted; yet he has all sorts of excuses and comforts himself, as others do, with the kind of comfort that will not hold up in the hour of death and before God's judgment seat. This news was welcome to me because I had considered this man to be one who is preparing his salvation in good order; and therefore, during his frequent complaints about his corrupt heart, his indolence,[109] disloyalty, etc., I have preached more from the gospel than from the law.[110] His wife is honest-hearted and fights the good fight of faith with great loyalty.

Friday, the 5th of May. Necessity has required us to dig a small cellar in the orphanage and to provide it with a roof, because in this hot season neither milk nor other things can be preserved anywhere but in a cellar. However, if we dig only five feet, we strike water; and it is therefore hard to get an effective cellar in this water-rich land. We have equal need of a regular well; but, since we must first wait for another supply of divine blessing, we cannot yet make any arrangements for it at the present time.

Many in the congregation would welcome an opportunity to buy some cows, or at least one, with the money they earned in the past and have kept in reserve because they would be exceedingly advantageous for their maintenance. But one cannot buy cattle anywhere except in Carolina, and large marshes and the Savannah River are in the way so that they cannot be brought here except with great difficulty and with the loss of one or more head.

[Mr. Causton won't sell any of the Lord Trustees' cattle in Old Ebenezer and is also making no arrangements for the third transport to receive the cattle and other livestock that the Lord Trustees have ordered. How much advantage the poor people would have had if it had been given to them soon after their arrival almost two years ago. It would have cost the Lord Trustees the same amount of money whether they had bought them now or then, and advantage would have accrued to the people if they had been bought then. What is difficult and impossible for other people is easy and possible for Mr. Causton. So far, there has been no lack of reminders, both written and oral, and, on his side, of good promises. We believe in a divine providence, according to which what the Lord grants us must be given in due time. I, for my part, would not like to overlook anything in this regard; and therefore I shall continue to ask and urge that the promised gift be delivered to the people, the sooner the better.]

In an open hut I found two suffering souls who were troubled that a large part of their planted corn has been dug up and eaten at night by wild cats, or whatever they are,[111] for the sixth time. Actually, however, it is serious sins committed in previous times, by which such grave wounds have been struck in their consciences that they leave them no peace by day or night. I presented them the gospel as simply as was possible and tried to lure them to this food that God has offered poor troubled souls according to His great love. And, when they said that the comfort of the gospel belongs only to penitent sinners, I explained to them what God actually demands for penitence, namely, that through the grace of God a person recognize his dreadful perdition, regret it, and feel a deep disgust and repugnance for the sins he has committed in having so grievously offended so good a God, who is worthy of all love.

The gospel says, I told them, what God has done for sinners, even for the greatest, namely, He has, through pure mercy, given them the Child of His Love as their Redeemer and Savior who has atoned and made good everything that could have oppressed us for ever. Now the Son of the Father is stepping through the gospel in front of the sinners; and He does not say, "Go hence, because ye are so full of sin and so evil," but "Come unto me, all ye that labour and are heavy laden." They should not wait until they are led, as it were, physically or in a sensual way to the wounds of Jesus, to the free and open well-spring against sin and uncleanness, and are brought to the application of the forgiveness of sins that is found therein; but rather, since they can trust the reconciled God with all good, they should also trust that He means them in the gospel and does not wish to exclude them. I asked them whether they did not find it to be the case with them that, if they could make good their sin through an external deed, through penitence, through an especially good work, they would gladly do so in order to be free of the sin. And when they affirmed this, I showed them that this would diminish the glory of God and the merits of Jesus, whereas God is greatly magnified in His love by granting forgiveness of sins through grace and accepting even the greatest sinner for the sake of Christ's merits. They should show Him the glory of finally believing in His gospel and throwing themselves bare and naked at the feet of Jesus. After the prayer I read to them the short but right comforting song "Oh, a word of Lasting Love."[112]

Saturday, the 6th of May. There are people among us who can always find something, and which they consider to be great and truly major faults, to reprove in even the most honest members of our congregation and who can pass judgment rather immodestly and unkindly. However, since it is unauthorized and contrary to truth, their judgment does not amount to much except that it tends to raise suspicions and give offense to those who are not familiar with the matter in context and according to all circumstances. Such calumniators set their piety in external and law-abiding conduct and know nothing of the living faith in the hearts. When they see true Christians stumble or do not see them doing precisely those good works that they consider necessary and beautiful according to the inclination of their own temperament, then they consider them hypocrites and scorn the spirit of grace that truly dwells through faith in His children among us and knows how to chasten and correct them in their errors, not according to the way of this world, but in a heavenly and divine manner. Some of our dear people feel their sins and are also externally sad; and therefore their natures will not adapt to the frivolous and false evangelicals. Moreover, we wish that all among us would become more and more righteous, and then they would also conduct themselves more prudently (*akribós*) and thereby give the enemies of the Salzburgers less opportunity for sinning by calumny.

Sunday, the 7th of May. A young man visited me before the noon divine service to discuss his spiritual circumstances with me. He shudders and is horrified at the sin that he previously committed; and, since he feels its poisonous serpent bite, he is running ever further from the Lord Jesus. He thinks it is good for him if he can be right sorrowful; for otherwise he will merely become frivolous again. He does not feel himself good enough for what he heard today from the gospel of John 16:23 ff. about the Lord Jesus' comforting assurance of the Father's love toward even His weak children, and he does not think it suits his circumstances. However, the clarity from the loving heart and countenance of the Lord expelled some of his inner darkness; and I attempted to apply to him some meditations and verses that had been read today, such as I John 4:8–9: "God is love. In this was manifested the love of God, etc.", also Jeremiah 3:12: "Return, thou backsliding Israel, saith the Lord; and I will not cause mine anger to fall upon you, etc." cf. Luke 15:20 ff. At last I prayed with him and presented to the Lord Jesus in prayer especially His own words: "I am come to seek and to save that which was lost." I also gave him the first *Kösteritz Memorial*[113] of the late Professor Francke concerning Romans 8:1 ff., in which this person's present spiritual condition is beautifully depicted and necessary instruction is given to reach an experience of the power of the gospel.

May the Lord teach me how to associate wisely with such heart-troubled and bowed souls so that they will not become enmeshed in the law or relapse into the state of worldly security. How much I myself have realized my ineptitude and inexperience in dealing with such souls who should not merely remain in their first awakening but should be led entirely to Jesus, the only helper! Last week I was greatly humbled by this. Were I permitted, I would like to choose the least place in the congregation and make room for another, who has received more wisdom and experience from God. One thinks much too little of the importance of the office before letting oneself get placed in it. I would gladly remain in the Lord's vineyard in

Ebenezer, if only I did not have to be minister and preacher. But may the Lord's will be done! Acts 21:14.

Monday, the 8th of May. Yesterday and today we have had such a mild continuous rain that we could not wish for a better one. The soil was very dry, yet the planted corn and sweet potatoes were not damaged. If our dear Lord holds back a while with good weather, it does no harm but merely means: "These wait all upon thee; that thou mayest give them their meat in due season" (Psalms 104:27), also in Book of Wisdom 16:21, "When one waits upon thee, it reveals unto thy children how sweet thou art."

Our dear Lord revealed to me both yesterday and today that He did not let His word be preached without noticeable blessing. The sweet love of the Father that He bears in His Son for miserable men pressed many tears from a man at his work, whereupon he remembered what he had heard eight days ago about well meaning and obstinate souls; and he had to confess that he had meant well so far, to be sure, but had lacked serious struggle to be saved. A man who came to me told me some facts about others which I shall be able to use for much good through God's grace, especially for Christian prudence in preaching the divine word. Oh, how much one still must learn! May Jesus take us into His school and teach us through His spirit to share His word correctly and to give each and every one his own! The listeners are often instructed to apply the truths we preach in a proper manner, and therefore it is necessary for them to endeavor to implore God for a recognition of their spiritual condition and be content when they are told by their ministers or other pious people what their actual condition is if they do not recognize it themselves. Then it will come to pass in accordance with God's will that they will acquire what is especially appropriate for their spiritual condition.

Tuesday, the 9th of May. For several days I have been impressed that, out of love for God and for their own salvation, several people have recognized their lack of righteousness and have promised to free themselves of it through restitution. May God let these awakened souls go so far as to hasten straight to Jesus, the righteous Helper, through their faith and allow Him to save them truly and entirely.

[Certain domestic conditions required me to go to Purysburg at noon, whence I returned already in the evening. I had to speak with the preacher[114] there on behalf of a Reformed Swiss who lives near Savannah. However, we did not find him at home but had to seek him at his plantation, from which he comes occasionally (not even every Sunday) to read a sermon. A new house and a church next to it have been built for him, for which money is said to have been collected in Charleston. The hut we use as a church is gradually becoming more and more unsuitable for holding divine services; this the Lord well knows and can easily grant enough so that we too can receive a somewhat more comfortable place for our spiritual assemblies, like the arrangements that are being made in Savannah and Purysburg.

[Wednesday, the 10th of May. The Purysburg man whom I recently mentioned brought his daughter to our school today. God give His blessing to this! A certain physical problem is again burdening us in the community, of which we would at this time rather complain to God than to report more clearly. The dear Father in heaven has already helped us through much; in this case too He will look upon our sighs with mercy and give help.]

Thursday, the 11th of May. On this Feast of the Ascension, as always happens, we have edified ourselves from God's Word both morning and afternoon. We visited a few people, in whose homes we ourselves received some [much] edification. They are usually very intimate with us and tell us everything that is on their hearts, and thus we can better provide them with instruction from God's word. On Sundays and holy days we find them at home, whereas on work days we must seek them in the fields.

Friday, the 12th of May. The two soldiers who have to reconnoiter in our region have received orders to return to their fortress after, as they tell us, six hundred royal troops arrived last Saturday in Savannah who are to be transferred to the new fortresses that have been established against the Spaniards.[115] One of them, who was born in Hamburg, asked me this morning to help him to settle in our place.[116] He is tired of the soldier's life; and, because he finds German people here and an opportunity to practice his profession as a tailor and to attend divine services, he would gladly live among us. His enlistment is finished next September. I do not yet know what I should do about this. I shall consider it with several informed members of the congregation so that I can hear their opinion about it too. Next Sunday the word of God should again be preached to the German people in Savannah and, because I have something to settle with Mr. Causton, I shall undertake the journey. May the dear Lord stand by me so that I will at last accomplish something that I have long wished to accomplish.

Saturday, the 13th of May. During a visit[117] I spoke with a person who was full of yearning to receive some assurance of God's mercy and her Savior's love. She is looking forward keenly to Whitsuntide and wishes with great longing to be filled with the Holy Ghost. She says that, when the bell rings in church for prayer meeting or other things, she is happy and thinks that now perhaps is the hour when your Jesus will look upon you with love.

Sunday, the 14th of May. Today through the grace of God I have learned better to understand how necessary the Holy Ghost is in order to arrive at a living recognition of Jesus Christ. When it gives testimony in the heart about Jesus Christ, and especially of His death, blood, and wounds, then all pain vanishes and one achieves new strength to continue merrily on one's course. May our dear heavenly Father truly transfigure His child Jesus in us and for this bless the office of the Holy Ghost!

Monday, the 15th of May. This afternoon I returned to Ebenezer from Savannah. Mr. Causton was very kind and donated various provisions and blankets to our orphanage, for which the name of the Lord be praised! He will now take serious steps to send us the cows that were ordered by the Lord Trustees for the members of the last transport. The pigs and poultry will surely also come in due time. He is pleased that the soldier who was born in Hamburg wishes to live among us and take up land. Our Salzburgers give him a good recommendation; and therefore I shall let it happen in the hope that it will be to the poor man's good, especially spiritually.

Among the German people in Savannah, to whom the word of God has again been preached, things look right miserable;

and because of their own fault, I do not see what can be done
for them. [We learn of the most dreadful sins they have committed in Germany and on the voyage over here, and they all
live together in such discord that it cannot be described. The
Trustees also receive little good from their work.][118] This time I
let them give me the names of those who intend to partake of
Holy Communion in four weeks, when we come to them again,
so that they can better understand and test themselves in advance.

A new preacher[119] has arrived in Savannah, who was actually
destined for Frederica but is now remaining in Savannah for a
while because there is no preacher there. I had an opportunity
to become acquainted with him and I learned that he is an up-
standing [pious and Godfearing] man. [It is uncertain whether
Mr. Wesley will return.]

Tuesday, the 16th of May. On one of the ships, which are
bringing not six hundred but three hundred soldiers from Gi-
braltar to garrison the frontier fortresses, there are two chests
for us that were sent to the Lord Trustees via Hamburg. The
ships are now standing off Tybee Island, and therefore I have
not been able to get them this time. After Whitsuntide our boat
will fetch the remaining provisions that Mr. Causton has given
to our orphanage, and then the chests can be brought along
too. Presumably they contain medicine for Mr. Thilo and something for the congregation from Senior Urlsperger. We received no letters this time, except that Mr. Verelst mentioned
the chests in two lines and referred me to Mr. Causton about
them.

Mr. Delamotte, former schoolmaster in Savannah, is now returning to London, after having been replaced by another,[120]
who has come with the new preacher. He has performed his
work on the youth in Savannah with great loyalty and self-
denial. [He is honest at heart but adheres too much to Mr. Wesley and his personal principles, even though I learned that he
does not attribute as much divine power to episcopal ordination
as Mr. Wesley does.[121] Nor does he approve of Mr. Wesley's taking so much trouble in rebaptizing those people who were not
baptized by an episcopally ordained preacher, as he did to several on the sea voyage, especially to a locksmith who was born in

Ulm, as is mentioned in Mr. Ingham's journal, and as he also wished to do, but without receiving his permission, to the carpenter Volmar,[122] who is well known to Court Chaplain Ziegenhagen.] In Mr. Delamotte we have a safe opportunity to send our diary and various letters to Europe. [It is now Whitsuntide week, in which the people are reporting to me to register for Holy Communion but I must see to it that I write at least a few letters in order for our dear benefactors and friends to receive some news about the condition of our congregation.] He is leaving shortly.

[The clockmaker Mueller's] two [oldest] children registered for Holy Communion.[123] The word of truth penetrates into their hearts and is making them into new creatures. The girl was publicly confirmed and blessed here and partook of Holy Communion for the first time after previous preparation, from which time the dear Lord has begun His work in her and will surely carry it out gloriously if she remains true, as she has resolved to do. [The two children work untiringly with their feeble father in the field, but they received such a bad lot that not a fourth part of their work is repaid. Last year, while the oldest son was still alive, they cleared and planted two more acres, which they are now abandoning, because the land is far too poor and dry. We have tried often enough to see whether this sandy soil will bear anything or not; and now no one will persuade us that any person can maintain himself on it properly, unless he can improve it with manure; but we still lack enough cattle and means of transportation to improve the fields.

[This Mueller with his large family now has only a year-old calf, the cow that he bought having died. I am sorry for the good man and would gladly do what is in my power if only he could be helped. He would have been better able to support himself in Germany than here, for here his wooden clocks are worthless and there are no paper mills here in which he could practice his profession (for he is actually a paper-maker). He is frail, his wife is old and weak, both are unaccustomed to field work, and they have four children, of whom only the two oldest can work a little, while the two younger girls are still in school.

[If a new transport should come, it would be good if the Lord

Trustees would give permission for the people to seek out their land in our region themselves and not have to accept it according to the surveyor's chain.[124] We are requesting nothing on the far side of Ebenezer Creek, because this is supposed to belong to the Indians; but we only wish freedom to take up land down the Savannah River in the direction of Abercorn and Purysburg. The surveyed area extends no more than two English miles downstream, measured from our place, and it is only sandy and infertile soil.]

Wednesday, the 17th of May. Now that the listeners who wish to take Holy Communion on the coming second day of Whitsuntide are reporting to me, some of them are confessing their sins so frankly that they would probably be much too bashful to do it in the confessional booth. In particular, one young man revealed to me that, already in his ninth year when he had had to guard the cattle, he had been tempted by others to some right loathsome sins and that afterwards, when he was in service in Germany, the temptation had continued.[125] Once infected by it, he could not get rid of this disease right away here; and some time ago he had freed his heart of some of it through confession, but he had been afraid to confess the truly gross things. However, since a worm was always gnawing at his conscience and he was becoming more and more miserable in his silence and could find no tranquility, he now confessed clearly more than I wished to hear. But this confession was made with such expressions and in so pitiful tones that I could well recognize from them the deep humiliation of his heart. What a wilderness of sin lies in the hearts of even untutored children that grows and breaks out so early, if any opportunity presents itself. Whoever has children might well watch over them; for we have learned from many examples in our congregation that this is most necessary.

Thursday, the 18th of May. Mrs. N. [Arnsdorf] told me what comfort and trust in further divine aid has been wrought in her by the experience of God's wonderful ways that He has gone with her and her family in this country. It pleases me very well that she is able to use everything that occurs to her in a Christian manner and does not ascribe it to luck or to this or that person. She does good service in the orphanage with laundry and washing the children, for which a certain stipulated sum is paid to her. She asked me to help her get a better hut set up for her and the two children who are still with her, and for this some Salzburgers have already offered themselves to help her for nothing on certain days. Before his departure the carpenter Sanftleben prepared as much lumber and shingles as are necessary for a spacious hut and brought them right to her door, so that now it merely needs to be fitted together, raised, and finished as a dwelling.

Mrs. N. [Schweighofer] is greatly troubled that her children are still so frivolous and do not wish to obey the gospel of Christ. She would consider it her greatest joy and superior to an empire if one of the three would begin in truth to love the Lord Jesus and to live in His truth. While visiting me she remembered what joy she had had some time ago in her oldest girl because she had begun to pray seriously and to give her heart up to our dear God. She [the girl] had then told her that she was awaiting me with longing and wished to jump towards me with joy when I returned home from Savannah to tell me that God had begun to give her His grace for conversion. She had also said she would no longer resist her mother if she wished to chastise her because of her naughtiness. But now she was again frivolous. I comforted this pious mother concerning her children and spoke with her about the marvelous yet blessed guidance of our loving God which a true Christian experiences, once he has begun his pilgrimage, and how one finally comes from unrest to peace and from struggle and victory to triumph and the crown. She desired from her heart soon to be at home with her Lord; and today she twice thought that the Father would fetch her, His miserable maid, because, while praying in the cowshed, she lost almost all strength and breath. This God-fearing and richly anointed widow is dearer to me in the orphanage than a great capital, for her prayer is strong and brings the Lord's blessings over our little institution.

Friday, the 19th of May. Now that Whitsuntide is so near, we have been able to write only a few letters, namely to Court Preacher Ziegenhagen, Senior Urlsperger, Professor Francke, Court Chaplain Butjenter, and to the merchant in Switzerland, Mr. Schlatter, to whom I must report that Mr. Causton wishes to send the payment for the linen he received in money or in rice as soon as Mr. Oglethorpe arrives, whose directions he wishes to follow. To the Lord Trustees and the Society I wrote only a short time ago and will do so again as soon as I have more time.

[The shoemaker from Purysburg, Reck, is bringing his little son back to our school and is having it boarded in the orphanage for a small payment. He is denying strongly that he played any part in the disorderly behavior of the renegade Riedelsperger and promises to be more prudent in his conduct. Because we have no shoemaker and because ready-made shoes in Savannah are not much good and are also not to be had, we can hardly do without the man. I have come to an agreement with him that he will put aside especially good leather for our orphanage, from which he will make durable shoes for our children, and I prefer to advance him the money for buying such good leather. He attended yesterday's prayer meeting about the last part of Numbers, Chapter 12, with us, which, he claimed, had touched his soul. God grant that he will finally become wise!]

Saturday, the 20th of May. The poor people in the congregation, of whom there are many, are now asking us for linen for summer clothes, for we are accustomed to buy, as we have previously done, coarse linen that is said to come from Osnabruck. An entire piece of ninety-six ells that costs about four pounds sterling is quickly distributed. Praise be to God, who has still granted us so much through the generous hands of some Christian persons that we have been able to help widows, orphans, and other poor people with it. Such offerings please God well. In today's preparation I used the words from Numbers 14:22–24 as a basis for our communal awakening in order to recognize our salvation in these days, but in such a way that I touched upon the main points of the entire chapter, as well as the story of the guidance of the Children of Israel from Egypt. The main exposition was meant to show what ways God is accustomed to go with the people whom He is leading from the spiritual Egypt to the promised Canaan and how the pilgrims should behave and how they are accustomed to behave.

The story especially suits our listeners, who also have many vexations and temptations because of the land and external

matters, and who should be warned not to fall into the very
same example of disbelief but rather concern themselves righ-
teously with the spirit that dwelt in both Caleb and Joshua and
inclined their hearts to obedience towards the commandments
of God. Psalm 143:10, Sirach 46:12. This preparation was held
from four to five o'clock, so in the evening at the time of prayer
meeting we had plenty of time to bow ourselves with our congregation before God and to invoke Him (our kind heavenly
Father, Luke 11:13) for the promised spirit in the name of His
Son. Before the prayer I read them Book III, chapter 16, from
Johann Arndt's *Book of True Christianity*, which occurred to me
during the sermon and which I recommended to them for later
reading. May God make us into a spiritual mother hen, who
presents her biddies the little grain she has found for their
nourishment and praises it with her clucking.

Sunday and Monday, the 21st and 22nd of May, were Holy
Whitsuntide. Two Evangelical-Lutheran families[126] came from
Purysburg yesterday before the preparation to attend the divine service during these holy days and to go to Holy Communion with the congregation. We preached movingly both to
them and to all our own dear listeners from the dear gospel
straight to their hearts to become true New Testament Christians and fruitful trees in the garden of the Lord. The dear
Lord will not let it all be entirely in vain. [Perhaps the people in
Purysburg can hear a good word now and then, since] the old
Mr. Zouberbühler,[127] a Reformed preacher from Switzerland,
has arrived in Purysburg with the intention of remaining there
with his daughter. He preached there on Exaudi Sunday, and
the people there tell many edifying things about this sermon.
This preacher actually belongs to New Windsor near Savannah-
Town, where his son[128] has had a town and the land appertain-
ing to it surveyed for the Appenzellers; [but he remained for so
long in Charleston, I don't know for what reasons, that meanwhile most of his congregation in the above-mentioned city had
died. People tell a lot of evil stories about this old man, whom I
do not know; but they cannot be considered true. Love hopes
the best.

[Some provisions were brought to us for the German people
in Old Ebenezer; and our people would have been burdened

with them on the two holy days, if it had been permitted. The desecration of Sundays and holy days is as common in this country as any sin may be and is not even noticed. We do not wish our people to be dragged into such improper and profane behavior. Honest people have a repugnance against it, and we are after the frivolous ones with warning and chastisement.] I was prevented from visiting our dear listeners in their homes and seeing whether the sown seed of the divine word has sprung up and is bringing forth good fruit. Nevertheless, I visited one family, where I myself found so much edification that I returned home praising God. The wife told me how the dear Lord taught her to pay attention to little things that He is undertaking in her, for she will find in them many traces of divine wisdom and goodness for the strengthening of her faith. Yesterday, she said, God had given her a blessing from His own word; but today she has been entirely barren and complained to her husband, who was present, that she could not go to Holy Communion with such a heart as she now had. Thereupon she went into a corner and wept about her condition and asked God with great simplicity that He might grant her to recognize and feel all her sins truly; and, she continued, He had looked upon her tears and prayers graciously and during the prayer had revealed her sin to her and had greatly comforted her. At the beginning of the divine service, when a psalm was being read to the congregation, He had greatly comforted her through the assurance of the forgiveness of her sins. But, because she had previously wept greatly and been very troubled, she had suffered many pains in her body because of her pregnancy and had thought people would have to carry her to Holy Communion, but she had reminded the Father with tears of His promises and of the spiritual help she had received shortly before then, and God had, she said, soon heard her and strengthened her, to her great amazement. This pious woman knows how to get along so simply and childishly with the noble promises of God (as she expresses it), that she can certainly win something from God through her faith. She told with especial emotion what a great blessing God had granted her during the last Easter festival, which blessing He had maintained so far and increased according to His great mercy. She so greatly enjoys hearing us sing the song: "Hallelujah, laud, praise, and glory,"[129] and hopes to be able to sing the "Holy, Holy, Holy" with true holy reverence before the allhighest God.

Tuesday, the 23rd of May. This morning we sent our boat down to Savannah on account of provisions for the orphanage, at which time our letters and diary were forwarded to Mr. Delamotte, who is returning to London. I had recently asked Mr. Causton to buy twenty cows and calves for our congregation and to have them sent here along with the cows that he wishes to send for the third transport. Now I had to tell him that our Salzburgers request 30 milk cows. The good people save their money as best they can to buy cows with it, for the gain from them is very great.

A pious woman sent me word that she wished to speak with me when there was an opportunity, and I soon made one for her. She told me that on Whitsun Monday the dear Lord had granted her such refreshment from His word that she could have constantly laughed with joy, but had restrained herself. However, in the evening all this had vanished again and she had, she said, become so miserable that she could not express it; and in this regard she was in such bad spirits only because she was afraid that Satan might tear the good word from her heart, against which the listeners have been warned in the repetition hour. She had not been able to go to bed, she said, but had prayed and implored until God had shown mercy upon her and had granted her another sight of His grace, although not such a perceptible one as previously. She marvelled at this goodness of God, namely, that she had been able to remember everything that had been preached in the sermons, since she is usually so weak in her memory. Everything had been fresh and alive for her, and she would have liked to remain that way forever. I told her that she should not consider the good word, which she now no longer perceives so clearly, to be lost or torn away; but rather the dear Lord had let it fall like a good seed into the furrow of her heart so that it would not be lost but would surely reveal itself in due time. God, I continued, wishes to accustom His children to trust without feeling and to believe without seeing and the word of the promise must be more certain for her than the feeling of joy. I read her the 35th chapter of Isaiah and gave it to her after the prayer to take home. She remembered with much melancholy her father and other relatives, of whom some are in Salzburg and others in Germany, and she is not a little worried about their salvation. She prays unceasingly to God that He might bring all men, including her acquaintances, to penitence and bliss, since she knows from her own example how great the danger of self-deception is. Previously she had not doubted that she was saved; yet she would have gone to hell if she had died that way.

Yesterday I heard a married couple praise the dear Lord for having brought them in this wilderness to the recognition of the way to bliss and to faith in His dear Son. They marvelled that they had been so blind at their departure from Salzburg and afterwards that they had considered themselves good Christians; how greatly the dear Lord had revealed to them only later that they were still lacking a firm foundation. To the glory of God they said that the Bible stories that we contemplate in the evening prayer hour profit them so much and reveal to them various previously unrecognized sins. The woman admitted that, while we were still camped in Abercorn, she had been very restless in our depressing circumstances and had not considered it the will of God but rather a human error that she had come here from Germany. Her late husband had reminded her of the wonderful and *a priori* unknown ways of God and had assured her from the divine word that everything would turn out all right. The dear Lord had done so well by her that she was ashamed of her disbelief and believed with certainty that this journey would serve her for her salvation and bliss. She praised God for His patience and forbearance, and her husband did so too, and added "God wishes to teach us through His example how we should behave with other people, namely, we must have patience if they cannot accept everything or if they betray some discontent in case of want, sickness, etc."

Wednesday, the 24th of May. Since the last rain we have had no more for over fourteen days, but only hot weather. The nights are cool, and the lovely dew is of great help to the crops. [Rauner's son, who had been placed in apprenticeship in Savannah, has run away from there and travelled to Purysburg with a little boat which he had taken, and thence came back to us as soon as an opportunity offered itself. The boy complained much about his master's treatment of him, in that he had to work hard, even on Sundays, did not receive enough to eat, etc. I do not know at this point whether the man in Purysburg[130] will have him back, and what should be done with this naughty child of an equally frivolous mother.]

Necessity has required me to buy in Savannah for the orphanage a large cast-iron cauldron that holds forty gallons, since it is indispensable for washing and brewing beer.[131] To be sure, the second and third transports have each received a copper kettle through the kindness of Court Chaplain Ziegenhagen and Mr. Butjenter, which, however, we hesitate to use too often, since they are used by the entire congregation for beer boiling and partly for washing. This iron cauldron weighs two hundred pounds and costs 2 £ 10 sh. sterling. Now we are having bricks made, as well as they can be made here without kilns, so that the said cauldron can be properly set in a hearth and made convenient for use. To be sure, the money for this, as for several other things, had to be borrowed; yet the hand of the Lord has not been shortened to grant a new blessing, and His fountain[132] has an abundance of water.

Thursday, the 25th of May. Today a man reported to me that he had freed himself of the sin of unrighteousness, about which he had recently confessed to me, through restitution and that the person whom it concerned was well content with it. I told him the most important thing that had to happen, namely, that he would not stop at that but take his wounded conscience to the only Helper, the Lord Jesus, as a poor sinner and seek forgiveness in His blood. He requested a small separately printed sermon by the late Professor Francke; he had seen one at the house of another person, and it had pleased him very much.

Friday, the 26th of May. Today our boat came home again; and, because the things that had to be loaded on it were too much, another boat had to be taken in Purysburg. Among them are the beautiful blessing that is flowing to our orphanage from the storehouse in Savannah, with it the large iron cauldron and the two chests from Europe, one with medicine for Mr. Thilo and the other from S. U. [Senior Urlsperger] for the congregation. May our loyal God repay the dear Orphanage in Halle for all the good in the form of medicine and other benefactions that we have received so far from it through the hands of the most worthy Professor Francke. May He also repay the dear Mr. S. U. [Senior Urlsperger] for his remembrance of love and let the gifts received have the sought-for effect on the whole congregation.

In this chest there are just as many kinds of useful things as we received for the congregation at the arrival of the third transport; and, since much joy and praise of God arose then, I do not doubt that this considerable benefaction will have the same lovely effect. The chosen Frau von Heslin has doubtlessly contributed the greatest part of this considerable benefaction this time, as she did last time; and may our loving God repay her, like all the rest of our worthy benefactors, according to His great mercy in time and eternity! In the chest we also found the late Schaitberger's book, in which this dear benefactress' whole name was written, which gave me occasion for some good thoughts about its honest purpose. We are accepting it as a gift for our church library. Likewise, Mr. Schauer has thought of our congregation with much love by sending them sixty vials of his well proven balm, which the Salzburgers greatly respect. We and the Salzburgers wish him the rich blessing of God as a rich compensation for it. Toward evening we had a storm with a gentle rain, which stopped again about midnight. It has greatly refreshed the soil, even though it penetrated the earth only a hand deep.

Saturday, the 27th of May. [Among the objects received there is also something for Stephan Riedelsperger's wife, née Valentin, which was wrapped in a special package, sealed, and addressed to her. All the things were a little damp, and therefore we had to open this package too in order to preserve the things in it from spoiling. We are keeping it with us because we do not know where this degenerate woman has run with her miserable husband. We are herewith asking Senior Urlsperger what we are to do with the package if in time we discover where she is staying, and if it is the benefactor's intent that it should be sent to her. The two are surely to be pitied, and without doubt they will cause sorrow by their offensive conduct to those who knew them in Germany.]

In distributing the received benefactions, among which are forty-six yards[133] of linen, six axes, stockings, much yarn, needles, fasteners,[134] knives, hooks, ribbons, combs, etc., it has been our policy to distribute everything in such portions that even the smallest child has received something, and therefore it has caused general rejoicing. The children, both large and small and even down to infants, received their gifts first, after I had first spoken to them for their awakening from God's word and had prayed with them. I told them that they should recognize from these benefactions from afar that godliness is useful in all things and promises much in this and the next life. I told them that God had inclined the hearts of many pious people in Germany to our congregation who were pleased to help us and would be most joyful to hear that our children are walking in Christian truth and that they would gladly reveal their joy on occasion by sending various physical benefactions.

I also reminded them again that a few years ago a certain benefactor had remembered the names of four children of whom he had heard good reports and had sent them something. They should let the present gift serve to make them 1) praise God for it humbly, 2) pray heartily for their benefactors, even though unknown, 3) be content and satisfied with their gifts even if they were small, since they had to be divided among so many people; for they should consider themselves unworthy of even the least of God's benefactions. If they make good use of the small gift, the dear Lord could very easily grant something larger. As soon as we were finished with the children we distributed to the men and then to the women, after having spoken briefly to them about something that served this purpose. Each family received a vial of Schauer's balm. God be praised for all his goodness. He lets it be known through this His benefaction that His hand has not been shortened but still reaches out over us to do us good. Soon after the distribution two Salzburgers called on us again and asked us to send many thanks to our benefactors. The joy was great on all sides. There were also a few articles of clothing which our benefactors had intended for us and our helpmeets just as they had done the last time, even though there was no letter or instructions concerning the disposition of these things.

Sunday, the 28th of May. During the afternoon divine service a violent storm wind and cloudburst occurred, which inconvenienced us somewhat in the church, but it soon passed by. Mrs. N. [the old Spielbiegler woman and her son] was [were] somewhat cheerful today in noting what I had told them in a private visit for their salvation. She accused herself greatly because of the sins of her youth and praised the fact that in our place the path to salvation is so clearly marked that neither she nor anyone else can blame the ministers if they are not saved. She seems to feel displeasure at the godless behavior in N. [Memmingen], where she was [for many years]; yet, in spite of all that, she will not make an effort to convert herself to God honestly but knows how to give herself enough comfort despite all her self-accusation. She has a few old books, which she considers very important. There may be many divine truths presented in them; but perhaps the order of salvation is not indicated as it should be. There are several people in the congregation who think they really have something if they possess an old postil or some other book, which perhaps doesn't even have a title page. They consider such books very valuable, but we also learn that many of them are not used correctly and that the truths they present are not applied rightly.

[Monday, the 29th of May. The Englishman in Old Ebenezer, who is in charge of the Lord Trustees' cattle,[135] has withheld our two horses for as long as he has been there; and whenever we have wished to use one we have had to ask him. Because he has now almost ruined them and because friendly reminders are in vain, I asked Mr. Causton last week in a letter to make a judicial investigation into this man's unjust behavior and to protect us in our possession. He wrote him a few, but very emphatic, lines, which I sent to the man; but today I received the answer that he refuses in spite of it to release one of the horses, which he has been able to use very well until now. I have given him eight days to reflect; and, if he does not obey orders within this time, I shall denounce his disobedience in Savannah. We need the horses now in order to haul up the sawed boards.]

Mr. Delamotte, until now schoolmaster in Savannah, would like to see our place and the Salzburgers' arrangements; and he would have come up with our provision boat already last week if it had not been loaded too full. Tomorrow I shall send our small boat to Savannah to fetch some meat that Mr. Causton is giving to our needy from the storehouse; and I am inviting him to come to us on this occasion. Perhaps it will be useful, because he intends to tell our friends in London directly how he found things here. Last Sunday a couple of men from Savannah were with us who were here also about a year and a half ago, and they could not marvel enough at the great changes that have taken place meanwhile in the huts and cultivation, even though they saw only the front part of our place.

Tuesday, the 30th of May. Today the dear Lord has revealed in several people that it has pleased Him, for the edification of our congregation, to bless that which was presented in the last repetition hour on Sunday and again inculcated in them. In the morning I preached on the regular gospel for Trinity Sunday, using the initial words of 2 Peter 1:11, and presented the entrance into the everlasting kingdom of our Lord Jesus Christ, which, to be sure, men do not know by nature or from their own reason, but will be shown by Jesus in His school. We were told especially by N. [Rothenberger] that God had awakened him mightily to care for his salvation earnestly and that he had great need of frequent visits, and I soon did this. I found another eager man at his house, and I soon found occasion to edify myself with them through a simple conversation and prayer. N. [Rothenberger] heard the word of God and the prayer with many tears. His spirit is so softened by the word that the Lord will soon be able to plant His image in him if only, as we hope, he will remain true to the grace he has received.

N. [Pichler] has had a relapse, and he seems in great danger. He has the most excruciating pains and vomits up all medicine. While I was visiting him today he grasped my hand and wept greatly, and at the same time he thanked me for my efforts and appeared very moved. When I asked him the cause of his tears and his humility, he said: "If only God will not reject me, if only I were soon there, etc." I had given him the verse: "The son of man is come to save that which is lost." At the same time I reminded him how loyally Jesus has sought him so far and how He had sought him so much on the recent holy day that he could well perceive it. Even now, when He is seizing him on his body, He is seeking him; he should merely turn himself entirely with everything he has, even with all his sins, to this merciful Savior and sigh to Him unceasingly that He prepare him properly for a blessed departure. And, since he well knows how much is necessary for a blessed death, he might give a good admonition or warning to those people who visit him or watch him at night. He knows, I continued, how necessary this is for some people who wish to be his friends and acquaintances.

At my request last Sunday he had revealed to me some disorder which had occurred before Whitsuntide among some of the young people, which news was very necessary for me. I was very pleased when he told me that he had seriously reproved a disorder that had occurred, and he also told me the actual words and expressions. He can express himself very orderly, clearly, and impressively. After he had been prevented from his design of moving away he noted that, through the word of the gospel, he had made room in his heart for grace; and since then he has not been embittered toward us, as one feared. May the Lord look graciously on our prayer for him and help him fight his way entirely through the narrow gates and through everything that must be overcome before one can come to the entrance into the everlasting kingdom of the Lord Jesus.

Wednesday, the 31st of May. An Englishman brought a woman down to our place from Savannah-Town and wanted to leave her at our place until he could return from Charleston. However, he took her with him again, because he could find no lodging for her; and this pleased me when I learned of it. For this reason I made a necessary admonition in yesterday's evening prayer hour that people should not burden themselves with such riffraff, who might cause us great harm and bring the displeasure of our benefactors upon us.

My dear colleague lent a woman the printed preparation for Whitsuntide concerning the dear words of Revelations 22:17: "Let him that is athirst come," in which she has been reading and from which she has felt such edification that she could highly praise it with much emotion and many tears. She always carries the booklet with her and reads, kneeling, one section after another to her Savior; and she does not do this hastily but first ruminates on one piece for a good while before she reaches for the following one. She is a right needy soul, yet does not know it. She is very impressed by the passage when the blessed preacher is very friendly towards those who feel no thirst and tries to awaken them.[136]

The sins of her youth humiliate her greatly; and, because of their magnitude and loathsomeness, they make her afraid to apply to herself the gospel of God's forgiveness, which the Savior has won for all poor sinners. Her husband was standing there and said that a certain Salzburger, who had been working with him for the past few days, had told him that he had been dragging himself around for a long time with his sins and had been held back by them; but, after he had cast down all his burden at the feet of the crucified Savior and had come to him bare and naked, he had achieved peace.

JUNE

Thursday, the 1st of June. In answer to our letter Mr. Delamotte replied that he did not have enough time to come to us before his departure, since the ship wished to leave in two days. I had written another letter to Senior Urlsperger which I would have given to him, along with two others to a couple of the Salzburgers' benefactors in Augsburg if he had come to us. I have also written to Mr. Plaschnig, cadet preacher[137] in Petersburg and given him, at his request, a report of our congregation and its spiritual and physical circumstances. [We shall see whether we cannot manage to have these letters sent off, together with the last portion of this diary.]

Pichler has come very close to his end. Yesterday and today he has had the most violent convulsions and has lain several times without consciousness. As far as possible we have shouted many comforting words to him and prayed for him with others in his hut. He has made no provisions for his child and material affairs but has left it all to me. During Whitsuntide he had asked Kiefer in Purysburg for his daughter in marriage, therefore he must not have imagined that his end was so near after he had recently recovered.

Friday, the 2nd of June. Pichler, who had come so close to death yesterday, recovered so much last night that he is fully conscious again and is gaining new strength. His pains are gone, and the entire sickness seems to have been broken by an unusually strong sweat that followed his epileptic seizure.[138] It was probably not medicine that did this, because he has received no medication since Sunday except for two prescribed enemas, for which I hope our medico has his well-founded reasons. We diligently call to him "Today, if ye will hear his voice, harden not your hearts." He well recognizes that it is a great grace of God that he still has time to prepare himself properly for a blessed eternity. I also read him the parable about the wise and the foolish virgins.

Saturday, the 3rd of June. Yesterday I reported something in a letter to Mr. Causton about the evil conduct of the man in Old Ebenezer who did not wish to obey his orders concerning our horses, whereupon the man again received a very serious command not to hold back our horses from us under any pretext. He is said to be very angry at me about this, but that does no harm. I have been very patient and have been unable to accomplish anything by good words.

[For a couple of days thunderstorms were threatening, but they soon pass on. It may have rained and thundered heavily in other places, but the wind did not let it come up here. The soil is very dry because it has not rained for a long time.] A couple of times we had a little rain, which, however, was soon dried up by the great heat. Nevertheless, the crops look fine, only the people cannot plant their sweet-potato vines as long as it is so dry.

Sunday, the 4th of June. Our sermon today was about the gospel for the first Sunday after Trinity, repentance and faith being preached as if from the eternal kingdom. Our dear Lord has blessed today's message in several listeners, as was revealed to me during visitation. A Salzburger told me in the presence of his wife that he cannot come to any certainty of his state of grace and he believes that he has been greatly hindered by having kept something among his things that does not belong to him, but to the storehouse, after he who had owned them had long since been dead. After the repetition hour this man's wife came to me and asked me to awaken her husband when the op-

portunity presented itself; because, she said, he was lax and
made no serious effort to be saved and caused her much struggle. She would like to break through and experience the great
salvation in Christ, but she found it so difficult. I was pleased
with the news from the husband, and I referred her and her
troubles to what I had said in the repetition hour for the comfort of the penitent and remorseful sinners.

Another Salzburg woman deplored her present condition so
sincerely that she could hardly speak for her sobs. She regrets
that she has been living for so long in uncertainty. Her husband, she said, admonishes her well and can remember and repeat what is said in the sermons better than she, and she herself
is always mightily moved. Nevertheless she never reaches the
point of being certain that she would be saved if she died now. I
admonished her to continuous and zealous prayer, to quiet
vigilance over herself, and to obedience to the discipline and
chastisement of the Holy Ghost; and I asked her not to adhere
to any sin with her heart and to free herself honestly from any
filth of unrighteousness, if she has any in her, as we have become aware of in many members of the congregation. Her husband was not present; and she said that he would be sorry, since
he enjoyed our encouragement. She assured me that he does
not go out elsewhere to spend his time evilly, since he well
knows how harmful it is if one gossips too much, especially on
Sundays.

[Monday, the 5th of June. Today we had an event that has
not yet occurred in the performance of our office, for which we
wish to enter all the circumstances here with the request that
our dear Fathers who read it will correct us according to their
experience if we have not acted wisely. On Exaudi Sunday, Paul
Zittrauer and Barbara Maurer (two unmarried and at the same
time unconverted people) were together in the evening in a
Salzburger's hut and sinned by frivolous talk in the presence of
two other men, who probably helped them in it. After they had
separated, Zittrauer accompanied the Maurer woman to her
house under the pretext of fetching his shirt from her, but he
remained with her for a half an hour. A man in the neighborhood noticed it and told the watch, which is held every night to

keep good order; and after some time it was reported to me, not immediately after my return from Savannah but only after Whitsuntide.

[I had both the witnesses and also the two suspected people come to me, but separately, spoke emphatically to their consciences, and hoped to elicit a confession of their presumed uncleanliness. They did not deny that they had been together for almost half an hour at ten o'clock in the evening in the Maurer woman's dark hut, which the righteous Schmidt had given up to her next to his own hut for her to dwell in. However, they had not done anything except that the servant girl had looked for the young man's shirt but had not been able to find it, and then they had chatted together about trivial things and then parted from each other. I gave them both time to think it over until today and, before holding an exact examination, I wished to let pass yesterday, which was Sunday, when such an important matter touching our salvation or damnation was treated, in hopes they might reconsider and come out all the more readily with a confession.

[This morning they both came as they had been summoned to our hut, where seven other men had come who knew of the scandalous event or at least of the very wicked appearance of evil. First we prayed together, then I invoked the dear Lord to let it resound deep into our hearts that He is not only a gracious and merciful but also a holy and just God who will not bring us to salvation but in His holy order. I also asked Him to let us, especially these two people for whose sake we had come together, well consider what this means: "You destroy the liars, the Lord abhors, etc.,"[139] likewise, "He is not a God who is pleased by godless ways." Then, in the presence of my dear colleague, I conducted the matter as follows:

[1) I told them briefly why I had had them assemble here, namely to clear up the occurrence and the scandal that was known to them, for which reason I wished to have no one present except them who knew about it. 2) I indicated that I had spoken to the consciences of Paul Zittrauer and the Maurer woman according to my office and duty and wished to do so again in the presence of several witnesses, whereby I was asking them in advance not to sin and to burden themselves with God's dreadful anger by denying. 3) We stood up, and I read the two people the following slowly and clearly: "Note what I say: God says in Proverbs 28:13, 'He that covereth up his sins shall not prosper.' You know what suspicion has fallen upon you and how, because you were together late at night for almost a half an hour, people can not help but think that you have sinned through fornication and carnal union. Now should it happen that you have let yourself be seduced to such disgusting sin of uncleanness by the devil and your own worldly hearts, then I beg you for God's sake, if salvation is dear to you, not to deny it, for God says in the quoted verse that you will not succeed if you deny it, you will fall into His judgment and will certainly lose your blessed state, for it is expressly written: 'Whoremongers and adulterers God will judge.' Do not think you can pray away this sin if you deceive me, that the disgrace would not allow you to confess it, for you would be disgraced before the entire congregation."

["But now listen, is it not better to be disgraced here in this world before a few people than to appear one time in everlasting shame and disgrace before the judgment seat of Christ and to be damned there before all the angels and people as a whoremonger and scoundrel and to be cast for ever and ever (oh listen!) into the eternal tortures of hell? I am not speaking to you now in my name but in the name of Jesus Christ the future judge of the quick and the dead, who has said: 'He that heareth you heareth me; and he that despiseth you despiseth me.' Think how Ananias and his wife Sapphira fared according to the 5th chapter of Acts, who brought a dreadful judgment from the Lord on their head. Your 'yes' or 'no,' which you will now answer? to my question, which I am posing also in the name of Jesus Christ, (mind you well) in the name of Jesus Christ, is before God just as much as an oath; and you well know (and should well know) what a dreadful sin a perjury or false oath is, through which a man can surely be everlastingly lost if he does not recognize and confess his perjury and do penance for it while there is still time."

["Therefore, in the place of God and Christ, I ask you, Paul Zittrauer, in the presence of these people, who will someday be witnesses of your statements at the day of judgment, whether you have had carnal relations with this Barbara Maurer and committed the disgrace of fornication with her or not. Answer 'yes' or 'no' with great deliberation. Barbara Maurer, I also ask you in the place of God and Christ in the presence of these people who will someday be witnesses of your statements at the day of judgment whether the said Paul Zittrauer has had carnal relations with you and whether you have committed the disgrace of fornication with him or not. Answer 'yes' or 'no' with great deliberation."

[Because both of them denied it, the next address to them was as follows: "Now you have it on your conscience, before God your 'no' is equal to an oath. If you are guilty of the deed, God will surely not leave you unpunished. The Lord Jesus says in Matthew 12: 'Every idle word that men shall speak, they shall give account thereof in the day of judgment.' How much more you will have to give account for your present denial, if you really did the evil deed. And it is written in 2 Corinthians 5:10: 'For we must all appear before the judgment seat of Christ; that every one, etc.' You are all witnesses that I have performed my office on these people, I can do no more."

["Now that they have so solemnly shown that they are innocent of this misdeed it is our duty to drop all suspicion and to warn others not to sin through judgments of these two people. You can tell those who know about the scandal that they have declared under oath before the living God that they are innocent; and therefore everyone must leave them in peace. Meanwhile, it is a shameful matter that you have been together at night; and, because you have caused much vexation and harm and have caused us ministers much distress and sorrow, you have cause to confess such a sin penitently and to invoke the dear Lord humbly and zealously for the grace of penance and henceforth to be diligent in all Christian prudence." 4) We fell on our knees together and prayed.]

Tuesday, the 6th of June. A young man wanted to borrow an implement for farm work from us; and, when we gave him an old one, he was very joyful about it and said, "It shall last this year, to be sure; who knows whether I will need it any more in another year." I said that it does not matter if a man dies soon, if only one is deemed worthy to see the good that cometh (which were the opening words last Sunday from Jeremiah 17:6). Hereupon he began praising God for having given him grace not to fear death any more, since he was now certain of his state of grace. "Oh," he said, "I did not know formerly how blessed Christianity is and what a gracious and loving God we have. Alas, that not everyone wishes to believe it! They do not wish a new birth, but remain in the world; and therefore they cannot experience the good."

I asked him to work on N. [Herzog] on occasion and to dissuade him from the suspicious thoughts he has about God, since he is otherwise so well acquainted with him. This very man said to me some time ago when I visited him that once in an attack of his severe fever it had seemed to him that he was at the gates of eternity and that, if he had been just a little more wicked, he would have fallen into the abyss. He had used this to be right sure of his state of grace and to penetrate into the rich grace of God in Christ. I thought of the verse: "And if the righteous scarcely (*molis*) be saved, where shall the ungodly and the sinner appear?" 1 Peter 4:18.

[Pichler has recovered and goes out again, but he is again walking his previous apparently sinful paths even though I reminded him of his duty, now that his recovery has begun, with the verses: "Behold, thou art made whole: sin no more, etc." and "Offer unto God thanksgiving; and pay thy vows unto the most high." If he had died in his present condition, he would have fared very badly, because before his sickness he had sinned by writing an angry letter to Barbara Maurer and after his sickness he had compounded this sin with the right horrible sin of disavowing and of involving other people in his wickedness. Yesterday evening he could not escape me here, even though his clever mind usually helps him do so; and because the circumstances were so deceitful, hypocritical, and heinous, I have seriously preached penitence to him in his hut and on the street. He will not succeed in his wickedness, which he commits under good appearances; and it is a divine mercy that his deceitful heart is so clearly revealed, for now one can understand him better, whereas he can usually wiggle out. From this fact we can easily conclude that he has not yet done penance for the disorders he committed with the renegade Riedelsperger at his planned departure. On the occasion of yesterday's examination much was made known that was, to be sure, unpleasant, but which was necessary for us to know for the sake of the souls who are concerned and on which we must work.]

Wednesday, the 7th of June. Yesterday there was an outburst of anger between two families that could have caused a harmful break between them, if we had not intervened in time with love and seriousness. I was not a little distressed yesterday evening and this morning when I had this squabble on my hands; but finally God helped me calm the tempers and bring them to a recognition of the cunning of the devil, who can fan a great fire from a small spark. Finally it cost many tears, through which the hearts became all the more gentle and intimate again. I remembered that which is in Apostles 15:37–39.

In spite of the longlasting drought, the corn in the fields, as well as the rice, are still beautiful. The deer do much damage to the beans, which are planted between the corn and are still young, by eating away whole areas at night. Yesterday evening and this afternoon several people have joined together to search the woods around the fields and to flush the game. Perhaps they will be lucky enough to shoot something, and for this purpose they have supplied themselves with muskets. They work in the fields during the day until they are too tired to keep watch over their fields at night, which would help little, especially when the moon is not shining.

Thursday, the 8th of June. [The surveyor is again breaking his promise. At his departure he promised to be with us soon again and to put the people's plantations into final shape; and even though I have reminded him about it several times he always turns us away with good promises. The Salzburgers wish to divide the good land and then later to distribute the bad plantations too, which, however, cannot occur without a surveyor; especially since he has not yet completed all the surveyed and distributed plantations on his sketch. God willing, I shall go at noon tomorrow to Savannah on account of the German people to preach them the word of God, and I shall seek out this surveyor in Purysburg or remind him by letter of his promise.]

When I read the cordial wishes sent to us and our congregation by the worthy Master Hildebrand, a simple but honest

Salzburger remembered this righteous man as well as other dear benefactors known to him in Augsburg and wished to know when we were going to write again to Germany, since he wished to send a thank-you letter along and report, to the praise of God, that he is faring well, and he wished to mention in it the cattle and field with which God has blessed him.

Friday, the 9th of June. In visiting the people we find souls thirsting for grace in different degrees, who have no greater desire than to be certain of their state of grace. The dear Lord gives them many a glimpse of His love; but, because the sins of their youth are always lying in their minds, they do not rightly know whether they may be truly assured of the grace which the Lord has shown them. They would like to come to certainty yet also not deceive themselves, because they well know that many thousands will someday be damned who had good hopes here for their salvation. For eight days I have been much impressed by the words from I John 1:9, therefore I have told and shown such diverse souls how they should act very simply and go to the dear Lord with all the sins of their youth, confess them frankly, and also, if it is necessary, reveal special circumstances to their ministers or to others in whom they have confidence, especially if the dear Lord Himself give them an impulse to do so. If they would only do this in all simplicity and if God would see that they honestly wished nothing but His grace, then He would be loyal and just, forgive them their sins, and cleanse them from all vice. Yea, even if they could not notice right away that all their sins had been forgiven, they should believe it if for no other reason than that the Bible promises it to those who confess their sins in truth; and they should merely persist in prayer, for, when God sees the right time, He will grant them to perceive and enjoy the comfort of the forgiveness of their sins.

A week ago, as I was about to make my way to the orphanage to hold the prayer meeting and to speak the said words to the hearts of those present, I met three women on the street to whom I said these words too, whereupon one of them, who is especially sincere, answered that they had just been discussing together how loyal God is and that they need only to have complete confidence in Him, come to Him, and believe that He will receive them.

Saturday, the 10th of June. Toward evening I was visited by a woman whom I admonished to be right serious in her Christianity. She told me that she had had great fear in her heart some time ago and that she had wished to come to us, but she thought, "What will you do there? You will not be able to speak because of your great distress." Then the dear Lord brought it about that her daughter had to come from the orphanage and, as soon as she had seen how depressed her mother was, she took her hymnal, looked up a song, and said: "Here, mother, is a song. Read it, and you will be comforted." The song is named "Ah, my heart, be undaunted, don't you know God's love?" [140] Because of this she marvelled that it was precisely her child who had to come and be her occasion for some encouragement. But now she had to admit that she had not loyally used such grace.

Sunday, the 11th of June. The dear Lord granted us much blessing from his gospel today and especially called to us: "Come unto the marriage." [141] Toward evening I had to bury a child, at which occasion I showed from Revelations 19:5–9 how well off those will be who properly accept the call of God or had already accepted it through His grace. It is H. Flörel's child. I had just come into their hut yesterday evening when the child was about to die, and the mother asked me to pray with her and those present. She said that she loved the child, to be sure, but she preferred for the dear Lord to take it to Him, for now she knows that it is dying a blessed death. Hardly a quarter of an hour passed before the Lord had taken it to Himself.

Monday, the 12th of June. This morning I returned from Savannah, where I had gone in the performance of my office. We made use of last night, and this speeded up the trip. Again I have had an opportunity, both Saturday and Sunday, to proclaim the word of the gospel publicly to the assembled German people there [both Reformed and Lutheran]; but it is known only unto the Lord whether any blessing has been caused by it. One entices, calls, warns, and chastises as the circumstances demand; but up till now it has not borne the fruit that we wished. Because the meanness of most of them is quite apparent and the office of the gospel is merely blasphemed because of them, I let them know during the afternoon sermon with what a heavy heart I come to them because of the want of resulting

fruit and that, if it continues in this way, I would rather remain
at home. I would try it, I said, a couple of times more and see
whether or not anything could be gained in a few of them, even
if it were only one person. Four [nine]¹⁴² weeks ago some had
registered to go to Holy Communion this time; but a couple
were angry and irritated and a couple were sick or had been
prevented from coming; and therefore Holy Communion was
postponed for four more weeks.

After the morning service a couple of these people were married; and another couple, whom I had referred to the minister
in Purysburg, [because the bridegroom was of his flock]¹⁴³ persuaded me through Mr. Causton to marry them after the afternoon services. Because we cannot declare their banns every
Sunday in succession, the intended marriage is announced to
the assembled congregation; and they are asked in the presence
of the couple whether anyone knows a just reason why they
should not be married. If there is no obstacle, the marriage
takes place in the presence of the whole congregation. Also, we
must have the oral or written consent not only of the parents,
but also of the master in whose service they are.

It is too bad that we do not have a place where these ignorant
and misbehaved German people could come to us. It is much
too hot for visitation, and when we visit them we do not always
find them the way we would like them to be in order to say a
good word to them. Before my departure some of them spoke
to me and wished to assure me that God had already blessed in
them the sermons preached so far, they had felt it in their
hearts, and things had already changed, etc. They asked me not
to stay away from them because of those who are so wicked;
after all, for the sake of a few righteous people, God did wish to
show patience with all the rest in Sodom and Gomorrha. I gave
them some admonitions according to their circumstances and
dismissed them.

[This time I made the acquaintance of the new preacher in
Savannah, Mr. Whitefield, who gave me many proofs of an
honest friendship and affection. God gave us an opportunity so
to join ourselves in the Lord that I promise myself much profit
from it. He is only a deacon and therefore cannot hold Holy
Communion: he would like to return to London within six

months to be ordained as priest. He was actually called to Frederica; but, because there is no preacher in Savannah and one
is needed more here than elsewhere, he has remained here at
the request of the city council until he is replaced by Mr. Wesley,
as people hope, or by someone else. This Mr. Whitefield is zealous in his office, and he gives awakening and edifying sermons.
He has no regard for peculiar opinions that do not concern the
essentials and only instigate unrest.]

Tuesday, the 13th of June. The dry weather is still continuing
and is a new tribulation on the country. May God grant that all
among us learn to resign ourselves to it better than others in
this country, from whom we occasionally hear only unbelieving
complaints and despair. In our contemplation of the Bible
stories we have come to the fourth[144] year of the wandering of
the Israelites; and in today's evening prayer hour I gave a re-
capitulation of the content of the story of the first two years
after the exodus from Egypt, namely, God's exceptionally loving care and goodness toward His people but also their ungrateful conduct toward their Benefactor, upon which nothing
else but many physical and spiritual judgments could follow;
and, since people of this time still behave so ungratefully toward the kindness and goodness of God, it is no wonder if God
is sitting in judgment, which fact, however, is not recognized by
blind men, who attribute the evil that befalls them to the nature
of the country, the climate, other people, etc., even though one
should apply such an experience as it is written in Daniel 5:22.
The chastisements that the Lord inflicts on his children, now as
then, have a very salutary purpose. God is accustomed, I told
them, often to punish here and to spare there, and often to
spare here and punish there.

Wednesday, the 14th of June. Mr. Causton sent me word that
he had bought as many cows for the third transport and for
other people as I had requested and that they would soon be
brought to us. A cow and calf come to two pounds, thirteen shillings and four pence, which the Salzburgers are glad to pay if
only, as has been promised, good and tame cattle are brought;
and in this one must take one's chances. The third transport received twelve cows and as many calves; ten head were donated
almost two years ago by Mr. Ogelthorpe, of which five have

either run away or died; those that survived were so distributed among the people that two persons share a cow and a calf, even though the Lord Trustees had provided for only a cow and calf for five people. Mr. Causton has again assured me he will send pigs and poultry shortly, for which we have long been waiting. The dear Lord has always treated us this way, He does not grant us everything at one time but lets us receive one thing after the other so that we will be reminded by each benefaction of His providence and praise.

In this evening's prayer hour we have again had much to note on the occasion of the story in Numbers 20 about the Israelites' lack of water, especially the fact that this is still the way of God to test his people with many wants so as better to reveal the foundation of their hearts, which one knows far too little in good days or rich enjoyment of physical benefactions. True believers learn thereby to recognize that they still live in the imperfect world and not yet in the all-sufficient paradise of God, where God Himself will be their everlasting portion and inheritance, for which they should strive all the more zealously the more they are burdened by want and misery.

I showed them that, in the present lack of rain, God has the salutary purpose as in the Israelites' lack of water, namely, to show what a benefaction water is, and therefore also rain, of which one does not think when there is no lack of it. Our wise God wishes to test our faith and confidence through such lack, and when He has achieved His purpose, it will be as easy for Him to give rain as it was for Him to bring forth water from the rock, for His hand has not waxed short. Worldly people have an opportunity to recognize their thoughts and language in the example of the worldly Israelites, who not only uttered the harshest words against Moses and Aaron but also called the wilderness a bad place because it did not go according to the desires and devices of the body even though God had shown them so many physical and spiritual benefactions there and had been present Himself as the highest good among them. On the other hand, in their language they call it a good place and a good time where their flesh and blood fare well, even if they have less or no opportunity for conversion or the salvation of their souls.

Thursday, the 15th of June. The Frenchman who has established a brandy house in our neighborhood in Carolina must sell all that he has on account of his debts in order to pay his creditors. His large barrel of rum, of which he is said to have sold very little, was taken back to Purysburg recently, because he had borrowed it from another and cannot pay for it. Such a profession, which is undertaken for the harm of other people, can have no blessing and no long duration. After the harvest he will probably go away entirely, because he did not achieve his purpose.

The widow Helfenstein needs a dwelling; and, because she is poor, she is asking for some help to be given her from the poor box. Some men of the congregation will help her for several days without pay when they have completed their field work. She has two children in the orphanage, the oldest daughter serves in my house, and she still has in her care three children, of whom she needs two, and the smallest, about three years old, for whom she receives aid as far as that is possible.[145] [Baron von Reck picked her up in London with her late husband and brought them here, whereas with her many children she might have been better provided for in London.] The widow is honest and attends public worship diligently, and she also works with her children as much as she can, but she accomplishes little since she and the children are weak.

Friday, the 16th of June. Toward evening today the dear Lord again showed us a rain in the clouds, but soon took it back again. Several times a dark thunderstorm gathered, which gradually passed on. As easily as He can give, as easily He can take it away. Well for him who is fully happy with His guidance. In reading the 4th chapter of Numbers, which we are now reading in the evening prayer hour, I marvel that it would have been so easy for the dear Lord, when He had brought His people to the frontiers of the earthly Canaan, to lead them to complete rest and great comfort in the promised land if only he had compelled the Edomites to permit them to pass through; yet it had pleased Him to let them wander again from south to east with many tribulations so that their souls would be even more revealed through such new trials and the Lord would have an opportunity to open his merciful heart even further at a time when things looked especially sad and depressing. Compare Numbers 21:8–9. Our wise God doubtless has a salutary purpose if He does not let our crops grow this time and thereby let the Salzburgers come to rest and comfort. In such new tribulations, many hearts would be revealed and God would be sure to reveal His glory even when things look outwardly most depressing.

Saturday, the 17th of June. A Salzburger, who had returned some property several weeks ago that did not belong to him, came to me and deplored his miserable condition, which he now recognizes better than previously. He is sorry that he retained it so long and that he had sinned so grievously in his youth and had now become so old; and now it seems to him that God will not accept him because he has waited too long and his sins are too many. He thanks the Lord that, while he was sick a year ago, He did not snatch him away like an unripe fruit; he would not have been saved, because he knew of no real conversion. To be sure, after being awakened by God's word, he had begun several times to pray and be serious; but again and again nothing came of it, and all the fault was his. I told him some of what, God willing, I shall present tomorrow from the Gospel of Luke, 15:1 ff., namely, that the Lord Jesus rejects no poor sinner but seeks each and every one with much effort and finally receives him with a thousand joys. Thereupon I referred him to a right simple, zealous prayer, in which he should join diligently with his wife, who is very much preoccupied with being saved. Then the promise will be fulfilled of which the Savior speaks in Matthew 18:19.

[Kiefer of Purysburg came to us with his family and will remain here several days. Pichler had asked for the hand of his oldest daughter even before his recent sickness, and she came up here too to post her banns and to be married to him. The said man has long wished for all his daughters, of whom three are grown, to be married to pious men in our congregation; but for a year he has not been able to achieve what he wanted with his daughters, although there have been several opportunities for him to marry off his two oldest girls here. May God grant that it turn out well for this one! She is very ignorant;[146] but she will be able to be cured of that gradually through this good opportunity that God is now putting in her hands, provided she will accept instruction.]

In today's evening prayer meeting, in telling the story of how the Edomites, the close relatives of the Children of Israel, had been the cause that they had been prevented from a prompt entry into their promised Land of Canaan (Numbers 20:18–20), I reminded the listeners that often either their best friends hinder them from entering and penetrating the Kingdom of God or else they and their best friends hold each other up; and I reminded them what the duty of each of them was, namely, to hasten to save his soul and not to go backwards. N. [Pichler] confirmed this after the prayer meeting from his experience, in that during his wife's lifetime he had had more hindrance than furtherance in his Christianity. I wish he would recognize on whom the blame lay and on whom it still lies, since he still allows himself to be held up and does not penetrate into the kingdom of heaven with violence.[147]

Sunday, the 18th of June. Today God gave us much edification from His word, especially from the soothing booklet and source of comfort of penitent sinners, namely, from Luke 15; and we hope some blessing will remain therefrom until blessed eternity. Both yesterday and today Kiefer [and his sons, who are also with him][148] was so mightily awakened by the word of God that you could see the effect of the heart-penetrating word in the church, and he also came to me after the sermon and informed me that he was fully resolved to resell his plantation, which he bought only a year ago, and to move here; for it is a delightful thing, he said, if one can be with the word of God and prepare oneself for eternity. I was especially pleased at this, because he has many children who need church and school; yet I admonished him not to be too hasty in his decision but to consider everything well and particularly to pray about it. I said that I too hoped that his design would be recommended to me in prayer.

Many of the congregation take great pleasure in the new, good, and to a large extent unknown songs in our hymnal. Although we have taught some of them to the congregation through the children, with whom we learn them in school, it is not so easy to do so now that the grown children whose voices have changed have been dismissed and no longer do so well. Therefore I have resolved to apply an hour on Sundays after the catechism lesson for learning the unfamiliar melodies, for which a beginning was made today in God's name. Only the female persons, and of those only those who possess good voices and some ability, sing out loud with me, the men and children softly after us. Today we had the song "Where is my little lamb that I love?", also "Where is the fairest whom I love?",[149] which two have the same melody. The spiritual enjoyment that I had in this was a rich compensation for the easy effort. God bless this undertaking and also what I quoted about the authoress of the first song, the late Fräulein von Schuttin, for the edification of those present, especially for those of the female sex!

Monday, the 19th of June. Toward evening a storm gathered, which brought us a splendid rain. Yesterday afternoon we were encouraged to cast all our anxieties upon our heavenly Father, who has promised to further our true salvation without any of our doing; and we well see even this physical benefaction as a sign of His fatherly care, which encourages us to His praise and to further trust in His divine help. It pleased Him to lead the people of His covenant under many tribulations into the promised land; so why should we demand any other treatment?

Tuesday, the 20th of June. After the rain the air has become so cool that one must marvel, if one thinks of the previous heat. Such rapid and striking changes tend to bring fever, if one does not guard oneself. So far, God be praised, we have remained free of fever, although this is the time in which last year and two years ago almost the entire congregation was sick with it. Our life and health are and remain in God's hands; therefore may our land and the crops upon it be further commended to His blessing! The longlasting drought has damaged much corn and spoiled it while it was flourishing. Yet it is easy for the Lord to bless the remainder so that the apparent loss can easily be replaced. The present rain has not been able to soften the soil through and through; yet, now that it has rained a little bit, the people are very busy planting sweet potato vines in the heaped-up earth, because it is high time. Perhaps the dear

Lord, who knows our needs, will soon grant us a fertile rain again.

Wednesday, the 21st of June. The tailor Hernberger has moved into his new house; and he invited us there because he wished it to be blessed and consecrated with the word of God and with prayer. We sang a song of praise; and then I read the 19th chapter of Luke, and from it I made useful to me and others especially the words of v. 9, which were appropriate for the purpose. Then I showed what kind of a mind the Lord Jesus demands of us if He is to come to us and move into our dwelling and what an incomparable profit and blessing we have from that if we are deemed worthy of His gracious presence (for which He is sincerely ready, cf. Revelations 3:20). This honest man surely practices his profession the way it was required of the Christian servants in Colossians 3:23–24. He works without interest and personal profit, adjusts himself to the poor, and is content with little pay for his well done work. He lives with his helpmeet, whom he married not long ago, in such quiet, love, and contentedness, that others could follow his example. He is now always sickly, and this state he uses to prepare himself all the more earnestly for eternity.

Thursday, the 22nd of June. The water in the river is now lower than it has ever been since we have been in the country. Usually the flood tide reaches Purysburg only during low water; but now it comes to the so-called Indian Hut, which lies an hour away from us by water. Our people are using this opportunity to dig wells, because they can dig deeper in this dry weather. At other times the water comes, to be sure, quickly, but it disappears again with lasting drought. They have also agreed to clear the creek toward Abercorn of its many trees, and this will be very useful for those who have their plantations on this river. This creek comes out of the Savannah River two English miles from our place (calculated by land) and flows back into the Savannah below Abercorn, so that it makes a big island between Purysburg and Abercorn. On the map of Georgia this creek is indicated as an estuary of the Ebenezer River, as if the latter divided into two arms and flowed thus into the Savannah River. We hope to have better passage back from Savannah when this Abercorn Creek, as it is called, has been cleared and made convenient for travelling, and when the saw mill, which was built a few years ago by a native Swede, Purker [Parcker], not far from Abercorn, has been torn down as an unusable and useless thing.[150]

Friday, the 23rd of June. This afternoon Mrs. N. [Schweighofer] was at my house and let me underline in red ink those verses in the Bible for her that she had already marked with a pencil as noteworthy. I read her one verse after the other and explained those to her that appeared difficult to her. She watched and listened with many tears and wished nothing more than for God to save her out of mercy for Christ's sake, since, as she says, she is the greatest sinner. She yearns for her death, even though she suffers no want in physical things. Her yearning arises entirely from her longing desire to be able to serve her dear Father and Savior in blessed eternity without sin and to thank Him for the benefactions He has shown her so abundantly. She truly considers herself to be the greatest sinner and knows nothing of her own merits, but only of the free grace of God in Christ. The prayer meetings in the orphanage, which are held by us alternately at five o'clock in the morning, bring her much edification; and we hear from her words that she is always thirsty for the word of God.

Saturday, the 24th of June. At about noon Col. Stephens and a magistrate[151] from Savannah came to inspect our place. The first-mentioned gentleman has been sent by the Lord Trustees to this colony to inform himself exactly about all the circumstances of the people whom they have sent here at their own expense and to send back reports about them. As far as the heat of the day would allow, he viewed our people at their field work; and he used such good words about it that we may well praise the dear Lord for having let such an impartial man come to us, who will without doubt report to the Lord Trustees honestly what he sees here and what pleases him so well. He considers our Salzburgers superior to all others in this colony in their field work and the arrangements of their town; and he is happy that, in what he has reported to the Lord Trustees from hearsay, he not only has not erred but has even reported too little. He showed a particularly great pleasure in our orphanage and its external and internal arrangements, and he wishes to recommend it diligently to the benefactors as a useful and blessed work.[152] God be praised for this benefaction too!

Sunday, the 25th of June. Before the afternoon divine service it pleased our dear Lord to send me a slight fever, by which I was prevented from continuing the singing lesson we had begun. I had already announced the hymn, "My Father beget me,"[153] the text of which the listeners were supposed to learn before we assembled. May God let me reflect that man's life is nothing and perishes like a flower.[154] By evening I had recovered enough to hold the repetition hour, which we do not like to miss. The two gentlemen travelled this morning to Old Ebenezer and returned again this evening.[155] They found great pleasure in our melodies, which are very different from the English ones. We told them how we conduct things in the school and in the entire community and what is the most blessed means to keep external good order, which they had noticed particularly. They are both honest people and would not have journeyed from Savannah over Sunday if their circumstances had not required it. They went to Old Ebenezer this morning only so that they would not be a burden to us here or cause any inconvenience, since they cannot understand our German service.

Monday, the 26th of June. This morning the magistrate rode out with my dear colleague to inspect our herds, which are being grazed an hour away from here; and I was busy with Col. Stephens giving him a written list of the names of our people and the work they have done, of which he must give an adequate report to the Lord Trustees. He himself inspected a great deal of corn plantings in the fields; and what he could not see has been reported to him by the other gentleman, who has seen more with my dear colleague, and all this to the praise of our people. He wished that more such people might come into this country; and, because he heard that lack of good land is an important obstacle, he has resolved to request the Lord Trustees to extend our township[156] a couple of English miles further downstream, where there is still much good land for any latecomers.[157] Both of them were greatly pleased that our people have agreed to divide the good plantations so that everyone will get a good piece, and so that a large forest can be all the better

cut down and fenced in; and they will speak about it diligently
to Mr. Causton so that we will not be thwarted through some
misunderstanding because of this design.

Now that they have seen Old Ebenezer, they are not astonished that we moved away from there, since they, like us,
find it entirely impossible to build a regular town there, to say
nothing of the soil itself and the remoteness of the place. Toward evening the two rode back to Old Ebenezer to inspect both
the Trustees' cattle and the saw mill. Tomorrow they intend to
journey back to Savannah via Abercorn and a few other places
en route, which are not yet well settled, however. They have let
us see many signs of their love and affection, and we do not
doubt that God will bless their report both in Mr. Causton and
especially in the Lord Trustees, so that they will give less cre-
dence to those who calumniate us under whatever pretenses
but will continue to show all possible aid to our poor Salzburgers. We spoke a great deal with them regarding the best interests of our listeners and also regarding the support of the entire
colony, and they fully approved of everything.

Tuesday, the 27th of June. We heard that Samuel Eveleigh,
Senior, a wealthy merchant in Charleston, died two months
ago. He always showed himself very friendly toward us and forwarded our letters, which we had addressed to him, to London
by the safest opportunity. Before Sanftleben's departure we
sent a couple of small packets of letters in succession to him but
received no answer as to whether they had been correctly delivered to him or not. We do not yet know whom we can now find
to entrust our letters and diaries safely. [We would now write at
least one letter to Court Chaplain Ziegenhagen, if there were
any opportunity. God is again letting us experience something
new that can have no good consequences and which we would
like to report soon with the request for good advice.]

Rain has been lacking for a long time and therefore the corn
is suffering in the field, and the sweet potatoes too are suffering
much damage. The two gentlemen from Savannah who left us
yesterday have well seen our Salzburgers' great industry in the
fields and have assured us that they have not seen such beautiful corn in the entire colony and that, if they should have a bad
harvest this year too, it would again be without their fault. The

colonel especially wrote down the point that our harvest last year was spoiled by worms and caterpillars, in order to ask the Lord Trustees to give the Salzburgers some assistance, especially since they have actually received no provisions from the storehouse since September but have lived on what was due them from previous times. Some time ago Mr. Causton sent four kegs of meat for the poor in the congregation; but, since it is only for the poor, some people are bashful to ask for any.

Wednesday, the 28th of June. I was shown a couple of ears of corn that a certain vermin had eaten up entirely, and they say that entire areas along the woods and swamps have been damaged in this way. During the day these harmful animals remain in hollow trees, and at night they go out robbing.[158] In a newly established colony there are many difficulties and strange unexpected circumstances; and for that reason those who have had to break the ice with so many troubles should be given the freedom to seek out the best land for themselves and to enjoy all other advantages.

We plan to go next Sunday to Holy Communion, for which sixty-one people have registered. My fever, which was severe yesterday, prevented me from speaking to the confessors privately, and my dear colleague had his hands full with the school; yet he visited our listeners as far as time allowed. Therefore I admonished our dear listeners with all the strength that God gave me to guard themselves well during this week and to prepare themselves right carefully for this holy undertaking. A few of them will have to be held back for good reason.

Thursday, the 29th of June. [Michael Rieser's wife now wishes to go to Holy Communion with us for the first time. Otherwise she is Reformed,[159] and when she was in Purysburg two weeks ago the Reformed people there exhorted her not to apostatize but to remain with the faith of her fathers. She has now been listening to the word of God for some time with us and has been able to recognize the way to heaven as it is preached among us. I have now spoken to her about the difference between us and the Reformed with regard to the dogma of Holy Communion; and I warned her not to go against her recognition and conscience, because God would have no pleasure in it and she would have no gain but great loss. Purysburg is not far, I said; if she has more confidence in the Reformed way, she was free to go to Communion there. She was quite pleased with the given explanation, appeared to accept it well, and promised to prepare herself carefully for it. She also received Luther's *Catechism* in order to familiarize herself with the questions in it. She can read well and attends the preaching of God's word.]

The dear Lord showed us a blessing both this morning and especially in the evening, when a great thunderstorm arose, but it soon passed on again both times.

Friday, the 30th of June. According to the way this country is set up, our town owns only a small parcel of free wood, which will be cut away in a short time and used for building and fuel. The Salzburgers are beginning to build houses of solid thick trees that are flattened on the sides. These may make very comfortable houses in this hot country, but they demand much wood. It remains to be seen whether or not Mr. Oglethorpe will give more forest to the town if we ask him for it. Otherwise things will remain according to the prescribed plan. There is said to be no more free wood in Savannah; but it must be bought from the plantations, for which reason fire-wood is already right expensive.

[Mrs. Rheinlaender is receiving no news from her husband, who has been away from us for a year, as to where he is or how he is faring. I am afraid that it is a pre-arranged matter, which will soon be explained. I understand that she has agreed with an Englishman, who carried supplies to Savannah-Town, that he will take her to Charleston when he passes by and that she is planning to leave the two oldest children around our neck, to which, however, we are opposed and about which we will notify Mr. Causton. She still pretends that she is converted to God and is therefore a child of God, even if we notice in her none of that spirit which such people should have.]

JULY

Saturday, the 1st of July. A Salzburger woman complained to me that she had wished to pray and prepare herself [on her knees] for Holy Communion but had felt no strength to do so.

Therefore she had wished to come to me so that I would refresh her with a good Biblical verse and so that she might pray with me. She was full of spiritual hunger and thirst, and her words were so expressive both before and after the prayer that I was very pleased with her visit. She complained about indolence most of all.

During our confessional, which my dear colleague held today in my place, a thunderstorm arose and brought us some rain at the same time, which, however, did not penetrate very deeply because of the long drought. Yet it is a benefaction of the Lord which He can increase according to His gracious will and our need. Today we assembled in the orphanage, as we are accustomed to do before taking Holy Communion, to prepare ourselves even better through prayer for our holy undertaking.

Sunday, the 2nd of July. On this day fifty-eight members of the congregation attended Holy Communion, which our gracious God may bless in them all for their eternal salvation. Last night my fever caused me discomfort in my stomach like that which I had a year ago when I had to keep to my bed for almost eight days; yet our loving God heard my and other pious souls' prayer and let me get up again rather healthy and with new strength so that I could perform my duties all day today unhindered. May His name be humbly praised both for this benefaction and for all physical and spiritual good.

In our scheduled singing-lesson we sang the song "My Father beget me" with uncommon joy.[160] Many people of both sexes joined us, and some of them learned the lovely melodies quickly.

Today's gospel largely concerns St. Peter's and his companions' work, which appeared to have been in vain yet was not; and this gave me a good opportunity to instruct the congregation about the steps that God is taking with His children in regard to their worldly profession: namely, He sometimes lets them work in vain and, when He shows them a blessing, He takes it away from them as a trial. However, if a man remains loyal and patient in his work and does not immediately give up entirely but casts his net out again at God's command, then He finally lets the hour of His help and blessing come. Yet it is already a blessing if a man knows that he has done his work in the fear of the Lord and in faith; for it is written: "Whatsoever he doeth shall prosper," as that future harvest shall show. A pious worker could sing every evening: "Thine be the Glory that all has turned out well, NB according to Thy counsel, even if I do not understand," etc.[161]

[Monday, the 3rd of July. Several thefts have been committed in our community, and a strong suspicion has fallen on the Austrian Grimmiger. Last week a few things turned up that make it rather certain that more than two years ago he had already taken more than 3 £ sterling in money from Pletter's chest. We examined him last Friday, and he was very bold in denying it, as he has been previously; and would have gone to Holy Communion in that state of mind if I had allowed it. I well know his devious nature. Not only did he come to us entirely ignorant, but he also brought along a very wicked nature, which may not have been known in Regensburg.[162] He began an irregular marriage with his wife, who died two years ago, in that he was married to her not long before his departure from Regensburg, yet already in Frankfurt had a child baptized, which he then brought here.

[Because this ill-behaved man noticed that people would further follow up the clue that had been discovered about his previous thefts and would finally convict him fully, he suddenly absconded and has not been seen again since Saturday afternoon. He is said to have taken along an old boat that has been lying here, in which he probably travelled to Purysburg. He will perhaps follow Riedelsperger, even though he is entirely without money. In his work he is also unintelligent, lazy, and disorderly. He would surely have let his child perish, if we had not taken it in and borne the expense of maintaining it. He has not taken any of his clothes and things with him but ran away in the clothes he then had on. Everything has been brought into our storehouse for safe-keeping.]

Tuesday, the 4th of July. All sorts of suspicion and misunderstanding had spread through the community about a certain unexpected matter; and, because we did not know what we were to believe about it, and wish to prevent all the harm that may come from such matters, we let the most experienced men of the congregation assemble in my hut in order to inform ourselves of the circumstances and to hear their appraisals and judgments. Such things often occur during the conduct of our office; and we can size up the matter only after we have discussed it with the congregation.

Wednesday, the 5th of July. Toward noon we had a fruitful penetrating rain, for which we had been looking for a long time. Since this weather coincides with the new moon, we hope it will last, it being very necessary for the parched soil. Just as we have prayed so far to the Giver of all good gifts for this benefaction, we now wish to praise Him publicly for it too.

Mrs. N. [Schweighofer] had an unnecessary worry concerning her late husband; she had remembered this and that in his previous behavior that had not pleased her, even though she also knew of clear signs of his patience, love for God's word and prayer, readiness to die, etc. Concerning herself she has often said that she was blind during her husband's lifetime and that she had reason to thank the merciful Lord day and night for not tearing her away but for bringing her to a recognition of her disbelief and also to a belief in her Savior.

Thursday, the 6th of July. [Christ, the Jew who was baptized in Germany, was accepted into the orphanage from compassion; and, before that was done, he was given a long period to think it over in advance and was admonished to become orderly, since previously he was never steady in any work but was accustomed to bumming around and being idle. For several weeks he behaved in an orderly fashion and thanked God for the benefactions that came to him in the orphanage; but soon thereafter he again longed for his earlier way of life. Intelligent people advised him as best they could against his obstinacy, and this held him back for a couple of more weeks; but now he has departed without my knowledge and cannot give any real reason, except that he cannot stand the submissiveness any longer, likewise, that the children annoy him. He will recover the provisions that he brought to us, and a bit more in addition; but he will probably soon learn how thoughtless he has acted and to whom he has caused the greatest harm with his departure.]

We have not yet had a well in our orphanage; and up to now carrying water has been a right difficult matter, especially since much water is required in such a household for washing, brewing beer,[163] etc. Whatever water happened to collect in the newly dug cellar is very little and also dirty and disappears in dry weather. Therefore we found it necessary to think about a regular well. During the dry weather we have been able to dig a hole twenty-five feet deep and seven feet wide on each side, and we have found a living and very fresh source. This week the carpenters have been busy putting the well into a right usable condition. To be sure, it is costing a lot of work, but it will be of great use. It is quite near the kitchen[164] and garden; and, since it had a couple of feet of water even during the long-lasting drought, we hope we will never lack water. Our dear Lord (as we trust Him in Christ for this and all good) will surely grant the expenses for this.

Friday, the 7th of July. Our people are now beginning to build better houses, for the old huts are about to rot because the corner posts are stuck into the ground and the lower beams are lying on the earth. At first they could not build anything better, because time was very short and there was also their long lasting fever; but now they take more time for it, lay a regular foundation of pine wood that does not easily rot, and build a regular house on it. In such constructions each helps the other; if one of them has helped another for several days in the field or in some other work, then the latter helps him for the same number of days in his construction. The carpenters do it this way too; and, even though they earn sixpence more than other workers, they are willing to let it go.

Saturday, the 8th of July. This year the fever does not last long; even if someone catches it several times, it soon abates again. It is that way here in Ebenezer and also in other places. They say that many people in Charleston are dying of smallpox; this is something unusual among the English and therefore all the more frightening. We in our place, praise the Lord! have been spared from it so far.[165]

Sunday, the 9th of July. The dear Lord has again blessed this Sunday in trying to magnify in us His Son with His righteousness and entire merit so that our hearts have well felt the power of it. May He salve our eyes with eye-salve so that we will learn ever better to recognize both ourselves and also the great salvation in Christ and to consider everything else, even our own righteousness, as loss, dirt, and filth in comparison with such superabundant recognition of Jesus Christ. Great is the mercy that He shows us.

Monday, the 10th of July. This morning I took a stroll a short distance into the forest, and there I met a man at his work who soon began to talk about the good that the Lord had granted him from His word on the previous day. He was very happy that the Lord Jesus has earned for us a [marvelous] righteousness that well suits poor sinners. The dear Lord in His mercy had, he said, strengthened him even more through such contemplation; and he trusted that He would always show him even more goodness and not leave his prayers unheard. Even though he could not always feel perceptibly that he had received what he had prayed for, he nevertheless believes that he had it because His word, which is so friendly, says so. Soon thereafter I met another pair of workers with whom I spoke according to their circumstances, especially with one of them who cannot persevere because of his great sins. I told him that the righteousness of the Son of God is the kind of righteousness that cannot be daunted, even if it summons the greatest rascal to the judgment of God. May the Lord help this man persevere too according to the wealth of His mercy, with which He has loved us.

Tuesday, the 11th of July. Last Friday I travelled to Savannah in order to hold divine services there with the Germans (as has occurred every four weeks so far) and to take Holy Communion with some who have recently registered for it. Yesterday evening I returned to Ebenezer well and happy under God's protection and brought with me the preacher from Savannah [Mr. Whitefield], who is to return to London in a few months but first wishes to see our place and establishments himself, even though Colonel Stephens has already told him much good about our Salzburgers and their fine conduct during divine services and in their work. [God gave us another opportunity to join our hearts again most closely.] He showed his love for me, my dear colleague, and our congregation not only through this friendly visit but also through many other proofs, especially through physical gifts that he had brought with him from London for this colony. He had been so pleased by Col. Stephen's report about our orphanage and all its arrangements that he has given it all sorts of things such as stockings, hats, ribbons, knives, spoons, tin pots, bonnets for boys and girls, and as well about a hundred pounds of large raisins, in which the sick people in the community are also to share.

This morning after the prayer I distributed everything but the raisins in my hut in his presence, and, to be sure, in the following manner: I told the children something about God's fatherly providence, according to which He does much good for all His creatures, especially for human beings and most of all for His children. He is also doing it for them, even if they are not, as they themselves must recognize, His dear and obedient children. How much more gladly He would do it if they would offer up their hearts to Him and devote all their time to His service and glory. I also told them something about the purpose that He had in the distribution of His benefactions, namely, to lead ungrateful people to penitence and a change of heart, but to cause His children, who have so dear and benevolent a Father, to be even more zealous in His service. He has, I said, this very purpose in these physical benefactions that are lying before them and which He has so kindly granted contrary to my and their expectations.

Because I learned on this trip how miserably some people in Purysburg are faring, I could not help but tell the children that such want was also afflicting the parents of the four children who are with us in the orphanage and that therefore they had all the more reason to thank our Father in heaven for inclining to them the hearts even of strange people who grant and give them good. Hereupon we knelt down together, thanked the dear Lord for all His goodness, and especially for the present benefactions, and prayed for all divine blessings as a reward for this and other benefactors. Finally, I let a couple of children pray and closed with the last stanza from the song "Praise and Glory be to the Highest God." [166]

The gifts were distributed only generally, and something was placed in the hands of each child for him to carry, for which they thanked the minister obligingly with outstretched hands; and then they went home, where each child received his own particular gift. The dear man expressed great satisfaction with what he saw and heard during the distribution and praised God for letting us come so far. And, because some gifts did not suffice for all children, he wrote it all down and promised, at the next opportunity, to send every child a full amount in proportion to the number of children.[167]

He inspected our entire place, the fields of the Salzburgers, and especially the orphanage; and above all he praised the goodness of the Lord, to whom alone we should ascribe all blessings in the houses and fields. We had to give him complete reports about everything, even about the wants of our dear listeners, all of which he wrote down; and he voluntarily promised to look out for us as he does for his own congregation. He said that, when the ship arrived, we would share in the things that he bought in London for 15 £ sterling and loaded on a ship that was coming here. [He is not yet ordained, and this is the chief reason for his return, at which time he will again have an opportunity, as previously, to recommend this colony and the poor inhabitants in it, as well as our congregation and orphanage, to charitable persons in England.]

He has a beautiful talent for preaching, and he is said to have enjoyed large attendance and approbation and to have seen the good effect of preaching in many charitable gifts. He performs his office very zealously and with much advantage. Next week, after having made good arrangements in the church and school in Savannah, he will travel to Frederica, where he will remain for about a month in order to establish a school; and soon thereafter he will go to London. He brought three schoolmasters with him, who have no other purpose than the glory of the Savior. We had to tell him something about the arrangements of the Orphanage in Halle, which pleased him very much. Toward noon he departed from us in the company of my dear colleague. God bless him and remember him kindly.

Mr. Causton gave our orphan girls two spinning wheels and five pounds of wool and gave the widows and orphans a large piece of linen of 139 yards and a piece of colored material of 35 yards, each yard reckoned as three mathematical feet. In addition he is ready to give the poor of the community aid in meat and corn as often as I request it. God be praised for His ineffable mercy!

As far as the performance of my office is concerned, I held a preparation hour for Holy Communion and used as a basis the gospel of Matthew 5:25 ff., which was scheduled for Sunday and in which our Savior explains the fifth[168] commandment and gives direction how people who live in enmity and anger with one another are to behave if they wish to do the will of God and to go to Holy Communion with profit. This is a matter that is very necessary for the quarrelsome and ill-behaved people there [for those who belong to the quarrelsome and ill-behaved sort].[169] After the prayer an old woman stepped forth and offered her hand to a young man with whom she had quarreled and asked for forgiveness because she had taken to heart the word about reconciliation with one's neighbor being the fruit of reconciliation found with God (which also belongs to good order). Because I knew that some people had caused great annoyance through drunkenness and disobedience, I publicly separated these and deferred their Communion until their true improvement. There were five persons. A child who had received emergency baptism from the English preacher was brought to church, and the emergency baptism confirmed. After the afternoon service a couple of young people were married. My text on Sunday morning and afternoon was Titus 2:14. [It is very hot; and, because I was busy administering Holy Communion and marrying and confirming the emergency baptism, the sermon lasted not much over three quarters of an hour each time.]

In Purysburg I visited Pastor Zoberbiller, who lay very sick with fever. He appreciated my visit, even if I could not remain with him much more than a quarter of an hour. His wife died two weeks ago and his daughter one week ago. His son is also sick; and now he and his sick son are being cared for by his oldest daughter, whose husband died in Purysburg a few months ago. His words were very edifying; and he well sees what the Father's purpose is in this apparently severe chastisement, which he and his entire family have had to feel according to His will. I told him what kind of a diet I have been accustomed to keep, even the last time, with fever; and I promised him at his request to send him some medicine, which my dear colleague has taken to him.

Wednesday, the 12th of July. Yesterday evening we had a violent thunderstorm with much rain and strong wind; it all passed on without any damage except that some roofs were torn apart. Our roofs are all without nails, because the people did not receive any for building in New Ebenezer.

N. N. [Grimmiger], who is not a Salzburger, could not escape the hand of God by running away. He got lost in the forest behind Purysburg and ran around hungry and thirsty for four days and tore his few clothes and the skin of his hands and feet on the thorns. Because during his wandering he could see nothing ahead of himself but death and hell and suffered extreme thirst, he began to recognize his sin and promised God in his need to confess everything frankly if only He in His mercy would help him back to Ebenezer. Thereupon he caught sight of a small footpath that brought him to a small plantation. Here the people refreshed him for a day and, as soon as he had recovered, brought him to Purysburg, from whence he was brought here last Sunday at his own request but full of fear, by the shoemaker Reck and two other people.

When he came to me, he fell on his knees and begged us not to send him to Savannah but to proceed with him mercifully. He said he wished to confess everything freely, and this he did; and he admitted the theft that he had committed against the poor Pletter and had so shamefully denied at repeated questionings. He wishes to submit, and to pray and implore until God converts him from his wickedness and accepts him into His grace for His dear Son's sake. He also confessed the lewdness [unchastity] he had committed in N. [Regensburg][170] before his marriage and showed remorse because of it. People are now getting after him to make him confess other thefts, because at various times objects have disappeared from our place, even if they were petty things. We will consider together and with the congregation what is to be done further regarding his punishment. I have not yet reported anything to Mr. Causton about his running away and other offenses; and, since the matter has taken such an end, I think I shall not do so in order to avoid embarassment, especially since he does not like to pass judgments on the members of our community or to intervene in our affairs. May God give us wisdom and not let His name be blasphemed, but glorified, and let Satan's kingdom be more and more destroyed.

Thursday, the 13th of July. [Christ, who recently left the orphanage and its regular way of life, soon recognized to whom he had caused the greatest harm. He has again requested me through various people to be accepted again and has now called on me himself. He complains of his inconstancy and obstinacy, is ashamed of his folly, and wishes to promise before witnesses to accommodate himself to all good order if I will just accept him once more. Kalcher and his wife have in him, to be sure, a great trial of their patience; yet they will gladly accept him again through compassion, or else I would not force this person on them. He gladly hears God's word, and not without profit. However, he is accustomed to fooling around and idleness; and therefore he sometimes considers good order to be a yoke.]

Today we had another beautiful rain, which was very convenient for planting sweet potato vines. The corn that appeared half dried out is becoming green again and is getting ears; and thus the dear Lord knows how to preserve easily that which He hath given. Damage will be caused this year by the fact that our people, as well as others in this colony, have let themselves be talked into planting yellow corn, which is often brought here from New York and Pennsylvania but does not bear so abundantly here as it may in the North. In the future such corn will probably not be planted any more in this country, because the loss is apparent. It grows very short stalks; and therefore the fruit can be much more easily damaged and devoured by wild animals than on the corn of this area, which grows a good nine feet tall. Col. Stephens and the councilman who were with us recently could not complain enough about the loss that people suffered in Savannah because of this foreign corn.[171]

Friday, the 14th of July. The rain has lasted until today. I received news that the Salzburgers' cows had been brought to Old Ebenezer, and therefore several people were sent to fetch them.

[Today our widows have distributed the linen and colored material that God has granted them. Mrs. Helfenstein received the most because of her large family, just as she and her children always receive more good in physical gifts than anyone among the Salzburgers; yet we have to suffer that she too judges these simple and honest people harshly. She betrays herself ever more clearly in that, while she may not be lacking in good words, she does not have a right foundation. She herself told me that her house in Heidelberg had been as good as the common meeting place of the Inspirationists[172] and other inordinate people; and, although she claims that she took no part in their disorderliness, we believe her less now that she has revealed that she excuses strange Enthusiastic opinions, indeed, even approves of them ipso facto. She lets her children have their own way and will make very little good of them.]

Saturday, the 15th of July. Our people have now divided their new cattle. The third transport received twelve cows and the same number of calves, and the other seventeen were bought by individual Salzburgers. Thirty-five head had been ordered; but the man lost six underway while driving them here and therefore six families must have patience till some other time. These cows do not look so fine as we had hoped from the man's promises and from the high price, for every cow cost 53 shillings 4 pence sterling, whereas people usually buy them for 40 shillings sterling. The third transport now lacks hogs and poultry, concerning which I have sent Mr. Causton several reminders.

Sunday, the 16th of July. Today after the morning sermon N.'s [Grimmiger's] annoying case was tried publicly, and he was cut off from the Christian community like a rotten limb until his true conversion. First I told the congregation that the theft that N. [Grimmiger] had committed against poor N. [Pletter] had occurred somewhat more than two years ago and that at that time the gravest suspicion had fallen on him because he had been at home alone in the same hut in which Pletter lived and no one else had come into the hut. I had, to be sure, made every effort to persuade the man to confess this injustice and had often spoken with him movingly, especially while he was dangerously sick; but he had always referred to his conscience, to divine omniscience, etc., and so it had been impossible to get anything out of him. In this state of mind he had gone to Holy Communion various times in two years; and even in the preparation hour he could not be moved to free himself of such a curse, concerning which the listeners were frequently admonished sincerely and with all our strength. His heart had always remained hard and insensitive, even though the dear Lord had blessed such admonitions to this purpose in several others, who had confessed their own sins of injustice and had restored what they had stolen. What indescribable forbearance and patience God has let this man experience on his sinful path!

Yet God has shown that He is a holy and just God, who will not always let the godless man succeed but surely knows how to reveal his wickedness. The opportunity for this was a chisel or smoothing iron that Pletter had seen being used by another man who had gotten it from Grimmiger; and, because he remembered that it had lain in the chest with the lost money, he brought it to me. I immediately examined Grimmiger on the street in the presence of two men; but he again boldly claimed, with an appeal to divine omniscience and legal justice, that he had brought this steel tool with him from Germany. With this new suspicion it became known that he had spent much money in Savannah and here as well and had bought all sorts of things that amounted to two guineas.

Because of this we summoned him to a hearing with three elders again and spoke to him sincerely but could not accomplish anything. Because the suspicion was very strong and because another, albeit smaller, theft had come to light from the time of our voyage, I excluded him from taking Holy Communion that time. This excommunication must not have prophesied much good for him, so on that same Sunday he took an old boat from our landing and went with it to Purysburg with the intention of travelling to Charleston and thus escaping the physical punishment for his theft. But he was unable to escape the hand of God; for, when he had become entirely lost, God let him come into such straits that, in his great thirst and extreme physical weakness, he swore to confess his sin gladly and to submit to the proper punishment if only God would save him from his wandering and mortal danger.

Hereupon I asked him the following questions: 1) Whether everything I had said was true? 2) Whether he admitted that he had taken poor Pletter's money and denied it for so long? 3) Whether his conscience did not tell him that he had committed other thefts as well? Answ. "No." 4) Whether he knew that such theft is a serious sin? I confirmed his "Yes" by reading out the verses 1 Corinthians 6:9–10. 5) Whether he also knew that God in His word insists upon the restitution of what is stolen? I again confirmed this from Ezekiel 33:14–16 and Numbers 5:6–8. 6) Whether he agreed to such restitution? 7) Whether he wished to submit to the [spiritual and physical] punishment which he had merited through such repeated wickedness? He affirmed all this with humble spirit. Hereupon we announced his exclusion from Holy Communion and all privileges that Christ gave His church and told him that we could not accept him again until we could detect infallible signs of a true conversion and until he had freed himself from his ban by an effective restitution. However sorrowful his exclusion was for us now, I said, his reception would be just as joyous for us. 8) Since, as an example for others, such a wicked deed must be assigned a physical punishment, I asked him where he would rather be punished, here or in Savannah? Answ. Rather here.[173]

I shall speak further with the congregation as to what is to be done. With the increase of our herd we need a new herdsman, and it might well be N.'s [Grimmiger's] punishment to guard the cattle until Christmas without pay. He would receive clothes and provisions, but no money. However, this has not yet been announced to him. I finally admonished him to a complete change of heart, for which purpose he would have to use the means of salvation better than up to now. For he himself had to admit that he often missed the prayer meeting and has therefore not heard what he needed. I also told the congregation how I hoped from my heart that others who had sinned against the Lord in this or in other bad ways would be revealed so that they could be helped.

It was no misfortune for poor N. [Grimmiger] that his wickedness had come to light and he had been disgraced: better here than there before the judgment seat of Christ. Now we would have all the more time to work on him in his condition, I said, and now he could comfort himself with the help of the prayers of all the righteous people in our congregation, which would be denied to those who kept their curse hidden. And because, as N. [Grimmiger] had done to his own harm, several people had stayed away from the evening prayer hour without compelling reason or at least had missed it from time to time, I admonished them to reflect on their salvation and to take advantage of the good opportunity in which they could receive so many necessary admonitions from the Biblical stories. Also, they should drop all suspicions that N. [Grimmiger] might have been the thief who stole other secretly taken things, since he had declared not only publicly now but also privately to me and others that he had played no part in the other thefts, in which here and there a few not very important things had disappeared. Finally we closed with prayer.

Monday, the 17th of July. During the proceedings with N. [Grimmiger] yesterday a man remembered a certain injustice he had committed in his youth, for which reason he came to me today and confessed and paid four shillings for the poor as restitution. Another who was present remembered a similar sin and also paid four shillings, which money was sent as aid to the poor carpenter who had received the worst cow along with a sick calf that soon died.[174] This will doubtless awaken him to much praise of God for His fatherly care. He lives in the fear of the Lord and works diligently, even though he is very weak physically. [The schoolmaster, Ortmann, has been conducting himself very well for some time, and it appears that the dear Lord has again begun His work of mercy mightily in his soul. He follows God's word diligently, prays seriously, and tends to his duty loyally in the school. His wife has been dragging herself around for some time now with bodily weakness, which probably contributes to the fact that she is more orderly, for in previous times the schoolmaster was incited against us by her and much evil was committed. She speaks good words, but she gives no indication that she regrets in her heart the sins of her youth and the vexations she has caused among us.]

Tuesday, the 18th of July. For several days we have been having many but not lasting rains, which, however, is not too much because of the drought we have had for so long. A Salzburger told me with much praise of the Lord that his corn and beans are growing so beautifully that he promises himself a rich harvest, provided the Lord continues His apparent blessing. He had not wished to trust the alien corn but had preferred to plant our native corn, which he thought would turn out best.

The parents in Purysburg who have their children in our orphanage and school are so poor that they cannot send them any
clothes, as was stipulated; and therefore we will look out for
them too in this matter. The physical want among the people in
that place is very great; and their spiritual want, which is the
chief want, they recognize much less [not at all. We hear no
good reports at all from there.]

Wednesday, the 19th of July. The soldier[175] of whom mention has once been made wrote to me from Fort Prince George
and asked whether he could rely on the fact that he would be
permitted to settle among us. In that case he would like to find
someone who would build a hut for him and fence in his lot.
Our Salzburgers still have much confidence in him; and therefore I would like to report to him that he can come when his
service is over. He is a tailor and will have enough work among
us if he will work for a fair price. The alien corn is already so
ripe in some gardens that it must be picked. The native corn is
now in its finest growth, and our dear people promise themselves a good harvest under divine blessing.

Thursday, the 20th of July. I had a conversation with a
Salzburger woman that was edifying for myself. She was full of
love and praise of God for the rich grace of God in Christ. She
remembered the beginning of her conversion and said that one
can well know whether [and at what time] God works a true
change and reform of heart in a person. She can well remember, she said, the circumstances of her conversion and will
never forget it. While the persecution of the pious people was
taking place in Salzburg, she felt a yearning in herself to learn
who had the true faith, the Catholics or the Protestants; and
therefore she sighed diligently to God. However, she was
prevented by her /arch-/ Catholic father from becoming acquainted with honest people, and she herself and others of her
family could not read. At the same time, she said, a great deal of
voluptuousness was committed at a wedding in her neighborhood that she heard from far away; and she had been so troubled by this worldly joy, by which the dear Lord was so greatly
insulted, that she fell into a very serious sickness and lost her
consciousness from worrying about her own sins. With all this,

as other people could tell by looking at her, she had great pains; but she herself did not feel anything except that it seemed to her that a very pleasant change had occurred in her, which she could observe very clearly when she had regained consciousness.

Ever since that time, she said, her senses and spiritual strength had always been directed at matters above this world and temporal things had been a burden for her. She had also felt such zealousness for the truth that she would not let herself be held back from being better instructed in it; and in this a man in the neighborhood had done excellent, although secret, service. And after he had been expelled, God had sent her another friend who read to her and others from the Bible and Arndt's *Christianity* in the forest on Sundays while other people were in church. She would never have found any rest until she herself had emigrated; only when she came to the gospel did she realize how much she was still lacking. But through God's grace things were getting better with the state of her soul the longer she lived. The gospel of Christ is becoming so dear to her that it seems to her that an entirely new and sweet gospel is now being proclaimed, which she had never heard before, even though it is surely the old one. She knows how to snuggle with all her frailties into Christ so that she is still a poor deeply bowed sinner, to be sure; yet she is full of comfort in Christ and full of God's praise.

Friday, the 21st of July. [Mr. Thilo has been almost bedridden for about four weeks with quotidian fever. He does not cure according to the method of the late Dr. Richter, which, as I have been able to tell him, has until now always succeeded for us with divine blessing.] So far this year the congregation has been almost spared from the fever, with the exception of a few people. May God be praised for it!

N. [Grimmiger] is very humble and obedient now that God has brought him to recognition and confession of his grievous sins. Good people are also working on his thorough conversion. He has returned most of what he took and does not refuse to guard the community's cattle until Christmas as a punishment, for which he will receive clothing and provisions but no money.

In this way, provided he shows loyalty in his herding, he can re-gain his credit in the community and in the future be regularly appointed as a herdsman.

N. [Ernst] may also have many injustices on his conscience but will not admit it. Today, when he picked up some meat, I asked him to think it over with his wife and unburden himself; because this is God's serious wish. However, he remained silent. Mrs. N. [Rheinlaender] also has much muck on her conscience which she has confessed to my dear colleague; yet she persists in using excuses and is full of tricks. She was at [a count's] court for a long time and learned and carries many court sins, for which she has never done penance. Nevertheless, she claims that she has been converted at our place, but she has never won our approbation in this. During all the time that she and her husband have been with us God has often knocked mightily at their door.

Saturday, the 22nd of July. For a few days now, sunshine has replaced the blessed rain, and the weather is good for the growth in the fields. The nights are cool, and there is a heavy dew.

N.'s [Hans Floerel's] wife is among those who run forward with all earnestness to the jewel that God holds forth to them in His dear Son; and it is an uncommon sorrow to her that she has spent so many years without seriously aspiring to the kingdom of God and that she now finds so many obstacles in her body and in many external matters. The patience and forbearance that God is showing to her daily as a great sinner let her grow every day, and she is very careful not to misuse them the least bit for security or indolence. During her service she took a little piece of cloth for her own use, more from simplicity than wick-edness, and this is now lying on her heart like a millstone be-cause it is unjustly owned wealth. I spoke and prayed with her according to her condition and finally referred her to the two first chapters of Johann Arndt's second book to read later on, which suit her circumstances very well.

[Sunday, the 23rd of July. Spielbiegler and his mother are surely incorrigible in every way. Both of them are mired in the most miserable blindness and yet do not use the means of salva-tion in order to be saved from it. Both of them are seldom seen

at church; and, when they are there, they listen to the word
without any application, as we well realize during our visitation.
Barbara Maurer is also just such an ignorant and at the same
time wicked person. To be sure she is often present at divine
service, but because of her frivolity she notes nothing or does
not apply it to her spiritual needs. Recently, through malicious
stupidity, she had someone tell me that she did not mind that I
had not wished to let her go to Holy Communion the last time,
and that she was not sorry that she had had the letter written to
P. Zittrauer (it was a disgraceful and abusive letter, in which she
had even misused my name.) She has played even more silly
and annoying tricks among us so that she is scorned in the
community, and there is probably no one among us who will
desire her as a wife. We must bear with her and chastise her as
long as God suffers her. To be sure, God can easily create sweet
fruit from a bitter root. Who knows but that He may someday
succeed with her.]

Monday, the 24th of July. This afternoon our land had
another fruitful rain. The thunderstorms this year are quite
bearable in comparison with those of other times. The heat of
the day is so tempered that our dear people could not wish for
better climate for their work, now that they have gradually become accustomed to it. They can work in the fields both summer and winter and they can graze their cattle the whole year
through in the forest. These are two very fine advantages.

To be sure, the Frenchman in our neighborhood in Carolina
has taken some of his brandy to Purysburg because of his debts;
yet he is still selling such things, as we learned today. One of the
two millwrights who built the saw mill in Old Ebenezer[176] requested our boat in order to go to this man; and since he had to
admit at our questioning that he wanted to fetch rum, the boat
was refused him along with good and adequate reasons, which,
however, he did not recognize as adequate. Instead, he used
very daring expressions against the regulations concerning this
strong drink that were made by the Lord Trustees, in whose
service he earns much money, more through indolence than
through work.

[The Englishmen in Old Ebenezer, who are in charge of the
Lord Trustees' sawmill and cattle, live right brutishly; and the

previously mentioned millwright is said to run around entirely naked like a drunk Indian with only a piece of cloth hanging in front. Col. Stephens saw some of the brutish disorder there himself and has, I hope, submitted a report. Rum is the ruination of the people.]

[Thursday, the 25th of July. Quite early this morning] A few days ago a man from the congregation asked me to come to him; and he confessed to me on his sickbed many sins of injustice that lay on his conscience like a hundred-weight, yea, like the weight of the whole world. The treatment given to N. [Grimmiger] has given the right emphasis to the previous warnings against remaining in such muck so that he had become ill through disquiet and worry. He has been in my hut once in order to confess everything on his heart, but he was prevented from it by other people who were there. In the last few days he has experienced well enough what David confessed about himself in Psalms 32:3, "When I kept silence, my bones waxed old through my roaring all the day long." During the previous night he had passed hours of fear because of his misdeeds as if he were lying in hell, because he had gone to Holy Communion with them several times against his conscience although he knew better.

[In the presence of his wife, who also had some part in it], he confessed everything he had done here and in his homeland against the seventh and sixth commandment;[177] and he declared himself ready to make a complete and superabundant restitution, in which the poor carpenter, who has lost his cow and calf, shall again participate. He will gladly be disgraced before the entire congregation, if I find it good to do so. However, this is not necessary, because no one has been scandalized by him, but rather they have been edified so far by his diligent use of the means of salvation and his present pious Christian behavior. No one would have looked in him for such misdeeds, to which the deception of sin has led him; and therefore the righteous nature of Christianity would be greatly blasphemed by its enemies if these sins should be revealed.

He is truly penitent and right contrite, so that I believe God will separate him completely from his sin in this crucible and make of him a pure vessel to His glory. I demonstrated to him the horror of his sins, especially his having gone to Communion several times with a burdened conscience, since he surely knew better than others what God requires of a man for a worthy use of Holy Communion and for salvation. I also assured him, from Holy Writ, that God would nevertheless not reject him because of such deeds and disloyalty but would show him mercy for the sake of Christ, who had completely paid for his sins. For this purpose I quoted several verses such as Ezekiel 33:15, "If the wicked restore the pledge, give again that he had robbed, walk in the statutes of life, without committing iniquity; he shall surely live, he shall not die." 1 John 1:9, "If we confess our sins, he is faithful and just to forgive us our sins, and to cleanse us from all unrighteousness." Matthew 11:28, "Come unto me all ye that labour and are heavy laden, and I will give you rest." At the same time I admonished him to lay himself, with all his pangs of conscience, into the wounds of the Lord Jesus and to give more rest to his body, which has been entirely weakened from sighs, fear, and sleepless nights. I prayed with him and promised to visit him soon again.

This example confirmed in me what I had admonished publicly to the congregation just last Sunday, namely, that there are still many in the congregation who have muck on their poor consciences which hinders them in their fundamental conversion to God, on which we always insist. Because of fear of disgrace and loss they do not wish to confess and give back until finally our dear Lord, who loves their souls, so attacks them that they cannot dodge Him but will entangle themselves in all sorts of pretenses and excuses; and this, as this man well recognizes, is a boundless and superabundant mercy of God.

Wednesday, the 26th of July. I called on several Salzburger families to encourage myself with them, in the Lord Jesus, to apply diligence so that we might someday be able to complete with joy both the course of our Christianity and our external profession. I found an honest spirit in all of these; and it is their daily concern to withdraw more and more from themselves and the world with the help of the Holy Ghost and to live only for the glory of their Savior. They not only recognize what they are lacking and what obstacles lie in the way of their forceful penetration into the Kingdom of God,[178] but they direct their prayer and struggle toward breaking their way through even better and to become quite familiar with their Lord Jesus.

A woman complained bitterly and with tears about the dreadful fantasies she has at night, even though she sincerely implores the Lord Jesus to guard her from them and to fill her mind and heart with His love. Such fantasies and dreams drive her all the more zealously to her prayer in the morning, and she learns more and more to recognize what a chaos is lying in her heart and stirs when she is not even thinking about it. Today she told me that several times it seemed to her in her sleep that she could hear the voice: "Just come to me. I am Joseph, your brother, etc.," which had been very comforting to her spirit after all the previous difficult struggle. This woman goes to bed with an ardent yearning to experience the grace of God in Christ; and she gets up with the very same yearning and does her chores, but tears herself away several times during the day to pour forth her troubled heart in prayer. Oh how she longs for grace and for the gracious forgiveness of her sins!

Thursday, the 27th of July. It is a great sorrow for some people that they cannot achieve certainty of their state of grace despite all their struggle. In the case of some of them, their own disloyalty is probably to blame; because they do not fight vigorously and constantly the struggle to which the Lord has once awakened them but become comfortable and lax whenever there are difficulties or obstacles or if they must suffer somewhat. In general these people well recognize that they are to blame and are pleased if we admonish them and pray with them. Others continue in the loyalty that God has given them and take their struggles right seriously; and they are already actually crowned with grace, as experienced Christians easily recognize for their own edification and to the praise of God. Yet our marvelous God has His salutary reasons for not letting them taste the grace they have won but lets them dig deeper and deeper in the recognition of their corrupted hearts. In their case, in order to strengthen them in their faith, we must apply all diligence in raising them up with the gospel and in revealing to them the grace that they cannot see in themselves. God is doing the best thing for those souls on whom He is especially working; and He often lets the rays of His sun of grace and of His father-heart that loves them so dearly shine forth on them so sweetly from among the clouds that they at last observe how far they will finally come through God's boundless mercy, according to which He will fail no man. So far one verse has been a refreshing and strengthening balm for a struggling soul, namely Isaiah 27:5–6: "He may make peace with me, and He *shall* make peace with me. He shall cause them that come of Jacob to take root: Israel shall blossom and bud, and fill the face of the world with fruit."

In addition to these souls, in whom God blesses our office in His fatherly mercy, there are various obviously lazy people who see their Christianity in the use of the means of salvation and in external probity and at the same time let themselves believe, for their worldly comfort, that one cannot go so far as to be sure of one's state of grace or salvation but must believe from the gospel that God will save us through His great mercy and for the sake of Christ's merit. We seek in all ways to cut through these dangerous snares of Satan with the sword of the spirit and to convince our listeners of the contrary from the unambiguous word of God and also from Biblical and other [edifying] exempla.

In some prayer meetings I have had an opportunity to say one thing or the other on the occasion of the lovely story in Numbers 27, which also made an impression through the grace of God. As soon as this exemplum is finished, I shall read the very impressive exemplum from the thirty-fourth *Contribution to the Building of the Kingdom of God*[179] in order to clarify and confirm the truths that have been presented.

Friday, the 28th of July. The man who was mentioned above [on the 25th of this month] has, ever since that time, confessed away from his heart still more things that he had wrongfully taken both here and in Germany, and I must marvel at the deception of sin that has revealed itself especially in this case. As long as he has been among us he has conducted himself right exemplarily and equaled the honest people among us in his serious use of the means of salvation; yet all that time he had borne such a dreadful muck on his poor conscience and had even increased it. After his confession and restitution he attested that his heart had become lighter. However, it did not last long before he fell again into the greatest quandary and kept complaining that not the least bit of divine comfort would stay with him.

We have visited him diligently these last few days, and he has sent for me various times both by day and by night to complain of the great fear in his heart and to ask me to read him a verse from the gospel. In his fear he prays constantly and grasps strength-giving gospel verses with his spirit, but they will not remain there. However, he still has some hope that the Lord Jesus will have mercy on him and will not entirely reject him because of his great sins. Also, he always keeps in mind the verse: "Come unto me all ye that labour and are heavy laden, and I will give you rest." Likewise, "Mine hour is not yet come."

A few days ago N. N. [the old Rieser] was admonished by my dear colleague to prepare his salvation seriously and to test himself well to see whether he knew anything about conversion and rebirth, without which no one can enter the kingdom of God. Instead of accepting this with love, he contradicted him in a bad temper and committed no little sin. I called on him several times in his hut and, since I did not find him at home, I spoke with his wife and children as necessary to avert vexation. His wife has also scolded him about such sinful contradiction and resistance but just made the bad in him worse.

This morning he called to me on the street that he could neither eat nor sleep nor work until he had spoken with me, for he did not know how he stood in regard to his salvation. I made an appointment with him for noon; and, when he came, I showed him, at his sincere insistence and in all gentleness and simplicity, the way in which he would be able to escape future wrath and be saved in his old age. What pleased me about him was that he was already convinced from God's word that 1) there must be a true change in a man if our holy and glorious God is to be united with him both here and there, and 2) that such a change was still lacking in him, even though until now he had prayed and read, heard, and done much good.

I read to him, with ample clarification, the first six rules that the late Collin had taken from God's word and put into the hands of those who wished to be converted and that are to be found in the *Contribution to the Building of the Kingdom of*

God.[180] I also gave him, to read later at home, the late Professor Francke's sermon about the righteous nature of Christianity concerning the gospel John 3 : 1 ff. and Pastor Freylinghausen's penitential sermon "God's Counsel concerning a Godless Sinner."[181] God grant that the Truth shall someday be in this man. If he fights his way through and becomes a true new-born Christian, it will more easily be possible to accomplish something with his children. What the mother builds up the father often tears down, as she told me with many tears while giving examples of his bad disposition, but with the request that I keep them to myself.

Saturday, the 29th of July. Three soldiers called on me and said that they, along with two others, had roamed through our forest as well as other regions in order to find three men who had broken out of the jail in Savannah and run away. They had shot cows and pigs and had caused much damage and were therefore going to be hanged.[182]

An old Swiss from Appenzell Canton, who is now staying in Purysburg, came to us yesterday with his little son, partly to inspect our place and partly to ask to be accepted by us. He is faring very miserably in Purysburg and must suffer much hunger; and he has no opportunity to earn anything even though he wishes to work. He is a carpenter and can do all sorts of cabinet making and barrel making. He brought about 600 florins cash with him but lost it all in one year, and he also lost two married daughters with their husbands through death. His wife and six children are still back in Switzerland in good condition, and he would like to return to them if he could raise the money. I pitied the miserable man and therefore wished to serve him in any way possible. Because he is not satisfied with food and clothing /but wishes to have money/, he will not fit in our orphanage. We could well use him in our work, yet he is fifty-seven years old and rather debilitated from his recent hunger and other difficult circumstances.

[Mrs. Helfenstein is his compatriot and good friend; and we are afraid that he might let her turn him against the Salzburgers, since she is not at all satisfied with them, although she and her children should have good reason to thank God for the good that she has so far enjoyed among and from them. The two Zueblys adhere greatly to her; and, if this man joined up, her following would become even larger and many troubles could result. The tailor Metzscher of Purysburg is also request- ing to be accepted at our place. He is faring very miserably there, and he and his family have to live in the woods without divine services. He has two children in our school and is very pleased with that. I told him 1) that he should deliberate with good friends whether or not he could subsist and earn his living on the poor soil that is all that remains here, since our people have already divided up the good land among themselves, and 2) that it is the order of the Lord Trustees that anyone who wishes land in this colony may not have any in Carolina, and therefore he would have to sell his land if he wished to move to us, and 3) that he could not be accepted here without the con- sent of the congregation, for I accept here none but those in whom we have confidence that they can harmonize with the members of the congregation.]

Sunday, the 30th of July. Last night we began the 28th chap- ter of Numbers; and I showed, to the profit of myself and the congregation, the relationship between this chapter and the two previous ones, which also apply well to our circumstances. Ear- lier we have learned that God let the people be counted and made arrangements for the land of Canaan to be divided among those who were counted. Also, Joshua was chosen to fight the Lord's wars and to bring Israel into possession of the Promised Land. Now, instead of prescribing rules of war for His people and making arrangements for their campaigns, the dear Lord has them instructed in the methods of divine service and how they should bring their daily, weekly, and yearly sac- rifice to their God of the Covenant in order to indicate that their divine service and care for the Kingdom of God should be their chief concern during all their military difficulties and in the occupation and cultivation of their land. From the prophet Haggai I explained what damage is done by the neglect of such things and how a curse, instead of a blessing, is brought down upon a land and people.

Our people are now talking a great deal about their desire to move to their plantations and live there, as necessity demands. For many plantations lie at a distance of four to six English miles from our place, and it will not be possible to come here every evening. They will have to take all their live-stock and their entire households out there with them. However, since they emigrated from their homeland not for the sake of land but for the sake of the word of God, they should well deliberate together as to how they could arrange to retain the diligent public practice of God's word and prayer without hindrance from their external occupations. My dear colleague and I would be most happy to adjust ourselves to anything so that such a purpose might be realized. The only way to work with God's blessing is to consider first the Kingdom of God and His righteousness.

Monday, the 31st of July. [Now that she probably wishes to move away soon, Mrs. Rheinlaender is making every effort, after all her gossip, lies, and slander, to set people against each other from time to time and cause trouble; at the same time she wishes to appear in the right and to keep up good appearances. She has been practicing her wickedness, and sometimes her hypocrisy, long enough among us; and the Lord will not suffer this for ever.]

Our people are now hastening to harvest their ripe corn, because it matures and spoils in the rainy weather that we are now having. This occurs more easily to the foreign corn, which they have planted in considerable quantity, than to the local variety. A man who planted only such corn assures me that he has lost at least twelve bushels. Some Salzburgers who have planted only or mostly the native corn see the advantage clearly. This will ripen only after two months and now has the best growing weather.

AUGUST

[Tuesday, the 1st of August. Rauner has now been with the word of God for a long time, but he is not becoming any better but remains the Old Adam. I reminded him today of several wicked deeds that he did not care to contradict, nor does he wish to improve himself seriously. He is hand and glove with the Frenchman on the Carolina side and is said to commit all sorts of disorder; but I cannot accuse him of this, because I must first inform myself better about it. It is certain that he likes to drink and lets himself be used for all sorts of things for a small gain. When he has plunged into disorderly conduct and it becomes known, he weeps, to be sure, and again promises much; yet no change results from it. He shall not come to any good end if he continues, as it appears in his disloyalty toward the signs of God's mercy.

[Of just such a kind is Ruprecht Zittrauer, both in regard to his Christianity and in regard to his housekeeping and external work. Along with his wife, Anna Leihofer, who came to us with the third transport, he is lazy and indolent in all physical and spiritual occupations. At the same time they like to drink and eat well, make private debts, and are a burden to other people. We admonish, implore, and chastise them as often as we have an opportunity; and therefore they will have no excuse if things turn out badly for them.]

Wednesday, the 2nd of August. A woman had something to do with me because of her husband, at which time she revealed, with many tears, things that she had been too bashful to mention before. So far the word of God has penetrated so deeply into her that she is full of disquiet and worry and cannot come to the preparation for the coming service of Holy Communion until she has relieved herself of everything through confession. These were various sins against the seventh commandment.[183] Her masters had trusted her too much and let her have charge of everything; and, because she had otherwise been treated too strictly, she took various things that she now wishes to restore. Indeed, she wishes to restore everything in excess and give it in the form of money to a needy pious person.

We have learned from several examples how true is the proverb: "Opportunity makes thieves," and likewise: *objecta movent sensus.* This has taught me to keep a constant eye on all people whom we employ in the house and not to give them a sure opportunity for sinning by putting too much trust in their honesty. Often something is considered very trivial; yet, because it is stolen, it causes great disquiet when the conscience is awakened. Last week a man complained to me that the wine cellar had been left at his disposal, and as a result he had taken many drinks furtively, whereas he had previously had carefully

measured drinks [measured by himself], with which he could
have been satisfied. When many such petty things, as they seem,
are collected in one register or debit book, the *facit* and *summa*
will finally be rather large. We like to warn against the deception of sin.

Thursday, the 3rd of August. One of the former friends of
Baron von Reck, a young German man, called on me as he was
travelling past us from the Indian nations on his way to Savannah.[184] For the purpose of trading he has roamed many hun-
dreds of English miles among the Indians, both the Creeks and
Chickasaws and also the Cherokees;[185] and I learned from what
he told me that the Indians up there have the same life style as
the local ones and that they drink themselves full and cause disturbance just as often as they can get strong drink, which, however, it is difficult to take to them on pack horses. The French
import much spirits among them wherever they can go. The air
is said to be very good, and no other diseases prevail among the
Europeans or Indians but venereal diseases, which they con-
tract through their dreadful libertine life.[186] The Indians there
have always waged wars among themselves, one nation against
the other, and they cannot live long without war; and therefore
many hostile Indian slaves are brought and sold to the Europeans. Negro slaves do not come there. This year the drought is
said to have been very great, and this must be the reason that
the Savannah River has become as small as the oldest inhabitants of the country can remember it.

Friday, the 4th of August. Now that the wood and boards for
my dear colleague's house are dried out enough, the carpenters will begin in earnest to raise it, and they will not undertake
anything else until it is completely built. There is one difficulty
in this matter, namely that we do not know at exactly what spot
the house should be erected; the surveyor from Savannah who
surveyed our town[187] should indicate it to us, as we have already asked him to several times. But everything goes very
slowly with these people. Our plantations are not completed
either, and we have neither heard nor seen anything of the
surveyor who was engaged for them.[188] God willing, my dear
colleague will go to Savannah tomorrow for the sake of the German people in order to preach the gospel to them, and I shall

mention these points in a letter to Mr. Causton. I shall also report to him the disorders that the Frenchman in our neighborhood wishes to cause by secretly selling rum among us [with Rauner's aid], now that I have gotten to the bottom of this wicked business.

[Mrs. Rheinlaender has departed in the boat belonging to the man who was with us yesterday and has left her children behind. She does not wish to improve but causes much vexation here through her gossip and intrigues, so everyone would be very happy if she would leave with all her belongings. Shortly before her departure she was resolved to leave a stench behind her, but she did not succeed in this. God will gradually free us of all these wicked people.

[Mrs. Helfenstein has been very close with her during the last months; and because, as her custom has been from the very beginning, Mrs. Rheinlaender has often uttered lies and calumnies in her hut against the Salzburgers, Mrs. Helfenstein has come into discredit with them and they have little affection for her, and this gives her an opportunity to sin with even more such judgments against the Salzburgers. Her credit with us has also dropped very low ever since she began trying to marry off her oldest daughter to Mr. Thilo, who would like to marry her if there were not one obstacle in the way.[189] She[190] is Reformed, but so far she has attended our services diligently. Nevertheless, we have perceived, both while Mr. Spangenberg was here as well as on another occasion, that she may have absorbed much from her numerous associations with all sorts of erring and disorderly people who had their assembly in her house in Heidelberg; thus, she approves of everyone who has love and good appearances. Her children, of whom she has two in the orphanage, are naughty. The oldest daughter[191] is beginning to fear God. They all must have had a poor education in their external life; because they cannot cope with their work well, and they are lazy. Their mother is very indulgent with them. Because she is a widow and also very poor, we give her much help and also are having a good hut built for her; yet we cannot help but bring her to order when we see her committing excesses because of her lax principles, even if she will later consider it persecution.]

Saturday, the 5th of August. An old Indian with his wife and son followed me into the orphanage, to which he gave a piece of venison in return for some bread, [beer],[192] and rice. I led them to the orphans' dormitory, which was so clean and orderly that they were amazed. I have already let several Indian parents know that they should leave one of their children with me, but they only laugh at this. Their love for their children is very great, and therefore they allow them every freedom. There are now several families of such heathens here, who conduct themselves very quietly and respectably. They bring meat and honey here, for which they receive all sorts of provisions.

I have had several attacks of fever, and I also note many other kinds of weakness, which are preventing me from going to Savannah this time, for which reason my dear colleague undertook the journey this morning. May the Lord accompany him with much blessing in his affairs. So far I cannot say that I have even made a good start with the German people. Whether any good has been accomplished here or there secretly is known only to the Lord. They cause much trouble for the authorities and for their masters; and, when we come to Savannah, we hear many complaints about their disobedience, defiance, waste of supplies, laziness, etc.

Sunday, the 6th of August. Our song-hour, which is held on Sundays after the afternoon service, is proceeding well; and God grants his blessing to it for our edification. The people come very regularly and are all the more encouraged in their acquisition of songs when they notice that it is possible to learn one melody after the other; for we have already sung several newly learned songs publicly in church without error and with much pleasure, for example: "Where is my little Lamb?", "My Father, beget me," "How well for me, oh Friend of Souls," etc.[193] Some female persons among both adults and children have bright and well ordered voices and express the melodies very well and clearly; and they sing to the remainder, who learn more slowly, until they too have gradually learned them. The charm of the melodies and the lovely content of the songs gives joy and pleasure to the attentive spirits. There will be few unfamiliar songs and melodies in our hymnal that can be sung by public congregations that we do not already sing in our congregation. This is a major advantage in edifying the entire congregation. God be praised for that! Today we learned the beautiful song "Here lies my soul before Thee,"[194] which the people quickly mastered. Finally I read to them "May my soul flow in the Blood and Wounds of Jesus"[195] and showed how these two songs are associated in the experience of a Christian. Whoever first learns to sing the former in spirit and in truth will be able to say the latter, which we will learn next week, with equal truth.

When we have finished with the songs of the first part, we plan, if God grants life and strength, to undertake the songs in the *Extract*, which have been taken from the second part. Some of them are truly incomparably beautiful, such as "Thou, the Light of my Eyes," "Mary chose the Better Part," and "Jesus, Lord of Splendor."[196] We would like to have the melodies that were printed separately in Halle so that we can remove the mistakes that have crept into even the well known songs whose melodies appear in this little book, for this could be easily done in our congregation. We ourselves have formerly learned many melodies wrongly in various passages, which we only realized when we had the music in our hands. The old songs are equally dear to us; and many that were nearly forgotten are again sung here, e.g. "Awake, oh Man," "In the Midst of Life," and "Worldly Honor and Temporal Wealth."[197]

Monday, the 7th of August. I was given a couple of peaches that could not find their equal in Germany for size and delicious flavor. Here in this country there are many kinds of peaches, which differ in size, color, and taste. The trees grow up very quickly and some bear fruit in the second year but most of them in the third year. We had already supplied ourselves with a number of such trees in Old Ebenezer, which we have brought to our new place; and from these we enjoyed some fruit already last year. In the spring of this year all the trees blossomed exceptionally beautifully, but then several severe night frosts and cold winds came so that only a few remained. However, because we have many trees, we are getting as many peaches as we and our families need for our refreshment. God provides us in this wilderness with all sorts of good things that we could not have imagined when we first arrived. Everything comes, my Lord, from Thee!

We have again received rainy weather, which is good for the rice and sweet potatoes. God is giving us the weather we wish; and our dear people would have a beautiful harvest despite the long drought if only they had not planted the foreign corn. The orphanage itself has lost from thirty to forty bushels. The said corn has small ears and grains; and it begins to spoil and go to seed before it is ripe. A few people have planted only local corn, which, in places where adequate work was done, is more beautiful this year than we have ever seen it. May God preserve for us the blessing He has shown, and may we enjoy it to His glory and with hearty gratitude.

Tuesday, the 8th of August. This morning we laid the foundation for my dear colleague's house, after having spoken and prayed with the workers on the building site. Shortly before that, in the regular lesson in the orphanage prayer meeting, I had spoken the words from Matthew 8:20, "The Son of Man hath not where to lay his head;" and I used this verse at the laying of the foundation to the benefit of myself and the others. For we must thank the voluntary poverty of this loving Son of Man, our Savior, that our heavenly Father grants us so much good from His rich treasures from His kingdoms of nature and grace, and it is a great benefaction as well that He now wishes to grant my dear colleague a regular comfortable dwelling, from which He will receive much praise and thanks for this and other benefactions and in which much other good will be accomplished to His glory and for the good of the congregation. Since autumn is coming, I have had my hut repaired once more and will spend enough on it to have glass windows set into the open holes, because my weak constitution suffers much from the air, moisture, and variable weather. If it is the will of the Father that a house be built for me, then these glass windows can always be used again.

At about noon my dear colleague returned to us safe and sound. Mr. Causton has given a favorable answer to the letter I sent him; and, at my request, he has also sent large and small nails to Mrs. Arnsdorf and Mrs. Helfenstein for building their huts.

Wednesday, the 9th of August. [Mr. Thilo is still sick with fever. We would like to serve him in every possible way, and we often offer ourselves for that purpose. We have put at his service everything God has granted in the way of foodstuffs, medicines, and other refreshing remedies; and we refuse nothing that he asks for or send for if it is at all possible to do it. We cannot approve of his diet and therapeutic method, because they do not concur with the methods of the late Dr. Richter or of Prof. Juncker, whose cures, as I know, have had good results for me and others through divine care.]

We are planning to go to the Lord's Table next Sunday; and therefore I take every possible opportunity to talk, according to their condition, with those who registered for it last Sunday. The prayer meetings are also aimed at this undertaking. A man asked me whether I would let him go to Communion. I told him he should know himself how he stood with his Savior and whether he was seriously resolved to prepare himself with His mercy for this important undertaking. He gave as his answer that he felt sick and needed a physician and medicine,[198] and that he hoped the Lord would accept him too. He was well able to tell me what he was lacking and what he had to do, and wished to do, to achieve salvation in Christ. The song "Here lies my Soul,"[199] from which I clarified and applied verses seven and eight last Sunday, were most impressive for him because they suited him very well.

The condition of the housekeeping and of the children in the orphanage requires that one thing and another be investigated, put in order, and solved at a given time; and for this purpose I have assigned an hour after dinner on Wednesdays and Saturdays. Sometimes my dear colleague is also present. A book is kept in which the good or bad behavior of each and every child is written under his name; and, if he has deserved punishment, the nature of the punishment is also added. We hope that some good will be accomplished through this method and that misbehavior can be prevented. May the dear Lord grant His blessing to this, as He is asked to do at this conference at both the beginning and end of the hour.

Thursday, the 10th of August. A woman had wrongfully acquired a couple of strings of black coral in Germany, which she brought to me. They must have cost very little; and, because I did not know what to do with them, I gave them to an Indian, who soon thereafter sent his wife to me with a beautiful piece of venison, which was given to the orphans. This was better than if we had given the useless necklace to a poor child.

Friday, the 11th of August. A man complained greatly because of his lack of faith, in which the dear Lord has now put him to shame. Because the drought lasted so long, it seemed to him that he would have an even poorer harvest this time than last year, and in his distrust he said this to my dear colleague; but now God is granting him so much corn and beans that he can be very content. I reminded him of what we had read from the Gospel of St. Luke 5:1 ff. concerning the very dry weather at that time and the apparent crop failure, namely, that the dear Lord continues to treat His children as He did Peter and his friends: He let their net tear, as if he wished to take back the blessing He had given, yet He could also preserve him in the face of all danger, if it served for His glory and man's salvation. He had done this with Peter, and now He is doing it with us; and this should strengthen us in our belief and faith in our almighty and at the same time abundantly good God.

Another young man complained to me that he recognizes all too little his miserable state of sin, for which he can shed no tears even though he hears that others do so. Likewise, he often goes to his neighbor to edify himself with him by reading and praying; but he finds that the other, who cannot read, receives no edification from his reading, because he occupies himself with other things, speaks frivolously, etc. He wished to tell me this so that I would know whether or not he and the others were following the advice I had given them about this. I gave him the necessary instruction and prayed with him. God began His work in him some time ago, and he shows sincerity in well applying the grace he has received.

Saturday, the 12th of August. A Salzburger sent his wife to us with a plate full of virgin honey, which he had taken in great quantity from his beehive in his garden. More than a year ago he had set a swarm of wild bees into a hive, and it had remained with him. This honey is more beautiful than that which the Indians and our people sometimes take from the trees in the forest. They usually find it in the tallest trees, which, in addition, stand in swampy areas; and the bees die because they must cut down the trees to get the honey.

[Because of his disorderly behavior, of which some mention was made on the 4th of August, Rauner has been rather disgraced in the community after we got to the bottom of the matter seriously and made some references to it in the prayer meeting. He promises to break entirely with the Frenchman and send him back his old boat that he had lent him (Rauner) for evil purposes. And, whereas he and his wife have sold bread here for this man for several weeks, he will have nothing more to do with it but, at my discretion, will himself bake—and, to be sure, with larger loaves and more conscientiously, than this man does. For which purpose we will make the necessary arrangements, because sick people and some others occasionally need bread, and someone in the community might as well have profit from it, especially this Rauner, who accomplishes very little with his farming even so and therefore hits upon all sorts of schemes. This is better than for the hostile and shameful Frenchman to make money here and cause disorder secretly.]

An unfriendly altercation occurred between two men because of external matters, but I had been prevented from settling it and calming their angry tempers. When I wished to investigate and settle the matter today, they had already reconciled themselves and recognized their rashness on both sides. It is easy for anger and misunderstanding to arise between neighbors because of chickens, pigs, and other livestock, since the people have to live too close beside and behind each other. A house lot given according to the arrangements of the Lord Trustees to each family for its house, stalls, and yard is not more than the eighth part of an acre and is ninety feet long and sixty feet wide. A quarter of an acre would be very convenient for a family and its housekeeping, but this will probably be difficult to change.

Sunday, the 13th of August. Yesterday evening two families of Evangelical Lutheran people came to us to go to the Table of the Lord with our congregation.[200] They arrived only after our penitential and confessional service, so my dear colleague undertook such a service with them this morning. This time thirty-one people in all took Holy Communion. Our loving God has granted us much edification from His gospel all day long. In the morning the listeners were asked, in the name of Christ, to let themselves be reconciled with God; and in the repetition hour I read them an edifying exemplum, in which they could be reminded even more emphatically of the excellent and salutary dogma of the necessity and possibility of reconciliation.

Monday, the 14th of August. The surveyor, who has surveyed our gardens and plantations but has not yet completely finished them, came to us on Saturday, because Mr. Causton had sent him a letter about it. This morning I came to terms with him about a matter that means a great deal to me and am now letting him go, because he claims unavoidable business on his own plantation in Purysburg. He promises to come back within four weeks and to put everything in order for the good of the community, according to our judgment. It is probably too hot for him now to survey; besides he fears the snakes, which are now very dangerous.

Tuesday, the 15th of August. Mrs. N. [Spielbiegler] had me called to her yesterday evening and asked for private Communion, because she thinks herself near death. She complained bitterly about herself and her corrupted heart and evinced remorse and shame for her so numerous sins she committed against all the Lord's commandments since her youth. I admonished her to ask God zealously to reveal to her the dreadful corruption which is found in her too because of man's fall, and through which she has so often offended her benevolent God and Savior, also to bring her to a sincere remorse and suffering because of it, and to bring her to a true faith in her Redeemer. If she would prepare herself in this way, I said, then I would administer Holy Communion to her early this morning. This I did, and she showed herself very humble and desirous of salvation both during the confession and absolution and also while partaking of the body and blood of Jesus Christ in the Sacrament. May God help her to prepare herself in time for blessed eternity, for otherwise things will look bad for her and her son. She wished to take Communion with other people last Sunday, but her physical weakness did not allow her to do so. She has been sick and weak for a long time, yet she has been able to walk around for a few hours of the day.

As time goes on, our dear Lord is further helping the man who recently freed himself through confession and restitution from the muck that God has gradually revealed to him in his conscience, with the result that his heart is coming closer and closer to a reconciliation and peace with God in the blood of Jesus Christ. He has suffered difficult struggles; and for a long time his wounded heart could not seize the least comfort from the gospel, even though he listened to the most significant Biblical passages with constant sighs and prayers. Nevertheless, his trust in divine truth and mercy remained constantly firm, and he believed that our loyal God, who is a lover of life, would still let the hour come in which He would assure him of His grace, even if no comfort at all would take hold in his heart now. He well knew how very defiled his poor heart and conscience were and that they would have to be scoured and burnished if they were to become a vessel in which God could lay His mercy and the treasures of His salvation. And, because God has assaulted him so hard both inwardly and outwardly, yet not as hard as he thought he deserved, he considered it a gracious sign that He had not yet rejected him but rather was working on him in this very way so that things might fare better with him.

Whenever edifying gospel verses [that were well known to him] were recited to him, he was very pleased with them despite all his pangs of conscience and his despairing condition; and he repeated them out loud very often and presented them to his dear God as his true thought. He also asked his family and the people who were helping him to remind him of such verses again if he should forget them because of his very weakened memory (because he had not been able to sleep during his entire sickness). He had received much splendid profit from the verse: "Look unto me, and be ye saved, all the ends of the earth" along with the story of the fiery serpent.[201] Because of his very weak memory I was accustomed to explain the verses through exempla and stories from the Old and New Testaments. To be sure, he has not entirely recovered; yet God is showing a marked improvement in his body and mind and he is actually feeling a few comforting rays from the sun of mercy. In his miserable physical condition and much suffering God is giving him great patience and an untiring desire for his salvation in Christ. At the same time he is grateful from his heart for every drop of water or anything else that is given him, and he considers himself entirely unworthy of any benefaction. Who could fail to perceive from this frame of mind that the new Creature[202] is appearing in him and that, if he remains loyal, he will finally come to a blessed end? If the Lord helps him through, then he will guard himself all his life long from such affliction of soul and never forget to warn others against the deception of sin and to tell them what the Lord has done for his soul.

Wednesday, the 16th of August. The surveyor from Savannah[203] came to us at our repeated request in order to see whether my dear colleague's house is being built on the right spot. He found no fault with what the carpenters had measured out; rather he was amazed and delighted that such a pleasant region had been made, in so short a time and through the people's industry and God's blessing, out of the wilderness that he himself had surveyed for our town. He gave me hope that Mr. Oglethorpe, who is now expected hourly in Savannah with several ships, will gladly advance the means for building me a house; and he promised to put in a word for us if the occasion arose.

Last night a Salzburger slaughtered a fattened ox and sold the meat in the community, which was very welcome to the people who were not well. Several people have raised young oxen that are now more than three years old and are therefore right for slaughter. They earn their money in this way just as well as if they sold them away in Savannah or to the Lord Trustees, and in addition the fresh meat is a great service to the community. It would be most advantageous if they could exchange such oxen for cows, but there is no opportunity for this since Mr. Causton will not let go of a single head of the Trustees' cattle in Old Ebenezer.

Thursday, the 17th of August. Our cattle herds, of which there are two, are now so large that they cannot find enough food; and therefore the community has decided to keep the calves, of which there are many, separate; and for this reason today and tomorrow they are building a hut for the herdsman and a pen for the calves. The cattle cost the people much to be sure, but they receive much advantage from them that should gradually increase. To help the community we do what we can with the benefactions that come into our hands, otherwise our people would not be able to afford to supply four herdsmen with clothes, provisions, and some money.

We have already received the sad news from Savannah several times that two men of the German indentured servants there have lost their lives miserably. The Reformed schoolmaster, who however has had no opportunity to run a school, has been killed by a tree in the forest; and another man has been shot to death by his comrade, with whom he wished to shoot a deer.[204] We hear nothing but unpleasant things about these people; and Mr. Causton and others in whose service they are suffer thousandfold annoyance from them. Of those who belong to our Evangelical Lutheran confession there are very few, and these we expect to be able to keep in order through God's grace and aid. We also work as much as possible on the others with all sincerity. [Most of them are Reformed and some of them are Catholic; but, because they are all German and most of them come to hear the word of the Lord, people in Savannah consider them to be our congregation and co-religionists, even though, whenever necessary, I have revealed to Mr. Causton and others the great difference in religion that is found among these people.]

Friday, the 18th of August. Because we have no carpenter and cabinet maker in our community, the clockmaker Mueller is applying himself to such work and makes everything very neatly and industriously. He has a large family, is very poor, and can accomplish little with his family in farming, especially since a very poor piece of land was alloted to him; and therefore I am pleased that we can give him an opportunity to earn something in this way. He can make almost anything that he sees; and he works not only in wood but also in bone, iron, and other tractable things. It is also easy to get along with him, since he and his family observe the Lord's word diligently and are pleased with what is good. His father may have been a very honest man with whom the late Mr. Elers [Oelers] had many dealings in the paper business. This clockmaker is actually a papermaker, who additionally learned to make wooden clocks and has also practiced other kinds of mechanics. Since he is very poor, I shall recommend him to Mr. Causton as a useful man so that he will grant him some assistance, as he is accustomed to do for such people. We are very pleased when we can have our work done by people in the community; for letting others do it causes too much difficulty and expense. If we had a shoemaker and smith, then we would be more or less supplied with artisans.

Saturday, the 19th of August. This afternoon word was brought to me from Old Ebenezer that a courier had ridden through there and hurried to Savannah to announce there that a troop of hostile Spaniards are gathered higher up in the country and that not much good was expected of them. However, we hardly believe that they would dare go so far into the country, which is full of forests and without beaten trails, since their retreat, as well as all provisions, might be cut off by the Indians, who are friends of this colony. People all over the country are congratulating themselves about the many soldiers and warships Mr. Oglethorpe is bringing with him, and as a result one may believe oneself safe here.

Sunday, the 20th of August. Since the Holy Communion service a certain person [old Mrs. Spielbiegler] has somewhat regained her physical strength and shows herself very joyful for the dear gift of Christ's body and blood that she received in the sacrament. In spite of that, the foundation of her Christianity is very weak, since she knows no more about conversion and rebirth than what she reads about it in the Bible and hears in our sermons and conversation/yet all this without experience/. She complains so violently about her youthful sins and attests so much remorse about them that, if we did not understand her language, we would think that she is penitent. When she tells something about her past life, we well hear that she makes nothing of various and even punishable deeds and injustices; or even worse, she laughs and is frivolous about this or that deed by which she has surely offended God. For example, in her homeland she broke the authorities' severe laws by receiving game and fish from the local poachers and hunters and selling them outside the country, whereby she earned much money. Likewise, much disorder and fraud took place in her other buying and selling [distilling and selling brandy], which she will recognize as a sin and ask God's forgiveness for, only as a favor to me. She well knew the verse "Submit yourselves to every ordinance of man for the Lord's sake," and also that you should obey even the "forward" masters, provided their orders are not contrary to one's conscience or the word of God.[205] Yet she does not think that she has actually committed a mortal sin in such deeds. How much we would like this poor person to be saved, since she [as good as walks on her grave and] is no longer far from eternity and the judgment. God give us wisdom! She admits much when we speak with her; but, once she begins contradicting and excusing herself, there is no end of it and it causes in her [in her son] more bitterness than edification.

Monday, the 21st of August. Yesterday Mr. Causton sent me a letter in which he requested our boat, with which four Salzburgers are to bring a family of indentured German servants up to the sawmill in Old Ebenezer, for which he wishes to pay. The Lord Trustees are spending a lot of money for the mill there, but it is still in a bad condition. If they obtain loyal people for this work, some day as many boards should be cut as they will need for the highway that is to lead from Old Ebenezer to Savannah, and also in the reverse direction to Palachocolas. For I hear that they will also use boards for it, perhaps in order to build bridges over various small rivers and the many swamps that are found all around. We would not and could not buy boards there and bring them here by land (for it is not possible by water) even if we received them almost as gifts. If a passage should be opened by land or on Ebenezer Creek, this would cause great expense, since, after the passage was made, large boats or horses and wagons would be required. At our place two Salzburgers cut a hundred feet for six shillings sterling. Perhaps more of them would apply themselves to board cutting if something were being constructed among us.

This evening in the prayer hour we had the 36th chapter of Numbers and thereby, God be praised, finished the entire Book of Numbers. I am looking forward eagerly to the beautiful Book of Deuteronomy, in which so much glory and splendor is to be found. And since our dear God has so far granted us much edification from our previous contemplation of the stories and from His statutes, for which His name has been greatly praised, we now promise ourselves His further aid and blessing, provided we are all sincerely concerned with the truth in them. During my first meditation concerning the Book of Deuteronomy I was much impressed by the fact that, in beginning His teaching office and in struggling against demonic attack (Matthew 4), the Lord Jesus first of all held up this book and three verses from it (v. 4, 7, 10), and used them as the sword of the spirit to overcome the enemy. If the Savior respected this book so highly, how much more should we cherish it? There must certainly be much in it.

Tuesday, the 22nd of August. N. N. [the younger Zuebly] was violently attacked about a week ago by a fever, for which our wise Lord must have a salutary purpose. His unvirtuous acts, which are sometimes intermixed with hastiness, are now clearly revealed to him and have almost melted away; and now he seems much more honest to me than he used to be. His new resolution is most sincere. He has acquired a new and very great love for His word, and recognizes with humility and hearty gratitude the blessing that our loving God has granted to our place above others in this country and its neighborhood.

[If he corrects his fault of polylogy[206] and and lets himself be brought to greater firmness in what is good and to discretion in his speech and general behavior, then he can become a useful tool among us.

[The old Zuebly is honest at heart; but, because of his weak understanding and natural simplicity, he is unable to test everything that is said to him, and therefore he was formerly misled by his brother along with others to transgress through premature judgments. I hope that God will turn both of them into the kind of people who not only behave honorably and honestly but will also be useful to their neighbors in spiritual matters and will be a joy for us. Since they are extremely poor and were rejected and abandoned by their rich brother in Purysburg, we help them as much as we can. Our poor box is now entirely exhausted, but the river of God is still flowing and will surely reach us in its own good time.]

The heat of the day has been very great yesterday and today; while the dog days were quite bearable the weather now seems to be making up for it intensely. We hope it will not last long, the nights are cool and very pleasant. Some people in the community are being attacked by fever, but they are soon free of it again. This summer God has graciously spared our congregation from the violent and longlasting fever which we have had to suffer for two years in a row in New Ebenezer; and this is a kind benefaction which is recognized by all honest people with heartfelt gratitude.

Wednesday, the 23rd of August. The conference hour, which I hold on Wednesdays and Saturdays in the orphanage, is very useful in promoting good order in the housekeeping and among the children. [Today we made an example of Mrs. Helfenstein's oldest boy[207] and of a girl from Purysburg, with a real punishment; and this made a great impression. The housemaster[208] has a great deal of work, and his wife is more often sick than well with her female complaints; and therefore the children sometimes lack supervision and misbehave. We are in great need of a supervisor for the children, but one cannot be found at the present time, nor can we hope for one, since we would have to pay him with money for his efforts. God gives one thing at a time; and we wish to recommend this important matter to His providence also.

[We likewise greatly need a maid in the housekeeping, since the girls are still very weak and must go to school. One of the oldest and most orderly of the girls helps Mr. Thilo outside of school hours and is sent by him on errands. Catherine Holtzer, who can almost do a full maid's housework, begged us insistently to let her move into the house of the Austrian Schmidt. The housemaster has always treated her as a father, yet she did not wish to recognize this but made many bitter complaints until we agreed to her moving out. However, she was scarcely out of the orphanage before she regretted it; and she has already begged me several times with tears to take her back again, because she now sees the difference in the work and other things. Nevertheless, I do not see that she is suffering any harm, rather she is made to observe order in all physical and spiritual ways; and therefore I will hardly let myself be persuaded to take her back into the orphanage, especially since, through her lies and calumny, she has caused trouble between Kalcher and Schmidt, who had acted quite a bit too hastily. Since then he has recognized and admitted his mistake several times, after having gotten to know the girl more closely.]

I was unable to get any clear idea of the surveyed plantations because I lacked a map made by the surveyor. Now that I have received it from the surveyor, I am astonished to see that he has extended our plantations more than half an English mile beyond Old Ebenezer [which surely is not a sensible thing]. As Mr. Causton has mentioned several times, the Lord Trustees intend to settle this Old Ebenezer; and for that purpose a sawmill has already been built at great expense. Moreover, the Trustees have a large herd of cows and calves there, from which all pasture would be cut off, and all land would be taken away from future inhabitants, if our plantations were to reach so far. Moreover, who would be able to keep his possessions in his field? The man probably did this in his own interest, because it is ten times easier for him to survey our land in such pine forests than on good soil that is covered with many trees, bushes, thorns, and reeds.[209]

On the left side of our village there is an island that doubtless is much, if not all, good soil, and on which our plantations would not come too close to Abercorn or any other place. In order to get some reliable information about this, I plan to send some knowledgeable people there as soon as possible to inspect the region for a few days; and then I shall urge the surveyor to survey here and to drop the four miles that he has surveyed in the area of Old Ebenezer. When I explained this to him, I noticed that he did not wish to undertake the work because he did not expect any pay from Mr. Oglethorpe; but we would rather pay the costs ourselves than do without the good land in our neighborhood. We had already told him several times that he should also survey a piece of land across Abercorn Creek, and therefore on this island, for the community; but at the time he excused himself by saying that he was not permitted to go across this creek as long as he could find enough land between

Ebenezer Creek and Abercorn Creek. But now we can well see that that was only a [miserable] excuse. He has not yet surveyed the land for the ministers, which is to amount to 600 acres, or for the schoolmaster, or the gentleman-lots /lots for people of high rank/; and I do not know where he will turn. [Such dishonest and selfish people do much harm, as is also the complaint in Purysburg.,]

Thursday, the 24th of August. [The Austrian Schmidt] the sick man on whose soul our dear Lord has been working so successfully for a fundamental conversion, and whom we have mentioned several times, God has now helped through in Truth; and God has let him experience what we could have assured him in advance from God's infallible promises: namely, "For peace I had great bitterness: /but thou hast in love to my soul delivered it from the pit of corruption: for thou hast cast all my sins behind thy back."/ He now clearly recognizes how well God means it with that soul which He attacks severely and allows to feel what great pain and sorrow it causes if one deserts the Lord God. Corruption lies deep, and therefore God must strike deeply. Someone had already told him of yesterday's prayer meeting; and I added to it today and showed him that the ancient Jews had not (alone) been kept from possessing the promised Canaan by transgressing against divine law and had also incurred God's wrath and punishment by the grave sin of worshiping the golden calf, and especially by unbelief, /which is the source of all sin/ (Hebrews IV). Likewise in the New Testament, those who reject the Physician Christ and His medicine through unbelief cannot possibly be saved, even though God in Christ is able and willing to save the greatest sinners. I read him the last page of the *Treasure Chest*,[210] which was incomparably dear to both me and him. The words are worth being read often to souls that are dumb and deeply bent with the feeling of their sins.

With our boat I received a letter from Savannah that requested me to come down and baptize the child of a German family. My dear colleague undertook the journey and hopes to be here again by Sunday. We like to serve the people if anything can be done for their souls. Our boat brought four of the German indentured servants, who comprise a family. They too are coming to the sawmill at Old Ebenezer and to the Lord Trustees' cattle. The women are free to do some planting for their own use, as those who arrived some time ago are doing loyally and diligently; but, because of the thin soil, they are accomplishing little without manure.

Friday, the 25th of August. The heat in the daytime is still very great, greater than at any other time this year. This weather is good for the rice and corn, which are now ripening; also, the beans and sweet potatoes are suffering no harm, because we had enough rain before this heat spell. It is burdensome for the working people. Until now six men have been working on my colleague's house and have not let themselves be held up by this very hot weather. They work most loyally and without any self-interest, otherwise they would spare themselves a bit more. The entire house is now fully finished, except that the floors are yet to be laid and the stairs, windows, and doors must be installed. To be sure, it has amounted to more than we first expected, but then it is a solid and well built structure. If the members of the congregation had not contributed much work without pay, if the carpenters had not exerted themselves exceptionally, and if the lumber had not been so near, then the costs would have easily come to 50 £ sterling, whereas they now remain between 30 and 40 £ sterling. However, it still lacks a kitchen, stables, and other necessary structures, which will demand new expenditures. Praise be to God, who has let it come so far with His fatherly providence that at least one of us already has a house; for the other He will also provide in due time. It was the same in Old Ebenezer; one had to wait for the other, and finally we were both provided for.

Because Senior Urlsperger and Court Chaplain Ziegenhagen are giving 14 £ sterling and the Lord Trustees have allowed 10 £ for a house, this house has been built on one of the lots destined for the ministers; and the other lot will remain empty until Mr. Oglethorpe has something built for me. There will probably be no lack of intercessions in this regard, since Mr. Causton, Col. Stephens, and others are affectionately inclined toward me and well recognize the need of a regular and well built dwelling because of my office and my physical and domestic circumstances. For good reasons I do not begrudge my dear colleague for coming first, for the hand of the Lord is certainly in this. If our heavenly Father should allow me to receive some temporal wealth that I did not need for my maintenance, I would like to build, on a private lot that would remain the property of my family after my departure, a durable house that would be only a few steps from my dear colleague's house. Meanwhile, may the Lord Trustees be moved to have a parsonage built. But nothing through my own will and self-interest.

[Mrs. Helfenstein's oldest son is not behaving well and passes his time in idleness and perhaps in many secret sins too. Therefore I spoke with his mother, who asserted that she was unable to keep him in order and therefore felt great sorrow that her warnings and admonitions from the word of God were having no effect on him. She let us understand very clearly that he had been corrupted among the Herrnhuters in Savannah, where he was to learn the shoemaker's trade.[211] However, we have long known him to be a good-for-nothing. I informed him[212] that we would gladly lend a hand to disciplining him and would take every precaution if she wished to send him to school, since he was idle most of the time anyway. This pleased her very much. I also spoke to the boy, who is already sixteen years old; and he declared himself willing to go to school and to the preparation for Holy Communion. Some time ago Mrs. Helfenstein and Mrs. Rheinlaender became very familiar; and since then their boys have been running around together to hunt and fish, and the Helfenstein boy has become even more disorderly.]

Saturday, the 26th of August. This morning my dear colleague returned from Savannah and brought the news that the preacher there [Mr. Whitefield] has just returned home from Frederica and is now resolved to travel next Monday morning to Charleston and from there to London on a ship that is lying ready. Some important circumstance must be pressing his voyage, since it had been set for a later date. I hastily wrote a letter to Court Preacher Ziegenhagen and the praiseworthy Society. [I also found time to write to Senior Urlsperger and Prof. Francke, if only hurriedly and briefly; may they forgive me for this in their paternal affection.] Mr. Oglethorpe is expected any day, and many more ships, at which time we hope to receive some letters. Because many ships loaded with rice return in the autumn, we plan to write in more detail then, if the Lord gives us life and health [strength]. My dear colleague has also written an inspirational letter to the last three missionaries in Tranquebar.[213] May the Lord bless all this to His glory!

Sunday, the 27th of August. We must praise the Lord and our Savior in that He has again blessed this day in us and some of our listeners. How the Lord fulfills His promise to bless richly the Sabbath in those who will but bring a heart hungry for mercy; this we see by the dumbest souls in our congregation. Therefore, those who remain without blessing in the glorious, blessed time of the New Testament, and thus on the days of the Lord, will one day have to blame themselves when they have to give an accounting.

Monday and Tuesday, the 28th and 29th of August. On these two days I had to go to Savannah because of the letters and diary. [Mr. Whitefield again received me with much tender brotherly love, inasmuch as he is as kindly disposed toward both of us as if we were his special colleagues.] The minister in Savannah told me how mightily the dear Lord had awakened the spirits of the people in Frederica through the Word of Truth, which he had preached there several times, how he had made many more listeners thirst for it, and how his pending departure had [therefore] saddened them and caused many tears. In Savannah, too, almost everyone showed respect for him, and he was accompanied by many wishes of godspeed and by requests that he return soon. In Darien, a town situated not far from Frederica, he had become well acquainted with the [Presbyterian] minister there.[214] He attested gladly that the spirit of Jesus Christ dwells in that minister and showed me a letter he had written [to Mr. Whitefield] from which I too could recognize [the beautiful foundation of his heart and] his [honest] intent to advance true godliness in his people and others.

This minister [Mr. Whitefield] left a note behind in which he instructed the schoolmaster there[215] (a likewise honest man [who is bound to us in love]) to give our Salzburgers various items from the things that would come with the next ship. He also promised voluntarily to remember our congregation like his own both before God and men. In addition to the ordination that he desires, the only reason for his present hurried return to England is that he wishes to recommend the poor inhabitants of this colony highly to the honest and charitable people there in sermons and otherwise. In this he promises himself divine blessing and good success, since he knows how willingly many Englishmen will contribute once they know for what purpose their money is being spent. In the meanwhile the schoolmaster is holding public morning and evening prayer hours until he [Mr. Whitefield] returns, which he will do as soon as possible.

Wednesday, the 30th of August. [Mrs. Rheinlaender has returned from her trip. During her absence things were very tranquil here; but now that she is here again, we are justifiably worried, from past experience, that she will again cause disturbance and worry. Nevertheless, she will probably not do this for long; for the Lord will take her from us when her measure is full. She and her family have enjoyed much good among us but have not showed the least trace of true gratitude toward God or man. Because her annoyances are so apparent and are not followed by any remorse, we no longer consider her a member of the congregation; and we shall no longer let her partake of anything that our dear benefactors in Europe might send here for the good of the Salzburgers. Mr. Causton is so disgusted with her that he would like to see her move away from this colony as soon as possible, since she, like her renegade husband, has caused only harm by her lying and calumny.]

The recent very hot weather has abated, and it is now cool and pleasant because of the rain that has fallen. Our people's rice is very beautiful everywhere, except that the birds[216] are doing much damage because the work elsewhere prevents the people from keeping watch over it. So far we have lacked a rice mill, and because our carpenters have never built one and it would cost much time and money if they did, I inspected a compendious rice mill in Savannah. In Purysburg I found a man who knows how to make such mills; and soon he will come to us to build one for the orphanage, which will serve as a model for others in the community.

Thursday, the 31st of August. I called on N. N. [Bartholomew Rieser] at his hut in order to awaken his family to earnestness in their Christianity and to remind them of what has been told them in recent days from God's word. The husband was not at home. The wife told me that her husband has been praying much more diligently for some time and that things were beginning to go better with him. The three children are sluggish with regard to what is good, even if they are now more orderly in external matters and in their work than they used to be in former times. The mother told me with many tears of a frightful dream, which gave me an opportunity to warn her children about the danger of their souls.

Four of our men have inspected the land across Abercorn Creek, which lies right in our neighborhood; they find it so low, to be sure, that it may be inundated every year by high water. However, it is so fertile and pleasant that one could ask for nothing better. We shall do our best to persuade the surveyor to take up here the four miles that now extend beyond Old Ebenezer. Also, the land that belongs to the church and the school for the ministers and the schoolmaster should be surveyed in this region.

SEPTEMBER

Friday, the 1st of September. Schoolmaster Ortmann has harvested a good supply of corn on the four acres that he has received from the congregation as two gardens, and in addition he can expect some beans and rice. He told me that he would have harvested about a hundred bushels had he not planted the alien yellow corn.[217] That is a general complaint that cannot be helped this time, but it may make people more cautious next time.

A woman who suffers many pains because of a certain severe physical injury told me that she could ignore all these pains if only she might reach certainty of her state of grace. The pangs of conscience that she feels because of her sins surpass all physical pains, etc. In her struggling prayer today, our dear Lord had granted her a glimpse of His mercy, and by this her depressed spirit was somewhat comforted. Some time ago God let her and her husband receive about 6 £ sterling from someone, which she would like to donate to the poor box as restitution for an injustice she committed several years ago. However, she had not had the heart to tell her husband and to ask for his consent, but had presented the matter to the dear Lord for so long in her prayers that He finally granted her a joyful heart and an opportunity to do it; and she found her husband fully ready and willing to do so. However, for good reason I hesitate to accept this offer right off: it must first receive more prayer and deliberation.

Saturday, the 2nd of September. My dear colleague journeyed to Savannah this morning, again to preach the word of the Lord to the Germans there. May God grant him to accomplish much good for His glory and the salvation of the souls there. I gave him a note for the English schoolmaster, which the latter is to forward if possible to the minister [Mr. Whitefield] who is departing. The clockmaster Mueller asked me to procure for him [through Mr. Whitefield] a mold for pouring pewter spoons and also strong wire for hackling flax (for which he also needs white lead). Both are very necessary, he said. Perhaps Court Preacher Ziegenhagen will help us in this if the English minister [Mr. Whitefield] has already left Charleston before the letter reaches him. It is a great advantage for the community when things that we need can be made at our place. It is cheaper in this way, and one person can support himself from the other. The shoemakers take much money from our place; and a Christian man could support himself very well here so that he would not have to work in the field at all during the entire year. He should also understand the preparation of leather; for then the advantage would be all the greater for him, and the people would be better provided for. An oxhide here costs only 2 sh. sterling, and such hides are easy to obtain.

Toward evening I received word that some of the cows that had run away from our herd a year or more ago had been brought to Old Ebenezer, and those who know them are urgently ordered to fetch them. This will cause them disturbance and inconvenience tomorrow;[218] but it cannot be avoided, since other cattle are going to be driven to Savannah. Mr. Causton had given orders that all cattle between Savannah and Palachocolas must be sought out and rounded up. Then those that belong to the Lord Trustees will be marked with a branding iron, at which occasion the cattle that belong here will turn up again.[219] We are still missing several head, and this gives us hope. To be sure, it will cause our people new expenses, since they will have to pay 3 sh. sterling for each cow or ox; yet it is a benefaction for them to recover their cattle.

Sunday, the 3rd of September. This morning we treated the regular gospel Luke 17:11 ff. concerning belief in the Lord Jesus; and we repeated this exceedingly necessary, salutary, and blessed material in the afternoon. In the actual repetition hour we read the beautiful and fundamental examination as to whether one believes in Jesus or not, which is found at the end of the precious little booklet: *Dogma of the Commencement of Christian Life*;[220] and we impressed this upon them with necessary application. Contrary to my expectations our dear Lord strengthened me very noticeably for holding the repetition hour; and He soon let me know the reason for this by blessing it most of all, as I learned this very evening.

A young Salzburger accosted me and attested that God is pulling on him mightily but that so far he has been so frivolous that the grace proffered by God could not take root. He had not, he said, been able to tear himself away properly from his comrades, whose material and worldly conversations always deprived him of what was good. I told him how loyal it was of God to allow him to recognize these obstacles to his penetrating into the Kingdom of God;[221] and I told him this and that about the possibility and salvation of true Christianity, and then I prayed with him. He requested a sheet of paper and ink in order to write down some of the verses and impress them on his mind. Our dear Lord reminds many souls through His Word that there is no lack of good resolutions and promises, as was the case with the Israelites in Deuteronomy 5:28; where it is also said from the mouth of the Lord, who trieth the hearts and reins:[222] "Oh that there were such a heart in them" (v. 29). This verse should be presented to the listeners at tomorrow's evening prayer meeting in its whole context, in that they should not be satisfied with resolutions and promises but should be concerned with a new heart and a solid foundation.

Monday, the 4th of September. In the hut of a sick married couple I examined a girl about yesterday's sermon and added this and that very simply for her edification, and the dear Lord blessed this in both of them to the praise of His name. Yesterday the wife had been troubled that she had not been able to come to the meeting; but she had given herself and her husband hope that I would come to them today and communicate with them. Both of them were overjoyed when I told her that, upon leaving the school, I had wished to remain in tranquility and pray privately to the Father and afterwards go to another family, but that I had been hindered in both and had been almost impelled to come to their hut. Before the prayer I cited for them the verse: "Lord, thou hast heard the desire of the humble;" and I said that the merciful Savior would not neglect any soul, not even a sick one, who earnestly desired Him and His gospel. I visited several more families, of which I found only some persons at home; yet even in them I noted that they had not listened to the word of the Lord in vain. May everything be commended to His further mercy and blessing, and to His glory.

Tuesday, the 5th of September. This morning before daybreak my dear colleague came back from Savannah and brought the news that Mr. Causton wishes to send pigs and poultry for the third transport as a result of my repeated requests, for which purpose several people should go down and fetch them. I asked Mr. Causton to send the livestock for the third transport in proportion to the full number of people brought by Mr. von Reck, without deducting for those who had left or died. In that way they would receive in all eleven hogs and a like number of turkeys and geese, and thus not five but four people would share in each. From the man who brought the cattle for the third transport I learned that Mr. Causton had ordered him to bring twelve head, which have now been distributed among the people.

[Today I read the letter from the Lord Trustees again and found that if five persons should have only one cow, then the first fifty-five persons who arrived should have been sent eleven, and for this reason I must speak with Mr. Causton. If he should not allow that many, I shall have to see how I can make it good.

[Christ is restless again in the orphanage and causes the

manager and his wife worry and vexation with his obstinate hardheadedness. He is tired of the food and complains about it. He is a right miserable soul whom we would like to keep in order in any way possible. If he is to leave the orphanage again, as it appears, then he is running into his perdition.]

Wednesday, the 6th of September. Mrs. N. [Schweighofer] revealed to me that her oldest girl had begged her to ask me to let her go to the preparation for Holy Communion; but the mother requested that she should not be allowed to go to the Lord's Table until she had shown sufficient proof of her conversion and worthy preparation. No greater joy could be given to the woman in this world than to live to see one of her children become a deserving guest at the Lord's Table. She came to me at just the time that our loving God had granted me much refreshment from the words of Isaiah 56:3–8, and with them I showed her convincingly that she did not have to worry about what she had often feared, namely, that God would have to reject her because of her many infirmities and because, as she thought, she was a withered tree, there was no help, etc. Here she would find it clearly expressed, I said, that God would not reject such withered souls as are dissatisfied with themselves. This grace-filled declaration of God gave her much joy, and she noted this chapter very carefully.

I based the preparation for Holy Communion on the order of salvation that Pastor Freylinghausen collected from Holy Writ. The children, of whom there are seven, learn the questions and answers together with the appended verses of proof and clarification. Out of these I present them with the truths of Christian dogma for the practice of godliness, and then I pray concerning these things. Sometimes I read them something edifying, if I chance to find it, so that the desired purpose can gradually be achieved.

[Christ has now changed his mind again and recognizes that he would be doing himself harm if he left the orphanage. Mrs. Rheinlaender had planted this and that in his head; and he himself now recognizes that he would run into his perdition if he were to follow her. Perhaps the poor woman thinks she is hurting me when she persuades people to follow in her footsteps and to move from us to some other place. Anyone who has a spark of goodness in him is disgusted with her insolence and entire nature. If a secular authority were here, would she have fallen into its judicial hands long ago? We have now excluded her.[223] The banishment will press upon her, even if she does not yet feel it.]

Thursday, the 7th of September. The surveyor Ross is now with us again. As he has received a letter from Mr. Causton instructing him to arrange his surveying as we think best, he is willing to survey the good land across Abercorn Creek and, in compensation, to abandon the four miles towards Old Ebenezer. He wished to survey the ministers' land right along the river, in which case, however, the Salzburgers would not be able to use the land they are now hoping for. As recently mentioned, it is inundated from time to time (even if not every year) by the Savannah River, so the people cannot actually build their houses and cow sheds there. Rather they wish to build them on this side of Abercorn Creek, where there is nothing but high land; in fact several of them would build on one plantation and also jointly own the plantation on the opposite side. Presumably good and perhaps even better land will be left for the ministers somewhat further down the river. Righteous people who are ministers here after us will neither think nor say that we did not further their interests, for a true shepherd of souls seeks the best for his spiritual sheep even in physical things.

The watchmaker Mueller and his wife showed me the physical blessings that God has granted them this year in the field and from the garden by their house. Both were joyful, especially because they had not expected what God has let fall to them. It was not really very much; yet it was much for them and a dear blessing of the Lord, which they ascribed to Him and not to their own work. It is a great advantage that our people have planted the gardens in and around the town, where they can protect the crops from birds and other vermin better than in the fields.

Friday, the 8th of September. The dear Lord is now granting us the most fruitful weather we could possibly hope for. Yesterday we had a penetrating rain all day, and today it has already cleared up so beautifully that the soil lacks neither sufficient moisture nor warmth and sunshine. The last corn and beans are now ripening, and this requires dry weather and sunshine. Although everyone has full time work with guarding and harvesting the crops, some people have been found willing to build a fine little house for the widow Arnsdorf. She is receiving much corn and beans and sweet potatoes that she cannot keep in her old and dilapidated hut. She is conducting herself very well among us, and therefore everyone loves and cherishes her even though she is not a Salzburger. For when ill behaved people are not allowed to have their own way in everything or to act according to their wicked and selfish intentions, or when they do not receive the affection of righteous orderly people, they always attribute it to the fact that they are not Salzburgers.

Saturday, the 9th of September. A [Salzburger] woman had great anxiety concerning her husband's and her own Christianity, which she revealed to me during my visit. She said that her husband wished to be the head in matters of work and housekeeping, but not in Christianity, in which he showed no seriousness, and that he was therefore more of a hindrance than a help to his wife in her Christianity. The dear Lord is letting her realize more and more how much is required if a person wishes to enter into heaven through the narrow gates of true conversion and imitation of Christ. Therefore she wished to have in her husband a true helper who would admonish and direct her, as well as chastise her when she was found wanting; and she had often asked him to do so. But he was, she said, too sluggish; and he took it very badly when she reminded him according to her recognition. For example, he became very angry a short time ago when she kindly reminded him in the presence of [two] other men who were in the house that, instead of useless conversation, he should take a book and read something to her and these people. The fact that they could detect so little divine blessing in their physical work was due to the lack of serious prayer, etc.

As she is causing much disturbance in doing this, even though in a legalistic way, and retarding herself in her Christianity, I told her that she was not doing wrong in lovingly and humbly reminding her husband of his duty to himself and to her, his wife. For the rest, she should commend everything to the Lord, pray for him earnestly, and penetrate ever further into sweet communion with the Lord Jesus and into the certainty of her state of grace. That way, I said, she would free herself of all disquiet and anxiety and be put into a position to work all the better on her husband with word and example. The husband conducts himself in an orderly fashion in external matters and is liked in the community. However, he lacks a firm foundation, and therefore he limps on both sides[224] despite all convictions and good resolutions, in which he is not lacking. As is often the case with beginners, the wife is rather legalistic[225] and may well be burdensome to him through unwise, even though never violent, chastisements, which only incite anger.

After the conference in the orphanage the manager showed me some squash in his garden at whose size I had to marvel. I do not remember ever having seen anything like them. They are still quite green and still growing and will presumably become even larger. The soil is very good, and we could not ask for better weather. If the Lord's blessing is added, things will have to flourish. A few days ago the watchmaker showed me a large squash he had taken from his garden, but it did not equal those from the orphanage in size. Everything comes, my Lord, from Thee! The most enjoyable thing was that I was told of two girls, Maria Schweighofer and Magdalena Haberfehner, that they had both begun to seek the grace of God with diligent prayer; and this makes an impression on others.

Sunday, the 10th of September. Both Chapter 8 of Deuteronomy yesterday evening and the regular gospel Matthew 6: 24 ff. today have given us a beautiful opportunity to remember the special providence of our heavenly Father, which has ruled over us so gloriously in this foreign land, and to awaken each other to obedience and righteous gratitude toward this dear and most beloved benefactor. He instructed His people fully forty years in the desert, gave them judges, guardians, and teachers, and chastised and tried them so that the foundation of their hearts would be revealed to their humiliation; yet at the same time He also provided them with bodily food, with clothes and health and, best of all, with the beautiful opportunity to achieve their salvation through well arranged divine services. And since the Lord has deigned to grant us similar spiritual and physical benefactions, we encouraged each other to raise up our Ebenezer once again to His glory.[226]

In the repetition hour, when we reached the opening words of I Kings 18:21, "How long halt ye between two opinions?", I reminded our dear Salzburgers of their former miserable condition in Salzburg; for then, from what they themselves had experienced, they could imagine the miserable condition of the Israelite church in the times of Elijah, when they served the true God in some measure out of respect for the prophets but also served Baal in order to please the godless Queen Jesabel and thus limped on both sides.[227] At the same time the few righteous souls were persecuted or expelled from the land. Now that God has granted them the noble freedom of conscience, I said, all limping and hypocrisy must cease, for God demands One Service and One Concern only. Those poor people are in a really bad way who remained in Salzburg for worldly reasons, although convinced of the truth, and who now follow their own opinion and secretly serve the true God /according to scripture/ while publicly serving the saints and human statutes [Baal and the Roman Antichrist].

[Monday, the 11th of September. Poor Mrs. Rheinlaender is continuing to practice her insolence and vexing behavior and to cause us and those in the congregation much sadness. Yesterday she was in church three times but apparently received not the least benefit from it, as her behavior today toward me, my dear colleague, and other people has shown. In the afternoon my dear colleague preached the divine truths from Galatians 7:7–10, "Whatsoever a man soweth, that shall he also reap" and took 2 Corinthians 5:10 as his exordium. However, she was not brought to any more reflection or even external improvement by this than she had been by the other things that had been preached publicly through God's word and with benefit to other people.

[Because she merely continues in her calumnies and reproaches and has cast off all shame, I told her that I shall write on various points to Mr. Causton and ask him to remove her from us because there is no hope for improvement and she will not even submit to the external order that we rightfully demand of her. She thought to prevent this and travelled with her son to Savannah about noon, presumably in an Indian canoe. In order for Mr. Causton to know how I have been carrying out his orders regarding her and how her behavior has been toward us and the congregation in general, I wrote a rather detailed letter that I sent down this evening in our little boat. It was necessary for my dear colleague to go with it, partly to request instructions from Mr. Causton, who does not like to write his opinion about such matters, and partly to prevent her from being subjected to any civil punishment for the coarse things she has perpetrated against us. Rather, he should merely remove her from us, and she will in any event fall into the hands of the judge soon enough, if no change is made on her part. We had a similar tragedy with Rott, who died miserably, and his wife.[228] When these people do not have their way and cannot act according to their carnal desires, they assail us with such importunity that you may hardly believe it. To be sure, they should offer such treatment to a secular judge! Now the Lord will redeem us from all evil!]

Tuesday, the 12th of September. I called on a pious family, where I found another pious woman who is accustomed to call on them for brotherly and sisterly edification. These dear people were just about to bend their knees before our dear Lord, and I did it with them. After the prayer they were very happy and praised [our good] God, who had blessed my encouragement and help in prayer. They are like hungry doves, which try to make use of every little grain. They also quoted this and that thing that they had found edifying and impressive in the sermon or in simple and private words of exhortation, not only from last Sunday but also from previous times. The wife reminded her husband of a verse that he had heard at a certain prayer meeting in the orphanage but had not understood correctly, so that he might ask me about its proper meaning. Among other things, the wife told me that, when she goes to the river, she thinks of the river of life and everlasting joy which God will grant to believers in eternal life. This gives her joy, and she has hope of reaching there. I told her that she should think of time which is rushing past, and of the verse from Galatians VI that we heard on Sunday: "As we have therefore opportu-

nity."[229] Thereupon she remembered the expression[230] from
the evening hymn "My days are passing speedily, etc. . . . Flow
hence, as does a river, etc."[231]

Wednesday, the 13th of September. [We have news of Mr.
Whitefield that he must now have been at sea some eight days.
In Savannah they have reason to say that Mr. Wesley has journeyed to Germany and will visit the Herrnhuter Brothers, also
that he intends to come to Halle. Letters have come from London to Savannah via Charleston in which the Lord Trustees
have sent orders that some changes are to be made in the
storehouse and in respect of the government of the colony. It
seems that Mr. Causton has many enemies who make all kinds
of accusations against him to the Lord Trustees. It seems to us
that he performs his office honestly, is favorable and helpful to
the industrious and orderly workers, but severe and grievous to
the disorderly. He has shown every possible affection for us and
ours.] People claim certain news that Mr. Oglethorpe can no
longer be far from Georgia. God help him to us safe and sound
and incline his heart to the expansion of our Savior's Kingdom
and the furtherance of all good order.

My dear colleague's house is now entirely finished, except
that it still lacks a door, staircase, and two windows in the upper
story. The people are overloaded with work during this harvest
period, therefore the remaining items must be completed at
another time. He would have occupied the house at this time in
God's name, in fact he invited the dear Salzburgers last Sunday
to its Christian dedication. However, an important obstacle has
arisen against that; and therefore he will have to do the best he
can for a couple more weeks in his former hut. To be sure,
when he moves, we will not be living so near together physically; for until now our two huts could be considered as one and
our yards and gardens as one. But through the grace of God
such physical changes will not separate our spirits the least bit.

His new home lies scarcely forty paces from my hut, so we
shall surely be together often. Perhaps the dear Lord will direct
Mr. Oglethorpe to have a house built for me soon after his arrival, then we will be near again even physically. Mr. Causton said
that the Lord Trustees had set aside 400 £ sterling for four
ministers, but he did not report any details about this or say

what their purpose was.[232] This much I know: at one point the magistrates and other prominent people have talked at table about the inadequate arrangements for the ministers in this land, and Mr. Causton has made very fine suggestions that he has probably made to the Lord Trustees too.

Thursday, the 14th of September. During this harvest season we have to put up with the fact that the older children remain out of school from time to time. They have to pick beans and guard the rice, which is often attacked by the birds. If rain hits the ripe beans (and we have had rain for two days), they burst open or become grey and worthless if they are not quickly picked and dried out again. Like some other people, we have planted cotton in our little gardens, which has prospered well. Out of a little seed grows a large bush, which bears many buds or bolls stuffed with cotton, which finally burst open and present the white wool for the picking. The most inconvenient thing is that the seeds, which consist of large greenish wooly kernels, cling very tightly to the white wool and therefore much picking and pulling is required in order to separate the two.[233] A year ago we received some cotton seeds from the West Indies, which were black and white kernels from which rather tall little trees grew.[234] These, however, all froze in the winter. The cotton is supposed to be taken from these much more easily; but, because they do not bear during the first year but must survive the winter, they cannot be used in this country, where a hard freeze occurs occasionally.

Mrs. Arnsdorf hardly knows how to give enough thanks to the dear Lord, who has inclined the hearts of the Salzburgers to build her a fine little house with sitting room and bedroom and to complete it right up to the doors, windows, and floors. She had requested it of some of them, who were quite willing to do it; and others came voluntarily and worked with great loyalty. She applies this benefaction well[235] and lets it keep her from ever vacillating in her trust in divine providence but uses it to make her ever stronger. She is sick now, yet very resigned to it.

Friday, the 15th of September. This morning before day the Austrian Schmidt's wife bore a young daughter, who was baptized before noon today. A few weeks ago things looked very miserable for this family; the husband was mortally sick, the wife had a high fever and another serious complication; and these and other troublesome circumstances lasted rather long. But now the dear Lord is returning with His help, the husband and his wife have both recovered, and she has delivered a daughter. They well recognize how salutary the previous rod of chastisement was for them, during which time much was revealed to them in their hearts that they would not have believed otherwise. I hope they will remain faithful.

The hut in which we hold church and in which Schoolmaster Ortmann holds school in the summer for the little children is very dilapidated, even though it has already been repaired by the congregation. If God lets Mr. Oglethorpe arrive safely, the first thing I should do is to solicit him for the construction of a church and a school. And, in order to cause less delay, I shall not immediately mention my house, that I much need. I trust that the dear Lord will help me to a dwelling in due time. Since our people must begin their work on their plantations and thus enter as into a primeval forest and initially very difficult conditions, we cannot presume upon them to undertake the construction of the church and school themselves, which, however, they would not refuse to do if it were necessary. This point was mentioned in the diary some time ago; perhaps the dear Lord will awaken benefactors in England and Germany to contribute something from their temporal wealth for this purpose in case the Lord Trustees were to hesitate to provide for church and school as we had been promised in Old Ebenezer. Others [Mr. Whitefield] will do their best to further our cause in this matter.

Saturday, the 16th of September. I came into a Salzburger's hut where the man showed me the beautiful supply of corn he had harvested and praised the dear Lord with humility and joy for this blessing, which he had not expected. We hear this in most of the huts; and the dear people are, to be sure, heartily glad that under divine blessing they are gradually becoming able to eat their own bread. He who is content with what the Lord grants will not yearn for any other land, since here, provided the soil is not pure sand but is black and rich, everything grows well and does not require nearly as much work as in Germany, as the Salzburgers well recognize. When the sandy soil is well manured, it also bears abundantly; but without manure it bears little or nothing, as some people have discovered again this year. Therefore they will not try it any more on such soil, as they have already learned this several times.

This week we have had frequent rain and little sunshine. The beans and rice need dry weather; but we must be satisfied with what the Lord does. This weather is very good for sweet potatoes, cabbage, and turnips.

This week the surveyor made a serious start with surveying the land across Abercorn Creek. This afternoon he came back home with three people who had helped him; and our people told me that the land is very good but very difficult to survey because of the abundant reeds, bushes, and thorns. This is surely the only reason that the surveyor would rather survey our land in the pine forest than here.

Sunday, the 17th of September. Because the surveyor heard that our boat is going to Savannah tomorrow, he asked to go with it back to Purysburg, where he will see to some business before he can finish surveying our land. I cannot stop him, especially since he is now demanding four men as assistants in his present surveying, whom I cannot supply because everyone is busy with the harvest. He will return again in four weeks and remain here until he has completed his work. By then it should be possible to find people to go with him. He claims it will take him some two months of work to survey our land; and therefore it would be rather expensive for us if we had to pay him and the people who help him. However, he himself believes that Mr. Oglethorpe will not object to bearing these expenses; and I too will request it of him. It would be a great loss for the congregation if they had to do without the land that is still to be surveyed and to retain the plantations that are already surveyed near Old Ebenezer. [Even if they receive this good land, they will still retain enough bad, which they will not refuse.]

Monday, the 18th of September. An Evangelical Lutheran man, who is overseer over some Negro slaves near Charleston, came to us on horseback in order to go to Holy Communion next Sunday with the congregation. He had ridden around a lot and, even though some Englishmen could have easily directed him to the right path, they did not wish to do it because, as they said, he was a fool to be travelling so far for the sake of the sacrament. He was in Purysburg three years ago and attended our church diligently. May God let him gather a blessing here that will remain with him into everlasting life.

[Mrs. Rheinlaender returned this afternoon from Savannah. She probably did not appear before Mr. Causton, who went to his estate on the same day that my dear colleague arranged his affairs with him. Her conscience must tell her that people will no longer put up with her wicked ways. She delayed six days in Purysburg, probably so as to again obtain the boat that she had borrowed for the trip down from the Frenchman who lives in our neighborhood, and which was rowed by someone, presumably an Indian. If she should cause new trouble the authorities will pay attention to our report and curb her wickedness. Even this time Mr. Causton had planned a well-deserved punishment for her that was, however, discouraged by my dear colleague. Since she is no longer pleased with our style and arrangements but only calumniates them and is a burden on the people, it would be best if she were removed from us, which we have requested both orally and in writing.

[Tuesday, the 19th of September. Yesterday evening God helped Mrs. Gruber and let her bear a little son, who was baptized this morning. She was in difficult circumstances; yet the Lord helped through everything, for which may His name be praised. Today Mrs. Helfenstein revealed herself more clearly than in previous times, since she can usually hide her secret purposes and dishonesties with well chosen words and other appearances. For a rather long time she has been consorting rather familiarly with Mrs. Rheinlaender, to the scandal of the congregation; and whenever they came together the Salzburgers were rather harshly judged, as one could well hear through the thin wall. Now, because Mrs. Rheinlaender has grown worse every day in her wickedness and calumnies against us and the congregation and has opposed all good order, she has been as good as excluded from our Christian congregation. After she had travelled to Savannah, Mrs. Helfenstein came to me and said she had freed herself from Mrs. Rheinlaender and had refused her this and that; she therefore would not and could not enter her house again. But Mrs. Rheinlaender had hardly returned before they were sticking together again.

[This morning I chanced to go past Mrs. Helfenstein's house and heard soft and secret voices in it; and, when I was about to enter, both of them hurried to put away their tea cups and other things and hide them. I told them that they had no grounds to be afraid of men if they had a just cause. I told Mrs. Helfenstein that she was doing nothing but favoring both sides and that vexation was being caused to the congregation and worry for us because she would still secretly consort with such a person who was entirely unbridled and shameless in all wickedness. Her children, who are quite naughty, are annoyed by her gossip and calumny. Along with that I cited several Bible verses in which the Lord and his apostles seriously urge us to withdraw from such disorderly and vexing people after they have been admonished and chastised several times, but without any effect.

[Thereupon I went away, and Mrs. Helfenstein followed me and tried to excuse herself again as best she could. Because she could not get very far with that and because comparisons of other people with Mrs. Rheinlaender did not help her, she began to talk of moving away and clearly showed, as people had previously noted in her and her oldest daughter, that it was all the same to her whether she were here or in Pennsylvania. She revealed quite clearly in other ways too that she was no lover of the pure truth of the gospel but of false ways and errors, which are now in vogue under an appearance of evangelical freedom of conscience. Those people who have clever speech and also an ostensibly good Christian behavior are usually the worst blasphemers, if one does not let them have their way but sees through their false argument and appearances and reveals them.]

Wednesday, the 20th of September. After the evening prayer hour yesterday, I received a visit from a Salzburger woman who had been prevented by fever from signing up for Holy Communion last Sunday and was therefore signing up now. God has granted her an exceptional hunger for this spiritual banquet, and she hopes He will be merciful to her soul and strengthen her through such salutary means in the good He has begun in her. Concerning her husband she told me that he had begun some time ago to pray seriously and that she was very happy in her soul because of this. Last Sunday he had been much awakened through the word of God, she said, and had been even more encouraged by a private visit from my dear colleague.

N. [Herzog] is also requesting to go to Holy Communion if we think it wise. He knows himself very well; and today he gave me examples of his evil and recalcitrant thoughts against the work and chastisement of the Holy Ghost that sufficiently revealed his dangerous condition. He wishes to be saved, he reads and prays diligently too. Sometimes he makes a serious start; but then, while praying and reading, he ceases the necessary vigilance over his heart and his serious struggle against the fancies and inclinations of the Old Adam and allows himself to be so disquieted by external matters that he casts everything away and harbors blasphemous thoughts. In a [evangelical] book he once read [Calvin's] dangerous error about the unconditional judgment of God in saving or damning mankind, that is to say, that He wishes to grant the grace of penitence and faith only to those whom He has chosen for salvation, and to no others. This [dreadful] dogma had set itself so firmly in his mind that he thinks it is being confirmed by his own experience. He says that he notices that God does not wish to give him His grace for conversion and has already predestined him for damnation. /From this example one can see what a very harmful influence that dogma has on the practice of Christianity./ Oh, how harmful it is for simple people when they read all sorts of books, and how dangerous it is when such errors are reviewed *cum rigore* in books and from pulpits but are then not contradicted clearly enough! This time too I spoke movingly with the man and showed him the obstacles to true conversion that are found both in and outside of him. I showed him how dangerous his condition is and how much the Savior, who is able and desirous to redeem all men, wishes to gather him under his gracious wings, if only he will bow to His order and use the means of salvation to that end.

Thursday, the 21st of September. [Some time ago a Swiss from Purysburg sent his daughter to our school, and now he has died after a long sickness. A man from there has told me that the girl's stepmother, a frivolous young woman, is squandering the dead man's legacy, which came from the first wife and belongs to the daughter alone, and that she would gradually sell everything if no one looked into the matter. Since there is no one who wishes to be responsible for the child, I wrote to a judge whom I know in Purysburg[236] and asked him to see that right and justice are done in the matter.]

I assembled the men of the congregation again to discuss some [spiritual and] external matters with them. The wolves are greatly harming the calves, which are now being guarded separately; and therefore better measures are being taken for their protection and security. Also, the carpenters will soon build a rice and corn mill. We have seen nothing of the carpenter from Purysburg who wished to build us a rice mill for a low price, and we also hear that there are more words in him than deeds. This year the corn is supposed to make lovely white meal; and, because the iron mills on which so much is ground every day are easily ruined, we have great need of a durable mill with regular millstones that can be driven by a couple of men. After having given good service so far, the third transport's stone mill now requires a repair.

[At this meeting mention was made of Mrs. Rheinlaender and her troublesome nature, and the congregation asked me to request Mr. Causton in the name of the congregation to remove her from us because we are having more and more difficulty with her. Her wickedness is getting the best of her, and therefore I am compelled to present Mr. Causton with the desire of the congregation and of us all.]

Friday, the 22nd of September. A young man on whom the dear Lord has been working mightily since Christmas complained to me with tears of his corrupted condition. He often renews his resolution to devote himself honestly to the Lord; but nothing comes of it because of his lack of vigilance, prayer, and struggle. As a major obstacle that is keeping him from true conversion, he cites worldly acquaintances that he has loved up till now and that have caused him great harm, even if he did not know it. He is very much affected by all the words in the sermons, as was the case last Sunday; and he was especially impressed by what my dear colleague recently read about prayer out of Professor Francke's *Epistle-Prayers*, p. 1152,[237] concerning the epistle for that day. This encouraged him not to despair entirely, even if he was progressing with only very small steps. He knelt with me, and we implored the true Savior for faith to go our way with conviction and feeling.

The cited words were as follows: "Man must not first ask for a long time whether he has any desire to pray, for then he would have to wait a good long while before feeling a real desire to do so. He must not wait until his sluggishness passes and he feels an especial impulse to pray; the more he notices that he has no desire to pray, the more necessary it is for him to pray. As we see, when the disciples were sluggish and sleepy on the Mount of Olives, our Savior awakened them and encouraged them most: 'Watch and pray, that ye enter not into temptation: the spirit is indeed willing but the flesh is weak' (Matthew 26:41). From which we should learn that we must pray most when we have the least desire to pray and when we are most sluggish to do so, because the need and danger is then the greatest. Man need not think that his prayer will displease the dear Lord because it is merely something forced. Indeed, dear man, you are being horribly deceived if you think that it will not please the dear Lord but even be repugnant to Him, if you thus compel yourself; for such compulsion is very agreeable to the dear Lord. Merely compel your Old Adam in every way. Such a struggle is very pleasing to Him when a man feels nothing but reluctance to pray yet compels himself and struggles with himself until he overcomes and thus goes and prays despite all contradiction in himself. Once a man has a desire and impulse to pray, there is nothing surprising in that he should pray. And it is, to be sure, very pleasing for God if a man thus converts into his strength and practice the very stimulus that he has received from the spirit of God. Yet in some ways it is even more pleasing and agreeable to Him if a man recognizes his misery and sees himself as naked and deprived of all comfort, of the feeling of grace and of the power of the Holy Ghost, but so greatly values the recognition of his misery and of his great danger through the mere admonition that God has granted him in his heart that he comes and confesses his misery and impotence and sincerely implores Him for more power and grace. Experience will teach that, if one does not indulge in one's indolence but actually struggles and thus often begins one's prayer without desire, one will receive the greatest power in prayer and will arise from prayer with pleasure and joy." Our loving God has blessed the reading of these words in several people. May the glory be His!

A woman wished for everyone to help her praise God, who was still granting her a period of grace and was working on her so mightily. She complained greatly of her sluggishness and said that she now had almost too much work, which might well be an obstacle in the course of her Christianity. She is full of honest poverty of the spirit, and she yearns for the Lord Jesus as a newborn babe yearns for milk. I spoke with her about several verses in Matthew 5, "Blessed are the poor in spirit," etc., "Blessed are they that mourn," etc., "Blessed are they which do hunger," etc.

Another woman was also pleased that I called on her; she complained to me that her husband has prevented her from going to Holy Communion this time. This week, as often before, he had quarreled with her and done everything to spite her and had even ridiculed her when she spoke to him from God's word. Because she shows no wisdom and humility toward her husband, I admonished her in this respect and to pray for herself and her husband; and I also requested her to tell her husband that I would admit neither him nor his wife unless they would reconcile themselves honestly in my presence and promise to treat each other better from now on. We have worked on him for a long time, but he is one of those frivolous people who cannot imagine that hell is so hot, or that eternal damnation is so long, or that the spiritual blessings of heaven are of such worth and value as God's word, the word of truth, tells us. The company he keeps also does him much harm, as his wife said.

Saturday, the 23rd of September. This morning Kiefer of Purysburg came to us with his oldest son and youngest daughter in order to go to Holy Communion tomorrow with the congregation. In yesterday's evening prayer meeting we had God's mysterious statute concerning the year of release from Deuteronomy XV, which gave me an opportunity to lay the verse Luke 4:18–19 as a foundation for the preparation; for in it our Savior presents Himself most gloriously as our only great prophet, physician, and redeemer in His glorious good deeds, who was granted us by the heavenly Father for the very purpose for which we needed him most.

Peter Gruber's little son died yesterday evening and therefore did not live even a week in this world. The parents are quite resigned to this dispensation of God and well see that He has done well with this little worm, since the mother had been unable to provide any nourishment for it, even though everything possible was done for her.

Schmidt's little child, who is a few days older, already has fever and is becoming very weak. So far we have done rather poorly in fetching up children, the reason for which may well be that the mothers in their poverty cannot take such care of themselves and their little children as such people require. We and the members of the congregation give them all the help we possibly can. (God will improve this situation too, as we certainly hope.)

Sunday, the 24th of September. Today forty-three persons attended Holy Communion. [Several, among them Barbara Maurer, were held back because they lack the proper preparation for such an important undertaking. The Maurer woman was also held back the last time, whereupon she caused annoyance through insolence and rough and ignorant words. When I remonstrated with her about them this time and tried to bring her to a recognition of, and remorse for, such sins, she again revealed her former wicked nature. She has a right foolish arrogance, by which she is misled into defiance and obstinacy. At the same time she is of very simple intelligence.]

The strangers as well as some of our regular listeners were abundantly edified again today, and they well felt its strength in their hearts, as we perceived. May God give them and us faith so that we may not only know what the Lord demands of us, since it is abundantly told us, but that we will also really keep his word, practice love, and be humble in our hearts before Him, which was the content of our morning sermon concerning Luke 16:1 ff.

Monday, the 25th of September. With the stranger, who is a

chief overseer over the Negro slaves near Charleston, I had a good opportunity to send a letter to the goldsmith Dannengiesser, who has been called as preacher by the people in North Carolina.[238] Already several months ago he sent me a letter complaining of the strange mixture of people he had in his congregation. The inhabitants there are said to be mostly wicked, dissolute, disorderly, and rather similar to the Indians of this country in external customs. He wrote me that many contradictions had arisen because of a catechism, in that every party wished to introduce into the school that catechism they considered the best and had perhaps heard of in their youth. Therefore he did not know how he would be able to unite them all.

I sent him the order of salvation that Pastor Freylinghausen had collected from Holy Scripture, whilst adding how I would act with such children of various religious persuasions. I would teach them the ten commandments, the seven petitions, and the dogma of the sacraments of the New Testament from Holy Scripture. Since the *Symbolum Apostolicum*[239] was accepted by everyone, it would also be easy to teach them. Moreover, I would treat the order of salvation and try to lay the foundation of a true Christianity in both children and adults. [I gave several little tractates by the late Professor Francke, especially the *Dogma of the Commencement of Christian Life*,[240] to the stranger, who is returning to his place today.]

Tuesday, the 26th of September. Last week and this week we have had no sunshine but only gloomy weather and occasional drizzly rain, which is somewhat hindering the ripening of the beans. Thunderstorms are usually very violent in this country, but this summer we have heard but few, and they were rather weak. The crops are said to have turned out very well in South Carolina, and corn and sweet potatoes are being sold in Charleston cheaper than ever before. The people around Savannah who planted yellow corn will have harvested little, as we here have also experienced in the case of this kind of corn.[241] God be praised for all the physical blessings He has granted us, and may He make us thankful for them. This year none of us will lack corn, beans, and sweet potatoes. And whoever has rice land will receive a considerable amount of rice. Our Father in heaven will also see to other things.

[Today Mr. Causton summoned Mrs. Rheinlaender to appear before the authorities in Savannah; and she was very insolent about this, as is her wont. In my last letter I reported to him various points concerning her great obstinacy and vexing and insolent nature and requested that he take her from us because she shows no desire for betterment and has already disregarded all charges of admonition and church discipline. Because she has comprehended some of the word of God literally and because she can speak glibly, she considers herself a newborn child of God; and she looks upon all the evil that she is bringing on herself by her insolence and disorder as the cross of Jesus and upon us as her persecutors. Such a blindness and obstinate wickedness was not to be found in the late Rott and his wife; rather the Rheinlaender woman is immersed in an even greater degree of blindness and wickedness. Tomorrow, when I send this woman down to Savannah in our boat, I will report her previous vexing behavior to the authorities in seven points, with the repeated request to remove her from us even though she has resolved, to spite and annoy us and the congregation, to remain in Ebenezer just because we would like to be rid of her, even if she will have to suffer want and hardship because she has no harvest as a result of her indolence and disorderly running around.]

Wednesday, the 27th of September. Before dawn this morning Simon Steiner's wife bore a little daughter, who was baptized today after school. The example of Mary, who according to the witness of Jesus Christ hath chosen that good part, is so noteworthy and edifying to this man that he let this beautiful name be given to his child. A short time previously in school the dear Lord had granted me a pleasant edification from this example and from the beautiful words of Luke 10:39–42, which stand in the *Order of Salvation* in the *Golden ABC* under the first words: "Attentive to the Words of Christ."[242] For this reason the man's reflection in naming his child was all the more impressive for me.

I found two women together in a room, one of them heartily

happy at the grace of the Savior which He has been granting her since she last partook of Holy Communion, and the other so very depressed because of the magnitude and number of her sins both on Sunday and on the following two days that she could hardly pray; but this gloomy cloud has finally begun to disappear. For the benefit of the latter I spoke a bit about the verse: "He that overcometh shall inherit all things," etc., and showed her that not so much the physical sensation of the grace of the Father and the love of the Son, but far more the constant and serious hate of and struggle against sin are an infallible characteristic of the state of grace, especially if the struggle is carried out loyally to overcome the temptations from without and within. During the conversation we touched upon the beautiful song, "Strive well when God's grace draws and converts you,"[243] which we sang together to my great refreshment. Then we commended our common need in prayer to our dear Lord with praise and thanks.

A Salzburger who had called on me remembered a special sin, which he had formerly not considered a sin because it was something common among the people of that place, particularly among the hired men and women. Now that our faithful Lord was bringing him to recognize better and better the strait way through the narrow gate to heaven, he showed a hearty displeasure and remorse for it. He still has a brother in the Empire, who is likewise tempted to such sins and will therefore come into danger of his soul; therefore he greatly wished that he might come here and prepare himself with him for eternal salvation. He was very happy when he heard that I could be of use to his brother so that he could become his nearest neighbor if he came with the next transport.

Thursday, the 28th of September. Since the surveyor is to survey four English miles for the Salzburgers across Abercorn Creek, he already wished to receive provisions from the storehouse in Savannah for his new work, even though he left us without finishing his business. Because Mr. Causton cannot believe everything the surveyor says and because the latter might report certain things to our detriment, Mr. Causton wishes to speak with me about it and to hear whether it is really so necessary for the above-mentioned land to be surveyed. But it is easy to show how necessary it is for our people to gain possession of this land: 1) Among the surveyed plantations there are not more than twenty-four on which the people can grow crops under divine blessing; on sandy dry soil nothing will grow, as we have already learned several times. 2) It is a great advantage if the entire community has its land together. Not only will they be able to cut down, fence, and plant a large forest quickly, but, since the Salzburgers wish to have the word of God along with their physical work, one of us can remain here and serve both old and young with his office while the other performs his office in the town. It is a great advantage in field work here in this country if the crops can stand open and not be surrounded with so many trees. What can the people accomplish if they take their plantations here and there wherever a good patch is. Shade and birds do much damage. 3) The land across Abercorn Creek is low and flooded so that no one can build a house or keep cattle there. Rather, whoever wishes to have his plantation there must live on this side of the creek. Consequently, no town or village can be built in the entire region there, whereas our people can use the land splendidly. They have agreed to build their huts and cowsheds on this side of the creek and to share the plantations where the land is high, and to share also in the plantations across the creek and work communally like brothers. 4) If they do not receive this land but have to be satisfied with the already surveyed plantations, then few of them could subsist. However, if they receive it, since no one closer than our town can receive it, then its value with divine blessing will be great for us and the whole colony. 5) If it is still intended, as Mr. Causton has assured us several times, that Old Ebenezer is to be settled with people, then there will be no land left over for this place, if the present surveying should remain, for our plantations reach a half mile beyond Old Ebenezer.

It seems to me as if the place where Old Ebenezer is supposed to stand belongs within the line of the plantations, only the surveyor denies this absurdity and has drawn the line on his paper past this place. Now if, as is meet and right, land is to be left for this place, then at least four miles must be surveyed for us at some other place; and now there is no other land except across

Abercorn Creek. The hamlet Habercorn (or rather Abricorn)[244] lies much further away so that our land would not reach into this region. This creek or arm of the Savannah River acquired the name Abercorn Creek because it empties back into the Savannah River two or three miles below Abercorn. the hamlet Abercorn does not lie on the island on which we desire the four miles for the Salzburgers' plantations, but lies on this side of the creek; and therefore no encroachment is being made on that place. Early tomorrow morning, God willing, I am going to Savannah for the sake of the German people and will speak to Mr. Causton about this matter so that our land will finally be put into order.

Yesterday afternoon my dear colleague moved into his new, very comfortably built house, and has dedicated it with our dear listeners with prayer and the word of the Lord. May our dear God, who has exercised His fatherly will over him in this matter also, give him and his dear family new strength in body and soul in these new quarters, so that he may live there for a long time in His honor and may benefit our congregation.

Friday, the 29th of September. After the morning prayer hour in the orphanage I called on a sick woman and inquired about her condition. She was quite resigned and told me how, in her sick condition, she had been so impressed and comforted by the verses where it says "[Zion said] the Lord hath forsaken me, and my Lord hath forgotten me. Can a woman forget her suckling child, that she should not have compassion on the son of her womb? Yea, they may not forget, yet will I not forget thee. Behold, I have graven thee upon the palms of my hands." She cannot read; but, when we spend scarcely a quarter of an hour with such a person, we receive more edification than if we spend three hours with someone else who only knows to chatter and with whom we can accomplish nothing because of their imagined piety. Such a person is poor Mrs. Rheinlaender, who scorns the Salzburgers because they do not chatter that way and do not answer so copiously to questions we ask them. Recently, in my dear colleague's hut, she said that the Salzburgers were people who had just come from Popery and therefore could not speak so readily from Holy Scripture as she and others in Ebenezer, who are not Salzburgers.

Saturday, the 30th of September. Yesterday evening Simon Steiner's little child died. It had come to the world somewhat too soon. This morning it was buried; and on this occasion, for mutual edification, a brief explanation was made of the words in Matthew 18: "Even so, it is not the will of your Father which is in heaven, that one of these little ones should perish."

OCTOBER

Sunday, the 1st of October. Praise be to the dear Lord, who strengthened me today to give witness of Christ. May He confirm this in all others! I have trust in our faithful Lord that he will let many of those who have not yet felt it so far feel that He means them too and that He would like to draw them as well to His son Jesus Christ. For then my joy too would be fulfilled, if Jesus the Bridegroom received many as his brides. Now He must wax, but I and all of us must wane.

Monday, the 2nd of October. At about noon I reached our dear Ebenezer again. In Savannah I preached the word of God to the Trustees' German indentured servants both on Saturday and on Sunday. For the preparation I used the words from Matthew 11, "Come unto me;" and on Sunday, both in the morning and in the afternoon, I led the people as simply as possible, using the regular gospel, to the essentials that are demanded for being saved. This time they appeared to be more attentive than usual; approximately fourteen people took Holy Communion. However, some of them who usually show a desire for it remained away this time and they told me their reasons for doing so. This much they know: that Holy Communion is a holy and important matter and that he who takes it with an unprepared heart sins greatly. Yet they usually place their preparation in the kind of things which, although they are pertinent, do not actually concern the principal matter; and therefore we try to give them sufficient instruction in this.

A pious Englishman inquired about our Evangelical dogma of Holy Communion; and, as he learned that it agrees with neither the Papist nor [Reformed] other opinions but only with the very clear words with which the Lord instituted it and therefore deviates neither to the left nor to the right, he asked

me to admit him too to Holy Communion; he had long had a
yearning desire for it but had been unable to enjoy it because
the English preacher here [Whitefield], /who is an Episcopa-
lian,/[245] has not yet received ordination [copulation] as a priest
and can therefore not administer Holy Communion. After
Communion he thanked me most appreciatively and assured
me that the Lord had strengthened him.

We hear everywhere the bitterest complaints about the German indentured servants [especially the Reformed ones] and
their loose behavior, and that their masters would be happy if
they could recover the passage money they had paid for them.
With their work they do not earn their provisions, much less
their clothing and what else is spent on them.[246] And, because
some Englishmen believe that they are Salzburgers and are actually people who belong to my congregation, and thus the
word of God [and our office] is maligned, I have been desirous
of admitting to our assemblies none but orderly people who accept the word of God and conduct themselves in a righteous
way; but I have wished to speak about it first with Mr. Oglethorpe and to hear his decision.

Mr. Oglethorpe arrived two weeks ago at Frederica with several ships; and, when people heard about it last Wednesday in
Savannah, they fired their cannons, which we could hear in our
place. He must have much important business there; therefore
it is said that he will hardly come to Savannah for another three
or four weeks. At his order nothing is now being given out of
the storehouse in Savannah because the previous accounts must
be brought into order and an inventory of the current provisions must be prepared. A new store keeper has been sent
here,[247] who is to relieve Mr. Causton of the burden of the
storehouse as soon as the storehouse has been put into order.
[Malicious people are passing severe judgments about this, and
all sorts of stories are being spread around the country. However, time will soon show that they are false tales; and people,
including the German indentured servants, will change their
minds, as they will probably be glad to do for Mr. Causton.][248]

The new storehouse manager came into the orphanage in
which I was lodging in order to make my acquaintance. His
chief purpose in this was to warn me against certain persons

[the Herrnhuters] who had been sent here [as missionaries by Count Zinzendorf] and had been with him on a ship, especially against N. N. [Mr. Böhler], because he thought that they would come to our community and desire our friendship (which has not occurred). He related that he, like other people in London, had at first thought highly of them and had believed there was a true fear of the Lord in them; but that he had later caught them in untruths and had also inferred from their discussions that they considered only themselves and the people of their party to be righteous and considered all others to be hypocrites and mouth-Christians who did not yet have Christ living in them.

He also said that they had been very severe and brutal in the discipline of a boy who seemed to belong to them, the likes of which he had never seen and which did not concur with the love that they pretended to have. He could not believe that they prayed, because he had never seen them do so. Several friends of N. and N. [Mr. Wesley and Mr. Whitefield] were present who said that those of these people [the Herrnhuters] who are already in this country are just as fault-finding and that they had wished to accuse Mr. N.N. [Whitefield] himself of damnable errors. However, they themselves had made it clear enough that they were very close to the Quakers, who are well known in England and especially in Pennsylvania, and at least cherish certain of their principles. Nevertheless, N. [Böhler], who was to be sent out among the N. [Negro slaves in South Carolina], had so blinded N. [Dr. Watts][249] and others that it was reported to Mr. N. [Whitefield] in a letter [which the schoolmaster opened in his absence and read] that Dr. N. [Watts] found in this N. [Mr. Böhler] all the qualities of an N. [missionary].

We must marvel that so much furor is being made in England and perhaps also in Germany about these people, since they live there very obscurely and seek their physical subsistence in every way they can. They do not seek to accomplish any spiritual good in anyone, much less in a heathen, nor do they speak any word to edify the Salzburgers, even though, when they are in Savannah, they visit and even lodge with them as Germans. What kind of a divine service they have and hold among themselves is their own secret. In their evening prayer meetings, which they hold in their regular living room or, in winter, in the

kitchen, things proceed so sluggishly, as I and others have observed, that I would be distressed if I saw anything like it
among us. One of them after the other is going to Pennsylvania
because this country does not please them. If they were concerned, as they pretend, with the edification and salvation of
their neighbors, then they would remain here and apply themselves to it more closely.

Mr. Oglethorpe had sent our letters to the storehouse in
Savannah, so I was able to read them there. I praise the goodness of the Lord who, through these edifying letters from our
Fathers in London and Germany, has again granted me and all
of us so much blessing for our edification and for arousing us to
a serious conduct of our office and our Christianity. As usual,
our dear congregation will share in this. This time, because of
the unexpected departure of Mr. Oglethorpe, nothing has
come but a thick packet of letters for us and Mr. Thilo; our
salaries and whatever else God has intended for us will be forwarded later with Captain Thomson. From Court Preacher
Ziegenhagen's letter I learn that two packets of letters from the
14th of October and the 14th of November, 1737, with two in-
stallments of our diary, had not yet arrived in May, when he
wrote his last letters; and they may be presumed to have fallen
into the wrong hands or to have been lost. They had been
placed together in one packet for forwarding and first given to
Mr. N. [Wesley], but afterwards, since he had resolved to remain here, sent to Mr. Eveleigh in Charleston. Mr. Eveleigh has
died, and therefore we cannot ask him about it. When I arrived
in Savannah on Friday, Mr. Oglethorpe's letters were being sent
to Charleston for forwarding, and I would have wished to send
a copy of the lost diary with them. Now we are occupied in
copying it. We will also take the copies of the letters written at
that time and send them to Charleston via Savannah as soon as
a safe opportunity is offered.

[Mrs. Rheinlaender was sent to jail by the authorities even
though I had requested only that she might be taken away from
us because she did not wish to fit into any spiritual order. She
sent a Jew[250] and several other people to me and had them ask
me to help her out again. She would gladly admit her misbehavior and humble herself; but now it is beyond my power,

and she will have to see to how she can straighten herself out. We have borne her for a long time and suffered much from her and at the same time have always shown great kindness to her and her family. However, since she remains ungrateful and causes much vexation and annoyance, God has shown that He is a Holy God who does not let evil endure for ever. This will make an impression on the insolent people among us and tame them in their wickedness, even if we have to let ourselves be judged because of it.]

In Purysburg a tailor,[251] who had kept two children with us in the school and in the orphanage but had brought them home for a short time to harvest beans, complained that his wife had run away and abducted two of his children, among them the girl who had been placed with us. It is the third time in this country that she has so shamefully abandoned him. It is uncertain whether he will soon be able to send the small boy back here to school, since his wife has taken the larger one, whom he greatly needs in harvesting his crops. Purysburg is in great confusion.

Tuesday, the 3rd of October. Yesterday evening in the prayer meeting I acquainted our listeners with the contents of Senior Urlsperger's beautiful, although short, letter. It was arranged according to the content of the gospel for the Second Sunday after Epiphany and well suited our circumstances. Oh, how often it has been true of us: "Mine hour is not yet come." Yet this hour of help has not remained away entirely; rather the glorious Savior has often revealed His glory most powerfully in our greatest need and want. With this we sang the hymn: "My soul turns quietly to God,"[252] which, together with the content of the letter, impressed me deeply. The heavy rain, which began some time ago and is getting stronger today, may perhaps hinder us in the prayer meeting today; otherwise I shall continue with the reading of the edifying letters.

Wednesday, the 4th of October. Yesterday and today I have been busy in answering the gratifying letters that have come to us from our dear Fathers, and also to send along the contents of the letters of the 14th of October and November, which seem to have been lost. May God let all this prosper for His glory and the edification of our neighbors and especially for the joy of our worthy benefactors and friends, and also for our own welfare. We write to Europe with heartfelt joy, for that always brings us greatly desired and edifying answers. Also, our dear congregation receives no harm, but rather much physical and spiritual good; for the letters from our Fathers in Europe are always read to the congregation with much blessing. To say nothing of the physical blessings, which God has always granted.

[During my absence Michael Rieser hired himself out as a rower on an English trading boat or as a soldier at Fort Augusta, after having begun to sell some of his cattle. I have reason to fear that he will take leave of us in the spring in the ungrateful and shameful manner of Stephan Riedelsperger, with whom he is especially well acquainted. He is not concerned with any of the land and is always malcontent; and it appears that he wishes to earn a bit of money and then depart. Some time ago he married an orderly and industrious woman from Purysburg, with whom he could live here well if only he desired to work like other orderly people. He has been a tricky and secretly hostile man from the first time that we got to know him. If he leaves, no one in the community will miss or mourn him. Spielbiegler is his neighbor and of one mind with him. He is even more worthless; and the two of them will surely run into their physical misfortune, since they already lie under the spiritual judgment of a pitiable blindness and resistance against all the grace of God that is chastising them and working on them.]

Thursday, the 5th of October. For about the last two weeks we have had rainy weather that has done much harm to the beans and rice. Neither can bear wetness while ripening but begin to sprout. The sweet potatoes too prefer dry weather, and today during my stroll I saw that some of them were damaged. Today the weather is beginning to improve, and may the Lord preserve it according to His will! He has shown us a fine crop in the fields, which He could withdraw if He wished even before it was enjoyed. Yet He is merciful and does not treat us according to our sins. Those people among us who have learned to look not for the visible but for the invisible know how to resign themselves in this and are well content with the government of the Lord.

Yesterday evening we heard many cannon shots; and from

this some conclude that Mr. Oglethorpe has arrived in Savannah.[253] When I was there, people assumed that he would not be ready to come from Frederica to Savannah for three or four weeks. If we finish with our letters this week and if God keeps me sound of body, I plan to go down next week; then there will probably be an opportunity to see Mr. Oglethorpe. At first I shall not be able to mention my house, since I must ask him for something concerning the congregation and also urge him to cover the expenses for my dear colleague's house, which stands on the public square for the ministers.

[Court Chaplain Ziegenhagen well knows the mind and circumstances of the Lord Trustees, and how careful we must be with them in our requests and demands.] Since the Trustees' expenditures here in this country are very great anyhow and they are restricting their management of the storehouse more and more, he will find it difficult to add anything substantial to the 10 £ that the Trustees have allowed to each house. [If he adds anything, he will promise me boards from the sawmill in Old Ebenezer for my house, and it will cost me more to bring them here than they are worth. The mill is not yet in an operative condition, and therefore considerable time would pass before I get my house if I were to wait for these boards. And how would I be any better off with regards to my poor physical and my official condition if they build me a house of boards as in Savannah, in which one is protected neither from the heat nor the cold and in which one can hardly say a loud word? I shall postpone the construction at least until December and meanwhile see how Mr. Oglethorpe may be disposed toward it. Yet I must build in such a way that the house will be ready not later than April when our people plant, not only because they will then have their hands full with their fields but also because the entire region in front of my house and to the Savannah River will be planted, and I would be in their way if I built later.

It is believed that I could have a secure house if the walls were made of clay and lime and covered on the outside all around with thin boards for keeping the rain off. In this way I will distribute the pay not only among the carpenters but also to others in the community, who can earn something by cutting boards, digging and treading the clay, etc.[254] To be sure, I have no money now for this construction, but perhaps the dear Lord will move Mr. Oglethorpe to advance me something for a few years without interest, which I will gradually repay him from that which God grants. I am planning to set the house on my own lot, and thus I can best arrange it for the use of my family. We also have great need of a good house for the church and school, which I must likewise solicit from Mr. Oglethorpe. The schoolmaster's hut is also quite dilapidated. If only the Lord Trustees wished to give something for all these, I would be glad to keep quiet about my house.

Friday, the 6th of October. Yesterday evening I applied Court Chaplain Ziegenhagen's letter of the 14th of May of this year to the benefit of the congregation; and this evening I applied one of Professor Francke's letters, namely, that of the 21st of December 1737. By means of their edifying content we mutually encouraged one another to learn, through the power of the Holy Ghost, to believe well what everyone confesses: "I believe in God the Father, almighty Creator of Heaven and Earth, etc." If anyone unites himself in faith with this almighty God, who at the same time is in Christ our reconciled Abba and rich in mercy, he can leap over the walls of all difficulties with his God like David and is calm in all tribulations, for he says: "Everything cometh, my God, from Thee." On the occasion of these edifying letters the dear Lord has again let us hear much concerning the necessity and usefulness of tribulations. May He grant it, like a good seed, to bear much fruit, and may He abundantly repay our dear Fathers with spiritual and physical blessings for the effort that they have taken in writing such long and edifying letters, which flow with the honey of the gospel.

Our dear Salzburgers would warmly thank Pastor Breuer if, as he has been admonished by Professor Francke, he would write something concerning the Salzburgers in Prussia.[255] What a blessing he and his congregation could receive from that! The little effort, which can scarcely be called an effort, that we joyfully make in writing letters and sending the diary is rewarded for us a thousandfold. If we had not reported our trials and tribulations, then there would not have been so many prayers for us according to our circumstances, also we could not have been so greatly helped with counsel, intercession, and deeds. And, so far as we can see from the worthy Court Chaplain Ziegenhagen's and Mr. Butjenter's letters, upon the reports of the good among us our loyal God gives His blessing for our edification, and by this God is glorified. How much our congregation would be encouraged to pray for the Prussian Salzburgers if they learned some details, after which they are constantly inquiring from us. I do not know how they can justify this their silence [before God and man].

The next time I shall continue with reading out of Professor Francke's letters and also from the very pleasant letter of the dear Court Chaplain Butjenter. Soli Deo Gloria!

The song: "Up, upwards to Thy joy"[256] has encouraged us to call upon the everlasting loyalty of the Lord Jesus in all vexations. When it is sung devoutly, it is as if the dear Lord Jesus himself were reaching forth His gracious hands for us to grasp and were offering His wounds as a fortress. I was much impressed that, although the danger because of the Spaniards was very great in this country, our dear Fathers had faith in the dear Lord that He would turn the danger away from us and protect His little flock, as He so graciously did, and look mercifully on the prayers of His servants and children. The danger was great, as was reported in the letter to Court Chaplain Butjenter; but our Lord's help was still greater. He can help even without men and their aid. And as we read in their letters that they trust in the almighty and loving God to do glorious things for our Salzburger congregation, He will certainly do such good in His time, if only we do not hinder Him in His work. May He preserve us in His mercy!

Saturday, the 7th of October. We have again received beautiful dry weather, which is very convenient for the people in gathering their beans, which would have been entirely lost if it had rained longer; for, as the people say, they are half spoiled as it is. Last night it was rather cold, so they feared a freeze, since the time has now come for it to be quite fresh and cold in the evening.

I was told by a pregnant woman that she had suffered serious bodily harm through her lack of shoes and stockings, which she had relinquished to her husband. The woman is very timid and did not wish, as many do, to reveal her want. We are badly off with regard to a shoemaker; and this time I have urged Court Chaplain Butjenter to seek out a good man in London. [The Purysburg shoemaker who works for us is a dissolute man and carries off much money for his often shoddy work, and there is nothing we can do about it.] Our orphans are barefoot [too].

We have now written again to various dear benefactors and friends, namely to Court Chaplain Ziegenhagen, Senior Urlsperger, Professor Francke, Secretary Newman, Dr. Watts,[257] Court Chaplain Butjenter, and Baron von Reck. I am planning to travel to Savannah next week and to look for a safe opportunity to forward to London these letters and a double diary, namely the present one from the 27th of August to now and the copy of the diary that was lost in September of last year.

Sunday, the 8th of October. This morning two Christian women were churched with their little children, one of them before and one of them after the public divine service. In the Augsburg Church-Agenda we cannot actually find anything about how we are to deal with women who are to be churched and wish to praise the dear Lord in a public assembly, to pay their vows, and have themselves and their little babies blessed. Therefore we have drafted something as best we could; and, because we cannot remember whether we have incorporated it into the diary for the judgment of our worthy superiors in the Lord, we have considered it necessary to do it this time and thus to make the conclusion of the diary that is to be sent off. In this act we are accustomed to sing the beautiful song "Praise and honor be to the highest Good."[258] After it ends the mother steps before the altar with her little child and the one of us who is to give the sermon, or who has just done so, speaks in the following manner:

"Dear Friends in Christ:

"You have come to this place with your little children to thank our dear Lord heartily for the many benefactions that He has shown you and your child before, during, and after its birth in spiritual and physical ways. In this you are doing a Christian and God-pleasing work, since the dear Lord demands in His word that we be thankful with heart and mouth for all of His benefactions, especially since we cannot repay Him in any other way for his loyalty and goodness. Also, you have before you the example of pious people in the Old and the New Testament who have not only prayed diligently in their physical and spiritual circumstances but have also cordially praised and lauded the Giver of all good and perfect gifts after the divine help and assistance they have received. In this the example of the blessed Maria, the mother of our Savior, is especially recorded in the Bible as one who appeared in the temple at the set time with her child Jesus and presented this her dear child to the Lord and brought the dear Lord her sacrifice of praise and thanks.

"We read almost the same thing about the mother of the prophet Samuel in the first and last chapter of the 1st book of Samuel: she had not only requested this her son from the Lord with sincere diligence; but also, after she had been granted her wish, she praised the Lord publicly and gave her son back to the Lord. From these two examples you can learn what your duty is, too, after God has not only blessed you with the fruit of your bodies but also delivered you at the proper time and received your child into His covenant of grace through Holy Baptism and also graciously diverted so much hardship and danger from both of you. Foremostly you should recognize that these are purely unmerited benefactions of God, which He could have kept from you and your child just as easily as he granted them to you: there are many mothers and children in the world whom God in His wondrous counsel and justice has not let enjoy such benefactions.

"2. Since God demands no other repayment from you than that you thank Him for it from your heart, it should be your occupation not only now but during your entire life to praise Him, your Creator and Keeper, with all your body and spirit.

"3. You should sacrifice your little child to the Lord, that is to say, you must direct all your care and efforts to raising it in the fear and of and respect for the Lord so that it will lead its life according to the promise made in Holy Communion to let its light so shine before men that God will be honored, your neighbor edified, and its own salvation advanced, in this order. It was spoken out of the mouth of the Lord: 'Direct my children, the work of my hands, unto me.'[259] For you should well note that this little child now belongs to the Lord Jesus in that He not only created it but also redeemed it as His own property with His own blood with infinite physical and spiritual suffering and has washed it clean of all its sins and sanctified it in Holy Baptism. Therefore He says unto you even as the daughter of Pharaoh said unto the mother of Moses: 'Take this child away and nurse it for me, and I will give thee thy wages.' Through His mercy God will not leave unrewarded the loyalty that *you* show in raising the child; rather, if it is neglected through your fault, He will demand its blood from your hands on the day of judgment.

"4. Because you now need much divine grace and wisdom for the Christian nurture of this new blessing of your marriage, let a serious prayer be recommended to you through which you build a wall around yourself and your child, and, through the power of God, drive back Satan with all his cunning and wickedness, while he runs around like a roaring lion to swallow up your little child. Also, in all your cross and miserable circumstances that are accustomed to afflict married people in this vale of tears, you could do nothing better than to comply with what God tells you and us all: 'Call upon me in the day of trouble: I will deliver thee, etc.,' likewise, 'Cast thy burden upon the Lord, etc.,' also 'Commit thy way unto the Lord.' And now too we wish to raise our hearts to the Lord and pray thus:

"Merciful and loving God, we give Thee hearty praise and thanks not only for blessing this person in her marriage with the fruit of the body but also for mercifully guarding her all during her pregnancy from all misfortune and danger and for delivering her at the proper time from her bodily burden. Yea, we also thank Thee, Oh merciful God, that Thou hast let her child be reborn through holy baptism and hast received and accepted it as Thy child and hast guarded it so far in life (and health). For the sake of Christ may the spiritual and physical condition of this mother and child be commended further to Thy mercy and mayest Thou bless their going out and their coming in and guard them on their ways and paths with Thy holy angels and grant Thy divine blessing on the Christian nurture of this little child so that it may grow like a plant to Thy praise and bear much fruit of gratitude for all Thy benefactions. Behold, we are now bringing it to Thee, mayest Thou accept it closer and closer and fill it more and more with Thy Holy Ghost and make such a person of it as will keep Thy commandments for many years and observe Thy laws and act according to them. Grant that, oh [dear] God, and everything else for which Thou shalt be asked, for Christ's sake, amen!

"Our Father, who art in heaven, etc.

"The Lord bless you and keep you and your child, the Lord make His face to shine upon you, etc. The Lord bless your going out and your coming in from now into eternity, amen!"

Monday, the 9th of October. N. [Pichler] is sick again. I visited him and found that the dear Lord had left witness of Himself in his soul. He was present last week in the prayer meeting when my dear colleague, Mr. Boltzius, read the letter from Mr. N. [Senior Urlsperger], which greatly touched his heart because he realized that the worthy N. [Senior] is so earnestly caring for us, praying for us, and thinking of us. He well recognizes that at the time that he wished to leave us with N. [Stephan Riedelsperger], he was doing himself much bodily and spiritual harm.

During the evening prayer hour I read the two letters which our worthy Professor Francke had written to me and which I found to be most blessed letters! The dear Lord did not let them go without blessing on other people too; for someone came to me soon after the prayer meeting and told me so with joy, whereupon we awakened each other even more and joined in prayer. At the same time I read out loud the 19th chapter of the 3rd book of Johann Arndt's *Of True Christianity*, in which the dear Lord is presented and shown to us especially in His love. If His children believed that better, they would have real confidence in Him and pray to Him for all His blessings.

Tuesday, the 10th of October. This morning at the prayer meeting in the orphanage I chose, as the basis of edification, the words from Luke 12:32: "Fear not, little flock; for it is your Father's good pleasure to give you the kingdom." While I was returning home, I saw N. N. [Simon Reuter] working on the street and cited this verse to him. Thereupon he told me with joy that he had been wishing to come to me and tell me what God had recently done for his soul. God had been working on him, he said, for nearly five years; yet his state of grace had always seemed bad and he had never been able to be sure of it. The last time he went to confession he did not know whether he dared go to Holy Communion; but he had persisted in praying and imploring, and the dear Lord had shown mercy upon him. He had been unable to believe that God could be as merciful and loving toward poor sinners as he was now discovering. He could now truly say with right: "I thank Thee Lord, that Thou hast been angry with me and that Thou hast turned Thy anger from me and comforted me."

This N. [Reuter] had formerly been unable to read, but he learned to from my dear colleague in Old Ebenezer. Often he had been certain that God had accepted him; but, as customarily happens with children of God, temptation[260] had come and he had not known for sure how things stood. Therefore he had prayed all the more, and now at last he was fully assured. I could see by looking at him how joyful his heart was about it. But I also told him that the temptations to doubt would not remain away. "Yes," he answered, "I know that well, I have experienced it; but I have just come to a chapter in Johann Arndt which discusses the fist-blows of Satan, and from this I well recognize that it can't be otherwise, that is the way it goes with God's children." I admonished him to praise God and be steadfast and left him at his work.

Wednesday, the 11th of October. Yesterday there was a very cold wind, and last night it was very cold. This cold is lasting throughout the day. In the evening prayer meeting I discussed the conversation of the Lord Jesus with the Samaritan woman in the New Testament story in John 4; and our loving Jesus did not leave the contemplation of this story without a blessing. From it we see how the heart of the Lord Jesus is disposed toward poor sinners and how He wishes to reveal Himself to them with all His mercy, love, and affection, indeed, how He really does so.

Thursday, the 12th of October. This morning after the prayer meeting I went to a grace-hungry soul, namely to N. N. [Mrs. Peter Gruber] and told her what I had discussed in it, to wit: "Come, for all is ready,"[261] and showed her how kind the dear Lord is and how He is asking us to come to Him. From this we should recognize that He would like to give us everything if we were to come to Him. That should so win our heart, and therefore also hers, to our so kindly God that she could put her whole faith in Him. She was very pleased to hear this and said immediately that she wished to tell me something; it was very minor, to be sure, yet she wished to say it. N. [Margaretha Gruber] (whom she had had in her house constantly since the death of her parents) was at first very naughty, especially at night during their sleep so that they were unable to get any rest. They had tried admonitions and punishments on her, but nothing would help; and they were finally determined to send her away.

However, after the dear Lord had taken their little child unto Himself, they had preferred to keep her and look upon her as their own child. Therefore she had told her husband that she wished to go to the right Man, who could help them. She did that, and the dear Lord had been so loving and had heard her poor prayer so that she was now very tranquil. She told me this; and her husband, who had just arrived, was overjoyed at the kindness that God had shown them in looking upon her simple prayer so mercifully. She also said that she cherished the verse that I had recited to her on Sunday morning: "Oh Israel, trust thou in the Lord." Ever since that time our loving God had, she said, shown Himself especially merciful toward her. However, she also added, "Things change so much with me all the time, it can't be any different, it can't be otherwise in Christendom."

In the morning after school a person came to me and said that a great weight was lying on her heart and that she was therefore suffering much anxiety. She said that she had been greatly refreshed yesterday evening in the prayer hour but that now everything had vanished. Sin was stirring in her and was causing her to believe that she still had no grace. I told her the story from John 4 in more detail and showed how lovingly the Lord Jesus had shown himself to this woman, who was a great sinner, and how He had finally revealed Himself to her. Therefore she too should set her trust in Him and continue it, and then the Lord Jesus would also show Himself thus to her. This person often receives a glance of grace from the Lord Jesus, but this soon disappears when she thinks back on the multitude of her sins and she cannot yet believe firmly and constantly that His mercy far far surpasses all her sins. Therefore she must still struggle to be right certain of her condition of grace. Among other things, she said that she thought last night that she would be able to believe it and make the Lord Jesus her own but that she had now lost such joy. I told her, however, that to the honor of the Lord Jesus she should believe that He had granted all His grace even to her because He had, as she knew, promised it and had offered Himself so lovingly in the gospel to poor sinners. I told her she should persist in her prayer, it would come about in due time that she was certain of it.

Friday, the 13th of October. My return to Savannah was delayed this time longer than usual; but I do not regret it, especially since with God's divine blessing I pretty well accomplished the purpose of this trip. Our letters are in good hands and will be sent off to London at the first opportunity via Charleston by Col. Stephens. I shall always make use of this safe opportunity and, hopefully, be doing the surest thing. General Oglethorpe was not yet in Savannah; but he arrived in Savannah unexpectedly last Tuesday toward evening in an open boat despite strong and very contrary winds. Mr. Causton had received news of his impending arrival a few hours in advance, so everything was arranged for his reception.

The inhabitants lined up in good order with their muskets opposite his house, which is situated at the place where everything that comes to Savannah by water must land. As soon as he came ashore twenty-four cannons were fired, the magistrates received him at the water's edge and accompanied him up the bluff and into his house. Mr. Oglethorpe showed himself very friendly toward these as well as toward the other people, who were gathered in a large crowd, and spoke to some as he passed them. The whole city expressed its joy until late in the night with shooting and fireworks; and various important people of the city welcomed him in his own home. He retained these for a long time in his house and told them some very pleasant things concerning the welfare of the colony.

Mr. Causton led me in, and Mr. Oglethorpe received me very cordially; and finally, after he had dismissed the others, he kept me there in order to talk with me about this and that privately.

The next day, namely Wednesday afternoon, he granted me another audience, at which time we could talk some more on behalf of the congregation about the good land across Abercorn Creek. He must have already inquired of others about the condition of our congregation, and he revealed to me his joy and pleasure that the dear Lord had helped so much; and he was entirely willing to give us the afore-mentioned land. He soon spoke about it to the surveyor and gave him orders to reconnoiter the entire island and to bring him reliable information. I also mentioned the orphanage and the necessity of such an institution among us, and of this too he seemed to have already heard some reports. He assured me of his affection and aid and gave me some advice as to how and in what manner I should solicit the Lord Trustees in writing for a contribution for maintaining the orphanage and how I should refer in my letter to him (Mr. Oglethorpe) and his approbation. He did not doubt, he said, that the Lord Trustees would willingly contribute toward it.

Kikar, a former soldier in this colony who was born in Hamburg and wished to settle among us, had travelled with me to Savannah in order to speak with Mr. Causton or with Mr. Oglethorpe himself about his design. Because he has a good testimony from our people, I mentioned him to Mr. Oglethorpe; but he did not wish to dismiss[262] him until he had given more proof of an orderly life, for which purpose he should sojourn with us for a while.

At the same time he told me that two young married people, whom he met underway on a boat, wished to join our community but that he did not think much good of them; I should inquire into their circumstances. By this he meant N. [Grimming],[263] who was accepted [by Baron von Reck] into the third transport in London but left us within a half a year and finally married a Scottish woman. He is very humbled, and he assured me that he is seeking nothing in the world but his and his wife's true salvation, from which, however, he had been entirely prevented in Frederica and Darien; [for he did not know of a single soul there who had even begun to journey on the narrow path to heaven. Rather everyone there lived according to the flesh, and the minister there was quiet.] His wife is young [of handsome appearance] and in great danger of seduction. However, because her spirit is pliant, he believes that she can be won if she can come to good people and live in tranquility. It had cost him much to tear her away from her father and other people and bring her here. I told him that I did not wish to prevent him from settling with us, but he should seek and be sure of the divine will in this matter and consider everything carefully so that he might not regret it later if he found difficulty in earning a living.

I also told him that Mr. N. [Whitefield] was a righteous man whom the Lord will bless in his office when he returns; so it would perhaps be better for him if he remained in Savannah, since he could earn something there for himself and his wife and since she would profit better from divine service there because she understood only English and her Scottish mother tongue.[264] However, he has no desire for this but is determined to come to Ebenezer. When Mr. Oglethorpe asked me about him again, I told him how I had previously known him and why he had left our place and what he now had in mind. Mr. Oglethorpe was pleased to hear this and promised to give him and his wife the reduced rations for a year. Nevertheless, this N. [Grimming] must speak with him personally before then. Moreover, Mr. Oglethorpe assured me that he would not allow anyone to move to our place unless he were previously known to him and to us as honest and orderly. This time he will not remain for more than eight days in Savannah, but will return to Frederica. Next time I intend to mention the church and school, which we need so much, and also my dear colleague's house. Of my house, I shall not make any mention, and that for good reason. I will also postpone the construction until I have more certainly convinced myself of God's will and shall have received some tangible proof of His providence. Our father in heaven knows what we need. Perhaps Mr. Oglethorpe will visit us himself one of these days; and then my own poor hut will speak for me, as it were.

As I understand from the merchant Purry in Savannah, as well as from Mr. Oglethorpe's reports, the Lord Trustees intend to be quite economical in their expenditures, as much has been spent in recent times, and as the rich people in England, having received [unpleasant] unfounded news of the poor state of this colony, no longer wish to contribute anything, except that which is being allocated by Parliament, i.e., 12,000 £ for the maintenance of the troops here, and 8,000 £ for expenses of the colony, which is little enough for such large undertakings. Mr. Oglethorpe has given me permission to write to him, which I shall do if he should not return to Savannah for a long time. [It is being said, in this respect, that he is not well content with the inhabitants of this place, for which he has ample reason.

[Mr. Purry does not wish the merchant Simons in London (whose representative he is) to send him any more goods but wishes to suspend his business here because there is no money among the people and consequently his goods will spoil if he does not sell them on credit and thus lose money. People think the whole scheme of things will have to be changed if this colony is to prosper.[265]

[For Mrs. Rheinlaender, who was still in jail, I asked both Mr. Causton and also Mr. Oglethorpe to have her let out, as was done last Tuesday.] Because the above mentioned Kikar has not yet received the desired answer from Mr. Oglethorpe, he remained in Savannah; and I had to return home with two men, of whom one was very weak. This was very slow, but, God be praised, successful!

[In Purysburg I learned that four Herrnhuters had brought Count Zinzendorf's two missionaries, Böhler and Schulius, to Carolina on a boat to start their office among the Negroes in Purysburg and other places in Carolina. They had sojourned a short while in Kiefer's house, and he inquired of them about their profession and intentions; but they did not wish to say anything about it. Later, however, he learned the cause of their arrival in Purysburg from a letter that Mr. Mueller, the former servant of Baron von Reck, had written to him (Kiefer) on the 3rd of May of this year in care of those two men. After learning this, with further details from me, he was aggrieved by their dissimulation because he would have been glad to give them good advice for their undertaking if they had told him something about it. He showed me Mueller's letter, from which I could clearly infer that this man, on whom God was working here not in vain with His word, has been entirely drawn by the

Herrnhuters to their side. He wishes Kiefer could feel about these brothers, of whom Böhler is the deacon, just as he feels; and now he wishes to go to Herrnhut.]

Because the cold weather is starting, I had to buy some heavy cloth for the orphans on credit so that winter clothes can be made for them. I had no money on hand, but I remembered the words of the Father: "I will never leave thee, nor forsake thee." Also, the shoemaker from Purysburg came to us and made shoes for the orphanage, which had not been necessary in warm weather. God, whose goodness is everlasting, will see to the payment in His good time. Meanwhile, the merchants in Savannah are glad to extend us credit because they do not doubt that they will be properly paid. The schoolmaster in Savannah, Mr. Habersham, promised to give us for the orphanage some of the winter clothing that he will receive for the poor there from a ship that has just arrived and which has been left entirely at his disposal [by Mr. Whitefield].

Saturday, the 14th of October. I found N. [Eisberger] sick in bed and began to tell him something about God's salutary purpose in His chastisement. When I showed him how much effort the dear Lord had to make with a miserable man before He could tear his heart away from everything and fit it for his dwelling of grace, he wept out loud and said that his greatest worry was that he had not yet been able to achieve any certainty of his state of grace. The trouble lay, he said, in himself. He did not wish to give up everything, and he showed no sincerity in creating his salvation, for which he was sufficiently admonished in Holy Scripture. In his soul-suffering he was comforted by the fact that he had often heard that God would not forsake his soul, that He loved it far too much. This love of God, which showed itself so gloriously in suffering him, sparing him, and calling him, forced a plenitude of tears from him because God could love even such a disobedient and disloyal person as he was with such steadfastness.

I reminded him of what I had preached to the congregation before my departure in the repetition hour and which God had again blessed in him; and I told him that I had had him especially in mind at that time and had wished he would earnestly

seize upon the dear promises of God and would not rest until
he too had found a little nook as a resting place in the wide-
open father-heart of God. He should not despair because of his
sins, because God had promised and added an oath that he did
not wish the death of a sinner, but rather that he be converted
and live; and he had many examples of God's merciful help in
the Bible. As I recently advised the congregation in the prayer
meeting, in reading in the Bible of these comforting examples
of those whom God helped out of spiritual and physical hardship, he should add: "His goodness lasteth for ever. The God
who hath helped this man and that, indeed many thousands, is
still the same one who is most willing to help us."

Sunday, the 15th of October. I had to inquire of a [young]
man about something that occurred during my absence,
whereupon he told me that during his work in the fields he had
remembered the sins of his youth, which had caused him much
worry and sorrow. At the same time he was now learning the
meaning of the words: "If Thy word had not been my comfort,
I would have perished in my misery."[266] However simple this
man is, he still well knows how to make use of his Savior and the
reconciliation He instituted through the power of the Holy
Ghost and to crawl into His wounds like a little worm. In this
way he will be preserved both from all anxiety caused by his
feeling of sin and mounting carnal desires as well as from all
false self-made comfort and frivolous application of the gospel.
He showed me the physical blessings that the dear Lord has
granted him this year, and he was more satisfied and grateful
for it, as a true blessing of the Lord, than unconverted worldly-
minded people are accustomed to be with their wealth and
superfluous supplies.

For several days, and therefore on this Sunday too, one of the
millers[267] from Old Ebenezer has been staying here and, according to his wicked nature, had little good in his mind. Yesterday evening after the prayer meeting he began to sing all
sorts of frivolous songs on the street in the English language;
and I prohibited this earnestly because it was causing disorder
and was aiming at a parody of the Salzburgers' singing. And,
because today he spent his time in shooting and thus wantonly

desecrating the Sabbath, I warned in the repetition hour that I was much displeased by the sheltering of such disorderly people and that the congregation would not be acting contrary to charity if they refused hospitality and company to such people as are annoying and cause disquiet and harm in the community. This person does not need to be here, for he belongs to Old Ebenezer; but he may have his own evil purpose in spending these days here. Later he came to me himself and let me know that he had understood that I had warned the congregation against him, and he wished to know the reason why. I could tell him this easily, with the declaration that Mr. Oglethorpe would seriously banish from our place such disorder as he had committed. Since I am the minister of the congregation and its spiritual shepherd, he should not be surprised if I watch over my flock and attempt to prevent all danger of temptation. He was satisfied with this explanation and made a frivolous excuse for his disorderliness. Tomorrow he will go his way. Apparently this man, with others, earns his money at the sawmill in Old Ebenezer with idleness.

Monday, the 16th of October. This morning I learned that the dear Lord had blessed his lovely and grace-filled gospel in various people and that several had assembled after the repetition hour to edify themselves with an edifying conversation and with singing and praying. /They praised the spiritual profit from this for the glory of God, and desired such simple assemblies for the future./[268]

During this dry weather our people are very busy bringing in the rest of their beans and rice. This year some of them will get more rice than they will need in their households. We are now preparing to make a rice mill.[269] Our carpenters have never built such a thing; and therefore I am having a qualified man come from Purysburg who will build such a mill for the orphanage, which has also raised some beautiful rice. Afterwards, we can use it as a model. No stones will be used in it, rather two wooden hammers instead of stones.

Tuesday, the 17th of October. It was very pleasant for me to hear that a certain Salzburger could rightfully repeat Isaiah's words: "He hath clothed me in the garments of salvation, He hath covered me with the robe of righteousness." However, he was worried by the fact that he did not feel his misery as much as he heard from other people. But I told him he should be content with what God had let him recognize as much as He himself thought necessary for his thorough humiliation and that he now had nothing more to do in the world but to be concerned for his Lord Jesus and his grace. It was good, I said, that he was never satisfied with himself, he should merely continue with his struggle and look up to Jesus, the Beginning and End of our faith. God never tries a man beyond his abilities; he should merely cling quietly to God.

Wednesday, the 18th of October. This morning I learned that the dear Lord had not failed to bless yesterday's evening prayer meeting, which again dealt with the fourth chapter of the Gospel of St. John. May His name be blessed because He still accompanies His Word with His blessing, just as He blessed the word that the Samaritan woman announced in the city. A certain woman had had this chapter read to her a couple of times, and thus it impressed her all the more. She told how the Lord was following her just as He had followed the Samaritan woman at that time. The day before yesterday another woman said that she thought she would have greater progress in her Christianity if she herself could read and search in God's word. She had asked her husband whether she might be able to learn; and her husband answered that it might well take place if she desired it and if she called upon God for His blessing on it.

Thursday, the 19th of October. N. [Herzog] has been in a serious condition for a long while.[270] This evening he visited me and said that he could not deny that God was working on him and testing his soul; yet it still always seemed to him as if God did not wish to bring him to salvation, for nothing wished to change in him; rather, things were getting even worse. But he also had to confess that he himself was to blame, because he was not treating faithfully what God had granted him. As I can gather, he must have let himself be drawn into much sin in Salzburg, from which he does not wish to be freed through a true confession. I recited for him the words from Acts 17: 30–31: "And the times of this ignorance God winked at; but now commandeth all men (and also him) to repent," and the Lord wished to effect penitence and faith in him too. Likewise,

I Peter 4:1-2. At the last part of the third verse, he said that that was just the way things went in his homeland. I also spoke with him further, and may the dear Lord place His blessing upon it!

[Friday, the 20th of October. This morning I learned that some souls had remained together until late in the night and read a chapter from Johann Arndt and sung and prayed; and this so encouraged them that they all wept and wished to spend almost the entire night together. So far, God has been blessing His word powerfully in Veit Lemmenhoffer. He has let him strongly feel his deep perdition but has also refreshed him again.]

Saturday, the 21st of October. This morning N. N. [Simon Reuter] said that, as long as he lives, he will never forget the gospel that was treated yesterday in the prayer meeting and stands in Luke 4:18-19; for this was the very word that the dear Lord had blessed so splendidly in him the last time at confession. It had never refreshed him so much as that time. To be sure, he does not feel this comfort all the time; but he was greatly struck by what he had heard the day before yesterday: one should trust and hold to the word of God without feeling. He had never known this, he said, and therefore he had suffered much anxiety at not being able to feel any divine comfort. A woman who had recently heard the verse: "For the Son of man is come to seek and to save that which is lost" said that she well noticed ever since then that the Lord Jesus was seeking her and had accepted her especially.

Yesterday there were some adults with me with whom I could edify myself. N. [Simon Reuter], who was formerly unable to read and still understands only a little about it but has learned to know the Lord Jesus in truth, can speak so cordially and intimately with the dear Lord in his prayers that I can truly edify myself from it. N. [Mrs. Schweighofer] was also there, but full of distress. She said she had been so well on Friday that she could not proclaim it. My dear colleague, Mr. Boltzius, who went down again on Tuesday to Mr. Oglethorpe, had said in the last prayer meeting before his departure that the congregation should wax fat on the pasture of the Lord during his absence so that, when he saw it upon his return, he might praise the dear

Lord for it. She then thought that this would be fulfilled in her, but now it was all gone again. I told her, however, that the dear Lord wished to keep her in her humility in that manner and prepare her for a greater grace.

Monday, the 23rd of October. In the evening during the prayer meeting a boat full of people arrived,[271] and at the end of it I was given a letter that my dear colleague had written yesterday in Savannah, with the following contents: "I hope that, with divine aid, I shall be with you and my dear ones at noon on Tuesday. I am sending you a little flock of people who, apart from the shoemaker and his family, have been presented to the community by Mr. Oglethorpe to serve as herdsmen. The old woman has been entirely abandoned and is therefore assigned to the orphanage.[272] If these people arrive before me, please shelter them with Christian people and give them some meat according to weight and some beans according to measure from the barrel that is accompanying them. The old woman, who is said to be very industrious and useful in material circumstances, can soon be put into the orphanage. My text today was from Romans VIII: 'And we know that all things work together for good to them that love God.' This I explicated in the afternoon with the story of the regular Sunday gospel. I believe that the Lord has blessed His word. Greet mine, yours, and ours with the following words: 'Be it as it may, my Father in heaven knoweth counsel and aid for all things.'"[273]

Tuesday, the 24th of October. It has again become so cold that last night the leaves on the sweet potato vines began to wilt or to look as if they were half boiled. In the evening prayer hour I gave the story from Luke 5:1–11, and at its end a woman from the Germans who arrived yesterday told me how happy she was that the dear Lord had brought her to this place where she had the pure word of the Lord. She wished me many blessings. I told her how the dear Lord wished to help us to apply our short time in this world well in order to prepare ourselves for blessed eternity and therefore not only to have His word but also to use it rightly. The dear Lord also blessed this prayer meeting in one of the Salzburgers, who told me of it joyfully as he passed. The Lord's name be praised for this!

Wednesday, the 25th of October. At the beginning of last

week I went to Savannah to see Mr. Oglethorpe for the sake of the congregation and widows and orphans, and I only came back this evening. My reasons for waiting so long in Savannah were in part various business with Mr. Oglethorpe and the storehouse and in part the arrival of Capt. Thomson, whose ship[274] was, to be sure, in the river, but not yet at Savannah. And, because our money was here, I preferred to settle everything I had to do with the storehouse rather than to journey down again.

[In Savannah there is nothing but troublesome circumstances, which are a reason for us too to pray diligently, even though the need and want there do not affect us as much as the other people in this country. Therefore we are all the more obliged to thank our eternally loyal and merciful God for His care, for which we wish to awaken ourselves through His grace.

[On the very day that I arrived in Savannah Mr. Oglethorpe assembled the people of the city of Savannah and announced to them that all the sums of money that were to be spent in the colony this year had already been expended, and more, and that the Trustees had incurred great debts. Therefore these debts will be paid, as far as it will go, with the provisions that are now in the storehouse.[275] Otherwise nothing can be bought for the storehouse or sold from it until the coming month of June, rather everyone must see to how he can get along on his own. Also, no other people will be employed for the Trustees' undertakings except their own indentured servants, because there is no money to pay day laborers. If anyone wishes to leave the country, he may do so if he is not in debt to the storehouse; otherwise he must pay or give sufficient assurance of payment. Mr. Causton must be to blame for this, since he went too far in buying and distributing the provisions; yet it would look worse for him if he had not done it and the people had had to starve or leave the country because of lack of provisions.[276]

[In addition there is the equally great distress of] The poor people whom Capt. Thomson brought along as indentured servants for this colony [They] are Palatines and Württembergers, a whole ship full—men, women, and children. These are to be sold for a period of five years, but the inhabitants of this land have neither money nor food for this. An adult costs 6 £ 5 sh. sterling. After I had preached the word of the Lord to these poor people, partly from Romans 8:28 and partly from the gospel for the 21st Sunday after Trinity, a great crowd of them ran up to me and asked me to take them to our place, which was, however, not within my power. I asked Mr. Oglethorpe to free an old widow of fifty, who had lost her husband at sea and had been rejected and abandoned because of her age; and I sent her to our orphanage.

We are in great need of a shoemaker. At my request Mr. Oglethorpe advanced the travel costs for one,[277] which the shoemaker must repay in two or three years. I am lending him as much money as he needs for his profession and food for the very beginning, for which he will make shoes for my family, for the orphanage, and for the poor in the community.

Because everyone in the congregation is planning to go to the new plantations this winter and no one wishes to guard the cattle any longer, I requested two herdsmen from Mr. Oglethorpe. He gave them to me and at first demanded, in the presence of Capt. Thomson, no more than that I should have to provide for their provisions and clothing. However, the next day I remembered what had happened to me several times in the past, namely, that after some time I was asked to pay for things that had been given to me previously. Therefore I thanked Mr. Oglethorpe for the gift of these herdsmen in writing, in hopes that no officer would dare to demand any payment for the people, because they had been given to us as a gift. [Hereupon I learned that Mr. Oglethorpe had no power to give away anything. However, he would request them from the Trustees; and I too might write to them and cite the reasons why we need herdsmen. He did not doubt that the Trustees would give them to us; however, if they would not, then we could still keep them for one year and not have to pay for them because we would probably gain little advantage from them during the first year, since they are not yet acquainted with the country and its way of life and might even become sick.]

I made a great effort to ask Mr. Oglethorpe to allow something for our widows and orphans, but only initially while our orphanage was in its beginnings and still owed some debts. [However, he made nothing but polite excuses and finally dismissed me with] /We received/ 200 lbs of flour, 200 lbs of meat, and some molasses or syrup. The Lord is still alive, [He will change His favors again and not disappoint us in our hopes but will send us help from afar if people nearby are hard and insensitive,] for in accordance with His love He has caused a beautiful blessing of money to flow to us from Court Chaplain Ziegenhagen, Mr. S. U. [Senior Urlsperger], and Mr. P. F. [Professor Francke], from which the poor in the congregation, and therefore also our widows and orphans, may expect much bodily refreshment.

I likewise see from Senior Urlsperger's letter that the dear Lord has also provided for us in the future; for we can expect from Halle and Augsburg many necessary things that are expensive in this country such as linen, Schauer's balm, books, etc., of which we have been sent an inventory already. God be praised! For from the very cordial letters we have received from our dear Fathers we have learned that Sanftleben has arrived safely in London and has been kindly received by Court Chaplain Ziegenhagen and that the letters from us and from various members of the congregation have caused much joy.

[Except for the many good things I enjoyed from the hand of the Father in Savannah and from the above-mentioned lovely letters, I was pained no little bit at being unable to receive payment for the linen sent by the merchant from St. Gall, Mr. Schlatter, and which Mr. Causton has accepted and also sold, with promise of correct and certain payment. The dear man himself has now even written to Mr. Causton and requested immediate payment, since otherwise his trade would suffer a blow. Mr. Oglethorpe wished me to ask the merchant to wait until next June or else to accept all sorts of provisions from the storehouse. If I had money, I should like to pay the good man myself, but at present I lack the means. Meanwhile I have asked Court Preacher Ziegenhagen to pay 30 £ sterling from my future salary to this merchant's correspondents in London, Messrs. Norris and Drewett. Perhaps Mr. Oglethorpe will repay me soon, for this colony cannot possibly remain much longer in its present circumstances. At worst I would have to accept provisions for it gradually from the store-house, even though one can buy elsewhere better and more safely with ready cash. But I should rather suffer than cause any more suffering for this dear benefactor, who sent four beautiful bolts of linen as a gift to our Salzburgers last year and promised still more. At least he will see my good intentions from this, even if I am quite incapable of doing any more. I myself have written to him.

[Matters concerning our land have still not been settled properly, and I do not know why Mr. Oglethorpe is so evasive.] Since the harvest is over and they are in good health, our people would like to go together to their plantations on Abercorn Creek if only the surveyor had orders to assign them to them. Mr. Oglethorpe is willing to employ the surveyor [but he does not wish to see him or speak with him because he finds him too long-winded and vexatious. And, because there is no money at hand and he does not wish to give any provisions from the storehouse, while the surveyor will not do anything without money and provisions, I cannot see how things will work out. However, I shall let nothing keep me from advising our people in God's name to begin work there, and I shall wait to see what orders come.]

Mr. Oglethorpe has heard much praise of the diligence and good order of our community, [yet I don't know how much that is to our advantage. But God is still Lord of the earth, the Refuge of the poor, etc., and, if people in Europe are praying and caring for our community so earnestly, can this be without effect? I do not believe so. Rather all false intentions and plots will be revealed and put to shame before God would forsake us or let us be oppressed. We tell the congregation nothing about these and other worries but continue to admonish them to observe their duty to God and man, and we try in all ways to give them courage. I requested payment for the construction costs for my dear colleague's house and also for the building of a church and school, but I was merely referred with helpful words to the Lord Trustees in London. I have not wished to mention my own house because it would have been in vain.]

He gave written permission to Sybilla Resch, who lost her husband in the forest three years ago, to marry again. It is already three years since her husband was lost in the woods, and nobody who knew his physical and mental condition assumes anything but that he died a few days after getting lost. Mrs.

Resch herself has two indications from which she thinks she can ascertain that he perished of hunger and thirst. Since everyone in the congregation believes that he is dead, it has long been wished that she might marry again, for this would be good both for her and for other people, who sometimes nourish unnecessary suspicions. So far she has conducted herself quietly and in a Christian way, as becomes a widow.

A new preacher[278] has arrived in Savannah [who, however, does not have the spirit or the gifts of Mr. Whitefield. He must not be a lover and furtherer of the good, and he preaches very insipidly.[279] Nearly everyone yearns for Mr. Whitefield, but he will probably be sent to Frederica].

Late in the evening a pious Englishman came to my bedroom and brought an English translation of the *Commentary* of the late Dr. Luther concerning the Epistle to the Galatians. In order to edify himself further, he read me a passage from it concerning the article of justification that had struck him as especially edifying. The dear Lord blessed all this so abundantly in me too that I found grounds to praise Him for it. On the following day I recommended this lovely material to the people with whom I was eating breakfast; and, because one of them was most interested and had received little instruction in this comforting Evangelical article, he continued discussing it with me. In order to ground himself better, he also read the late Mr. A. W. Böhm's sermon concerning justification.

Mr. Oglethorpe wishes us to continue serving the German people in Savannah with our office. Because we need people to row us down and back, I asked for provisions and for some payment for their efforts; and he agreed to this and approved what Mr. Causton has done up to now. Some of the Germans find the word that they have heard from us in the name of the Lord to be too difficult; and they make blind judgments about it, as I have been told.

Thursday, the 26th of October. The people who are now living among us and wish to serve the community were at my house, and I found that they are showing themselves to be very happy to be here and very grateful for this dispensation of God. [Mrs. Rheinlaender is here again, for which she has to thank only my intercession; and, because this wayward woman wished to draw some of these people to herself, I warned them against her; but they already knew something about her that they found to be suspicious and repugnant.]

As soon as the provisions come up, necessary measures will be taken for the herdsmen. [I wonder why the boat has not yet arrived that I sent ahead at noon on Tuesday, loaded with food and all sorts of things. I departed from Savannah at night with the flood tide and did not see that boat anywhere. Today some people fetched the remaining belongings of the new herdsmen from Purysburg with the little boat, but they did not see them[280] either. Whether they have perhaps gone to Abercorn, or how things stand, we will learn tomorrow, since three men wish to journey toward them in the little boat and bring back the provisions they are lacking.]

Friday, the 27th of October. [The schoolmaster Ortmann would like to have an indentured servant but cannot pay for one, and therefore he wishes to ask Mr. Oglethorpe for one. I did this in a letter that they should take down themselves as they wish to pick out the servant. He well needs such a servant. To be sure, I thought about it in Savannah; but I did not know whether I would be doing right if I looked into it because, if it did not go well, I would be to blame.

[The Purysburg shoemaker, who was to stay with us making shoes for the winter, will now leave us again because we have acquired a shoemaker for ourselves. He did not appear to be displeased, as our shoemaker is a compatriot of his, and he has plenty of work in Purysburg, even if he has little cash payment and too many wicked comrades and idlers around him. During my return journey I was in his hut in Purysburg, in which a Frenchman was lying sick. The wife complained to me that she had requested the preacher to come to the sick man to pray with him and to give him good instruction and comfort out of God's word; but he would not come unless one had payment in hand for his trouble. A man who was present said he was not a preacher but an overseer of Negroes or Moorish slaves, for he was keeping them hard at work on his plantation and did not trouble himself at all about his congregation.]

A man [A young Salzburger] announced that, since God had blessed him with a good harvest, he had remembered his for-

mer promise, namely, to make a restitution, from the blessings
he had received, for what he had purloined from his neighbor
in the years of his ignorance. He wished to donate something to
the orphanage and something to a poor widow in the congregation. Another person praised Luther's *Large Catechism* to me
and said he had received much instruction and edification from
it. It had caused him much reflection that the late Luther had
written that, even as an old scholar, he had still studied in the
Catechism and could never master it or learn it all.

Saturday, the 28th of October. Yesterday evening during the
prayer meeting a [our] large boat arrived, at which time we
learned that it had capsized between Savannah and Purysburg
so that all the provisions got wet and two barrels of flour, one
barrel of meat, an English woman's clothing, and my trunk
were lost. With great effort they were able to recover the other
things that had fallen out of the boat. In my trunk was a new
black gown,[281] and in its pocket was a leather portfolio with the
letters that had been brought by Capt. Thomson and also some
very necessary accounts as well as some linen and paper. We
greatly regret the edifying letters, which, to be sure, I had read
for my own edification but which I would like to have shared
with my dear colleague and the congregation. At the place they
landed at night with the boat there is a very dangerous spot
where our people have come close to great misfortune several
times.

This morning I sent some people down again in the small
boat and offered an Indian a white woolen cloth if he could
help me recover the trunk and other things. The sons of Kiefer
of Purysburg are also very skillful at diving in the water and
finding lost things in it, and I immediately called upon them
too. I also wrote a letter to the storehouse keeper in Savannah,
Mr. Jones, and gave him news of this unfortunate occurrence so
that he could pass it on to Mr. Oglethorpe. Perhaps he will be as
kind to us on this occasion as he was to a couple of families in
Savannah, whose huts and possessions were destroyed by fire in
broad daylight and to whom he gave something to compensate
for their loss.[282]

Sunday, the 29th of October. I learned from a widow and also
from others of the people who came to us recently and have

spent a Sunday with us for the first time today how the word I preached penetrated to their very hearts. I treated the gospel for the twenty-second Sunday after Trinity concerning the grace of God in two points: 1) that it is possible to achieve grace, 2) that it is, nevertheless, possible and at the same time highly dangerous to lose grace. My dear colleague, on the other hand, treated Chapter I of the Epistle to the Philippians concerning the fellowship in the gospel. Although it rained heavily in the evening and was dark, the dear people came in large numbers to the repetition hour. Even the children were as numerous as at other times, which impressed me very much. *Excitat auditor studium.* We are sometimes worried and depressed because of all sorts of occurrences; but, when we come to our dear congregation in church or at the prayer meeting and treat the word of the Lord together, their very presence and their great desire for the rational and pure milk so arouses us that we go home with serene spirits and therefore with praise of and gratitude to God.

Because most of our congregation will perhaps move soon to their plantations, it will be necessary for one of us to move there with them, as they have been requesting. Time and opportunity will teach us how we can then best arrange things in order to edify them from God's Word daily or at least often. All of those who move out will live together in a district of three English miles; and, because they wish to build a house for the preacher in the center of this district, they will probably be able to gather together often. Since my dear colleague has a well built house while I have a hut as a dwelling, it will probably be my turn to move there first. I am in the hand of the Lord and wish nothing more than to be right useful to the congregation in every way.

Monday, the 30th of October. From the blessings our loving God has granted in money this time, I have paid the debts of the orphanage; but of course it did not go quite far enough to pay them all. The well, which was indispensable for us, and also the cellar and the boards for the floor[283] have cost much money. Besides that I have had a beautiful piece of land cleared for the orphanage that lies all around the orphanage, and it would have caused much harm if the forest and the many trees and bushes had been allowed to remain. The money earned from this and from other services performed for the orphanage by our poor people, who have received no provisions from the storehouse for a whole year, can almost be considered a gift to them; and they all thank God sincerely for giving them an opportunity to earn with the work of their hands something for their sustenance and for their clothing, and for some of them to buy a cow, without having to remove themselves from our community and our spiritual care.

I trust the almighty and at the same time kind Father in heaven to support with His providence and divine blessings this house, which manifestly is meant for His service and glory and for the true spiritual physical advantage of our congregation and in which His holy name is worshiped, honored, and glorified. With our salaries we have also paid our own debts; and, because the praiseworthy Society has given us permission to receive money for a note on our salary and since our new salary begins as of November 1, we find ourselves required to borrow as much money from a merchant in Savannah as is due to us and the schoolmaster for half a year. I also plan to solicit Mr. Oglethorpe or someone else to lend me something for the orphanage.

Tuesday, the 31st of October. After the prayer meeting yesterday a pious Salzburger woman called on me and asked me to examine whether she could go to Holy Communion in the present barren and almost hopeless condition of her soul, in which she was, to be sure, aware of her sins and disloyalty but not of God's grace. She said that last Sunday she had not had the heart to remain with the others in church to have her name written down. I admonished her, for the sake of the love of Christ, who loves the hungry and thirsty and spiritually poor souls, not to stay back and to demand strength of spirit and a feeling of God's mercy for the use of this blessed feast and spiritual medicine. She told me of many inner trials that God had sent her from her first conversion on, of which He had made a beginning already in Old Ebenezer. During this she had been in poor spirits and almost despaired, but God had always looked upon her prayers and tears graciously for Christ's sake and had helped her so far. I reminded her of and impressed upon her spirit the parable that I had told her several times when she was complaining that she had again lost the joyful and comforting condition of her heart which she had received from the sweet tasting mercy of God she had felt, namely, things change in the kingdom of mercy just as the weather changes in the kingdom of nature, and all the contraries must flow together to help the fruit ripen and mature (Psalm 126).

[On Sunday Mrs. Rheinlaender too registered publicly to go to Holy Communion; I had to marvel at her audacity because she had vexed the entire congregation with her godless ways and otherwise opposed all good order and had cursed, execrated, and calumniated her ministers in the most shameful manner. I called her to me and showed her again that, as long as she remains this way, she is not a member of the community and cannot be admitted to Holy Communion. Instead of the curse that came over me from her mouth, I wish her all divine blessing for her instruction and wish to help her petition it from God.]

NOVEMBER

Wednesday, the 1st of November. The people are now very busy digging up their sweet potatoes, since they are endangered by the freezing of the ground at night. The sweet potatoes on the vines are rather small this year, for which the longlasting drought must be to blame. The cotton that some people have planted for home use has scarcely half ripened and is now frozen. It too had been held back in its growth by the heat and lack of rain. It blossomed late in the summer and bore buds, which then had little time left to ripen.

N. [Ernst] and his wife have conducted themselves quietly and exceptionally orderly for some time, and therefore we can let them go to Holy Communion at their insistent request, without much objection on the part of the congregation. Recently in my room I showed them what God demands of a man who wishes to be saved and also to go to Holy Communion. I also reminded them of what they had heard last Sunday about the example of the great debtor,[284] and then I prayed with them. I plan to speak with them further during this week in their own hut.

[The old widow and the shoemaker with his wife wished to go to Holy Communion too, but I advised them to wait until the next communion so that they will be better known among us and be able to learn the path to salvation, and they agreed to this.]

Thursday, the 2nd of November. The people whom we had sent to look for the things that were lost in the water have returned without having accomplished anything. I regret the loss of my trunk most of all, which contained, in addition to my gown, important bills and the last letters received from England and Germany. We got word in these letters that the mail sent through Mr. Sanftleben was well received and caused much joy. Also, our dear Lord caused some material blessings to fall into the hands of our dear S. U. [Senior Urlsperger], which he sent to Halle prior to posting our letters, and whence we shall expect linen, books, and other things as a renewed blessing. Prof. Francke[285] and Prof. Juncker had also enclosed letters for Mr. Thilo, which were likewise lost. Further, Captain Coram had written to me, and Secretary Neumann and the last three East-Indian missionaries from Madras had written to both of us. I shall inform the congregation of these letters as much as my memory will allow me, as I have always done, and we have received much blessing in edification and in the praise of the Lord therefrom. As we have a good opportunity to send letters back through Captain Thomson, who is to return in four weeks, we shall prepare ourselves to write letters as soon as we can arrange it.

The N. [Helfenstein] boy has withdrawn from all discipline in the school and from all good order in the orphanage; and, to evade punishment, he stayed partly with his mother and partly on the street, when she no longer wished to tolerate him in the house. This morning he was brought to me by his mother, and she herself asked that his obstinacy be broken and that he be punished vigorously. Since it had to take place publicly, I hope that this castigation will make an impression on him and on others. Obstinacy and disobedience are very common in children but must be suppressed like other vices by the means ordered by God; at least outbursts of these must be prevented and restrained. So far, the dear Lord has not left us without any blessing in our children, even if their frivolity spoils much good that has been begun.

Friday, the 3rd of November. The surveyor has now come back to us and has orders from Mr. Oglethorpe to survey the land on Abercorn Creek for us as I asked. He promised me firmly not to quit before it is all completed and our people have been assigned the ownership of their plantations. This gives us all great joy and gives us new grounds for praising God, who has granted one blessing after the other and has now granted this one. For it is one of the principal physical blessings of the Lord that could happen for us in this land that this good piece of land has been given to our people, who so gladly work for the glory of God and the good of their neighbors. Without it some of them would hardly be able to subsist; and the congregation would not be able to /stick together and/ attend to their work and divine services communally and in good order. For it was a major worry of most of the people that they would have to do without the daily instruction from God's word that they had had in the evening prayer meetings if they went out to their plantations. For this reason some of them would have made out as best they could in the town rather than to live on the plantations without God's word, since this had been their chief reason for emigrating from Salzburg.

Now, however, the wisdom of God has so ordained it that the entire congregation can come to one place and live united together to their own, including physical, advantage. One of us will be there with the congregation in order to perform his office for both children and adults, while the other remains in the town, because some will remain here and others who move out will do some work here in their gardens and in other ways. Mr. Oglethorpe has given the surveyor neither provisions nor money; and, since he has nothing for his sustenance here, we will have to do what we can. Four people from the congregation go with him every day, and I give some meat to them and also to the surveyor and his boy.[286] The congregation sees to the other provisions. I hope that Mr. Oglethorpe or the Trustees will refund our expenses; for it cannot be demanded of our people, who were kept from their land for so long, to pay the surveyor and his assistant and bear all the expenses themselves.

Saturday, the 4th of November. [With the surveyor we have our troubles and worries. He set out on Thursday to survey the land and returned yesterday toward evening full of anger. He had not been satisfied with either the people, who certainly did their part sincerely, or with the provisions. The meat that I gave to him and to those who went with him he believes to be horse-meat. I bought it recently in Savannah as New York beef, and I regret that it has turned out this way. It has already happened to us several times that we have received horsemeat instead of beef from the storehouse in Savannah, between which some people can distinguish very quickly. I don't know what we can do to make the surveyor finish his work, since we are not in a position now to buy other meat or to pay the kind of people that he wants from Purysburg for his work.]

With the recently received money we have paid the debts of the orphanage and of the poor box, but not fully; so we must hold back as much as possible until God grants more. During the past year of crop failure everything has been so very expensive that both of us have spent so much that we have nothing left but debts. Because of other necessary expenditures for the congregation and the orphanage we have been unwilling and unable to use any of the money we have received but the 3 £ sterling from S. U. [Senior Urlsperger], which was specifically destined for us. Today, while paying the workers and other debts and closing the accounts, I became aware of the penury in which we now stand; whereupon, unexpectedly and with great easing of my mind, I remembered: "God's goodness lasts forever and in eternity. Beast and man He nourishes at the proper season. His mercy has proffered everything both early and late."[287]

In the prayer meeting yesterday, referring to the lost letters, I told the congregation how gloriously our true God has again provided for us in Europe by granting us, through our dear Mr. S. U. [Senior Urlsperger] and Prof. Francke, a supply of linen and other things, which is probably already en route. Likewise our good and pious God has also used the worthy Court Chaplain Ziegenhagen as a blessed tool to send us all sorts of gifts through him, which fountain will surely flow in future times at our need.

Our Salzburgers have collected the semiannual provisions for the herdsmen, in fact so abundantly that the herdsmen themselves are amazed at it; and I hope they will be compelled by it to serve the community all the more loyally. In this way these poor servants and our community will be helped. Instead of its costing 5 shillings herding fee for each cow, it now comes to about 18 pence (stivers)[288] since we have these servants. The community sees to their provisions; and clothes are furnished for them from the poor box, which the dear Lord continues to grant. The remaining people on Capt. Thomson's ship are said to be very badly off. The captain is no longer willing or able to supply them with food, and the people in Savannah are not able to buy them or to keep them in clothing or food. Especially the old people with children are having a bad time, for they must let the oldest children be taken from them while no one wants them themselves. If our people were capable of buying some of these people, then Christ's love would compel them to accept them and to give them the necessary support. We make such reports useful to our congregation in all ways so that they will recognize that the Salzburgers have every advantage.

This afternoon the surveyor called on me and gave his reasons for not being able to survey any more. The people are not used to him [and therefore they could not do anything to please him. Moreover, he lacked provisions, since he was nauseated by the meat.] He thinks he will need only eight or ten days for his work, and we must be patient with him for this short time. I have given him liberty to choose whichever people please him, for almost all of them are all ready to go with him so that he will finally settle the land problem correctly.

Some letters are now being written to England and Germany, which Capt. Thomson is to take with him. They are to the Lord Trustees, the praiseworthy Society, Court Chaplain Ziegenhagen, Senior Urlsperger, Professor Francke, and Mr. Schlatter, the merchant in St. Gall. [Because of our impecunious circumstances, I have to take back the letters I had written to Mr. Schlatter and his correspondent concerning his money (see diary under October 25), if they are still in Savannah; in these letters I announced that I had asked Court Chaplain Ziegenhagen to pay the 30 £ sterling. I am not able to have this money deducted from my salary, since I have had to collect my salary for the current half year in Savannah on a note, for which the praiseworthy Society has given us permission.]

Sunday, the 5th of November. Today most of the members of our congregation were present at Holy Communion. Yesterday I summoned N. [Rauner] to me and admonished him to examine his condition well before going so that he would not be judged. He knows himself well and promises much good; he blames his wife and children for his delay in conversion.

Yesterday evening we gathered in the orphanage where, before the prayer and to the great edification of myself and others, I read Court Chaplain Laue's[289] meditations on the words "But let a man examine himself, etc." as they stand in the *Contribution to the Building of the Kingdom of God*.[290] I also called attention to several points. This evening we began the prayer meeting in the orphanage after the repetition hour, as we are accustomed to do in the winter when the evenings are long, to the great advantage of our congregation. Before the prayer we usually read an edifying exemplum that fits the matter presented from the gospel, and then we pray [on our knees]. The song hour is being discontinued now that the days are getting short, and we sing a few unfamiliar songs in the prayer meeting.

Monday, the 6th of November. Today the Salzburgers began to build a hut for the widow Helfenstein. There were many who were working and, God willing, others will continue tomorrow. They are doing this work without pay. She has been given over 2 £ sterling from the poor box so that the clapboards and other things could be made. Some time ago, at our intercession, she received five hundred middle-sized and fifty large nails from the storehouse in Savannah.

Tuesday, the 7th of November. Today I visited a sick woman with her sick child. Formerly she was dissatisfied with God's dispensation, but now she is very content; for she sees it as a great benefaction that she has come to this country. The dear Lord let her husband get sick some time ago, she said, not only for her husband's sake but also for her sake; for He tried in that way to draw her all the more to Him, and the dear Lord is steadily achieving His goal in her. This woman cannot read, but she pays close attention to the voice of the Lord so that she well feels the strength of His word and therefore well remembers it. She told me something that she had heard long ago and still remembered. Among other things, she said she had once heard the verse "Except ye be converted, and become as little children, ye shall not enter into the kingdom of heaven." She said she now understood, to some extent, what this means. "Alas," she said, "how different a person becomes, so very small and almost nothing, when the dear Lord wishes to fulfill His work of conversion in him."

Wednesday, the 8th of November. My recently lost accounts and the delivery of our newly written letters required me to make another trip to Savannah last Monday, and there happened to be a safe opportunity to forward things to Charleston, with which a pious merchant in Savannah sent his and our letters to his correspondent for further forwarding. The letters that we had already written several weeks ago, along with the enclosed two diaries, were still lying in Savannah, because there had been no safe hands for forwarding them. Capt. Thomson has journeyed to Mr. Oglethorpe at Frederica and is very uncertain as to when he should return to London. So far he has forwarded our letters correctly. He cannot sell his German indentured servants [because there is neither money nor provisions in Savannah.]

The poor people in the ship are very miserable. They receive food only twice a week, and the rest of the time they have to get nourishment by begging or however they can. There are said to be many old people and children there whom no one cares for. Our Salzburgers are not disinclined to take on some of these people and to share with them some of what the Lord has granted them this year in the field, provided they could receive such people as gifts. I well assume that the captain would give them over if only Mr. Oglethorpe would pay some of the passage money.

[The authorities are doing nothing for these poor people, and they didn't even listen when I reported their misery. Savannah seems to be at the end of the road. Many are suffering great want and are selling their belongings and running away because there is no money there and the storehouse can neither pay old debts nor employ any workers. The new preacher[291]

is not walking in the footsteps of Mr. Whitefield but does more
to hinder than to promote what is good. He hates the honest
schoolmaster[292] and compares him with the scribes and phari-
sees in Christ's times; and therefore they do not live in one
house, as was the case with the previous preacher.]

I have been given good grounds to hope that, through the
intercession of those who wish us well, Mr. Oglethorpe will
be easily persuaded to give us something again from the storehouse to compensate us for the loss that we suffered, mainly
in provisions, on the recent voyage. If this is done, it will be
looked upon as a new gift from God. My trunk, clothes, accounts, and letters will probably remain lost, and this is the
greatest harm. An Englishman must have thought that I would
worry about this loss and therefore read me something out of
the English Bible, in fact from the prophet Jeremiah, which
could serve to help me recognize that God sometimes ordains
tribulations for our good.

Thursday, the 9th of November. This morning Thomas
Gschwandl and Sybilla, the widow Resch, were married. When
I declared the bans last Sunday I announced that I had reported the intended marriage to Mr. Oglethorpe because of the
disquieting circumstance that we have not been able to find any
actual evidence or report of Resch's death; that he had approved entirely and had given me a written statement authoriz-
ing me to marry these two people if no other obstacle were
present. Also, I had recently spoken with the congregation and
had heard no one who could make even the least objection to
this widow's second marriage. Rather, everyone who knew her
husband and his circumstances and also knows how easily one
can get lost and lose one's life in the woods must realize that it is
impossible for him to be alive, and that it is therefore advisable
for this widow to marry again, especially since she has already
been a widow for three years.

Mr. Oglethorpe's permission that he gave me for performing
my function at the marriage is worded as follows: Upon the
Petition of Sybilla Resch, Widow for License to marry Thomas
Gschwandl, setting forth, that her late Husband was lost in the
Woods three years ago, where he died et never returned,
neither was his body found, et that she hath abstained from

Marriage during the afore said three years, making Enquiry after the Body of her said Husband: and the Matter having been referr'd to be inquired into et reported to me by the Rev'd Mr. Bolzius, that the Marriage of the said Widow will give no scandal, but the whole Congregation are desirous, the said Marriage might take Effect. I do therefore hereby licence et impower you the said Rev'd Mr. Martin Bolzius to perform the office of your Function, in joyning the above named Widow Resch in Wedlock with Thomas Gschwandl afore said.

Given under my Hand & Seal

To the Rev'd Mr.   21st of October 1738
Martin Bolzius   James Oglethorpe

A woman told me that she had hoped to cause me a pleasure upon my return by reporting an improved spiritual condition; but things were still as they had been, namely, nothing but great sins and disquiet in her conscience. Another one who was present made the same complaint. I reminded both of what we had learned on Sunday about the words "Good and upright in the Lord: therefore will He teach sinners in the way," namely, that this is the first lesson that the Lord Jesus gives to sinners to learn, namely, the recognition of sins. But one must not stop at that, one must progress further, namely, to the blessed recognition of Christ, who will save a man from his sins if only he will remain steadfast.

Friday, the 10th of November. [Christ has become obstinate again, is defiant and self-willed and does not wish to remain in the orphanage. He does not like the regulations, nor does the food please him; and Kalcher can do nothing to please him. I spoke to him and told him that he would please me and all of us if he would be satisfied with our regulations and the food. At present they must be content with the products of the country such as rice, beans, Indian corn, sweet potatoes, squash, and cabbage, until the dear Lord will again provide some money, and then they would from time to time have food and sweet dishes made with flour. I could not permit him to cook secretly outside the orphanage or to have all sorts of delicacies brought up from Savannah, as he had done to the scandal of other people. However, he would not change his mind but moved out today. I will let him take his winter clothes that were made for him at this time and I shall continue to do everything possible for him so that he will not perish. He cannot earn his living with his work. He cannot work in the field, he lacks the strength and he also lacks patience; he also does not understand his tailoring profession too well. Without supervision he is lazy, and he gets bogged down with unnecessary things. In the orphanage he would have work that he could do, and thus he could help his neighbor.]

I came into a Salzburger's hut where I found several pious people gathered who could not work because of physical weakness and had therefore assembled for a good conversation. We encouraged each other simply by singing an edifying song and by praying together to learn to know the heart of the Father in Christ the Beloved better and better and to climb down with all our misery, however great and thick it may be, into the free and pleasant wellspring against sin and uncleanliness which is opened to us through the dear Savior, and to let ourselves be washed thoroughly. A man prayed with us so simply and from his heart that it was truly a great pleasure for me. I learned that, because the public prayer meeting could not be held last night, some people had been at the home of my dear colleague and had enjoyed much edification. The hungry always find something for their refreshment.

My dear colleague's house is very convenient for consorting intimately with the simple souls, and therefore there is a small gathering there every Saturday evening. Today I very vividly recalled the verse "Obey them that have the rule over you, and submit yourselves: for they watch for your souls, as they that must give account, etc." (Hebrews XIII);[293] and God is letting me recognize how much I still lack and how much further I must come if I wish ever to stand joyfully before the countenance of the Judge with my congregation. God help me through and teach me to care for my own soul and that of others! One has enough to do in saving his own soul. "He who hath much else, how can he make intercession?"[294]

[Saturday, the 11th of November. The surveyor is still a very restless man who cannot get along with anyone who goes with him to survey. Every week I must look for new people to go with him because those whom he has once had do not wish to go with him again and he finds some fault in every one of them. As I hear, he will not be finished as soon as he told me the last time; and therefore we will have to be patient with him for a while longer. The weather is very comfortable for his work, it is dry above and below and not too warm by day. Even though it is very frosty and cold at night, this is not considered important, because he has a big fire built at night for himself and his people. Also, he is not content with the usual food but wishes to have bread and butter. We do what we can in order to achieve our purpose.]

Sunday, the 12th of November. Old Mrs. N. [Spielbiegler] is almost always bedridden now, and her strength is consuming itself more and more. Therefore she herself can notice that she is coming very close to her grave and eternity. She recognizes that it is an unmerited benefaction of God that He did not overtake her with sudden death but has granted her until now both time and opportunity for penitence. She told me that she regretted that she had devoted her youth and her previous life to the course of the world and accused herself greatly for doing so; yet she was very quickly comforted by the forgiveness of sins through the merits of Christ. I implored her not to be too hasty with this comfort but to beg God unceasingly to reveal her corrupted heart clearly to her and to let her recognize and feel what it means to sin against the good Lord and to insult Him who has never done us any harm but only good. Indeed, she had to recognize, I told her, that she had caused Christ much martyrdom with her sins and had even killed Him. She approved all this and was pleased that I prayed with her.

Monday, the 13th of November. N. [Cornberger] and his wife became estranged a while ago over some little matter which, as they themselves had to admit, had caused them much harm in their prayer and Christianity. To be sure, they had already reconciled themselves on the same day; yet they found it good to tell me of the matter so that I might be able to speak and act with them better according to their circumstances. The man is very quick tempered, and the wife was also inclined to be so. However, as she confessed today, God had so blessed in her the verse "For the wrath of man worketh not the righteousness of God" (James 1:20), which I had marked for her last year in her Bible, that from that time on she had never let herself be overtaken by anger. However, this had cost her much prayer. Therefore she greatly hoped that things might go better with her husband too. Because of her physical condition the woman is sometimes slow in spirit and lets herself be bogged down in petty matters, whereby she causes herself much unnecessary worry. Her husband acts annoyed and angry at this because he does not yet understand her mind. I reminded him of his duty to show patience and gentleness to his wife as a very weak tool, and one who has especial weaknesses now in her present circumstances yet really means well all the time. They also had an unnecessary worry about the future, which I quickly talked them out of.

This afternoon Ruprecht Zittrauer's wife brought a little son into the world who was already baptized today, before the prayer meeting. We are pleased that our congregation are cautious and diligent in bringing their little children to baptism soon. Among the other people in this country there is great procrastination in this as in other religious matters.

Tuesday, the 14th of November. Muggitzer has been away from us for almost a whole year and has worked as a laborer in the service of the Lord Trustees. He is now returning with the resolution never to go off again because the profit that he has from outside work is very slight. His pay is on the books in the storehouse in Savannah; and now, like other people, he cannot get any payment. Michael Rieser too had hired himself out for one month and is now returning without any pay. This has made a good impression on the others; and they see that, when we advise them against leaving, it is only for their own good.

Recently I bought a good supply of wool in Savannah, with which I can provide Mrs. Helfenstein, her children, and a few others in the community and the orphanage with useful work in spinning and knitting, since the evenings are now long. The stockings /that we buy/ are expensive and yet of hardly any value. In this way the poor will be provided with something durable and some will have an opportunity to earn something here among us. We hope to plant much flax here next spring, since it grows well if the heat does not last long and is not too great. We also plan to try hemp, if I get these seeds, along with wheat, barley, oats, etc., early enough from Pennsylvania, as I have been promised by a merchant.

Wednesday, the 15th of November. We have had rainy weather since yesterday, and this has required the surveyor to return home. Also, because the water in the river is getting deep, several places on the new land have been flooded, and this makes the surveying difficult. Consequently, the surveyor does not wish to continue until it is dry again. However, he will indicate the plantations in such a way that everyone will know his own and will therefore be able to begin his work unhindered. He is afraid that they [Mr. Oglethorpe] will pay him nothing or little for his present work, and our people should not expect him to pay those who help him in the surveying. Indeed, he even demanded of me that I give him as much for every mile as they [Mr. Oglethorpe] had promised him for the rest of the work. I refused him this, however, since he is now doing his work on the orders of Mr. N. [Oglethorpe]. This much our people will do: they will not demand any payment from him. I shall give him and his assistant provisions, and he can look out for his own payment himself.

Because the evenings are getting long again, the awakened and salvation-hungry souls among us are again beginning to assemble in the evening after the public prayer meeting for prayer and good conversations; and God has greatly blessed this in me and my family as often as they have come to me. There are only a few each time whose circumstances allow them to come, and among these few it goes all the more simply.

Thursday, the 16th of November. Today we had such a cold wind that we could not expect the children to come to school this afternoon, since the wind was strong and very cold. For lack of a firm house we are still holding school in two huts in which it is very inconvenient to build a fire, because the smoke discomforts the eyes and we cannot keep the attention of the children, who must sit all around the fire if they are to enjoy any warmth at all. Nor can we hold the public prayer meeting during a strong wind because the light is blown out: for the large old hut in which church is held is badly protected from the wind that blows through it. Everything will gradually improve under divine providence.

Several pious people came to my hut and prayed with me and thus spent the evening hour well. They pray with such sincerity, industry, and childish simplicity that I too receive no little edification; and I consider it an especial blessing of God that they join with me and my family in prayer. From their prayers we can learn what lies in their hearts and what God is blessing especially in them. They always remember our dear benefactors in Europe; and, since those who pray, in so far as I know them, are His children, I do not doubt that He will hear such intercession. This morning I found another little flock of pious people in a hut who requested me to pray with them. May God bless this conversation and prayer for much communal edification.

Friday, the 17th of November. An old Salzburger woman shed tears of joy at the kindness that has reigned so far over her and her family. In her homeland, and when she was leaving it, she had been unable to imagine what she was now experiencing: she could not imagine anything but want of those things that she had had in her own country, and she had resolved to resign herself to this if only she could be with the gospel until the end of her life. But now God had granted her as much foodstuff, even milk, as she needed for herself and her family; and He was working steadily on her soul through His Word to prepare her for blessed eternity.

A young man also showed me what God had granted him in the harvest and at the same time he wished that God might keep his heart from all adherence to and trust in temporal wealth, for these were not the true treasures. To the great praise of God he remembered what He had done in his soul. He had revealed Himself to him as his Father in Christ and given him a full assurance of His mercy and the forgiveness of sins. As long as he lived he would remember that day and the circumstances connected with it. To be sure, he said, he no longer felt the sweet taste of God's love that had poured out into his soul at that time and made him so merry and joyful; however, he did notice that the Lord was continuing His work in him. For his instruction I spoke to him a bit about the words "For we walk by faith, not by sight." He showed me the place in his yard where he had knelt secretly before God whenever He wished to prepare him more closely for experiencing His mercy. Here he had been quite barren and incapable of spoken prayer, whereupon he went into his hut and fought his way through in prayer until God let the sun of His mercy shine upon him.

In today's prayer meeting, in connection with the words of Deuteronomy 24:13, I reminded the listeners of their duty and told them how they were obligated to bless their benefactors and to pray for them, since, among other things, many benefactions in the way of clothes had flowed to them in which they would be able to keep warm in winter time. When a little flock of people came to me in the evening after the prayer meeting, I asked them what good thing they could tell me out of their experience; and they answered that, before coming to me, they had spoken together about the goodness and providence of God, according to which He had granted them clothing among other benefactions. For everything they had on them, they said, was a blessing from Him through the hands of the benefactors, for which they praised God.

Before the prayer I read them a very edifying passage from the late Scriver's *Soul Treasure*;[295] it was the application of the third sermon in the first part, and it brought us all much edification. From their prayers we note that nothing in the world is dearer to them than Jesus and His reconciliation. Among them was an old widow of whom I learned that she now passes most of her time in prayer and reading, since she cannot do much work, and that she does not let the cold weather in her room prevent her, to the great amazement of other people. She often remembers, she says, what I once told about a pious theological student in Halle, who, whenever the cold discomforted him, always prayed to keep warm in his cold room, which he was too poor to heat. The love of Christ and the blessings that she received from prayer and from the sweet gospel warmed her, she said.

Saturday, the 18th of November. My dear colleague journeyed to Savannah this morning to proclaim the word of God to the Germans there tomorrow. May the dear Lord reveal to us more closely whether it is His will for us to bother with these people any longer, because of whom this and that in our community must be neglected. We hold school together and try through the grace of God jointly to edify the congregation on Sundays. /Each of us needs to hear something for himself and to edify himself on the other's talents./ We fear the day that the congregation will have to separate on the plantations for the sake of their work, when most of them will move to Abercorn Creek and a few will do their work on the plantations close to town but will reside in the town. However, because we are here for the sake of the congregation, we too will have to separate, one moving out with them and the other performing his office in the town with both adults and children. May our kind Lord Himself show us which of us should move out with the congregation. It has been requested of me, and I feel myself obligated to be where the larger part of the congregation is to be found; and, since I have no house or good dwelling in Ebenezer anyway, this seems to be indicated. Nevertheless, several things have arisen that might almost require me to remain here and to visit the congregation on Abercorn Creek frequently. Everything will be considered better in the fear of the Lord.

So far as I can hear, nothing would please the people better than if the evening prayer meeting could be continued, since God has usually laid an abundant blessing on it. I also hear that the dear listeners are taking the new hardship on their new plantations on themselves because they will get one of their ministers in their neighborhood and right among them. Our foremost duty is to see to the edification of their souls for their eternal life and then to contribute in every possible way so that they may earn their bread in Christian order and that the purpose may be more and more fulfilled for which the Lord Trustees sent the Salzburgers into this colony, all of which will be very useful for the present inhabitants of this place as well as for their successors.

If I too should move out with them, then I wish I could have a regular dwelling in the town, because I would also have much business in Ebenezer and would have to visit the parishioners

living here. We cannot allow the town to lie unbuilt and everything to return to forest, as in Purysburg, for this would give
the Salzburgers a bad name, especially since they have enemies.
I also hope we will gradually receive more craftsmen, who will
all live in the town. The orphanage is here too; and perhaps
God will grant us a physical blessing so that we can someday
build a church and school, of which we are surely in great need.
If the Salzburgers continue to enjoy divine blessings in their
work on the new and very fertile land, then I believe they will
be able to take on hired hands, and the householders will do
their work in the town.

Best suited for this would be honest and loyal people who are
tired of their all-too-great hardships elsewhere [in Germany]
and would therefore like to move to America: they would be
better cared for in our community than at any other place in
America. They would not lack for food and clothes, if God continues to bless us; and, if they served loyally, they would be assisted so that they could soon eat their own bread and live
among us as free people. Yet at the present time our dear people are not in that position but still need outside help. Even
though they have just harvested a bit, for which they are heartily pleased and grateful to the dear Lord, there is no money in
the country now for which they could sell the things that they
do not need themselves [including what God has granted them
this time.]

[Last summer the storehouse bought up so much corn from
some sloops that it will spoil; there is no money on hand for
buying anything, even if this supply of corn were not available.
Most of them need everything that God has granted them this
time for their own use; and, if they receive any clothing or
other assistance, they accept it with many thanks. The Lord
Trustees should have given the Salzburgers their land sooner
and of a kind on which they could have raised something. Also,
they should not prescribe rules for them as to how they should
do their field work and force them to observe their impractica-
ble regulations, but rather give them freedom to work according to their judgment and personal experience. In this way
much would have been improved.]

May God incline the hearts of the Lord Trustees to be pleased with the present arrangements of the Salzburgers, which are surely of such a nature that something really good and useful can be developed. [We say nothing of this to Mr. Oglethorpe because he just makes so many objections, which he considers irrefutable.] The land on the other side of Abercorn Creek is low and is flooded about once a year, and therefore no house can be built anywhere in the region. Also, according to the judgment of knowledgeable people and our own experience, it would be unhealthy to live there. In order for this very beautiful land to be used, our people have agreed together to take up the entire strip of high land on this side of Abercorn Creek and to build their houses and cowsheds on it in such a way that three families will live near each other on one plantation, with each family on a separate piece of land. Here, to be sure, stand mostly pines and firs, which they will use for building; and the land on which cane-brakes are scattered about they can well use as cattle pasture, as up till now most of our cattle have been pastured in this region.

There is no timber on the river or across it, but much high cane, thick oaks, beeches, nut trees, and a great quantity of thorn bushes; and knowledgeable people find this land of such quality that they hope to raise all sorts of local crops, as well as hemp, flax, wheat, barley, oats, etc. Because it is flooded annually and the Savannah River carries much fertile silt, they never have to fertilize such land or leave it fallow but may use it every year. The test has already been made with just such land in our neighborhood in Carolina.

The said three families, who are building on the high, dry, and also healthy land, have two plantations of forty-eight acres each on the land across Abercorn Creek; and, in order that each family will have a part of each kind of land, three equal lines are drawn through the three plantations so that each will know what is his. These three families work communally, in fact at the very place where their neighbors on both sides are clearing their land of trees. Because each family has for itself only a narrow, but therefore all the longer, strip, they are leaving no trees standing that could cast a shadow; and thus they will soon have cleared out a large open field. The figure of the three plantations, which are owned by three families, is as follows:

	Pe	ter		Gru	ber
e.g.	Tho	mas		Gschwan	tel
	Ru	precht		Kal	cher

Between the first and second plantations runs Abercorn Creek, on both sides of which, to be sure, two hundred feet must be left at the command of the Trustees. However, this land may be used by the owners of the plantations at least in the beginning. Behind these plantations there is still a large piece of very good land that has also been surveyed and belongs to us, but it has not been occupied by our people but is remaining for newcomers.

Although the Salzburgers have made such arrangements as were required by necessity and by their common interest, they have not violated the plans and order of the Trustees, since the old lines remain and the people are just adjusting them to their own advantage. At the end of the plantations towards Abercorn six [600][296] acres are being surveyed for the ministers if Mr. Oglethorpe approves it. This will be extremely advantageous to our people because of the cattle pasture, especially at first, since it will lie uncultivated for a considerable time. If the useless sawmill in Abercorn Creek would rot away or be torn down, we would have a very convenient and short passage to Savannah, since the flood tide comes up to our new plantations and we could therefore return home from Savannah in six hours.

Sunday, the 19th of November. On Sunday evenings our orphanage is exceedingly convenient for simple edification and prayer with our listeners of both sexes. We have enough room: the men are on one side and the women on the other; and we, who give them the opportunity for edification, are in the middle room. Again today we shared hearty enjoyment with each other. May God preserve this His work and let us further feel His blessings in physical and spiritual matters.

During the past few days in the prayer meetings we have learned from the 24th chapter of Deuteronomy how dear the poor, strangers, widows, and children are to the heart of our dear and merciful God and how pleased He is when their needs are cared for. This has strengthened me in my faith that He will continue to awaken benefactors from afar, if the people nearby are [hardhearted and] unfeeling, who will contribute to maintain this home for widows and orphans.

Monday, the 20th of November. A corn mill has now been made with the two millstones that Court Chaplain Ziegenhagen requested from the Lord Trustees some time ago for our congregation, and we hope it will give good service. Very few people are able to buy good flour, and they are satisfied with Indian cornmeal when they are healthy; but they have not been able to grind this fine enough on the ruined hand mills. This present mill is operated by hand by two people, but the corn must previously have been ground or crushed on an iron mill. In addition to the iron work, which God provided some time ago, it cost somewhat over 2 £ sterling, which Kogler and Rottenberger, two skillful and loyal workers, have well earned. Because there is nothing in the poor box, the community will collect the expenses. Otherwise we would have been glad to contribute something for the sake of the poor.

We should have two such mills so that one could be used in the town and one on the plantations, by those who move out there. If there are any millstones like this or larger in Savannah, I shall request them of Mr. Oglethorpe. Steps will also be taken so that rice can be prepared with this mill; and for this purpose the carpenters are preparing a round piece of wood the size and thickness of a stone, which will be used in place of the upper millstone, because rice is not freed from its shells or husks between two stones but is crushed and ground. In this way the orphanage will be able to keep its rice mill for itself, which is made totally of wood but is very usable.

Tuesday, the 21st of November. My dear colleague returned this morning from Savannah after travelling all night in order to be here all the sooner, because he had been delayed in Savannah longer than necessary. The Reformed minister from Purysburg had also come to Savannah to give Holy Communion to his co-religionists, at which time he read them something out of a book for their preparation but did not preach.

For this reason my dear colleague had only our own co-religionists as a congregation[297] [but the others remained away
through secret bitterness, and some of them probably enjoyed
themselves in worldly ways on the day of Communion. This is
a very mean company that cannot be allowed to have their way
but should be told the truth from God's word, even if they cannot bear this from a preacher who is not of their confession.
Most of them are obstinately Reformed and at the same time
miserably blind].

My dear colleague received much kindness from the storehouse manager, Mr. Jones. He sheltered him and kindly invited
him to stop in on him any time, especially after he has his own
house. He appears to have a true fear of the Lord; to be sure,
he is a Dissenter, yet he respects righteous ministers and especially Mr. N. [Whitefield. On the other hand he cannot stand
worldly-minded people, also including the present minister
in Savannah.][298] The schoolmaster in Savannah, Mr. Habersham, sent me for the congregation various good things such
as two pieces of linen, ten neckerchiefs, six ready-made linen
trousers, and six short flannel waistcoats, also a few tools, which
Mr. N. [Whitefield] had promised me and of which he had left
a list behind. The dear Lord has shown us the trail of His guidance not only in the gift itself but also in its application, in that
it now can serve the purpose of the whole congregation, but
could have been given only to some of them if we had wished
to distribute it like other gifts.

Up till now certain men of the congregation have had to help
the [annoying and obstinate] surveyor in surveying the new
land, and this has caused them great hardship. It had been
agreed that the entire community would pay them or compensate them with work, but we were already able to predict many
difficulties in advance, especially since the pay amounted to 5 £
11 sh. 10 p. sterling in addition to the meat that was given
from the poor box for provisions for the surveyor and his assistant. The surveyor surely has poor wages, since they [Mr.
Oglethorpe] gave him no more than one pence per acre, from
which he must supply provisions for himself and the people
who help him and pay a man sixteen pence wages every day.
When he surveys land in a forest with nothing but stands of

pines and firs, then he gets along all right; but, if he has to do his work on land that is entirely overgrown with thorns and bushes as ours is, and must measure such little strips as our plantations are, then he could not possibly get along on this pay, as everyone must admit. This is probably the reason why, from the very beginning, he made all sorts of excuses for not surveying this new land; and it would have been to the great detriment of our village if we had not agreed with him on a better method that was acceptable to him.

Now, because said work was doubtless to the best interest of our community and our successors and the work had to be paid for, I suggested that the things we had received and which belonged to the community be applied to paying the workers and covering the accrued expenses. In this way the entire community would profit, since otherwise the gifts could only be given to this or that person. This suggestion pleased everyone well, and all the items were appraised at 5 £ 13 sh. 5 p. so that only a little was left over, which will probably be given to the community's herdsmen.

In the evening prayer meeting we had the 26th chapter of Deuteronomy, the first part of which gave me a good opportunity to impress on the community this fact, among others, that God is well pleased if, while receiving and enjoying our present benefaction, we will also gratefully remember previous and past ones and encourage each other to His praise and to a loyal application of His gifts. I again told them how well disposed Mr. N. [Whitefield] was toward our congregation and the orphanage and how much good he promised me from that which God would grant him, and that we should therefore praise the present donor for the benefaction we have received and pray diligently for this and other benefactors.

Wednesday, the 22nd of November. There are still some families of German servants in Savannah whom no one wishes to buy. Various people in our community are inclined to accept children of both sexes and to take care of them through compassion and pity, if Mr. Oglethorpe will redeem and donate them on their behalf. I also hear that, while he was in Savannah a few days ago, he gave his consent for this and wishes to speak to me about it when he returns at the end of the month. This is also a benefaction for our people, since they will gradually acquire hired men and women, even if they will not derive much profit from them in the first years. If such children, especially of the female sex, behave themselves well, then they will someday be able to become good helpmeets in our community. We can hardly hope that a new transport, with unmarried women in it, will be sent, since the Lord Trustees are not now financially able to bear the passage money and maintenance for at least one year.

Thursday, the 23rd of November. Although the cotton did not ripen entirely because of the too early frost, I still see that many bolls are now gradually opening in which there is much useful cotton. Therefore it is good that we were not hasty in hoeing and weeding, for then we would have robbed ourselves of much advantage. Because everything in this country is expensive, one must make use of everything as best one can.

The old [Swiss] man from Purysburg who made a rice mill for the orphanage is still in our village and is used by the Salzburgers to make wheels for wagons and carts, for which they give him and his ten-year-old son food and a little money. He has a desire to settle among us and told me yesterday that he finds that there are peaceful and quiet people here, whereas there is no honesty in Purysburg. [But nothing but abominations among the sextons and simple people, and the preacher is no pastor of his flock, etc.] I note, however, that our people do not want him [because he is Reformed and very inclined to disputing, but this last thing I do not observe in him. Concerning his wife and children, who are still in Canton Appenzell, I learn that they are separatists. If they too should come here, we would have much affliction, as much as we would not begrudge the old and apparently honest man to spend his remaining days here.]

The Salzburgers wish very much for their countrymen to come here, for whom they intend to reserve some good land. No one doubts any longer that industrious workers can earn their bread here and can enjoy many advantages over others in Germany. The foremost treasure that we have in our community is God's blessing, which we see everywhere in abundance. I must often marvel at the goodness of God, because of which a right effective [noticeable] change has occurred among us in a short time. The Salzburgers were poor in every way and also appeared to be forsaken by the further assistance of the wealthy people in this land; yet everyone now has so much that he praises God and wishes the same good for others that he is enjoying here in spiritual and physical benefactions. The noblest thing in all this is their joyousness which makes even the least gift both dear and sweet for them. Among the material benefactions the foremost one is that they enjoy a greatly desired freedom. No one bothers them, no one demands anything from them, they are no one's servant; and all good regulations that are instituted and obeyed among us are made with everyone's approval and only for the common good.

Friday, the 24th of November. We have now accepted another child into the orphanage. It is a child of six[299] that belongs to our herdsman Hans Michael Schneider. The parents and their largest boy of twelve are showing the community good service and are loyal in their profession. In order that they will have no obstacles in caring for the community's cattle, which are being grazed in a lovely region an hour and a half away from Ebenezer, and so that they will be encouraged to even more loyalty and gratitude, we have taken this child into the orphanage as a boarder. It is a great pleasure for me that our pious congregation pray earnestly for our little institution, as I hear when they come to my hut in the evening to pray. I do not doubt that in His time the Lord will give everything that will be necessary and is now necessary for the maintenance and continuance of this His work. The river of God is full of water, and He lets it flow with great joy on miserable people, among whom widows and orphans have their place.

Because our congregation are showing themselves so pleased about the new land on Abercorn Creek and would like us to see it ourselves, we let them lead us around in it today, all of which tired our bodies, to be sure, but gave us much pleasure. The entire region where the houses are being built is exceptionally beautiful. It is high and mostly level land with enough timber and several live springs; and, where these are lacking, the river water is quite nearby and wells could be easily dug. Along the river on both sides, and especially across it, the soil is so good that they prefer it to all other land, even the best in our region. Therefore, according to all human expectations, its owners are promising themselves much good from it, provided God preserves their lives and gives His blessing to their work. Our dear Lord, who doeth everything in His due time,[300] be humbly praised for this new benefaction and fatherly blessing. May he keep the dear people in Christian unity and rule them through His spirit so that they will yearn for the true homeland and heavenly fatherland in all conditions of this life, whatever they may be.

Meanwhile I do not doubt that this testimony of divine care will strengthen our dear Fathers in Europe, just as it has us, in their faith in the living and extremely gracious God, who lets no one who waits on Him be put to shame.[301] They have suffered much distress from the previously sent reports, especially since enemies have been accustomed to make hostile comments about those tribulations and to gain pleasure from them and to calumniate others. However, since they have always clung to the promises of the almighty and kindly God in faith and cheered us in their letters with the strongest comfort, the present reports cannot but be right comforting to them because they have not been put to shame in their faith and hope. Whenever some of the members of the community have become weary of things in their time of tribulation and have wished to move away from us, to the scandal of others, we have made every effort through the grace of God to keep them from it and have always comforted them with the help of the Lord, even if we could not always see and tell how and whence that help would come. Along with many others, the verse Habakkuk 2:2–4 has been frequently presented to them. Now the Lord is showing that the comfort that has been given them was no unfounded human thing. May His praiseworthy name be worshiped for ever and ever!

The congregation have discussed together how they wish to go about building a house for one of their ministers who is to perform his office among them. However, because they will wish to erect necessary huts for themselves in the early period and to cultivate a good piece of land for planting in the spring and to use the fields near the town for another year, they will not be able to start building a parsonage sooner than about next May or probably later. Therefore, so far as possible, they will continue to attend divine services in the town and to work only from time to time on their plantations. However, if a house is built for the minister, then as many as intend to live out there will move at one time; the rest, who have their plantations on the Savannah River, will remain in the town.

The congregation is still requesting me to move out with them; but I could cite several weighty reasons which might almost compel me to leave the move up to my dear colleague, subject to his approval. Yet everyone recognizes that I would have to conduct my office again here if the congregation in the town should increase again and would not be able to be bound constantly to that place. It will be rather hard and burdensome, and in many ways disadvantageous for my office, for me to live another year in my old uncomfortable hut, whose beams and thresholds are almost rotted away. I will still need a house in the town even if I move to Abercorn Creek with the congregation, because all sorts of business will often require me to visit the members of the congregation in the town and to consider this and that matter with my dear colleague, as we have done so far, and especially if circumstances should require me to move back to town again. Perhaps the Lord will let me know His will more closely as to what should be done about building a house for me. I would have to borrow the money from Mr. Oglethorpe.

Saturday, the 25th of November. Our congregation are recognizing more and more what a benefaction it is that they have come to Ebenezer; so they consider themselves obligated to express their most grateful thanks to Mr. S. U. [Senior Urlsperger] for his fatherly love and for the great efforts he has made on their behalf, and also to ask him to be helpful by speaking in favor of the sending of a new transport. I first inquired as to what they actually wished to have written, whereupon I drafted something for them this morning and first showed the whole letter to some knowledgeable men and then read it aloud to all the Salzburgers and Austrians, who were

gathered in a hut, in order to learn whether they would consider this letter as their own and none other than as written by
themselves. They thanked me for my [poor] efforts and wished
to have all their names subscribed as testimony of their
gratitude toward Mr. S. U. [Senior Urlsperger] and other dear
benefactors, likewise as testimony that they would like nothing
more than that the Salzburgers and Austrians whose names
they listed, as well as other persons, might come here as soon as
possible and enjoy with them the good that our marvelous God
has granted them to enjoy after many kinds of tribulation. Because none of them can write clearly, my dear colleague was
asked to copy the letter and to subscribe their names so that
they might be clearly read. May the Lord be praised for this and
all His benefactions! We call out to one another: "Know ye that
the Lord he is God: it is he that hath made us, and not we ourselves; we are his people, and the sheep of his pasture." To Him
be glory for ever! During the reading of this letter our kindly
God brought forth many good emotions, which showed themselves through sighs, tears, and edifying expressions, from
which I could sufficiently recognize their full approval.[302]

In the evening prayer meeting we had the beginning of the
28th chapter of Deuteronomy, in which Moses explained the
two short yet very significant little words "blessing" and "curse,"
which had been presented to the people of Israel in the preceding chapter. From this chapter we learned in what order we
could comfort ourselves with divine blessing both spiritually
and physically, namely that we not only know God's commandments but that we conduct our lives according to them through
the power of Jesus. Although in the New Testament the Lord's
blessing on His children consists more in spiritual and celestial
than in temporal goods, still the Lord has promised that He will
bestow upon His children as many temporal blessings as are
useful and salutary for them and that they will enjoy what little
they have with a clear conscience in the grace of God and thus
with His blessing. I asked the congregation not to go to their
plantations unless they were certain of the grace of God in
Christ as the source of all blessing, for then it could also be said
of them: "Blessed shalt thou be in the city, and blessed shalt

thou be in the field . . . Blessed shalt thou be when thou comest in, and blessed shalt thou be when thou goest out."

On this occasion I told them what has always been lying on my heart, namely, that our wise and marvelous God must have had His wise and salutary reasons when He brought us together, both in Old and New Ebenezer, at one place, whereas, if it had been left to our own devices, everyone would have gone immediately to his own land and plantation and begun his work. Because the good lands that had been intended for our town during these years did not lie together in one stretch, the entire community would have dispersed for the sake of temporal nourishment; and this could have caused great damage to their souls afterwards. But in this way the Lord has done with us as He did with the Children of Israel: they had to remain together in one place for a considerable time before the Jordan, just as if it were their plantations, so that they might first be prepared through the Word of God for taking and occupying their land and be put into a condition to become partakers of God's blessings for their souls and bodies in occupying and managing their lands. Everyone among us must recognize, even if he is a weak beginner in his Christianity, that the dear Lord has dealt with us in this better than we could have planned it and that we thank this highest and ever loyal Benefactor far too little for His wise guidance and gracious purpose.

Sunday, the 26th of November. Yesterday evening after the prayer meeting the widow Arnsdorf consecrated her newly built house with the Word of God and with prayer, for which various adults and many children gathered. Previously, in the prayer meeting, we had said much about God's blessing that makes people contented and happy in spiritual and temporal affairs; and my heart was filled with this dear material and also with today's gospel for the 26th Sunday after Trinity. I also said something to the gathering and especially to the widow and her children about the beautiful words in Genesis 12:2: "And thou shalt be a blessing."

This afternoon I was somewhat disquieted by temporal matters. Capt. Thomson had sent an express-boat here from Savannah and reported to me in a letter Mr. Oglethorpe's will

and resolution with regard to the German people on his ship
whom some of the Salzburgers wished to accept. However, I
could not comprehend what he had written me; and therefore I
wrote him a brief answer and promised to come to Savannah
myself tomorrow, God willing, before he left for Frederica. I
shall also ask him whether he is going directly to London and
will take letters for us. I also have other business to tend to. In
addition, I am being importuned by the surveyor Ross, who
wants to speak to me and give a report about his surveying,
since he is planning to depart early tomorrow. May God bless
and further my journey and let me well apply on the journey
the good that He has granted me and others today from His
Word.

Monday, the 27th of November. As I was about to go to the
school this afternoon, N. [Spielbiegler] came to me and asked
me to call on the sick N. [his mother]. Therefore I went to her
after school, whereupon she told me that she was getting
weaker and weaker and wished for nothing more than for the
dear Lord to take her to Himself; for she always had good hope
in the dear Lord that He would take her into heaven, as she had
attested recently. But today it seemed to me as if she were no
longer so firm in her hope, for she may now better recognize
that things do not yet stand right with her. Therefore she said
that God must not have let her be sick for so long for nothing, it
must signify something. And, when I told her why God was
doing it and to what it had to lead and how far it could go
through the grace of God if she wished to be surely saved, she
told me among other things that she still had a wicked heart
and that the Old Adam was still ruling in her. Thus she has not
really gone all the way with her confession, and she no longer
comforts herself in her sins with the merits of Christ, as she has
been wont to do so freely before. May the dear Lord continue
to have mercy on her and illuminate her through His spirit and
bring her to a true conversion.

Tuesday, the 28th of November. Zant has been entirely blind
for several days, so that he cannot see except a little bit at night.
He is quite resigned to this and makes good use of his condition. The honest and pious widow Schweighofer had visited

him today and prayed with him right cordially, and this had given him great joy. He is improving a little bit. May the dear Lord help further!

Wednesday, the 29th of November. The day before yesterday I journeyed very early in the morning to Savannah in order to speak with Capt. Thomson in detail about the letter Mr. Oglethorpe had sent to him and me; and this evening I returned to Ebenezer with my travelling companions sound and satisfied. Both the captain and the storehouse manager, Mr. Jones, explained to me Mr. Oglethorpe's meaning, which is that I have permission to take as many small and large girls from Capt. Thomson's ship to Ebenezer as I wish to take, who are then to serve and be kept in good order at our place. If they behave themselves in a Christian manner and if any of the unmarried men in our congregation wish to marry them, such girls will achieve their freedom through this, and their husbands will have nothing more to do than to pay the interest that is customary in this country for the passage money, which Mr. Oglethorpe will donate to the orphanage. However, because this interest would cause some difficulty and would also amount to a large sum, I am free to exempt the people from it, since they would do a service for the orphanage anyway, especially as they are convinced of the benefit the entire community gains from the orphanage.

I selected six of these girls, who were fetched from Purysburg, to where Kiefer's boat had brought them. Two of them are nineteen years old, the rest somewhat younger; but all of them seem to have pleasant and docile dispositions and bring good references. They are all coming to Christian and charitable people in the community and will be well taken care of. At first the parents made some difficulties about letting their children go; and they hoped to move me in that way to take them, and therefore all their families, along as well; but I had no permission for this, and no one among us has the means for supporting them. However, when they saw that I would prefer to have no child than one that was forced on me and when they learned how things were among us, I could have acquired even more children if I had not had my own misgivings, even though there are still several people in the community who would have liked to take in a girl. The people were very worried that Capt. Thomson would take them to Frederica and place them here and there, and therefore they would have been very happy if there had been any opportunity of bringing them to Ebenezer.[303]

I tried to get Mr. Oglethorpe to free a sick old widow of fifty-four years, and also a man of twenty-two with a very frail daughter, and I shall learn whether he has given his consent to it. [All of them will be more useful with us than at any other place, and at the same time a work of charity will be performed.] The other swollen and sick people have been taken back on board in wheelbarrows, because the captain can spend nothing for their maintenance and no one else will take them on. These poor people are surely suffering great misery. If we had the means, which we don't, then we would gladly take on at least the poor widows with their children who have lost their husbands and fathers at sea and give them some work to do. May God let this physical plight contribute to their spiritual and eternal good!

Thursday, the 30th of November. Captain Thomson is returning to Savannah along with General Oglethorpe on 14 December, at which time there will be held a great court session that has been postponed until now. We have a safe opportunity to forward our letters and diary with him, so we are again getting down to writing even though a packet was sent via Charleston to London only a short time ago. It gives us great pleasure to receive letters from our dear Fathers and friends in Europe, since the dear Lord lets much good flow through them for our and our congregation's edification. Since they also like us to send in frequent reports of the congregation's circumstances and then write all the more promptly, we do not like to let a safe opportunity pass. God bless all this to His glory!

[The tailor Christ, who recently left the orphanage again, has had a hut built for himself with the little money I had kept for him, even though I had advised him strongly against it and had promised to help him get a private hut soon, since various people are beginning to move to their plantations. It appears that he desires not to return to the orphanage, where, if he requested it, we would have gladly done our best for him again through compassion for his poor circumstances. Yet we will never force our benefactions on anyone.]

DECEMBER

Friday, the 1st of December. This morning I found N. [Eischberger] in such a frame of mind that I am very happy and have good hope that God will still win his soul, on which He, as he well knows, has been working so far in every way and most loyally. During yesterday's prayer meeting, while the second half of the 28th chapter of Deuteronomy was being treated, He revealed to him the sins of his youth; with these he had merited not only his present afflictions, which for a long time now have been his lot and that of his wife, who, like him, is almost always sickly and incapable of steady work, but also all disfavor and curse of God. /He said it was only through the grace of God that he was still alive and was living in the time of grace./ [He said that until now he had thought far too little of the very miserable and pitiable condition of an unbelieving and worldly minded man, whereupon his eyes flowed over; and his wife confirmed that her husband had told her with much emotion about yesterday's prayer meeting and had admonished her to a serious achievement of her salvation.]

In every way I find that our dear listeners who are concerned with their souls like the evening prayer meetings more and more because our dear Lord is gradually letting us recognize so much that is splendid, marvelous, and comforting from the Old Testament that we did not know formerly; and I, for my part, wish to thank our merciful, loving God in eternity for the great mercy that He has shown me on this occasion.

As some pious souls were going home this evening from the private prayer meeting we held in my hut, a Salzburger woman remained behind and told me she wished to leave a beautiful verse with me for a good night, and it was from Psalm XIII: "But I have trusted in thy mercy; my heart shall rejoice in thy salvation, I will sing unto the Lord, because he hath dealt bountifully with me." Then she said, "Dear Sir, I am discovering in myself that God is so merciful and so gladly helps and is so good to me. To be sure, I feel in my heart much evil that always rises up and causes me much struggle and suffering; but I also experience that God is so merciful and helps so gladly and does me much good." This woman cannot read and also complains of a poor memory, but I find that she takes pleasure in God's word and is deeply concerned with the salvation of her soul and can remember beautiful verses and make good use of them.

Saturday, the 2nd of December. The weather is again very variable. We had very cold nights a few times and the wind was quite cold by day; but yesterday and today it has been as lovely as in spring. Some people have already started building huts on their plantations, which are indispensable at night and in rainy weather if they wish to clear their land. From bad experience they have learned to be more careful about their health, which suffered greatly in the first years.

Yesterday I visited Zant, whose eyes seem in a dangerous condition; but there were some pious people there who were presenting his and their troubles on their knees to our merciful Savior so that I could not speak with him this time. My dear colleague went to him just before the prayer meeting and let him know that we were inclined to accept him into the orphanage and to care for him as well as the dear Lord would grant the means until we knew how his sickness would finally turn out. I told him this today, but he wishes to present it to the dear Lord in prayer before he resolves anything. Yet he considers this offer to be a divine benefaction. He shows himself so patient and content in his suffering that he greatly edifies us.

In yesterday's and today's prayer meeting we continued with the 29th chapter of Deuteronomy. Because of its important content, we tried to utilize it in such a way at the end of this church year that, just as the Children of Israel remembered the manifold benefactions of the Lord that they had enjoyed up to then, we too would gratefully remember that He had saved us from many perils, and had led, fed, and clothed us. This we did so that we might once again be encouraged and obligated to obedience toward God and His commandments.

There are probably many among us about whom God might just as well complain that He had not yet been able to give them understanding hearts, seeing eyes, and hearing ears even though He had richly offered His grace from time to time; therefore it is a superabundant mercy that He is still working on us and is once again offering us His covenant of grace, from which He will no more exclude obstinate and disobedient souls than He did for the wicked Israelites, if only we will now recognize our wickedness and be willing to accept the offered grace in the proper order. If the covenant of grace then stretched out to all people, even to strangers, hewers of wood and drawers of water, and poor people, then the grace of the new covenant will not be less, rather God yearns in His heart for all, even the smallest, the least, and the most miserable, which is a great comfort for penitent sinners.[304]

Sunday, the 3rd of December. This first Sunday in the church year, which we experience again through the grace of God, was spent by us and our dear listeners with much blessing. The dear Lord has renewed in us our resolve to struggle with our listeners to reach a right New Testament nature in our Christianity and to apply our time and strength solely to His service and Glory.

[Before the prayer meeting Schoolmaster Ortmann caused me a worry that made it difficult for me to carry out what I had planned for my and the others' edification: namely, he sent me his wife with a long English letter that he had today addressed to Mr. Oglethorpe, accompanied with a postscript to me in German. I returned the letter to her unread, since I could gather from her words that he was pouring forth many complaints against the two Zuebli brothers and, as is his custom, was emphasizing the service he had performed as a former marine soldier for the English crown. The matter is not very important: About two weeks ago the younger Zuebli chose a plantation on Ebenezer Creek that another man, namely Hesler, had abandoned because he did not wish to remain there alone. Schoolmaster Ortmann had twice drawn lots but had not received any good land; and, because I had gotten to know him on the occasion of the two gardens, I asked him several times to seek out some other land that was acceptable to him, and also reminded the surveyor about it. However, he had procrastinated in this until he should have a servant, when, during my recent trip, the surveyor told him about the Zueblis' land and praised it to him.

[As soon as the surveyor told me that Mr. Ortmann had chosen this plantation, I attempted to prevent all misunderstandings but could never find the two Zueblis at home because they had begun to work seriously on their plantation. Since I understood that they had already been working for thirteen days, I asked the schoolmaster yesterday whether it would not be all the same to him if he left this plantation to the poor Zuebli brothers and selected the one that lies right next to it on the river and is not inferior to it in soil. Because I noticed right off that nothing could be accomplished since this plantation lies about a hundred steps closer to the town and was greatly extolled by the surveyor, I postponed the negotiations until Monday. Meanwhile he is becoming so restless that he not only wrote the letter on this Sunday and sent it to me, but also let me know that, to be sure, he had wished to register with other communicants for Holy Communion but that he had been disturbed by the fact that Zuebli wished to take away his land. I urged his wife that she and her husband should see to it that Mr. Ortmann would not act as in former times, when he would fall upon me with great violence from mere suspicion and meanness whenever he could not have his own way, and had caused me many sighs. If he wished to come to terms with these people in a Christian way, for which I would do everything possible, I should be most happy; but, if they wish to accuse each other in front of Mr. Oglethorpe, then I shall have to suffer them and will not get mixed up in it.

[In like manner we are having our troubles with Mrs. Helfenstein, who reveals ever more clearly that she has not been sincere in her previous appearances. Her impure intentions, which are harmful to the community and a hindrance to our office, cannot very well be set down here for good reason; but it will be mentioned for our instruction in our next letters. She and her children keep house in great confusion, and she lets them do as they want; and we can see in many ways that her supposed experience in Christianity consists less in truth than in many beautiful words, for which she, like Mrs. Rheinlaender, has a natural talent. Because she has not taken our good advice and warnings previously, but has persisted in her impure and vexing designs, I have advised her that I shall withdraw more and more and will have nothing more to do with her and her children, particularly in regard to material support. If she wishes to continue her behavior thus and cause me sighs and disquiet, then she should not be surprised if I send her two children who are being raised in the orphanage back home to her.

[Monday, the 4th of December. Although the two Zuebli brothers have done a considerable amount of work on their land, they wish to give in to Schoolmaster Ortmann in order to avoid all trouble and sinfulness, and to take another plantation in the neighborhood in place of it. But they rightfully want him to make good their work, which the schoolmaster appears to be willing to do. I read to the younger Zuebli, who called on me about it, from Matthew 5:5, "Blessed are the meek, for they shall inherit the earth."

[Toward evening I had the schoolmaster with me again in order to rectify the unhappy matter completely; and, because his wife had seen the two Zueblis' work on the plantation today, he was quite agreeable to pay the people for their work, for thus a debt that existed between them was entirely settled. I am happy that this matter has been arranged this time in such a way that the schoolmaster has not become angry at me, especially since I really could not judge him as being in the right.

[This evening I learned from my dear colleague that Mrs. Helfenstein had visited him and had complained to him about me considerably; but she learned nothing more from him than what I had told her, namely, that we cannot possibly be content with her impure and vexing behavior. Such people cannot bear the truth and will right away call us rough, hard, and angry if we clearly and seriously express our anger and displeasure in their behavior. This is also the language of Mrs. Rheinlaender, to whom we also appeared too rough and severe, whereas others in the community were amazed that we put up with her for so long and gave her benefaction after benefaction in order to win her. It is God's teaching to bear the wicked and not to bear them, each in its own season.]

Tuesday, the 5th of December. [Our shoemaker[305] was in

Purysburg for temporal reasons and drank some rum or brandy there against the cold weather that rose to his head and made him sick. He came to me himself and confessed his lack of caution and promised to be more careful in the future now that he has learned of the deceitfulness of this strong drink. Otherwise he works diligently and keeps himself and his wife very orderly in external matters, yet they are both nothing but natural beings. Our people find it very good that there is a shoemaker among us who not only makes shoes but also serves the people with repairs.] With others who were recently brought to our place, the shoemaker often declares that it is a blessing to live among us, whereas most of their travelling companions who have been sold here and there in the country have been treated severely; the large families as well as the old and pregnant and sick people whom no one wished to buy have been taken on to Frederica by Capt. Thomson, where, as happened in Savannah, parents and children have been separated and sold. When I was in Savannah recently, the people showed much misery at being taken further.

N.'s [The Austrian Schmidt's] wife is progressing very nicely in the grace she is receiving in her conversion: she recognizes her deep corruption better and better and is becoming ever smaller in her own eyes, but at the same time ever more desirous for salvation in Christ for poor penitent sinners. If we do not visit her for a few days she is sad and asks if we have seen anything in her or heard anything that displeases us. She is not a little bit disturbed that she herself cannot read and repeat the verses she hears; yet from frequent hearing and from her husband's reading aloud she has learned many verses, which now stand her in good stead. She requested permission to come pray with me and asked me whether Mr. Gronau would take it ill if she also went to him tomorrow to pray with him and hear some words of admonition. Such questions arise from the good people's shyness.

Wednesday, the 6th of December. The weather is very variable, now cold and now warm, yet we have not had any lasting rain for a long time so that the water in the river is falling very low. Now that we have become accustomed to the weather, the winter is very pleasant in comparison with that in Germany and does not hinder the field workers the least bit in their tasks. Yet it is at times too cold for the children in school, who have to sit for a couple of hours in one place, because we do not yet have a weatherproof schoolhouse.

We will not let any of the seven children presently in the preparation class take Holy Communion this time because we do not yet recognize in them any of the characteristics that must be found in worthy communicants. So far I have worked with them through the large *Order of Salvation*,[306] which they have learned by heart along with the most important Bible verses. Since they are also instructed enough in the word of God in church and school, they do not lack knowledge, but this is not yet enough, as they themselves recognize, for worthy participation in Holy Communion. From now on I shall diligently repeat the truths that have been presented so far and try at the same time to drill the children in the beautiful and edifying materials that are found in the attached *Golden A.B.C.*;[307] and afterwards I shall go through the questions from the catechism with them. May God accompany all this with His blessing so that such work will not be lost on the children!

Thursday, the 7th of December. Because Zant's eyes are not getting any better, he was taken into the orphanage today. It would have happened earlier at his request, but they have been threshing rice in the attic of the orphanage, and this makes a great racket down below.[308] It is now not in our means to build any other facility for this. We want to do all we can for the poor man, and we pray that God will restore his sight. To be sure, he is very crushed in these circumstances, yet neither restless nor discontented. I reminded him of the Bible story, and especially of the words in John 9:3.[309]

For the orphanage we greatly need a little house or at least a well protected room in which we could care for the patients and keep them warm, since the living room and bedrooms in the orphanage are protected only by thin, even if doubled, boards that are, after all, adequate enough for living and sleeping until God grants something better. However, since the patients must sometimes get up out of bed and it is dangerous to get chilled, a separate, well protected room that could be warmed by means of an oven would be a very necessary item for this purpose. But the Lord knows our needs better than we and will take care of it in His time. It is the same for me in my hut, for I cannot enjoy a tempered warmth in winter even though I have a hearth; and I cannot enjoy the fire except when I sit in front of the hearth, which is very inconvenient especially in time of physical weakness. I implore the heavenly Father to convince me more surely of His will as to whether we should make further arrangements for building a house for which neither supplies nor means are at hand.

Friday, the 8th of December. N.N. [Hans Floerl and his wife] are earnestly striving to seize Christ with His entire reconciliation and to achieve a certainty of their salvation. The husband makes himself very small before God in his prayers and knows how to divulge his heart so humbly before the Lord that everyone present at the prayer is not a little edified by it. Someday, when God has helped him through and brought him to a firmness in his grace, he will become a useful instrument in the conversion of others; and already he is working loyally with that which God has given him but which he does not recognize because of his poverty of spirit.

God has laid a longlasting quartan fever on N. [Veit Lemmenhofer] and his wife, which they always have on the same day and almost at the same hour and which weakens them and makes them incapable of physical work. So far as I can see, they know how to resign themselves by well recognizing God's salutary purpose in it. Several chapters of the late Arndt's *Book of True Christianity*, which concerns this, gave them a good opportunity to do so, as the husband told me this morning. Both of them were very happy that they will be free of fever tomorrow and Sunday and can therefore go to Holy Communion undisturbed.

Saturday, the 9th of December. Yesterday evening after the prayer hour Cornberger's wife bore a young daughter which was baptized today. I have been very much impressed that this pious woman was so concerned about the fruit of her body all during her pregnancy that she diligently called upon the Lord to give her grace to raise her expected child in the fear of the Lord and to His glory. She also admonished her husband frequently with tears to put away all frivolity and wickedness and to devote himself with her in time to a godly conduct so that, if the child lives and grows up, they may shine before it as a good example and pray for it right seriously and properly. God will be pleased with this Christian simplicity.

[Kieffer and his family came to us this afternoon to take Holy Communion with our congregation. He told me that Mr. Böhler[310] intended to instruct children in Purysburg and to preach to the people on Sundays if they wished to accept him and that he would not demand any tuition. Because he cannot accomplish anything among the Negroes he probably wants to try to make it with the white people and their children. This man[311] has no love for this new schoolmaster, and therefore he wishes to do nothing in the matter but watch and see what others do and how he arranges his teaching business. I could not give him any advice in this. However, since I do not doubt that he shares the ideas of Mr. G. von Z.[312] and the Herrnhuters, I told him what confusion and harm they caused in Germany even though they pretended for a long time, as this Böhler did too while at Kieffer's, that they are members of the Evangelical Lutheran Church. If it were possible for us to find a pious and skillful schoolmaster for Purysburg, we would gladly do our best to do so; but I believe that little can be accomplished there among the mixed and worldly-minded groups. The old Zoberbiller, the preacher from Switzerland, died a few weeks ago. He used to give edifying sermons to the people in Purysburg from time to time and would perhaps have gradually been able to do some good.]

Sunday, the 10th of December. In addition to Kieffer and his family, the shoemaker Reck and Metscher's oldest son also came here to take Holy Communion. Among the communicants there were sixty-two persons in all. On this day the dear Lord gave us very mild and pleasant weather, which stood us in good stead in the meeting hut, where wind, cold, and rain usually penetrate. In the next few days we will see how much blessing our dear Lord bestowed on the preaching of His word and on the celebration of His Son's last supper and how much of it the listeners accepted. Because the days are so short and we come together in the church three times on Sundays, we cannot visit many people on this day even though it pleases them very much and some of them wait for it with yearning. This time my physical strength did not suffice to hold the prayer meeting in the orphanage, although I usually attend with much joy.

By observing our listeners, I notice that they would rather spare us from moving out with them to their plantations, although at their recent request I, like my dear colleague, was ready to move out and perform my office among them. After deeper reflection they find that I could do more good by remaining in the town with my dear colleague, since I could hold the daily prayer meetings here but not out there. To be sure, they will not live that far apart on their plantations, but too far to come together at one spot for the prayer meetings, because their fatigue from their work and housekeeping will not allow them to make the trip.

On the one hand we have the orphanage, many children, and other people who will remain here to live and work on their nearby land, to say nothing of other business that we will have with people who come here on account of the congregation. Therefore we hope to achieve our purpose better on Sundays if one of us preaches the word of God to the congregation out there and one of us here in the town and if in addition a sermon and catechism can be held once a week at a given time. As far as visiting each and every family is concerned, it can be done from here just as well as if I lived there myself, since it is not at all far from here to the nearest plantation and the farthest ones in the direction of Abercorn will not be occupied until more people join us. That will help not only my health, which might suffer harm from the repeated change of place, especially since I would have to move into a new wilderness, but also our workers themselves, who will not have to build a parsonage on Abercorn Creek, and this would relieve them of much time and work and me of additional expenses. They will surely have enough work to do, especially since they will have to build there, as here, a well-protected spacious hut for a church. May God let us recognize better and better what His good and gracious will is in this! It is probably good if we can both live in one place, for our dear Lord has always blessed this so far.

Monday, the 11th of December. So far we have alternately held the morning prayer meetings in the orphanage between

five and six o'clock for the children and adults, which the dear
Lord has accompanied with His blessing. Each time after the
hymn we have read a chapter from the New Testament and
preached something edifying about it and then prayed on our
knees. Even though we have probably not spent more than
three quarters of an hour each time on these prayer meetings,
just as in the evening, our business will not allow us to hold
them any longer ourselves; rather we have delegated them to
the manager, who has already acquired a fine talent for praying
and admonishing from God's word. All sorts of business arises
all day long; and, if we do not apply the morning hours to
preparation and reading, then we are prevented during the day
from visiting our listeners or we must neglect something necessary, to say nothing of the fact that we must spend a part of the
morning hour in praying with our families and reading from
Holy Scripture. In doing this we are not neglecting the children
in the orphanage, since they hear enough of God's word from
us in school and during the evening prayer meeting and are
encouraged to pray.

[Things look pretty bad with Rauner and his family, and the
blessing of God seems to remain away from his house and his
work. There is probably no one in the community who is so
badly off as he, even though we have given him every possible
help. He still limps on both sides[313] and well recognizes that he
cannot be saved in this condition, yet he retains his lazy and
frivolous nature. Things will not end well with him. His two
children are the naughtiest and wickedest in the community. I
have noticed that he has not used enough precaution in regard
to these naughty children's sleeping quarters, so I asked him to
make other arrangements, and I will prefer to contribute something myself towards a blanket.]

Tuesday, the 12th of December.[314] Mrs. N. N. [Rheinlaender]
complained to me how painful it is for her to see others going to
Holy Communion while she is excluded. She again recited
much about her innocence and also asked whether she would
be allowed to go next time. But I could answer her no more
than what she had already heard, namely, that she cannot be
accepted for Holy Communion as long as she keeps her old
disposition. I told her my advice was to invoke God to let her

penitently recognize the corrupt condition of her heart that had been well enough revealed through her insolence and public disobedience in both words and deeds, to the scandal of the entire community. Then, if her penitence is of the right kind, she herself will desire us to cleanse her of these vexations before the entire congregation and to reconcile her with them.

Since she always considers herself innocent and shifts all the blame to others for having been punished with prison in Savannah, I dismissed her abruptly. Thereupon she changed her language and accused herself most severely, but this was all affectation. She claimed that someone in the community had said that it would not hurt her even if she were prevented from taking Holy Communion with the others: no one could take its strength (as she said) from her. But, she said, she would have no rest until she had taken it with the congregation too. Mrs. N. [Helfenstein] probably told her all these stories, since they keep intimate company; but she was not to be brought to any confession.

Wednesday, the 13th of December. Zant is getting along well in the orphanage, and his eyes are beginning to improve. He is seeking edification and companionship in the prayers that he finds here, and he is very content. Our listeners well know how much spiritual and physical good God [has showed and] is showing our community through this orphanage; and this is among the advantages that God lets us enjoy in this place over other people. The old widow who was freed at our request from Capt. Thomson's ship several months ago and taken into the orphanage is so content that she frequently thanks the dear Lord with tears for His care, prays diligently, loves the word of God, and does her work as best she can in quiet and with a willing heart. There is another old widow who is rejected and abandoned in Savannah and yearns to come here and would probably be accepted here if she survives her present sickness. [Christ, who left the orphanage and his poor but sufficient maintenance there a few weeks ago out of pure obstinacy, well sees that he thereby did the greatest harm to no one other than himself. However, he seems ashamed to request new admittance, which we will make somewhat difficult for his and other people's sake.]

The larger girls, of whom two are being prepared for Holy Communion, have good recommendations from the manager and his wife, so that the work that is being abundantly done in them is not entirely lost. They are already used for all sorts of things in the housekeeping, and, to be sure, with more profit now that they have begun, with the grace of God, to put aside their frivolity and volatile natures, in which was much laziness. We would have an opportunity to accept several children from Purysburg in whom we could accomplish some good with God's help, as with Kieffer's two youngest daughters; but at present there are no means at hand to accept more children. As soon as the Lord, who can do everything, gives them, we will have a sign to expand our little institution.

There are also some children in the community whose parents are unable to keep them properly and would be glad to see us accept one or the other child or contribute something to their support. The six girls who were recently given to our town from Capt. Thomson's ship with Mr. Oglethorpe's permission have nothing to do with the orphanage. They are in service with some of the Salzburgers, and one of them with me; and those who still need some instruction in reading and in Christianity are sent to school for a few hours. Except for one, who has very bad manners, they all conduct themselves well and are receiving much good here.

There are now in the community, in addition to us and the schoolmaster, twenty-eight married people, eleven boys, twenty-two girls, twenty-eight unmarried young men, and a single unmarried woman, Barbara Maurer [who appears to be behaving herself now better than formerly and to be more industrious in her work]. Mrs. Schweighofer, Mrs. Arnsdorf, Mrs. Helfenstein, and Mrs. Spielbiegler are the widows who have lived here, and we do as much as we can for them so that they do not suffer any want. Mrs. Helfenstein has two grown daughters and a boy of seventeen years [and could surely work more than she does, but much time is squandered in running to and fro and giving superfluous service to Mr. Thilo. I had bought a lot of wool in order to give her and her family a chance to earn something with spinning and knitting, but little or nothing has come of it so far.]

Mrs. Rheinlaender and her three children are not counted in this number. She has always defied us with threats of leaving; but, because no one is holding her back and she is not receiving the least reports from her husband, who moved to Pennsylvania in order to get rich, she would rather remain here if only we were willing and able to keep her. [There is nothing more we can do with her.] Also excluded from the above number are the six new girls, Mr. Ortmann's servant and maid, my servant with his sickly daughter, my dear colleague's maid, the newly arrived shoemaker with his wife and child, two cowherds with their wives and two children, twelve orphans, the old widow, and an English boy of eighteen,[315] who is cowherd for the orphanage and the congregation. Since we have been with the congregation, thirty-nine children have been born in Old and New Ebenezer, of which twenty-seven have died. Because the people are poorly housed and their dwellings are poorly protected, they have been able to raise up very few children. Gradually everything is getting better. From the very beginning, sixty-six adults and children have died in our congregation.

Thursday, the 14th of December. For a good while the weather has been as pleasant and gentle as it is in Germany in May. Also it is so dry that the people can tend to their field work unhindered. Previously at this time they have been accustomed to sow wheat and barley, which, along with oats and German corn, have also grown beautifully and abundantly, although the oats have produced more straw than grain and are therefore good cattle fodder. However, they find little gain in this sort of farming, since the wheat and barley are devoured by worms after the harvest and cannot be kept. They will sow much flax, and, if possible, hemp. If the weather is not too hot in the spring and if rain is not lacking, the flax grows very well, and perhaps it will go well with the hemp too.

We now have our letters and diary ready; and I plan to take them along to Savannah tomorrow, God willing, and deliver them to Capt. Thomson, who promised to come to Savannah with Mr. Oglethorpe about this time. We are writing to the Society, to Court Preacher Ziegenhagen, Mr. Butienter, Senior Urlsperger, Professor Francke [and also to Mr. Whitefield, who is probably still to be found in London]. Several letters from the congregation to several benefactors are also enclosed. Because of my office I have things to do with the German people in Savannah; and I shall both forward the said letters and try to get this and that from Mr. Oglethorpe. May God bless all this!

Praise be to God, who has let us finish the Book of Deuteronomy in today's prayer meeting and has thus let us complete an important piece of Holy Writ. May He let a blessing come from all that has been presented from it and may it last into joyful eternity! May He give us grace never to forget the beautiful example of the loyal servant of God, Moses, who recognized his Savior so vividly and sought nothing in the world more than glory of God and the salvation of the people of Israel, indeed, of all people; and may we never lose him from mind. Thus we, like him, will finally enter peacefully into God's joy. Amen!

Friday, the 15th of December. Yesterday the dear Lord helped Mrs. Kalcher in her difficult birth and let her bear a young daughter, which was baptized soon thereafter. The dear Lord did not leave the recent participation in Holy Communion without His blessing, as I learned especially from three persons; one of them said she had never been so refreshed as at that time.

This morning my dear colleague journeyed to Savannah to preach the word of God to the Germans. May the Lord be with him there and with me here, and may He bless our work!

Saturday, the 16th of December. During this week I spoke a couple of times with a simple person, who is a true Christian and who recited to me both times the beautiful verse: "I am come to seek and to save that which was lost." From that I knew that the verse was impressed right vividly in her heart by the Holy Ghost. I have previously noticed in this person that she carried a verse that has especially touched her heart for a long time and has heartfelt joy from it. She also remembered the recent Sunday gospel in which the Lord says, "And take heed to yourselves, lest at any time your hearts be overcharged . . . with cares of this life." "Oh," she said, "I have well noted that, oh how the heart always yearns for the world!"

When I went out towards evening to visit people, I was approached by a man who was going home from his plantation on which he was working this week, and he told me that he passes the evening hours after work in reading Johann Arndt's *Book of True Christianity* and that God is granting him much edification from it. Another man told how he and his fellow workers had said that it was a great benefaction that they had come from Germany where there was so much opportunity to sin.

Sunday, the 17th of December. On this day our dear Lord has granted us much refreshment from His sweet gospel. Although the weather was already rainy and cold, the congregation gathered diligently. In the evening I held the prayer meeting and read out loud the last part of the booklet called *The Gift of Christ*,[316] which shows the glorious fruits of Christ's birth; and the dear Lord blessed this. His name be praised!

Monday, the 18th of December. Last night between ten and eleven o'clock I returned with my travelling companions to Ebenezer healthier than I had departed and brought something with me which pleased all the honest members of the congregation, namely, that my trunk had been found by some servants of a merchant in Savannah. Because the master himself knew nothing about this, I was required to go myself to his plantation this morning and to inquire about the matter. To be sure, the servants made much fuss about it and demanded quite a tip, but they finally had to cough up the things they had found and had hidden in various corners and wait in Savannah for the reward they had earned. For neither their master nor another man considered it right that they had kept the things they had found hidden so long from everyone. It would seem that they did this in order to sell the black gown secretly, after having sold the remaining things such as some linen, wigs, etc., or having exchanged them for rum; for these things were lacking, along with my accounts, which were gathered into a rather thick book. They claimed that they had found the trunk open, at which time the missing pieces might well have fallen out. Our letters from England and Germany were all quite unharmed, to the great joy of all of us. To be sure, my black gown was so badly soiled that I had to have it turned inside out, yet I shall be able to use it again for a short time.

On the trip down to Savannah I got such a fever that I was almost forced to return to Ebenezer early Saturday morning because I did not expect to be able to accomplish anything with the people in Savannah. However, the dear Lord so strengthened me that I not only did not get the fever again but could even perform my official duties in good health. On Saturday evening I held a preparation based on Acts 17:30–31 for the people who wished to go to Holy Communion and presented them from it three clear proofs of God's mercy toward men. On Sunday, using the regular gospel for the Third Sunday in Advent, I tried to encourage them to a proper use of the present Advent and the approaching Christmastide and took as my exordium 2 Corinthians 6:2: "Behold, now is the accepted time; behold, now is the day of salvation"; and I repeated this in the afternoon. The dark rainy weather forced us to begin the divine service somewhat late; and, therefore, for the sake of the Englishmen who were coming to church immediately after us, we held Holy Communion in the preacher's house, and this was good because I had all the communicants close together. I always hold Communion here with a heavy heart because we can examine the people so little. To be sure, we inquire diligently into their behavior and conduct, but we learn little and only about their exterior lives. Yet there are a few there on whom the work through the Word is not in vain.

On Saturday evening a stranger of about forty years of age came to me and requested me to admit him to Holy Communion too. He spoke to me in English, so I told him that we held it in German and were Evangelical Lutherans and asked him who he was. He claimed that he had come here recently from Pennsylvania and was seeking a position; he was a theology student, was born in Sweden, and had studied in Uppsala. A certain bishop in Sweden had ordained him and sent him to Pennsylvania, but he found nothing to do there and had now come here, etc. A few weeks ago he had the misfortune to lose his letters, certificates, and recommendations. He speaks German; and, because he heard that the Reformed here need a preacher, he wished to serve them, etc. All this amazed me very much; and, since he can show no certificate and came to this country without being called, his case struck me as very suspicious. He attended our divine services both morning and afternoon and acted very devoutly. He asked me to recommend him to the congregation in the afternoon and help him get permission to preach in the Christmas holy days; however, I would have nothing to do with this but directed him both to the regular preacher in Savannah and to Mr. Oglethorpe. His name is Gabriel Falck.

Mr. Oglethorpe was not yet in Savannah; but his arrival was firmly scheduled for the 27th of December, so it will be necessary for me to travel down again. In the meanwhile I left my supplication for him and our letters for Europe in safe hands until they can be given to Capt. Thomson, who is not in Savannah either.

Tuesday, the 19th of December. Mrs. N.[317] is still asking to be admitted to Holy Communion the next time and will gladly cease annoying the congregation. We will have to examine her still better and learn whether her present claims have a better foundation than all previous ones. In the evening prayer meeting we began to make use of the edifying letters that have now been found. We have received much edification from them; and, since the dear Senior Urlsperger's expressions touched my heart deeply, I believe they will have the same effect on the listeners, who dearly love him. The El Schadai[318] has put our physical enemies and their attacks to shame as He has wished and hoped, for which reason we are encouraging ourselves again for His praise.

Wednesday, the 20th of December. Before my departure for Savannah I had given a Salzburger necessary admonishment to be cautious in consorting with all kinds of people so that he will not suffer harm or be annoying to other people. He accepted the admonition very well and requested us to tell him whenever we noticed anything wrong in him that is not compatible with Christianity. Yesterday evening he came to me again and told me that in my absence he had had so much worry and disquiet because of so many mistakes by which he might be annoying to other people even without knowing it that I had much trouble in raising his spirits. To be sure, even with honest souls one may not omit admonitions and friendly chastisements and one cannot simply rely on the best in them, but one must also be very careful not to cause them unnecessary worry or to harm them.

May the Lord guide us in all truth and practice us in His ways so that we can be useful to others!

Last night it became violently cold after we had had right pleasant weather this month. Usually, in this cold season, many ducks have come to our region, which have been shot by some of the people. It is said there are not so many this year, the reason for which may be that very few acorns have grown this year, which are the major part of their food. The turkeys, which also usually seek acorns, have come into the Salzburgers' fields often, especially where beans and rice have been planted. It has been said that last summer at least a hundred were shot in our fields. They are large and full of juicy, healthy meat; and they do good service for many a poor man who lacks meat. In Savannah I was offered an indentured servant who had made his living in Germany by shooting and fishing. He is in the service of the recorder.[319] Because this gentleman is just returning to England and fears more harm than benefit from his servants, he wanted to give me this man with his entire family, a wife and four children, and even some provisions to help out. But this man is a poor worker and he did no work in the field in Germany but just lived well and left his fatherland for worldly reasons, and therefore we would receive more harm than good from him. His shooting and fishing would only involve other people in such an uncertain and dissolute way of life. We shall remain on careful guard that such people do not come to our town.

Thursday, the 21st of December. Yesterday evening in the prayer meeting we were reminded by the letters from Professor Francke and Court Preacher Ziegenhagen of two especial benefactions of God, which may the Lord himself preserve in our memory and hearts for our trusting faith in His help in all need. The first concerns the especial supplying of our poor Salzburgers with a rich provision of foodstuffs that the storehouse in Savannah still owed us and which was revealed in an examination of the accounts at the beginning of this 1738th year and was then paid out, to the amazement of our listeners and to great praise of the Lord, and with which they could live until the harvest with divine blessing. The other especial ben-

efaction of God concerns the rescue from the attack of Spaniards, who, to be sure, had wicked intentions but were unable
to carry out their evil designs. Since our dear friends, when
they received news of it in Europe, used this danger of ours for
a sincere and trusting intercession, this experience of divine
aid, of which they have probably heard by now, will doubtless
serve to strengthen their faith greatly. The Lord, El Schaddai,
has not let them be put to shame in their hope and trust, and
this pleases us. We do not now hear that the Spaniards have any
hostilities in mind or plan to carry them out.

The weather has again changed; and last night and all day
today we have had a very cold rain, which will probably last all
night. The water in the river has steadily risen higher than it
has been in a year and will now probably climb even higher because of the heavy rain.

A journeyman tailor, who was born in Hamburg, is named
Kickar, and wished to join us some time ago but could not receive permission from Mr. Oglethorpe to do so, asked me to
come to him in Savannah and begged me with tears to take him
to our place so that he could be freed from the misery in which
his body and soul were mired. He would gladly work and support himself honestly: he demanded no wealth and good days
in this world but only the necessities of life. In Savannah he was
sick almost to death with dysentery and spent about 20 £ sterling for medicine and care in six weeks. Because this poor man
might perish here and because it appears that God has been
working mightily on his soul through this suffering and has removed him from all previous acquaintances and because our
people were willing to take him along, he was brought up yesterday in the large boat. He is now poor and has had to leave a
horse in Savannah as a security, yet I hear that the Salzburgers
are bringing him flour and butter so that he will at least have
some care in his great bodily weakness. A Salzburger, who has
fever along with his wife, has taken him into his well protected
hut; and they are both doing what they can for him.

Friday, the 22nd of December. In the evening prayer meeting, instead of the Bible stories, I am now taking those verses
that can give us a good occasion to prepare ourselves rightly for

the Christmas celebration. After the prayer meeting Rottenberger had his newly built house consecrated with God's Word
and with prayer; and many people, both old and young, attended. For mutual edification I said something about Philippians 4:5, "The Lord is at hand. Be careful for nothing." It is
very Christian and edifying that the first thing our people do in
their houses, even before they occupy them, is to pray and sing
with friends and thus seek for divine blessing so that it will
move in and dwell with them. This evening it became very cold,
but this did not hinder us here or in the prayer meeting.

Saturday, the 23rd of December. This evening we based our
preparation on I John 4:14, "And we have seen and do testify
that the Father sent the Son to be the Saviour of the world."
May God bless us all superabundantly for the living recognition
of His marvelous love. Before the preparation several people
held a prayer meeting in the orphanage, which I too attended.
Our dear listeners have called on my dear colleague diligently
this week as usual and have prepared themselves for the
Christmas celebration with much prayer. Because I have so little opportunity in my hut during this cold season and because
there is too little room, they find it more convenient in his
house. I hope that the dear Lord will also grant me a house
soon, which I intend to put to the use of those souls who like to
pray.

Sunday, the 24th of December. We treated today's gospel in
such a way that we learned from it, in the very edifying example
of John the Baptist, what is the foremost business of a Christian
at all times and especially at Christmas: 1) he makes nothing of
himself and worldly things, but everything of his Saviour; 2) he
does not seek to enjoy Christ and His grace only for himself but
directs others to Him too. During these four Advent Sundays
my dear colleague laid the glorious 118th Psalm as a foundation
for the catechisation and preparation for Christmas; and after
the New Year he will begin to catechize with *Luther's Catechism*,
since last year he had the Sunday and Holy Day epistles. I do
not doubt that fruit will remain from it into joyful eternity.

Monday, the 25th and Tuesday the 26th of December were
the Christmas Holy Days. Yesterday it was violently cold, but

today on this holy day such pleasant weather has occurred that we are not a little delighted at this goodness of God and furthered in our devotion during divine service. As a basis I took the Gospel of St. Luke, Chapter II, concerning the very best Christmas gift, which was 1) scorned and ignored by the world, but 2) dear and highly respected by God and His own. On the second Christmas day we had the Gospel of St. Matthew 23:34 ff. and discussed the grace of the New Testament, which was, to be sure, proffered but rejected, namely, 1) that God offers His grace in Christ abundantly, 2) that it is rejected by most men to their own judgment. On the first holy day my dear colleague treated the beautiful text Isaiah 9:6–7, likewise concerning the great gift with which God has honored mankind; and on the second holy day he treated John 1:1 ff. concerning the great good that we owe to the incarnation of the Son of God.

The congregation all attended church very diligently, and we hear that they would rather be sick on workdays than on holy days. My dear colleague held a prayer meeting with those who had assembled in the orphanage in the evening after the repetition hour, and it was very edifying for him too. I was too exhausted after the repetition, otherwise it is my pleasure to be there too in order to speak some with the listeners, to read to them, and to pray with them. After the afternoon service the children were with me and again gave me good hope they would desire and accept a new attitude from the Lord Jesus. One girl prayed with many tears and sorrowfully confessed to the dear Savior her previous naughtiness and disloyalty and begged His grace for improvement.

On the first holy day Mrs. Kogler bore a young daughter, which was baptized the next day before the morning sermon. After the sermon we churched Mrs. Cornberger, who accepts the word of comfort and admonition with great longing and thanks the dear Lord for every benefaction with sincere humility and recognition of her unworthiness. Now we often sing the song "We praise thee, Jesus, etc."; and, when this is sung in church, I feel as if I were amidst the blessed hosts of the chosen ones in the church triumphant. Our dear people sing it with an edifying tone and very devout expression in the way that we taught them some time ago with an easier melody than that which stands in the hymnal. We impart our melody with Christian simplicity:

Dich JESU loben wir, dich ehrn wir für und für, dir, o JESU,

wolln wir gebeu, Ruhm, Preiß, Danck und Herrlichkeit, hierdurch unſer

gantzes Leben, und darnach in Ewigkeit.

Wednesday, the 27th of December. I had wished to go to Savannah this morning to get an answer from Mr. Oglethorpe to the letter I wrote to him recently, because he had wished to be in Savannah before Christmas and to attend the court session scheduled for today. However, I learned yesterday evening that he had changed his mind and is hardly expected in six weeks, so I cancelled my trip.

Praise the Lord that I learned today that the Christmas celebration had blessed some people more than at any previous time. In the evening some honest people came to my hut to help praise the Lord, who, in Christ the Savior of the world, has shown mercy for them.

Thursday, the 28th of December. A Salzburger woman called on me and said that her spirit compelled her to come to me and to thank me for the Christmas sermon; something special had happened to her during the sermon on the first Christmas day, which she could not conceal from me. Recently it seemed to her that she was surrounded by a brilliance and her senses were as if drawn up on high; it seemed to her that she had heard a bright sound as if someone were speaking to her: "Thy sins are forgiven thee," whereupon she regained her senses and was filled with heavenly joy. I directed her to the Word, which is firm and certain; but I did not begrudge her her joy, especially since I know how seriously she has been struggling for assurance of the forgiveness of her sins. Among other things she said that the Savior is marvelous and goes marvelous ways with His children in order to lead them to glory and that it is good for one to make use, in a simple way, of everything that comes from Him or leads to Him even if it were but a sweet dream and to strengthen oneself in Him in every way in childish trust according to the rules of Holy Writ. For it is eternally true that He loves every sinner, especially the penitent one, with all His heart. And the Father too, who has sent us His Son, why should He not grant us and her everything with Him, including the forgiveness of sins?

I then told her she should just remain firm in her faith in God and His word; and I directed her to the first chapter of Joshua, which we began today in the prayer meeting and in which God takes great trouble to give Joshua courage not to fear but to continue vigorously with his ordained office and work with faith in the divine promises. I also reminded her of what we had heard in a repetition hour, namely, that the people who have come to the Savior, as can be seen in John I and Luke II, were, to be sure, not of one kind but were very different with respect to their recognition of Christ and of spiritual forces. Nevertheless, He never rejected anyone but has proved Himself to be a Savior who suits all people.

Zant has now moved back to his hut, after God has again granted him his sight and he has received much spiritual good in the orphanage during his sickness. His serious prayers for the orphanage are greater than any other compensation for what has been done for him. I was told by the manager's wife that, whenever he came out of church, he would kneel in a corner and recite to the dear Lord with many tears the words he had heard and would praise His glorious name. She felt put to shame by such earnestness, which she also perceived in the honest Mrs. Schweighofer; and therefore she wept bitterly that she could not find in herself the power, earnestness, simplicity, and zeal in prayer that she saw in him. I told her that one should, to be sure, let the examples of other believers incite one to emulation, but not to discouragement. Let each one faithfully use the grace he has received, and then he will receive more.

Saturday, the 30th of December. N., who had sinned some time ago against the 7th commandment and had to guard the community's cattle until Christmas as punishment, has now served his time.[320] He thanked me for this minor punishment, since he thought he deserved much more; and he promised to turn himself entirely to God. In guarding the cattle he proved himself as loyal as possible so the community has no reason to complain of him. Now that he is back with us, if he shows more fruits of penitence, he will be accepted again as a member of the congregation and admitted to Holy Communion.

I took the occasion to remind N. and N. of their recently committed wickednesses and annoyances and admonished them earnestly to penitence. I at once showed them that I could not admit them to Holy Communion until they had converted themselves to God and had brought the fruits of penitence. N. wished to justify himself but finally confessed everything and accused himself. Both of them assured me that they would not hold this procedure against me because necessity demanded it. I shall soon advise the congregation that I am proceeding thus with them (Mrs. N. not included) so that everyone will know that we should not let annoyances go unpunished.

Sunday, the 31st of December. When I began the first chapter of Joshua yesterday evening, I wished before God that the evening prayer meeting, which, with divine aid, will deal from now on with the Book of Joshua, will have an even greater blessing than the previous ones dealing with the Books of Moses. I could mention, to the praise of God, that this year has given us much edification in the evening prayer meetings and has furthered the Christianity of various people, who know how to tell of it to the praise of God. I could not, I said, conceal the fact that the word of God had borne no fruit in many and that this caused us much worry and pain. On the other hand, when we perceive good fruit, it brings us much joy and gives us renewed courage.

On this occasion I announced to the congregation what sorrow the above-mentioned two men and the woman had caused us through their un-Christian and vexing behavior, which was quite contrary to Christian teaching; and I told them that my office required me to use church discipline and to exclude them

from Holy Communion until they feel remorse for their godless behavior and great corruption, convert themselves honestly
to God, and bear fruit from this through a pious way of life. For
this purpose the honest members of the congregation should
work on them and try to preserve them from all bitterness,
which would only cause them great harm. Neither they nor
anyone else could wish for such vexing people to be admitted to
Holy Communion, they would go only to their harm on judgment day; and this we wished to prevent through this church
discipline.

The Lord has helped so far!

Thanks and Praise be to His name in all eternity for all the
good He has shown to our souls and bodies, Amen!

Appendix

The following three letters are appended as a sample of the voluminous correspondence from Ebenezer to England and Germany. The first of these is a request by Boltzius for the Trustees to contribute toward the building of the orphanage and also to pay for the passage of two indentured German families to serve in it.

Ebenezer Nov. 6th. 1738.

Dear Sir,

The Rev^d. M^r. Ziegenhagen has sent to me a Copy of a Letter, which you have wrote to him about the Money, which the Honourable Trustees have allow'd for Ruprecht Kalcher, Servant to M^r. Vatl.[321] The said Money, which is 6 £ 3 sh: 10d sterlg., is now placed to my Account by M^r. Causton, & I have satisfy'd the said Kalcher, who desired me to return the Honourable Trustees most humble Thanks for this favour. I had the satisfaction of acquainting General Oglethorpe with the Building & Intention of our Orphan-House beseeching Him for some Assistance in Victuals & Clothings. He is very we'll pleased by it, being perswaded of the Necessity & great Use of it in regard to My Congregation & other poor people, but having no power to allow any thing towards it without the Consent of the Honourable Trustees, He advised me to lay my humble Petition before them, doubting not but they would find out some Means for the Supporting the Orphan House, for which He promised me to write himself some Intercession to them. Be pleased therefore; good Sir to acquaint the Honourable Trustees that I want their generous Assistance in the maintaining our Orphans, Widows & other persons, who are imploy'd for the sake of the poor Children, our Saltzburgers being now not yet able to contribute any thing to it, tho' they are very willing being persuaded of the Usefulness of this Institution. Besides this I beseech humbly the Honourable Trustees to approve graciously of the generous Design of General Oglethorpe in shewing my Congregation a particular Favour. I intreated him for 2 families of the Dutch[322] Servants, which Cap Thomson brought over to Georgia, whom we want very necessary for being our Cowherds. Our Saltzburgers intend unanimously to go this Winter to their Works upon their Plantations, now fully laid out by strict Order of the General, for planting Rice & other kinds, & having a good Stock of Cattle, which they allways use to keep upon good Pasturages under the Care of some Cowherds, for want of which they would loose them as it happened in the Beginning of our Settlement to some, or to have them Wild & of a little use in the Woods, therefore they beseech the Honourable Trustees to allow those 2 families, consisting in 5 heads, for the use of our Town to be imploy'd for being our Cowherds. I have engaged my self to the General to find Victuals, Cloathes & every thing, necessary for them, intreating only the Honourable Trustees to pay their Passage, which as the General knows, neither I nor the Congregation is able to do. It is not to be doubted of, that this Gift of the said Servants will redound to our Saltzburgers great Advantage as well as to the said Servants great Satisfaction & Welfare, being now already mightily pleased & thankful to God & men for being brought by the General's Leave to my Congregation. M[r]. Gronan begs the favour of you to recommend his inclosed Letter to the Honourable Trustees. Pray present mine & my Congregations most humble Respects to them returning them many hearty Thanks for the many Favours & Benefits, that are bestow'd heretofore upon us, being in Hopes, they will generously add to the former Benefits this new likewise of allowing us the said Servants gratis, for which benefit we shall allways put up our fervent Prayers to bless them with good Health, long Life & happy Success in their praizeworthy Undertakings. Please to accept my hearty Wish & Prayers for your Happiness, who am

Dear Sir
Your most humble Ser[vt].
John Martin Bolzius.[323]

The following is the letter of 25 November 1738 that the Ebenezer congregation sent to Urlsperger praising their situation and requesting him to encourage and enable their kinsmen in South Germany to come join them. The German original was, of course, worded by Boltzius, but we may trust that he wrote only what they wished him to. This English translation was probably made in London.

Most revernd Sir.

Very beloved and honored father in Christ, we, the undersigned Salzburgers, and others of our brethren in Ebenezer, are reminded often to the glory of God, of his many loving and sacred gifts which were brought back by your worships in abundance to our poor souls and bodies not only in Augspurg; but also, as it were wafted to us from time to time even to America. Praised be the Lord, our God, for all the blessings that you have conferred upon us; for all the exhortations and consolations which you have given us by word of mouth and pen; for all the devout care, intercession, petition, and fatherly good will, with which up to this time you have always honored us; of these we have felt and continue to feel the need daily. So long as we breathe we shall not desist from praying to the merciful Lord each one by himself and in concert, that with a bountiful grace, he will reward your works in belief, your labors in love, and your patience in hope, both in this life and that to come and that at last when our wandering and pilgrimage are at an end we will be presented joyfully before the face of His blameless splendor with you as our pious father: how still later, without sin, we will praise our Redeemer with glorified voice for all the mercies He has shown us through your service to the healing of our souls and to gratifying our most cherished desires. In truth God has dealt kindly with us in so far as he bore us safely to Ebenezer, which now he lets us know better continually, on this account we have cause to be ashamed that at first we were not properly contented with His wise and good guidance but he helped us to understand that the former severe, though never too severe, but rather well-meaning test, was for our own welfare and He has also in a material way begun to bless us with such timely sustenance that we would be very sinful if we complained and did not wish to be satisfied. There is no one among us who has become poorer but remarkable to say, every one has received from God's hand so much since the last harvest as he might need for his necessities and something for clothing and living expenses; thus it will be easy for the almighty Lord to let flow to us here from other places, a substantial blessing; such is then our cherished hope from our last letters written to our beloved pastor: that we should receive linen and other necessary articles from Augspurg and Halle, for which we will value with due humility His holy care and merciful providence. we have percieved the fruit of your own prayers and of those of other godly teachers not only in the many benefits received of God which have been bestowed upon us here and indeed, also often sent to us from across the sea; but we see it also as a result of your heartfelt petition that we now again presume and suppose that the land already surveyed which belongs to the town but for the most part has been in bad shape such a good piece of Land on the Habercorn River[324] about one and a half hours journey from Ebenezer by chance we have procured, better then which we do not wish; therefore on account of our religious zeal it may be put into condition so that we will be able to hear the word of the Lord as plentifully as in the past while one of our beloved pastors draws hither to us where most of the members will live comfortably together in one place. When we reflect upon how much kindness the good holy Lord has done for our souls in the past by His sacred word how tenderly he has given us the entire treasure of his mercy through the Gospel during the whole time we have been here in Ebenezer and how faithfully he has worked on our hearts for the benefit of our own welfare, we could not believe otherwise than it was for a special benevolence, that we come so closely together and without becoming hindered in our external occupation, we are able to seek further the care and protection of God for our needs. In short the Lord has done great things for us and still continues his goodness and care; and because we know we differ in prosperity from our friends and brethren who formerly were also included to come to America, so we ask your worship to announce that.spiritually and bodily we are enjoying the care of our heavenly Father and in accordance with our love for them as our fellow-countrymen we wish that they were with us. So far as we can foresee in a human way, they would find already on their arrival here that they would have many a privilege to gain from us which we have acquired in a desert, unknown country and at first had to learn from experience in various ways with many a disadvantage and obstruction. The land is fully prepared to be cultivated, so that like us, they also, as soon as they arrive, can work on it; while we, on the contrary, had no land of our own for a long time, and had to do much work almost to no avail. They will find here well known people who would come to them with advice and assistance at hand and we could give them the experience that we have acquired of some things during this time; say that soon they could reward their work in like manner with profit and advantage; while, on the contrary, from lack of experience, we have had many sorrows and drawbacks. For cattle-breeding are all good arrangements now made whereby they, too, would have large profit. Through God's mercy we have now 200 head of neat cattle, besides hogs and poultry. At first so far as our dwelling was concerned seemingly we had a hard time, because in New Ebenezer as yet nothing was built; but now every one who might come here would be welcomed in houses and cottages already built until they could build something for themselves in the town on a lot which they could choose. We enjoy here entire Christian freedom in religious affairs and in every day life are subservient to no one; and we can conduct all our business in the best and most comfortable manner as it seems good to us. No one is allowed to harm us and there is a great difference between a free landholder in Ebenezer and a servant in Germany, even if he has a good master; indeed also between a farmer and a landholder in the same place. To the advantage of our place and company this is added that the noble General Oglethorpe recently without our request, has had given to us the gracious assurance that no one should come to our locality and settle among us before he is recommended and nominated by us and our pastors themselves. As in our case, could our countrymen also be sent here voluntarily in one year with provisions; also where possible, with tools and stock; thus we believe if they would fear God and would await faithfully the result of their labors, they will find here already their support and livelihood. It would be very enjoyable and pleasant if our region would be populated with such honest people of whom it is requested to do this only in order to save their souls and they would support themselves at last honorably by the work of their hands; then we would live together as brothers in great joy and peace. No true Christian looks for riches and luxuries in this world and the man who wishes to seek for these in Ebenezer must stay away; but he who is content with food and clothing and also his dear necessities can be advised to come here yet first must he consult with God in hearty prayer so that he shall come not of his own accord but by the will of God; when one is convinced thereof he is satisfied with all that God gives and such a one can trust indeed to the holy faithful Lord, that He will know how to protect him. Especially we ask your worship to offer the call to Ebenezer both to those neighboring Salzburgers and Austrians who are still well known to us and who, we know, would like everything here; we would rejoice heartily over their arrival.

They are:

1. From Lindaus
   Philip Wenger
   Nicol Rothenberger
   Georg Brandstetter
   Andrear Pittz
   Georg Wenger
   Peter Breitfusz
   Andreas & Jacob Brandstetter
   and their two sisters, Ursula
   & Anna
   Matthias Harmel
   Michel Steiner
   Matthias, servant of the Holy
   Church
2. From Memmingen
   Peter Dritscher
   Joseph Mitterecker

   Hans Eisenhoffer
   Matthias Bacher
   Hans Guldicker
   Simon Brandstetter
   Jacob Kranewinter
   Philip Eischbacher
   Bartholomeir Stickel
3. From Kaufbeuern
   Gertrand Lacknevin,[325] and
   many others whose names we
   forget.
   Wolffgang Baumgartner
4. From Nordlinger
   Anne Cornbergerin
5. From Augspurg
   Ruprecht Helpfferer
   Hans & Balthasar Ebner

Balth, and Wilhelm Gruber
Hans Grumpold
Christina Roshlacherin
Hans Reiter
6. From Leutkirch
George Hohmann
Lorentz Lickewalner
7. From Ulm
Michel Kasewurm
Paulus Kasewurm

8. From Liebrach
Veit Zefferer
9. From Kemten
Martin Grundner
Veit Hollaus
10. From Regenspurg
Bartholomeus Lerchner &
Frantz Ecker
Thomas and Martin Schmidt
Sebastian Topf Schuhmacher

If the company were together, then more safely among such could come over here some unmarried Christian Salzburger women or other honest members of the female sex who it is hoped would not regret to marry here and likewise to establish an orderly household.[326] Hitherto the young bachelors have endured much disorder in their dwellings rather than marry such persons in whom they did not discern the token of a genuine fear of God and an exceptionally honest life; and moreover our benefactors in England and Germany should know that they would not be served with indiscriminate people, but with Christian, painstaking, and honourable persons; how kindly their benefactors would grant this if they would help to settle our dear Ebenezer with genuine Salzburgers for the honor of God and their own good; and also how such Salzburgers would thank them for it at the same time as the arrivals; they would be glad to bestow their charity in such a way, that they would help a transport to America in the future if the honourable trustees should not be in condition to undertake it themselves. This is the colony, we have learned, that has been illy spoken of because no livelihood could be had here; indeed this might have been reported here through a great misunderstanding; but if every one seen that if still more Salzburgers were sent hither on request of the dwellers in Ebenezer, and one can hope to earn his living here; so would this be nothing else than a clear and sure defense of this country against enemies and slanderers. Still two points must be considered (1) That the people wishing to come here should not leave behind simple German implements and what they may bring along for tools and clothing, especially linen and shoes, because all such things are expensive here and hard to get. (2) They must so plan their journey that they will be here in Ebenezer at harvest time that they may get ready further and plant by degrees a bit of land that is ready, or that which is prepared around the town, so that something can be given to them for employment for some time until they have gotten their own in condition, which will be very useful to them. It was not so easy for us. The best and pleasantest time to work in the field is in the Autumn and Winter. And moreover they must leave Augspurg in April or at the latest in May or June; for thereby if they find a ship soon in England they can be here toward Autumn or at any rate before winter. But may the wise and kindly God bring them hither by his merciful and good will. May he rejoice your worship with all kinds of good tidings about our settlement which in the time of the reports that were first published about us, caused you much sadness on our behalf may He bless you richly and all servants of the Lord as well as the rest of the beloved benefactors and may our poor prayer for you in Christ seem good to Him. Herewith we remain, with a thousandfold greeting to all of you.

To his worship our very true and strong father in Christ, from his spiritual children fast bound to love and obedience.

Ebenezer November 25, 1738

1. From Lindau:
   Simon Steiner
   George Koyler[327]
   Matthias Brandner
   Christ. Riedelsperger
   Matthias Burgsteiner
   Ruprecht Kalcher
   Stephan Rottenberger
   Ruprecht Steiner
   Gabriel Maurer
   Rupr. Eischberger
2. From Memminger
   Thomas Bacher
   Martin Lackner
   George Bruckner
   Peter Reiter
   Meiggitzer[328]
   Zettler
      Thomas Pichler
   Paul Zittrauer
   Hans & Carl Floerch.[329]
   Leonhard Crause

Ott. Bach
Zant
3. From Augspurg
   Barth. Rieser
   Simon Reuter
   Ruprecht Zimmermann
   John Cornberger
   Christian Leimberger
   Veit Laudfelder[330]
   George Schwaiger
   Peter Gruber
   Veit Limmenhoffer[331]
   John Maurer
   Thomas Geschwandel
   Joseph Leitner
4. From Regenspurg
   John Schmidt
   Jacob Schartner of Kempten
   Christian Hester of
      Leipheim[332]
      by Ulm
   John Pletter

Ebenezer Dec[r]. 12th. 1738.

To M[r]. H. Newman.

Dear Sir

My last Letters to you are Sent by the way of Charles Town in Sept. & Oct. last by which I took the Liberty to acquaint You wth. the Receiving of our Salaries by Cap[t]. Thomson as well as to give you a little

Account of ye Condition & Intention of our Orphan house, which I humbly desired you to recommend to ye Honble. Trustees & Society.

I have now the Satisfaction to acquaint you that by order of Genl. Oglethorpe our Plantations are now laid out in such a manner, as it will be very convenient & advantageous to my Congregation. By this Generosity & Goodness of M^r. Oglethorpe our Saltzburgers will be enabled, if merciful God continues to give his Blessings to their Endeavours, to reap many good Fruits of their Labour in ye Ground, & are now so well Satisfyed, that the whole Congregation has desired me to give the Rev^d. M^r. Senior Urlsperger an Account of the many good things & Preferences which they enjoy now here under the Wings of Providence of ye Almighty. It will redound to our Towns & ye Colony's advantage, if our whole Town cou'd be Settled with Saltzburgers, as it was the praise worthy Intention of y^e. Honble. Society from the beginning. And Seeing that our Saltzburgers know a good many of honest & industrious Countrymen at Augsburg & Linden & other places in Germany, who are resolved to join wth. their Brethren here in their Worship & Labour upon the first good Acco^t. of their being settled well they give now wth. one Accord such an Account, doubting not at all, but they will ingage themselves very soon for being sent hither to Ebenezer. But being informed, that the hon^ble. Trustees cannot take up Saltzburgers upon the former establishment, I beseech the Gentlemen of ye Society to think on some means of gratifying our Saltzburgers humble Petition in paying a new Transports Passage & allowing Provisions & other necessary things for their Support and Subsistence in ye beginning. Our people's health continues pretty well, & have a mind to do a great deal of Work this Winter upon their Plantations for raising more Provisions for their & other Comers Subsistence. We shall endeavour our selves to the utmost of our Power to attend on our Congregation both in Town & upon their Farms, ministring to them the Gospel & holy Sacraments, which is the first and chiefest Thing, they constantly aim at.

My utmost necessity obliges me to build a house my Hutt being almost rotten, & very inconvenient for preserving my Health & doing my Business well & Successfully. I design to beseech Genl. Oglethorpe to lend me 40^lb Sterl. being in hopes, Almighty God will incline our Benefactors Hearts to contribute some to this very necessary & useful Building, by which I shall be enabled to return this Money to ye General in time. And as the Honourable Society are always very strongly inclined to do every thing to our & the Saltzburgers Welfare, I make bold to beg ye favour, of their intercessions at the Board of y[e] Hon[ble]. Trustees, to allow besides the 10[lb]. w[ch] they have allowd for one House, some thing more w[ch] Intercession will, I doubt not prevail very much wth. them to my advantage.

May the Lord Jesus bless you and all the worthy Gentlemen of the Society wth. good health and all manner of happiness, which is the sincere Wish and Prayer of y[e] Congregation, of M[r]. Gronan & mine who am

Dear Sir

Your most Obed[t].

humble serv[t].

John Martin Bolzius.

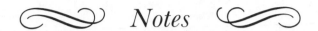

Notes

1. Samuel Urlsperger, ed., *Ausführliche Nachricht von den Saltzburgischen Emigranten die sich in America niedergelassen haben*.

2. Franckesche Stiftung—Archiv der Ostindischen Missionsbibliothek, Abtheilung 5 A–D.

3. For sojourn of Moravians in Georgia, see Adelaide L. Fries, *Moravians in Georgia, 1735–1740*. The term *Moravian* is misleading, since only a few of the sect actually came from Moravia. They claimed to be true Lutherans, yet they also claimed descent from the Bohemian Utraquists.

4. In this regard he at least writes better than Col. William Stephens, if we may judge by the syntax of note 204.

5. As good Lutherans, the Salzburgers served God both by working (*laborare*) and by praying (*orare*); but their detractors in Savannah said they spent their time in praying and eating.

6. When the Earl of Egmont tried to justify the Trustees' policies, almost the only success he could cite in the colony was that of the Salzburgers (C. L. Ver Steeg, ed., *A True and Historical Narrative of the Colony of Georgia*, pp. 4, 130, 160, 175, 345). The Malcontents, on the other hand, argued that the Salzburgers could not be held up as examples, since they "are yearly supported from Germany and England" (ibid., p. 136) and "they have been hitherto liberally supported both from Germany and England, and their rights and privileges have been much more extensive than any others in the colony" (ibid., p. 145).

7. See entry for 23 Sept. in George Fenwick Jones and Renate Wilson, trs. and eds., *Detailed Reports on the Salzburger Emigrants*, IV, 167.

8. "Advice came this day, that one Hughes, a Smith, settled at Abercorn, was newly gone off without the least previous Notice of his Intention, for Carolina, with his family." William Stephens, *Stephens Journal* (Allen D. Candler, ed., *Colonial Records of Georgia*, IV, 78).

9. Peter Rose. See Fries, *Moravians in Georgia*, 69.

10. See Jones and Wilson, trs. and eds., *Detailed Reports*, IV, 119. Entry for 28–29 June.

11. W. V. Davis, ed., *George Whitefield Journals*, 153–54.

12. These Germans, who were indentured for a period of service to pay for their passage, had arrived on 20 Dec. 1737; and some twenty were put under Mr. Bradley to work for the Trustees. *Stephens' Journal*, 60. Entry 31 Dec. 1737. See also Candler, *Colonial Records*, XXII, pt. 2, p. 21.

13. This was Anna Dorothea Helfenstein, widow of Johann Jacob Helfenstein, a Swiss tanner who arrived with the third transport. The Earl of Egmont reported Helfenstein as still alive on 13 March 1739 (E. Merton Coulter and Albert B. Saye, eds., *A List of the Early Settlers of Georgia*, 22), but Boltzius reports his death on 23 Oct. 1736 (George Fenwick Jones and Marie Hahn, trs. and eds., *Detailed Reports on the Salzburger Emigrants*, III, 232). Concerning his son Friedrich, P. A. Strobel (*The Salzburgers and their Descendants*, 117) says, "If the tradition in reference to him is correct, he was a lineal descendant of the Count of Helfenstein, who, with his wife (a daughter of the Emperor Maximilian) and their youngest daughter. . . ." Since Strobel was writing in the antebellum South, when illustrious ancestry was attributed to all of the planter class (to which the contemporary Helvenstons belonged) it was reasonable for him to mention this rather unlikely genealogy. On the other hand,

it is surprising that it was quoted as "probable" more than a half century later by Albert Bernhardt Faust (*The German Element in the United States*, I, 67).

14. This was probably her daughter Maria Frederica, who later married Thilo. The other daughter was Maria Christina. (Coulter and Saye, *A List*, 23.)

15. "She" apparently refers to the mother. Like many eighteenth-century writers, Boltzius was sometimes vague in his use of pronouns.

16. It is surprising that she says "both," since she had four sons: Friedrich, Johann Jacob, Jeremias, and Johannes. (Ibid., 23). Perhaps she is referring to the two living at home. See ibid., entry for 10 Jan.

17. Boltzius may have been misinformed and meant Capt. Hewitt, who brought the Germans on 20 Dec. 1737, according to *Stephens' Journal*, 54. Verelst also stated that several German families had left "last Saturday" on the *Three Sisters*, Capt. Hewitt (Verelst to William Bradley, 10 Oct. 1737, Candler, *Colonial Records*, XXIX, 579). Of course, Thomson could have been in port too, since he next arrived in Savannah on 15 Sept. 1738, which allowed quite enough time for a round trip. (*Stephens' Journal*, 212. Entry 15 Oct. 1738).

18. This surveyor, whom Boltzius calls Ross, was really Hugh Rose. "Read a Petition of Mr. Hugh Rose Surveyor That having been Appointed by Gen. Oglethorpe to be Surveyor of Ebenezer. . . ." (Candler, *Colonial Records*, II, 444).

19. For a brief but excellent account of the Ebenezer orphanage, see Lothar L. Tresp, "The Salzburger Orphanage at Ebenezer in Colonial Georgia," in *Americana-Austriaca, Beiträge zur Amerikakunde* 3 (1974), 190–234.

20. Egmont lists Johann Peter Amrsdorf [*sic!*] as still living on 13 March 1738. The widow's name is not given (Coulter and Saye, *A List*, 2).

21. "Capt. Daubuz in the *Georgia Pink*, arrived at Tybee laden with Provisions from Ireland" (*Stephens' Journal*, 66. Entry 12 Jan.).

22. Boltzius' faith in the Lord was justified. In answer to his petition for aid, Harman Verelst answered on 3 March 1739 that "the Trustees . . . have been pleased to direct that 40 £ should be paid into your Hands to be applied towards to Maintenance of your Saltzburgh Widows and Orphans." (Candler, *Colonial Records*, XXX (MS), 51).

23. Apparently Mrs. Pichler. See *Stephens' Journal*, 66, entry for 12 Jan.

24. To understand contemporary medical theory, we might see what the surveyor William Gerard De Brahm had to say about bozoardic powder: "The Operation of the Bozoardic is nearly thus: the tartar Vitriol dissolves the Phleme concreted from acids, sulphurics and Water; the Conchae absorbe the Acid, and constitute a sal cathardic, which leads the retained Secretion to Excretion. The tartar Vitriol likewise as a diuretic proceeds in the Lymphe and massam sanguinis, where it dissolves what is coagulated and promotes Secretion, the Niter as an antinephritium cools and lays itself in the Rain to give easy Passage to the secreted Salts. Antim, diaphor by gentle friction on the Stomach causes a perspiration of the Zinabarum is sublimed by the volatil sal comphori in the sinus cerebi, where its terra sulphurea contracts & strengthens their Dilatation" (Louis De Vorsey, Jr., ed., *De Brahm's Report . . .* , 86).

25. *Sammlung Auserlesener Materien zum Bau des Reiches Gottes* (Leipzig: Samuel Benjamin Walther, 1731 ff.). This collection consists of several contributions (*Beyträge*). See note 70.

26. *Andere nötige Bequemlichkeit*, a more delicate way of expressing the term *s. h. Abtritt* of 9 Jan.

27. *Eins ist Noth, ach Herr! dies Eine*, hymn by J. H. Schröder.

28. *Habe Danck für deine Liebe*, verse from *Seelen-Bräutigam, Jesu, Gotteslamm*, hymn by A. Drese.

29. *Bürgerliche Gerechtigkeit*, "civil righteousness" or "natural honesty," the sin of pride that makes man feel competent to achieve salvation on his own merits and without divine aid.

30. This means to stop vacillating. It is an allusion to Luther's translation of 1 Kings 18:21, *wie lange hincket ihr auf beiden Seiten*, which the King James Bible renders less picturesquely as "How long halt ye between two opinions?".

31. *Sey Lob und Ehr dem höchsten Gott*, hymn by J. J. Schütz.

32. See note 29.

33. David Zuebli, father of Johann Joachim Zubly, subsequently leader of the Georgia Dissidents and delegate to the Constitutional Convention in Philadelphia (Robert L. Meriweather, *The Expansion of South Carolina*, 40, note 19).

34. *Fällt die Sünd' ins Meer hinein, / Muss sie wie ein Nebel schwinden, / Wer will meine Sünde finden? / Nein sie soll vergessen seyn, / Jetzo, ja auf ewig hin, / Weil ich gantz in Jesu bin*. From an unidentified hymn.

35. Sanftleben did bring his sister, along with a shoemaker and four marriageable women, on 27 June 1739. In a letter of 11 Feb. 1738 to Robert Trevor, the British minister at the Hague, Benjamin Martyn gave their names as "George Sanftle Ben, John Caspar Ulick, Gertraud Lacknerin, Elizabeth Wassernaennim, Margaretta Eggerin, Margaretta Berenbergerin and her sister." Candler, *Colonial Records*, XXX (unprinted), 40.

36. Quite obviously Mrs. Helfenstein, since they were cronies.

37. "She" refers not to the widow, but to Mrs. Rheinlaender, whose husband had gone north. See note 15.

38. At the time and in the area the word "Frenchman" usually referred to French-speaking Swiss.

39. "In the Evening Mr. Causton told me, he expected a man from among the Saltzburghers at Ebenezer to-morrow, who was going for London, and thence to Germany, on some affairs of that Settlement, whose Name was George St. Leaver" (*Stephens' Journal*, 96–97. Entry 1 March 1738).

40. Quite obviously the tedious Mrs. Schweighofer.

41. *Entbinde mich, mein Gott, von allen meinen Banden*, hymn by L. Gedicke.

42. *Gecreutzigter, mein Hertze sucht*, hymn by J. E. Schmidt.

43. *Jesus ist das schönste Licht* (hymn by C. F. Richter); *Es ist vollbracht, vergiss ja nicht* (J. E. Schmidt); *Brich durch, mein angefochtenes Hertz* (J. H. Böhmer); *Zu dir, Herr Jesu, komme ich* (J. A. Freylinghausen); *Mein Gott, du weisst am allerbesten*, (I. Clauder); *Wenn dein hertzliebster Sohn, o Gott* (J. Hermann).

44. Both the Lutheran and the Roman Catholic Bibles number the commandments differently from the King James version. For them, the second commandment is to remember the Sabbath and the third is to honor father and mother. Through some clerical rationalization, the term "father and mother" included one's spiritual father, namely the clergy.

45. No doubt an indentured servant.

46. In Leviticus 19:3. See note 44.

47. The widow Ihler. See entry for 16 March.

48. Probably Samuel Montaigut, who maintained a store in Purysburg with Charles Pury until 1739 (Meriwether, *Expansion of South Carolina*, 38).

49. *verbis et factis*.

50. Col. Stephens also commented on the abrupt change in weather on 7 March (*Stephens' Journal*, 98).

51. Only the grace of God, not human nature, can achieve salvation. See note 29.

52. August Hermann Francke, *Lehre vom Anfang Christlichen Lebens*. A devotional tractate.

53. One could best depart downstream from Purysburg at high tide to profit from both the river current and the ebb tide.

54. She is referring to Luther's catechism, either the *Grosse Katechismus* or the *Kleine Katechismus*.

55. See note 27.

56. Capt. Roger Lacy and Lt. Richard Kent. See *Stephens' Journal*, 178. Entry 1 Aug.

57. It is to be remembered that the word *epilepsy* was applied to any sickness causing convulsions or paroxysms. Capt. Lacy died of "epileptick Fits" on 3 Aug. (Ibid., 179).

58. *die vor den Riss treten*, an unclear idiom that may mean "to step into the breach" or "to step up to the abyss."

59. August Hermann Francke, *Kösteritzisches Denkmal oder Ermahnungsrede* (Halle: Waisenhaus, 1726). Devotional tractate.

60. The Schmidts, like the Grimmigers, were among the religious exiles from Upper Austria (the province immediately east of Salzburg), who found refuge at Regensburg (Ratisbon) until being brought to Georgia with the third transport. They were treated the same as the Salzburgers.

61. See note 52.

62. *So bin ich nun nicht mehr ein fremder Gast*, hymn by J. E. Schmidt.

63. See note 42.

64. *Lass meine Seel ein Bienelein auf deinen Rosen-Wunden seyn*, apparently from a hymn.

65. August Hermann Francke, *Nöthige Prüfung sein Selbst vor dem Gebrauch des heiligen Abendmahls*. Devotional tractate.

66. See note 30.

67. See note 65.

68. Henry Bishop, son of a London grocer.

69. John 5:46 & 39.

70. *Der IX. Beytrag zum Bau des Reiches Gottes*. See note 25.

71. *Es kostet viel ein Christ zu seyn*, unidentified hymn. *Doch ist es wohl der Mühe wert.*

72. August Hermann Francke, *Vorbereitung aufs Oster-Fest*.

73. This sentence makes no sense in Urlsperger's edition, which has *wie* instead of *wir*.

74. At Ockstead, now called Causton's Bluff, situated near Thunderbolt. "Towards Noon I rode out, by Invitation from Mr. Causton, to his Plantation, which he has named Ocstead; where I din'd with him and his Family, and Mr. Anderson: I found he had built a very handsome House, fit for any Gentleman to live in, laid out by a pleasant Garden, cut a fine vista thro' the Wood, to a large Opening, and was going on with great improvements, both for Pleasure and Profit. (*Stephens' Journal*, 13. Entry 5 Nov. 1737).

75. Two centuries later the German exile Carl Zuckmayer had the same difficulty until his Vermont neighbors taught him to soak his seeds in tar before planting them.

76. The creek was still low when Col. Stephens described the mill on 27 June (Ibid., 161–62).

77. It is interesting to note that the settlers in Georgia already applied the word *trout* to the large-mouth black bass, as their descendants still do. Since carp were introduced to the United States only much later (from Germany), Boltzius must be referring to catfish, even though he should have known such fish in Germany, where they are called *Wels*.

78. Christ seems to have had consumption already before leaving Frankfurt. In his case, Georgia was perhaps healthier than Germany.

79. Urlsperger naturally deleted this aspersion on the morality of the people of Memmingen, the town in South Germany at which the first Salzburgers were recruited for Georgia.

80. Previously, Boltzius said the child was seven.

81. *Weg mein Hertz mit den Gedancken*, hymn by Paul Gerhard.

82. Paul Anton, *Evangelisches Haus-Gespräch von der Erlösung*. Halle, probably 3rd ed. of 1730.

83. It is not clear why Boltzius chose Matthew 2, which tells the stories of the Three Kings, the Massacre of the Innocents, and the Flight to Egypt.

84. See note 25.

85. See note 44.

86. She was most likely French Swiss, like most of the inhabitants of Purysburg. It is regrettable that Boltzius gave so few proper names.

87. Boltzius never mentions a dissolute character named Edward Dyson, chaplain to Oglethorpe's regiment, who held divine services from Whitefield's departure through 9 April (*Stephens' Journal*, 198. Entry 10 Sept. 1738).

88. See note 8.

89. *Heimsucht.* This ailment, usually called *Heimweh*, affected the Swiss mercenaries so severely that yodelling was forbidden in the French army lest it cause desertion.

90. This was John Regnier, an indentured Swiss who joined the Herrnhuters after they were established in Savannah (Fries, *Moravians in Georgia*, 80). "The name of the nurse (*Krankenwärter*) is not given, but he was probably John Regnier, who acted as physician, not only for the Moravians, but for many of their poor neighbors" (Ibid., 129). John Wesley reported that John Reinier had been robbed by the ship's captain and had been forced to sell himself for seven years. See Faust, *German Element*, I, 68.

91. Apparently the fifth chapter of Numbers.

92. Thou shalt not steal. See note 44.

93. *fremde Sünde (peccata aliena),* causing or conniving at other people's sins.

94. As we shall see, his name was Kikar.

95. See note 90.

96. One cannot always determine the sex of Boltzius' confessees. In this case the person is a "member" (*Glied,* neuter) of the congregation, then a "soul" (*Seele,* fem.). It was most likely a woman, since more women than men confided in Boltzius.

97. See note 96. This time the word used is *Person,* which is feminine even when it refers to a male subject.

98. The widow Ihler.

99. See note 90.

100. "A preliminary or elementary course or treatise," referring here, perhaps, to the first part of St. Paul's admonition.

101. Urlsperger's edition erroneously dates this entry as 25 April.

102. *Rein ab und Christo an, so ist die Sache gethan.* Unidentified verse. Theologically this means about the same as *Moral reicht nicht weit; zu Jesu hin, der gibt Gerechtigkeit und Stärcke"* (Cited by Boltzius in his letter of 15 Feb. 1738. See Urlsperger, *Ausführliche Nachricht, Dritte Continuation,* 2039).

103. This must have been a brother of the widow Ihler.

104. Urlsperger's edition erroneously gives this as Acts 7:57.

105. *Jesu du Trost der Seelen,* hymn by P. J. Spener.

106. Thou shalt not steal. See note 44.

107. Boltzius often used the word *äusserlich* to mean "of the world" rather than "of the spirit."

108. In goods or money.

109. Indolence (*Trägheit*) is the sin of *accedia,* failure to pray diligently.

110. More from the New than from the Old Testament, more concerning inner conversion and love for Jesus than outward obedience and fear of punishment. See note 29.

111. Certainly not wild cats, which are predators, but probably raccoons and fox squirrels.

112. *Ach ein Wort von grosser Treue,* hymn by J. H. Schröder.

113. See note 59.

114. Henri François Chifelle. Boltzius may have been too hard on this easy-going clergyman, for his parishioners in Savannah defended him and he was awarded 20 £ Sterling for serving them for five years, on 10 June 1743 (Candler, *Colonial Records,* XXIV, 31, 32).

115. At Frederica, Fort St. George, Fort St. Andrews, and Fort Argyle.

116. Kikar.

117. Urlsperger's edition has *Beym Beschluss* instead of *Beim Besuch.*

118. Col. Stephens often complained of their work (for example on 3 April); yet he and the Trustees still continued to buy them (*Stephens' Journal,* 117. Entry 3 April 1738).

119. "Sunday, May 7 . . . After this, I took a boat with my friend Habersham, and arrived safe at Savannah, at about seven in the evening, having a most pleasant passage" (Davis, *Whitefield Journals,* 144).

120. James Habersham, see note 119.

121. Wesley had offended many, including Boltzius, by his strict adherence to the principle that a priest could function only if ordained with the "laying on of hands" in unbroken succession from Christ and the apostles.

122. Volmar (Vollmar), a carpenter from Wittenberg, came from London with the Herrnhuters, deserted them and joined von Reck, then deserted Ebenezer. See Fries, *Moravians in Georgia*, 97, 102, 139; Jones and Hahn, *Detailed Reports*, III, 60, 88, 223, 243, 255. Egmont gives his first name as Michael and calls him a Moravian because he arrived with them (Coulter and Saye, *A List*, 54).

123. His surviving children were Johann Simon, Johann Paul, Johanna Margareta, Johanna Agnes, and Frederica (Ibid., 37).

124. This was one of the Malcontents' most justifiable complaints. Ver Steeg (*True and Historical Narrative*, 47) claims that, in Oglethorpe's distribution of land, "No regard was had to the *quality* of the ground in the divisions, so that some were altogether pine barren, and some swamp and morass, far surpassing the strength and ability of the planter."

125. Masturbation, incorrectly subsumed under the heading of onanism, was considered a heinous sin, called *die rote Sünde* (the red sin) in German.

126. Although never named, these two families are surely the Kiefers and the Metzschers.

127. The name appears as Zoberbiller, Zoberbühler, Zuberbühler, Zauberbühler, Zouberbühler, etc. This was the father of Bartholomäus Zouberbuhler, still in Europe but later the head of the Anglican Church in Georgia. See Candler, *Colonial Records*, XXXIII (MS), 318, 321, 333.

128. Sebastian Zoberbiller, leader of the New Windsor settlement although only eighteen years of age. He later brought settlers to Maine and became a magistrate in Nova Scotia (Faust, *German Elements*, I, 249–50).

129. *Hallelujah, Lob, Preiss und Ehre*, unidentified hymn.

130. This must be an error for Savannah, since the boy was apprenticed there.

131. The word *Bier* in such contexts usually designated some nonalcoholic beverage such as spruce or sassafrass beer.

132. *Brünnlein*. This image is more picturesque than the "river" in the King James version.

133. Boltzius kept the English word *yard*, which Urlsperger explained in a footnote as an *Ell* of three feet.

134. The word *Heft* has numerous meanings, but in this sartorial context it probably means "fastener."

135. Joseph Barker (*Stephens' Journal*, 160. Entry 25 June).

136. Apparently she is referring to the next sentence in Revelations 22:17, which reads "And whosoever will, let him take the water of life freely."

137. *Cadetten-Prediger*. This could mean junior or assistant preacher, but here it most probably refers to the chaplain of the cadets at the St. Petersburg military academy, many of whom would have been Lutherans from the Baltic states.

138. See note 57.

139. Luther has *Du bringest die Lügner um* (Psalms 5:7), King James has "Thou shalt destroy them that speak leasing" (Psalms 5:6).

140. *Ey mein Hertz sey unverzagt, kennst du Gottes Liebe nicht?*, hymn by J. G. Wolf.

141. Matth. 22:4. Luther has *Kommet denn es ist alles bereit* (Come, for all is ready). The King James version says: "I have prepared my dinner."

142. The Halle scribe wrote "nine," an error for "four." See entry for 12 May.

143. He was Reformed.

144. The Halle manuscript has "40th."

145. See notes 13 and 16.

146. For Boltzius "ignorant" most often meant "ignorant in theological matters."

147. Typical Pietistic rhetoric, perhaps suggested by the title of Friedrich Eberhard Collin's tractate *Das gewaltige Eindringen ins Reich Gottes* (Frankfurt/Main, 1722).

148. This Theobald Kieffer is not to be confused with the Theobald Keiffer whom Egmont lists as a Palatine trust servant, formerly a butcher, who arrived 20 Dec. 1737 with a large family. (Coulter and Saye, *A List*, 27.) See George F. Jones, "Two Salzburger Letters," *Georgia Historical Quarterly* 42 (1978), 52.

149. *Wo ist mein Schäflein, das ich liebe*, hymn by J. P. von Schutt, whom Boltzius calls Fräulein von Schuttin; *Wo ist der schönste, den ich liebe*, hymn by J. Scheffler.

150. It is claimed in Ver Stegg, *True and Historical Narrative*, 145, that this mill had cost the public 1500 £ sterling. The MS general index to the *Colonial Records*, 453, lists Parker's Mill under the heading *Parker, Henry*. By coincidence, the mill appears only on documents signed by Henry Parker (Candler, *Colonial Records*, VI, 186, 191, 251, 446).

151. Benjamin Martyn, secretary of the Society for Promoting Christian Knowledge.

152. "Saturday Proceeded up the River to Ebenezer, where we arrived about Noon. In the Evening walked over all the Plantations, which consisted partly of two-Acre Lots, and partly of Land lying in Common, which they had cultivated, and for this Year appropriated to themselves, enclosed mostly under one Fence, their proper lots not being run out till this last Spring, and then not perfected; lying moreover almost wholly on the Pine-Barren, where they apprehended it would be lost Labour, and therefore would wait in Hopes of better Land being assigned them farther down the River: What they had planted, appeared done exceedingly well; but by reason of the Difference of Seed (as every where else in the Province) great part of it was in no wise equal to that which was planted with better" (*Stephens' Journal*, 160. Entry 24 June).

153. *Mein Vater, zeuge mich*, hymn by C. A. Bernstein. The opening verse may have been inspired by 1 Corinthians 4:15.

154. Cf. Job 14:2, "He cometh forth like a flower and is cut down."

155. For their account of Old Ebenezer, see *Stephens' Journal*, 160–61, entries for 25–27 June.

156. Boltzius used the English word *township*, which Urlsperger clarified by inserting (*Stadtfluhre*).

157. Boltzius had written *Nachkommende* (latecomers), which Urlsperger changed to *Nachkommen* (descendants).

158. No doubt mostly raccoons, but also possums.

159. Most Purysburgers were of the Reformed faith.

160. See note 153.

161. *Dir sey die Ehr, dass alles wohl gelungen*. Apparently a hymn.

162. See note 60.

163. See note 131.

164. Boltzius had written *Küche* (kitchen), which Urlsperger mistook for *Kirche* (church).

165. Boltzius did not know, or suppressed the fact, that an Englishman at Old Ebenezer named Sommers had smallpox, which he had caught in South Carolina (Ibid., 161. Entry for 26 June). This may have been Joseph Sommers, who prospered and received grants for 200 and 300 acres in the District of Ogeechee on 30 Sept. 1757 and, having ten Negroes, received 200 more on 1 May 1759 (Candler, *Colonial Records*, VIII, 38, 216).

166. See note 31.

167. See Whitefield's account of this ceremony, which is quoted in the introduction to this volume.

168. Honor thy father and mother (and the clergy!). See note 44.

169. Although Boltzius has failed to make it clear, he is talking about the Germans in Savannah. Not realizing this, Urlsperger deleted the most damaging sentence in order to protect the Salzburgers.

170. See note 60.

171. See *Stephens' Journal*, 200. Entry 15 Sept.

172. *Die Inspirirten*, a religious sect in southwest Germany.

173. In Savannah he would have been flogged or hanged. See entry 29 July above with regard to hanging for shooting cattle.

174. Boltzius must have meant the clockmaker Mueller. See entry 18 Aug.

175. Kikar.

176. Either Cooper or Smithard. See ibid., entry 25 June. Verelst gives their names as Richard Cooper and James Smither. (Verelst to Oglethorpe, 17 June 1736. Candler, *Colonial Records*, XXIX, 281).

177. Thou shalt not steal; Thou shalt not commit adultery. See note 44.

178. See note 147.

179. See note 25.

180. See note 25.

181. Johann Anastasius Freylinghausen, *Buss-Predigt vom Rath Gottes über einen Sünder und Gottlosen*.

182. Hetherington, Elgar, and Bishop had shot the pigs. Hetherington and Bishop broke out of jail with a certain Wright, who had committed misdemeanors in the Indian Nations (*Stephens' Journal*, 12, 13, 171–73, 175–76. Entry 25 July).

183. Thou shalt not steal. See note 44.

184. Stephens in his *Journal*, 181, mentions this man on 9 Aug. as "one of our principal licensed Traders," but he gives neither name or nationality. In view of his calling Sanftleben "St. Leaver" (note 39), it may have helped but little if he had tried to give the name. Perhaps he was Lodowick Grant, "A Trader in the Cherokee nation" (Coulter and Saye, *A List*, 76).

185. Boltzius must have heard but not seen these names, which he writes phonetically as Criks, Tzschirkisaas, and Tscherrikies.

186. Boltzius was fond of the word *asotisch*, meaning "sinful."

187. This was probably Noble Jones, since Ross was from Purysburg.

188. This is Ross, who had surveyed the outlying lands.

189. This religious obstacle must have been overcome, because Thilo became engaged to Frederica Helfenstein on 17 July 1739.

190. "She" is apparently the mother, see note 15.

191. She is listed (Coulter and Saye, *A List*, 83) as Maria Frederica. See note 189.

192. The Halle scribe seems to have suppressed this word, which was actually quite harmless. See note 131.

193. *Wo ist mein Schäflein*, hymn by J. P. von Schutt (See note 149); *Mein Vater zeuge mich*, hymn by C. A. Bernstein (See note 153); *Wie wohl ist mir, o Freund der Seelen*, hymn by W. C. Dressler.

194. *Hier legt mein Sinn sich vor dir nieder*, hymn by C. F. Richter.

195. *Zerfliess, mein Geist, in Jesu Blut und Wunden*, hymn by P. Lackmann.

196. *Dir meiner Augen-Licht*, hymn by G. Kehlius; *Maria hat das gute Theil erwehlet*, hymn by C. F. Richter; *Jesu, Herr der Herrlichkeit*, hymn by J. J. Winkler.

197. *Erwach o Mensch, erwach, steh*, hymn by B. Crasselius; *Mitten wir im Leben sind mit dem Tod*, hymn by Martin Luther; *Weltlich Ehr und zeitlich Gut*, hymn by M. Weisse.

198. He is probably speaking metaphorically of spiritual medicine. The "physician" is, of course, Jesus. See entry for 24 August in this volume.

199. See note 194.

200. See note 126.

201. This is the "fiery serpent" that Moses set on a pole in Numbers 21:8. Luther translated it as a "brazen serpent" (*eherne Schlange*) and referred it to John 3:14, which states that Christ will be raised (*erhöht*) as the serpent was raised by Moses. Therefore Boltzius calls it *die erhöhete Schlange*.

202. This alludes to his being reborn in Jesus.

203. Noble Jones.

204. "Friday. Two German Servants, under Mr. Bradley's Direction in the Trust's Service, rambling out Yesterday with a Gun to look after Venison; one of them, by the Gun's going off through Defect of the Lock, as he had it on his Shoulder, shot his Comrade dead, who was behind him: Whereupon a Jury was summoned under the Direction of the Recorder, who acted as Coroner, to enquire into the Cause, & c. and the

Inquest gave in their Verdict accidental Death" (*Stephens' Journal*, 177. Entry 12 July). "Saturday. What only was remarkable this Day, was another unhappy Accident that befel a German who was going to work at Highgate; where standing by as they were felling a Tree, which he was not aware of; in falling, it crushed him to Death; leaving a widow and several Children at Savannah" (Ibid., 183. Entry 12 Aug.).

205. Luther's dogma that a Christian must always bow to temporal authority had its roots in the quietistic convictions of medieval German mystics like Johannes Tauler (1300–1361), who preached that it was useless for those seeking salvation to attempt any influence on external matters, i.e., the governing political forces. In Luther's case, it sought to quell the tide of discontent and rebellion that his teachings about the damnation of Rome and the empire had triggered among the people, and it was the tragedy of orthodox Lutheranism that it could not and did not come to terms with political authority except in terms of a complete abdication of influence on government. This tradition may be at the root of the inability of the German middle and professional class to effectively oppose Hitler and his radical reformers of the German body politic, who themselves had many of the antirationalist and antihumanist traits of the German and Austrian peasant movements. It is interesting to speculate how Boltzius and his group would have reacted to the events of 1933.

206. Garrulousness.

207. This was Friedrich. The thrashing must have been salutary, for he became a respectable citizen.

208. *Oeconomicus*. The housemaster or manager, in this case Kalcher.

209. German settlers were noted for choosing the densest, preferably oak, forests, as was noted in 1789 by Dr. Benjamin Rush, the "Tacitus" of the Pennsylvania Germans. (Faust, *German Element*, I, 132).

210. Carl Heinrich Bogatzky, *Güldenes-Kästlein der Kinder Gottes*. Halle, 17??.

211. No doubt from David Tannenberger. Rheinlaender had placed his son with him for a short while (Jones and Hahn, *Detailed Reports*, III, 243; Jones and Wilson, ibid., IV, 14; Fries, *Moravians in Georgia*, 156).

212. Clearly an error for "her."

213. They were German Pietist missionaries who were sent out from Halle just as Boltzius and Gronau had been. Their reports are found in *Der Königlichen Dänischen Missionarien aus Ost-Indien eingesandte Ausführliche Berichten* (Halle: Waisenhaus, 1735 ff.).

214. The Rev. John McLeod. "Friday, August 11. Went in the morning to, and returned in the evening from the Darien, a settlement about twenty miles off from Frederica, whither I went to see Mr. MacLeod, a worthy minister of the Scotch Church" (Davis, *Whitefield Journals*, 156).

215. James Habersham. See note 119.

216. Ricebirds (*dolichonyx oryzivorous*). The bobolink, a songbird in the North but a vermin in the ricefields.

217. The corn imported from Pennsylvania.

218. It being Sunday.

219. It would appear that the Salzburgers' cattle were not yet branded, even though Boltzius had requested a brand already on 26 October 1736 (Jones and Hahn, *Detailed Reports*, III, 233). By 3 June 1755 the Salzburgers had individual brands, which have been recorded in the Cattle Brand Book (MS Records of the Register of Records and Secretary; Marks and Brands, 1755–1778, in Georgia Dept. of Archives and History).

220. See note 52.

221. See note 147.

222. Boltzius writes "hearts and kidneys" (*Hertzen und Nieren*). From Psalms 7:9, which the King James version gives as "heart and reins."

223. From Holy Communion, which was tantamount to being ostracized in a theocracy like Ebenezer.

224. See note 30.

225. *gesetzlich*. She followed the law but not the spirit of the law. See note 110.

226. A reference to 1 Samuel 7:12, "Then Samuel took a stone and set it between Mizpeh and Shem, and called the name of it Ebenezer, saying, Hitherto hath the Lord helped us."

227. See note 30.

228. For Rott's sad fate, see index of Jones and Hahn, *Detailed Reports*, III, 345.

229. Galatians 6:10.

230. Boltzius wrote *Eindruck* (impression), which Urlsperger corrected to *Ausdruck* (expression).

231. *Meine Tage gehen geschwinde, . . . fleust dahin als wie ein Fluss*.

232. The Halle manuscript says 200 £.

233. Little did Boltzius imagine that this problem would be solved a half century later only a few miles from Ebenezer when Eli Whitney invented the cotton gin.

234. The German word for cotton is *Baumwolle*, literally "tree-wool," which suggests that the Germans first knew it as the product of a tree rather than of a plant.

235. In Pietistic terms this means that she let this benefaction convince her of God's love for her.

236. This would appear to be Johann Friedrich Holzendorf. See Jones, *Detailed Reports*, I, 64. It is stated in Meriwether, *Expansion of South Carolina*, 39, that he had moved to Charleston by 1737.

237. August Hermann Francke, *Epistl. Predigten*.

238. Boltzius meant to write Giessendanner. Johann Ulrich Giessendanner was at Orangeburg in *South* Carolina. He soon died and was succeeded by his nephew Johann, who foiled Bartholomew Zouberbuhler's attempt to oust him (Meriwether, *Expansion of South Carolina*, 47; Faust, *German Element*, I, 218–21). See Zouberbuhler's excuse in his petition of 1 Nov. 1745 in Candler, *Colonial Records*, I, 478.

239. The Apostles' Creed.

240. See note 52.

241. This was the unsuitable Pennsylvania corn. See note 217.

242. "*In der Ordnung des Heils im güldenem a b c unter den ersten Worten: Aufmerksam auf das Wort Christi.*"

243. *Ringe recht, wenn Gottes Gnade dich nun ziehet und bekehrt*, hymn by J. J. Winkler.

244. Correctly "Abercorn." The "H" in Habercorn was through confusion with *Haber* (oats) and *Korn* (corn).

245. *von der Bischöflichen Kirche*. Whitefield, like Wesley, was an Anglican.

246. To be sure, given the poor soil and the depressed state of the economy, the indentured servants could not earn their keep any better than the freeholders could.

247. Thomas Jones (Sarah B. Gober Temple and Kenneth Coleman, *Georgia Journeys*, 103).

248. Thomas Causton had held a thankless job, being accountable for the stores in the storehouse while Oglethorpe played the magnanimous benefactor. However, he does seem to have profited from it. See note 74.

249. *dem Herrn D. Watts und anderen einiges Glaucoma vorgemacht*. This was no doubt Isaac Watts, a man active in religious circles in London.

250. Benjamin Sheftal. "Wednesday. More Complaint from Mr. Bradley, who brought with him one Sheftal (a Jew, that had been appointed Interpreter betwixt him and his Germans)" (*Stephens' Journal*, 95. Entry 1 March 1738).

251. Metzscher (Metscher, Metzger). His son's name was Johann Jacob (Jones, *Detailed Reports*, II, 166).

252. *Meine Seele ist still zu Gott*, hymn by J. C. Schade.

253. Boltzius was mistaken. Oglethorpe did not arrive until 10 Oct. (*Stephens' Journal*, 212).

254. This is a good illustration of Boltzius' mercantilistic economic views, for he wished to keep money circulating in Ebenezer at all costs.

255. Most of the Salzburg exiles had been invited by the Great Elector to settle in East Prussia.

256. *Auf hinauf zu deiner Freude*, hymn by J. H. Schroder or J. C. Schade.

257. Probably the Isaac Watts of note 249.

258. See note 31.

259. Boltzius is quoting Isaiah 45:11, which Luther renders as *Weiset meine Kinder, das Werck meiner Hände zu mir*. The King James version differs greatly: "Ask me of things to come concerning my sons, and concerning the work of my hands command ye me."

260. The word *Anfechtung* denoted doubts sown by Satan to make one lose faith.

261. See note 141.

262. The Halle scribe wrote *dimmittieren*, which Urlsperger changed to *admittieren*. Oglethorpe probably wished to cashier the soldier only after his future was assured.

263. Boltzius meant Abraham Grüning (Griening) and his Scots bride.

264. The Highlanders of Darien insisted upon their Gaelic language for both prayer and battle. McLeod preached in Gaelic; and, when Oglethorpe wished to win the Scots over to his side, he sent Lt. George Dunbar "who speaks the Highland language, and has a very fluent and artful way of talking" (Ver Steeg, *True and Historical Narrative*, 98).

265. "People" (*man*) seems to be an early reference to the "Malcontents," a group of disaffected, mostly Lowland Scots, settlers.

266. Psalms 119:92. The King James version has "Unless thy law had been my delight, I should have perished in mine affliction."

267. See note 176.

268. It seems strange that Urlsperger would have added this insignificant sentence.

269. This was a mill for stamping rice, not grinding it.

270. Here, as so often, Boltzius is referring to spiritual, not physical, affliction. See note 198.

271. These were German indentured servants brought by Capt. William Thomson on the *Two Brothers* on 15 Oct. (*Stephens' Journal*, 212). According to Verelst, he was bringing them "at his own Risque" (Verelst to Oglethorpe, 4 Aug. 1738 [Candler, *Colonial Records*, XXIX, 579]).

272. Kunigunde Kustobader. Egmont gives the name as Knowart and the age as 54 (Coulter and Saye, *A List*, 27).

273. *Es gehe wie es gehe, mein Vater in der Höhe weiss allen Sachen Rath und Tath*. This sounds like a hymn.

274. The *Two Brothers*.

275. Boltzius describes this situation better than Col. Stephens does (*Stephens' Journal*, 215–18. Entries 23–25 Oct. 1738).

276. See note 248.

277. Solomon Adde (aged 30) was accompanied by his wife Margareta (32) and his son John (3) (Coulter and Saye, *A List*, 1).

278. William Norris arrived with Capt. Thomson on the *Two Brothers* on 15 October (*Stephens' Journal*, 212).

279. Boltzius must have been prejudiced by Habersham, who compared Norris unfavorably with the more eloquent Whitefield (Ibid., 219). "That a difference had arisen between Mr. Habersham, the schoolmaster, and our new minister, Mr. Norris, wherein Habersham was to blame, he endeavouring to hurt Mr. Norris's character, in favor of Mr. Whitefield, who is to return" (*Diary of the First Earl of Egmont* [London, 1923], III, 4. Entry for 31 Jan. 1739).

280. "Them" refers not to the belongings, but to the unmentioned occupants of the boat. See note 15.

281. *Kleid*. Boltzius wore the same black gown as the Anglicans did.

282. Boltzius fails to mention that one of the homeowners was the French baker, Gilbert Beque, who accompanied the first transport from Rotterdam to Savannah. See Jones, *Detailed Reports*, I, 47; *Stephens' Journal*, 214.

283. The word *Boden* can mean either "floor" or "attic" (*Dachboden*). Because of the use of the word *Boden* in the entry for 7 Dec., it would seem to refer to the attic.

284. Perhaps an allusion to Luke 7:41–43.

285. When referring to a living person, "Prof. Francke" is Gotthilf August, whereas the "late Prof. Francke" is his father, August Hermann.

286. It seems incredible that the surveyor could not provide himself with fresh game, which he must have confronted constantly in making his way through the woods.

287. *Aber Gottes Güte währet immer und in Ewigkeit. Vieh und Menschen er ernähret zur erwünschten Jahres-Zeit. Alles hat sein Gnad dargereicht früh und spat.* Apparently from a hymn.

288. Boltzius gives the word *Stüber* as a translation of "pence."

289. Samuel Laue had consecrated Boltzius in Wernigerode on his way to Georgia (Jones, *Detailed Reports*, 27).

290. See note 25.

291. William Norris.

292. James Habersham.

293. See note 205.

294. *Wer noch vieles anders hat, wie kan er das vertreten.* Unidentified verse.

295. Christian Scriver, *Seelen-Schatz* (Leipzig, 1687 ff.).

296. Boltzius wrote 600, which he must have meant. Despite the usual 50 acre maximum for freeholders, gentlemen with servants were granted up to 500 acres.

297. The Reformed, who comprised the majority of Germans in Savannah, ordinarily attended the Lutheran services, because ties of language were stronger than those of dogma. Chifelle was Reformed, but his German was inadequate.

298. William Norris.

299. This was John. The older boy was Hans Georg, aged 12; and the mother was Anna, aged 30 (Coulter and Saye, *A List*, 49).

300. *der alles fein thut zu seiner Zeit.* This saying, so dear to Boltzius, is from Ecclesiastes 3:11, which the King James version renders less happily as "He hath made everything beautiful in his time."

301. *der keinen zu schanden werden lässt, der sein harret.* Psalms 25:3, rendered by the King James version as "Let none that wait on thee be ashamed."

302. This letter, dated 25 Nov. 1738, appears in Urlsperger's *Ausführliche Nachricht, Dritte Continuation*, 2047–53.

303. According to Egmont's list of early settlers, the Salzburgers eventually received the entire family of the indentured Palatine farmer Philip Gephart, aged 45, including his wife Martha (43), daughters Magdalena (19), Maria Catherina (17), Elizabeth (14), and Eva (10), and sons Philip (6) and Hans-Georg (2) (Coulter and Saye, *A List*, 18). A letter by Conrad Held, who writes the name as Gebhard, states that originally only three girls went to Ebenezer, the father (and presumably the wife and three younger children) having been sent to Frederica. See *Ausführliche Nachricht, Vierte Continuation* (Halle, 1740), 2291. Egmont's list states that Conrad Held (written Heldt), aged 52, with his family consisting of his wife Elisabeth (53), son Hans Michael (23), and daughter Elisabeth (17) were employed in the Public Garden under Joseph Fitzwalter in January 1738/39; and Held's letter states that, after three months, he and his wife were brought to the orphanage in Ebenezer, where his son served a pious Salzburger and his daughter served one of the ministers (Coulter and Saye, *A List*, 22).

304. This paragraph, which is a single sentence in the original, is a splendid example of the rambling and asyntactical style that Boltzius affected when in a religious transport.

305. Solomon Adde. See note 277.

306. Apparently Johann Anastasias Freylinghausen, *Ordnung des Heyls*, 3rd ed. (Halle, 1725).

307. See note 242.

308. See note 283.

309. When Jesus healed a blind man and his disciples asked whether it was he or his parents who had sinned, Jesus answered, "Neither hath this man sinned, nor his parents: but that the works of God should be made manifest in him." As we shall see, God's works were soon made manifest in this Zant.

310. Peter Böhler, who later became a famous missionary (Fries, *Moravians in Georgia*, 201–20).

311. "This man" refers to Kiefer, not to Böhler, for whom he has no love.

312. Graf (Count) von Zinzendorf.

313. See note 30.

314. Urlsperger misdated this entry as 11 Dec.

315. This appears to have been John Robinson, who must have returned after being dismissed as incorrigible and sent to Frederica on 5 May 1736 (Jones and Wilson, *Detailed Reports*, III, 126; Urlsperger, *Ausführliche Nachricht, Vierte Continuation*, 2310).

316. *Christ-Bescherung*.

317. Since the Halle manuscript reaches only through 14 Dec., we can only surmise the names hidden behind *N* and *NN*. In this case it is clearly Mrs. Rheinlaender.

318. Boltzius wrote this epithet of the Lord as *El Schadai* and also as *El Schaddai* (entry for 20 Dec.).

319. This was Thomas Christie, who, however, did not actually depart until 8 March 1740 (*Stephens' Journal*, 530). For his career, see Temple and Coleman, *Georgia Journeys*, 145–60.

320. Grimmiger had stolen three pounds from Pletter. See entries for 7 July ff. and note 44 in the present work.

321. Jean Vat, leader of the second Salzburger transport.

322. It is to be remembered that "Dutch" always meant "High Dutch" or German.

323. From Candler, *Colonial Records*, XXII, pt. 1, 296–98. This second letter is found ibid., 342–50; the third, ibid., 356–59.

324. Abercorn Creek. The "H" was probably added through contamination with *Haber* (oats) and *Korn* (corn).

325. Gertraud Lackner, sister of Martin Lackner, already in Ebenezer. This poor woman, who seems to be the only one in the long list who accepted the invitation, arrived with Sanftleben and soon died of a painful and loathsome disease, as will be reported in the next volume of these *Reports*.

326. Sanftleben did bring four eligible women, including his sister, and all but Gertraud Lackner soon married.

327. George Kogler.

328. Hans Michael Muggitzer.

329. Hans and Carl Floerl.

330. Veit Landfelder.

331. Veit Lemmenhofer.

332. Christian Hesler.

 *Select Bibliography*

Candler, Allen D., ed. *The Colonial Records of the State of Georgia*, I–XXVI. Atlanta: various publishers, 1904–. Continuing under editorships of Kenneth Coleman and Milton Ready.

Coleman, Kenneth. *Colonial Georgia: A History*. New York: Chas. Scribner's Sons, 1976.

Coulter, E. Merton, and Saye, Albert B., eds. *A List of the Early Settlers of Georgia*. Athens, Ga.: University of Georgia Press, 1949.

Davis, W. V., ed. *George Whitefield Journals, 1737–1741*. Gainesville, Fla.: Scholars' Facsimiles & Reprints, 1969.

De Vorsey, Louis, Jr., ed. *De Brahm's Report of the General Survey in the Southern District of North America*. Columbia, S.C.: University of South Carolina Press, 1971.

Diary of the First Earl of Egmont. 3 vols. London: His Majesty's Stationery Office, 1920–1923.

Faust, Albert Bernhardt. *The German Element in the United States*. 2 vols. Boston: Houghton Mifflin, 1909.

Fries, Adelaide L. *Moravians in Georgia, 1735–1740*. Winston-Salem, N.C.: privately printed, 1905.

Jones, George Fenwick, ed. *Detailed Reports on the Salzburger Emigrants Who Settled in America . . . Edited by Samuel Urlsperger*. I, 1733–1734. Translated by Hermann Lacher. Athens, Ga.: University of Georgia Press, 1968. Wormsloe Foundation Publications Number Nine.

Jones, George Fenwick, ed. Ibid. II, 1734–1735. Translated by Hermann Lacher. Athens, Ga.: University of Georgia Press, 1969. Wormsloe Foundation Publications Number Ten.

Jones, George Fenwick and Hahn, Marie, trs. and eds. Ibid. III, 1736. Athens, Ga.: University of Georgia Press, 1972. Wormsloe Foundation Publications Number Eleven.

Jones, George Fenwick and Wilson, Renate, trs. and eds. Ibid. IV, 1737. Athens, Ga.: University of Georgia Press, 1976. Wormsloe Foundation Publications Number Twelve.

Meriwether, Robert L. *The Expansion of South Carolina 1729–1765*. Kingsport, Tenn.: Southern Publishers, 1940.

Spalding, Phinizy. *Oglethorpe in America*. Chicago and London: University of Chicago Press, 1977.

Stephens, William. *Stephens' Journal, 1737–1740*. Vol. IV and supplement of *The Colonial Records of the State of Georgia*, edited by Allen D. Candler. Atlanta, 1906, 1908.

Strobel, P. A. *The Salzburgers and their Descendants*. Reprint edition. Athens, Ga.: University of Georgia Press, 1953.

Temple, Sarah B. Gober and Coleman, Kenneth. *Georgia Journeys*. Athens, Ga.: University of Georgia Press, 1961.

Tresp, Lothar L. "The Salzburger Orphanage at Ebenezer in Colonial Georgia," in *Americana-Austriaca, Beiträge zur Amerikakunde* 3 (1974), 190–234.

Urlsperger, Samuel, ed. *Ausführliche Nachricht von den Saltzburgischen Emigranten die sich in America niedergelassen haben*. Halle: Waysenhaus, 1735 ff.

Ver Steeg, Clarence L., ed. *A True and Historical Narrative of the Colony of Georgia by Pat. Tailfer and Others with Comments by the Earl of Egmont*. Athens, Ga.: University of Georgia Press, 1960. Wormsloe Foundations Publications Number Four.

 *Index*